Data Conscience

Data Conscience

Algorithmic Siege on Our Humanity

Brandeis Hill Marshall

WILEY

To my husband, my parents and my ancestors

About the Author

Brandeis Hill Marshall teaches, speaks, and writes about the impact of data practices on technology and society. Her work contributes to data education, computer science education, and data science fields. She leads and runs a social impact business that provides educational resources and training designed to help data educators, scholars, and practitioners humanize data operations. She has advised and educated thousands in the public and corporate sectors. She also consults with organizations that are proactive in mitigating harmful effects of their data pipelines. Brandeis holds a PhD and master's degree in computer science from Rensselaer Polytechnic Institute and a BS in computer science from the University of Rochester.

About the Technical Editor

Dr. Triveni Gandhi is a "jill-of-all-trades" data scientist, thought leader, and advocate for the responsible use of AI who likes to find simple solutions to complicated problems. Her journey with data science began with basic statistics in grad school, and after finishing her degree she worked as a data analyst at an educational nonprofit organization, where she saw just how transformative data technology can be. It was not until she moved into the for-profit sector that Triveni saw the numerous shortcomings of the tech world—especially the lack of socioeconomic perspectives in the development and deployment of technology. As a result, Triveni has become a champion for diversifying voices in tech and teaching data practitioners how to discover and mitigate biases in their work. In her spare time, Triveni enjoys gardening, playing D&D, and spending time with her husband and puppy.

Acknowledgments

From information gathering to impact making, my passion for putting data into a humanizing context has been an over 20-year journey. The dotcom boom and subsequent bust showed to me the immense power of data actions and our society's reliance on a digital infrastructure. While others saw databases as boring and tedious, I saw them as a bedrock of our digital globalized world. Being this bedrock comes with it a deep responsibility. We all must be more careful in how we handle and manage data online and offline. After many interweb searches, I couldn't find a book that addressed this delicate and complicated, yet important, reality. Embarking on writing this book has been a dream of mine that could not have happened without so many people.

First, to my husband and life partner, Gemez Marshall, you are my biggest supporter and advocate. You've endured listening to me talk through ideas. You brought me food and drink when you saw I was in the "writing zone." You meet my anxiety and doubts with "one thing at a time" and "happy thoughts." You tell me I can do anything, and with your loving encouragement I do. I am eternally grateful for your patience and constant cheerleading. I know you're ready for me to write another book, but let's just see how this one goes.

To my parents, Carlton and Magnolia Hill, you both have been my go-to models on "doing the right thing even when the right thing isn't easy." You've been my fiercest champions and guided me through difficult situations. Thanks for the weekly pep talks, Dad. You know I needed each and every one. And Mom, thanks for always keeping it 100% real. You taught me to be candid. My love of data started with you as we rolled all your coin change on the living room floor when I was a kid.

To the Marshalls, you're my in-laws but you've always treated me like one of your biological children. Thanks for lifting me in your prayers throughout the writing journey, being quick to text an encouraging word, and checking in on me. You two were one of the first to preorder, and I already know where the book is going to reside in your house.

Iretta B. C. Kearse, thanks for being my work friend-turned-sister friend. From the many, many Instagram reel shares to the text messages, you kept me smiling and laughing this entire process, even when I wanted to stay in a sour mood. I got you and you got me. We ride together.

Kim Crayton, thanks for being the friend I never saw coming. When we met via Twitter, I would have never imagined all the powerful and insightful conversations we would have had. Our conversations go from the fun-silly to an audacious liberated society and back to fun-silly in minutes. You helped me push past my own bounds of what's possible. Thanks, once again, for allowing your guiding principles to grace this book.

Thanks to Ayodele Odubela for being the person who opened the Wiley door to me. I felt discouraged and uncertain whether I had a book proposal that a publishing company would deem publishable. For acknowledging my reservations and showing me an alternate path, I am sincerely grateful. Happy to be combatting algorithmic-based harms and fighting for equity and justice in automated systems with you.

To my acquisitions editor, Devin Lewis, you were my first point of contact at Wiley. From our initial call, I felt seen. Thanks for being transparent about the process, advocating for this book internally, and encouraging me to share my book writing journey through monthly newsletter updates.

To my development editor, Adaobi Obi Tulton, you have been my North Star. From the gentle nudge reminders to submit those latter chapter edits to the initial document formatting fixes, the care you showed me is much appreciated. I felt fully supported even when I struggled to find the words to express my thoughts.

To my technical editor, Triveni Gandhi, I'm forever grateful for your comments, thoughts, and insightful quips. You took on this project without hesitation and it has meant the world to me. I'm still amazed how effortless our first and hours-long conversation flowed at that Dataiku event. Every time we correspond, it's having a meetup with a good friend.

To the Foreword author, Timnit Gebru, I was frankly gobsmacked when you agreed to write the Foreword. I assumed you would say you were too busy. But no, you lead with a strength of kindness that continually inspires me. Thank you for lending your words here and your time always wholeheartedly.

To everyone at Wiley, thank you for helping me to fulfill my dream by contributing to the data and tech industries as the whole me—an educator-scholar-consultant who intentionally seeks ways to humanize data operations.

Finally, I'd like to thank those of you who read, share, and comment on this book. Hope this book helps you be more seen.

Contents at a Glance

Contents

Foreword

There is an assumption that we need to code switch, straighten our hair, get rid of that accent, get rid of those big earrings, not be too much of a Black woman, but instead assume an identity that is considered "the norm" in computer science spaces in the United States. This undertone exists in every single text book containing code snippets that I have read. There is a pretense that these books were written from no one's point of view, exuding an air of neutrality that we know doesn't exist, what feminist scholars have dubbed "the view from nowhere."

This tone is that of a cishet white man, seen as the norm while everyone else is considered a deviation. Dr. Marshall shatters that expectation. With DataedX, Black women in Data, the Rebel Tech newsletter, her many educational events and this book, Data Conscience, Dr. Marshall brings her full self to work and encourages us to do the same. Reading this book feels like we're having an honest conversation about data and code over our favorite food or drink.

Exclusionary views of who is considered a data expert, are one of the many ways that Black people are gate kept from a field that profits off of our datafication and criminalization. As Prof. Ruha Benjamin, sociologist and associate professor of African American Studies at Princeton University, notes, technology allows racism to enter through the backdoor: the false assumption of neutrality masks ingrained, discriminatory, systems, while at the same time we are told, implicitly and explicitly, that we do not fit into the computer science archetype.

This book tells us that we do fit, and helps us develop toolkits for responsible computing. It goes through all aspects of the data lifecycle including the processes of gathering, labeling, cleaning, storing, and governing data, explaining how each of these steps affects us. Dr. Marshall moves us away from the notion that everyone should be datafied and every problem should be solved by technology. Instead, she explains the complex societal layers that we lose when we attempt to convert everything into discrete data points. She asks us to consider, and resist, the many ways in which we are being taught to act like machines, and gives us tangible tips for how to actively push back to retain our humanness and Black identities in this world of data.

For those of us looking to hone our data skills, this book helps us do that with examples of what could go wrong, and how to avoid those paths. Contrary to textbooks that abstract out one aspect of the data lifecycle without any societal context, Dr. Marshall reminds us that "coding requires a 360 degrees of panoramic view that requires more than coders in order to see, understand, capture and partially address the social, technical and ethical considerations."

I hope you enjoy this book as much as I have. As Dr. Marshall says, every one of you is a data person, and you are enough. We need you to enter, and if you're already in, stay and thrive in this field so that we have a technological future that works for all of us and not only the select few.

—Dr. Timnit Gebru,
Founder and Executive Director of the Distributed Artificial Intelligence
Research Institute (DAIR)

Introduction

My journey to data conscientiousness started when I was a kid as I rolled coins with my mom and helped my dad organize his job's employee resource group's annual membership rosters. My mom would bring out the big Welch's jar, about half full of loose change. Sitting on the living room floor, she'd dump all the coins on the carpet and we'd start separating them by denominations. Mom would bring out all the coin wrapper rolls she'd gotten from the bank. We'd stack the pennies, nickels, dimes, and quarters—and talk about whatever moms and daughters talk about. She taught me how many of each denomination goes into each coin wrapper roll: 50 pennies gives us 50 cents, 40 nickels gives us $2, 40 quarters gives us $10, and 50 dimes gives us $5. When we'd filled as many of the rolls as we could, we'd count up our earnings. Sometimes it would be $30, and other times it would be closer to $100.

At first, I simply liked the counting, the talking, and stuffing the coins in those small paper wrappings. As I grew up, I started to associate these coins as a resource to get what I wanted. That 50 cents could be put to excellent use to get some SweeTARTS. Two dollars in nickels would keep my candy stash stocked for a week. Five dollars would pay for my favorite order at Swenson's and I'd have change left over. In college, $10 in quarters was gold because no laundry would have been done otherwise. Looking back, I realize it was her way of having me practice my counting, learning the many ways to make a dollar using coins and the value of saving.

My dad, for more than a few years, had this annual huge task of verifying each chapter's membership rosters for his job's nationwide employee resource group. The first year or two or three, Mom and I watched him. Somewhere along the way, I started to help out when asked at first and even volunteered, maybe once. My recollection is fuzzy. What I remember vividly was that the amount of mail he received took down a few forests. There were endless printouts on standard perforated paper from those old dot-matrix printers. The basement became overrun with boxes of unopened envelopes of various sizes, from letter-sized to overstuffed legal-sized.

While my dad was figuring out which pile to tackle, opening each envelope started my supply chain of organization and sorting: record the chapter location and region, clip the membership roster to the envelope, highlight the number of chapter members, leave the chapter's membership dues checks in the envelope, and add this new envelope to the other envelopes in that region pile. And yes, each chapter printed and snail-mailed their membership rosters. The cross-checking of the mailed rosters year after year was dizzying. Some chapters used a great printer and had access to plenty of printer ink. Other chapters weren't so fortunate. My young eyes were called upon to read the smeared and faded letters.

Reconciling these membership rosters took weeks of shifting from one pile to the next. Some people changed chapters due to job relocations but didn't update their membership affiliation. Other people decided to not be part of the employee resource group anymore and didn't follow the member pause/deactivate process. The employee resource group finally created an online database—my dad had something to do with this, I'm sure.

Rolling coins introduced me to data as numbers, math, and financial literacy without being intimidating. Organizing chapter membership rosters introduced me to data as people, context. and guideposts to decisions. Armed with this understanding, I found that school was just one cool place where reading, math, and general exploration of data things happened.

But while roaming the computer science hallways at the University of Rochester I came to recognize how data was viewed by the world. The Year 2000 problem, the Y2K bug, dominated the headlines my junior year. Everyone seemed so concerned about the computing infrastructure and whether systems would "hold up" after the clock struck 12 a.m. on January 1st, 2000. Businesses were desperately trying to back up their data on file servers, zip drives. and 3.5-inch disks. My classmates began signing big money employment contracts with signing bonuses by that fall. They were focused on refining their computer systems and networking skills. That's what employers wanted. I predicted that this dotcom boom was about to bust, so I elected to pursue graduate studies.

I saw the additional concern that businesses feared of not having their data. Everything I could think of had a critical connection to data, particularly why, how, and what we digitally house in systems. And society was singularly focused on the systems themselves. I believed then, as I do now, that data runs the world. I decided to go all in on data in graduate school and my career.

Data gets a bad reputation as a pseudo demon spirit creature because all the numbers and math are deemed complicated, confusing, and not relatable. Data is not a tangible concept to many people—those in computing, tech, and data spaces and those who are not in those spaces. We all, to some degree, are in digital spaces where data lives. Critiquing data uses involves all of us, but for those of us in the data trenches, there's a bigger pressure to suss out the issues and course-correct before the tech product goes public.

This book is for the rebel tech talent, those who acknowledge and are ready to address the limitations of software development. They recognize that tech's philosophy and practice of "move fast, break things" is inherently problematic, and needs to be changed, and they want to pinpoint the ways discrimination exists in this digital data space. The primary reader for this book, however, is the entry-level software developer or data analyst. But frankly, it should be considered a reference guide to making more responsible and equitable data connections.

Data Conscience translates theory to practice. The gaps in our current data infrastructure are spotlighted so that data practitioners know more precisely where issues exists. And I'm centering the most vulnerable, ethical issues and resolutions to address social, political, and economic implications and not just computational ones like optimization, load balancing, and latency.

What you will read in this book is a blend of social sciences, humanities, and data management with tangible, real-world examples. Consider it a modern antemortem describing specific instances of where ethical flags are raised and how data structures help or hinder ethics resolutions. I focus on being preemptive in handling data operation for inclusion rather than conducting conversational (generic) autopsies of case studies and algorithmic audits.

The book is divided into three parts. Part I, "Transparency" (Chapters 1–4), takes you on the rollercoaster of how outcomes and impacts of data, code, algorithms, and systems are revealed to all of us by companies, organizations, and groups. Part II, "Accountability" (Chapters 5–8), covers ways in which data and software teams can critique and explore interventions to make responsible data connections during the tech building phase. And lastly, Part III, "Governance" (Chapters 9–11), reviews the action steps taken thus far and ends as a public accountability manifesto on what all of us can do to humanize our relationship to data.

Here's a brief chapter-by-chapter overview:

- Chapter 1 explores the role data has played in our society, particularly in the United States—how we've handled it and our relationship to handling it well. Oppression tactics, in the law and in the sciences, are mere social controls to enforce a hierarchy positioning that doesn't exist.

- Chapter 2 describes for those of us on the "inside" of tech how we're torn by this realization that the code we write is likely contributing to a cycle of harm that we don't know how to curtail, stop, or dislodge ourselves from. Reconciling—and more to the point accepting—imperfection in data and tech needs a place in tech. The choice between error or no error doesn't exist anymore. There's a third choice: nontech-solvable.

- Chapter 3 tackles the term "bias" and its multitude of interpretations head on. I describe how bias shows up and ways to shift our mindset on how we recognize and handle it, even before we write a single line of code. Getting overwhelmed and disengaging in combatting bias efforts is no longer an option.

- Chapter 4 stretches our minds about what we've accepted as computational thinking and standard discussion points to fold in a more intentional socio-ethical tech understanding. Coding requires a 360-degree panoramic view that requires more than coders in order to see, understand, capture, and partially address the social, technical, and ethical considerations.

- Chapter 5 focuses on asking the "why" questions, especially as part of data collection and reformat practices. Tech does a poor job of handling data collection and reformat. Learning to ask questions early, often, and with real people in mind streamlines how we manage data operations as a data, computing, and larger tech community.

- Chapter 6 focuses on asking the "what" questions, especially as part of data storage and management procedures. We must come to grips with the fact that the data storage landscape is a culmination of intentional, yet sometimes harmful, decision-making exercises with social, computational, and morality implications.

- Chapter 7 focuses on asking the "how" questions, especially as part of data analytics. The algorithms, systems, and platforms are taken from the same playbook, by the same homogeneous people. There's much we can learn about data from our comrades in the humanities and social sciences.

- Chapter 8 focuses on asking the "when" questions, especially as part of data visualization. The allure of data visualizations is enticing, so proceed with caution with every chart, graph, and dashboard you encounter.

- Chapter 9 snaps us back to reality as tech moves fast while the law moves slow. Juggling the usefulness versus persnickety hindrances of the law dominates this chapter. Focusing on the fundamental building blocks of tech, like data and the algorithms that use it, has traction and momentum rather than constructing legislation that's fixated on applications of technologies.

- Chapter 10 discusses tech's dominance in our society and, in particular, as a culture that excludes other solution options. The rockstar tech workers, or algorithmic influencers, guide every industry one software update, code version release, or code library at a time. But clearly, we've hit a ceiling in what tech should do.

- Chapter 11 is my public accountability manifesto. We're each battling for our dignity in digital spaces, and we must do so with the same indignant veracity as we do in physical spaces. The tech industry's ability to operate, for the most part, without impunity puts more onus on us, as global digital citizens, to maintain intense pressure for transparency, accountability and governance in all spaces where data resides. Algorithmic processes, systems, platforms, and institutions won't become responsible or equitable without us making it a requirement, rather than a choice.

Transparency

In This Part

Welcome to Part I, "Transparency." Our society today is obsessed with *using* technology. The power that technology brings to people's ability in completing perceived mundane tasks is astonishing and lightning fast. The "hurry up and complete more tasks in a fixed time frame" mindset overlooks the cascading and compounding influences of those activities on the human condition. But this isn't the first time the outcomes overshadowed the people. There's an uncomfortable U.S. history of sidelining the humanity of certain people so that others can thrive. The journey starts at this uncomfortable place when technology wasn't prevalent. How we as a society are living through this technology era isn't new, but simply a reincarnation of how the world has operated in the past. Being transparent about the pre-tech era illuminates how tech systems came to be designed with so many flaws. The data, code, algorithms, systems, and platforms that make the tech industry thrive are a wicked web of assumptions, presumptions, and opaqueness.

Transparency (n) – Revealing your data and code. Bad for proprietary and sensitive information. Thus really hard; quite frankly, even impossible. Not to be confused with clear communication about how your system actually works.

—**Karen Hao, in "Big Tech's Guide to Talking About AI Ethics,"**
www.technologyreview.com/2021/04/13/1022568/
big-tech-ai-ethics-guide[1]

Transparency (n) – Revealing outcomes and impact of the data, code, algorithms, and systems by companies, organizations, and groups.

—**Revised Definition by Brandeis Hill Marshall**

Data is the fuel that runs our algorithms and systems. Chapters 1–4 have us get inside data as a construct, structure, and limiting factor when digitized. We struggle to wrap our minds around data within and outside of digital infrastructures. Ultimately, it's up to the collective we to be clear-eyed in our expectations of data and its uses.

Dr. Brandeis Marshall
@csdoctorsister

I feel like someone has said this, if not, here it is: you can't automate yourselves out of systemic racism, sexism and inequities. Meaning: this situation is beyond the scope of the quantitative. You'll have to face the qualitative perspectives too.

Source: https://twitter.com/csdoctorsister/status/1315376187632476161

Note

1. Hao, Karen. "Big Tech's Guide to Talking About AI Ethics." MIT Technology Review, 2021. www.technologyreview.com/2021/04/13/1022568/big-tech-ai-ethics-guide.

Oppression By. . .

Dr. Brandeis Marshall
@csdoctorsister

South Carolina's Black Code, from 1865/6, applied only to "persons of color," defined as including anyone with more than one-eighth Negro blood.

Anti-Blackness is built into the US laws, so why is it hard to believe anti-Blackness is built into algos+tech systems?

Source: Twitter, Inc.

In tech, the approach is to create a solution that works well for 80 percent of users. The remaining 20 percent have to conform, find workarounds, or suffer in silence. Those on the fringe aren't considered core demographic or essential members of the targeted population. So tech folks don't want to discuss or address racism, sexism, ableism, and otherism. Because each of these distinguishing characteristics are lifelong, minoritized people are not fully comfortable in society. In this book, we explore the role of data in digital spaces and our relationship to handling it well. The intended use of data, how it's represented in digital systems, and the resulting impact of outcomes play heavily in the moral fabric of data management. Leaning on this foundation, we'll work in ways to clarify assumptions, be more data-aware in our tech products, and flatten bad aftereffects. We'll share conditions to look out for to be more thoughtful and to carve out opportunities to make alternative design decisions.

We start head-on with oppression because it's not a new occurrence to our global society. Tech has simply reinvented it. To drive this point home, I'll describe how oppression manifests in the law and in the sciences. I share a brief snapshot of the history of oppression and how data is leveraged to solidify a social structure and order. I outline where society has been so we aren't more likely to repeat it. Calling out oppression by one's race, gender identity, and/ or class frees us from doing "nice diversity." I'm not just talking about things you know or have heard or have read. I'm digging into the impact of data use and misuse, over decades that turned into generations. This impact is not a collective of fuzzy faces and lives; it's always personal. It's you and it's me. The law and the sciences try to manage the intentional, calculated, and coordinated instances of oppression in different ways. Their words are empty: "They may forget what you said—but they will never forget how you made them feel," as said by Carl W. Buehner. The outcomes are what matter.

The Law

Anti-Blackness coupled with white colonialism is a global phenomenon. Strict and full domination by a group imposing ethnicity or race barriers has set the model that lives in every system, to varying intensities, that all of us use to navigate our lives.[1] The model reinforces itself and feeds on itself. It's a relentless pursuit to maintain that complete domination. Throughout history, policies and laws have removed, altered, or restricted the birthright humanity of Black people. Not that other ethnic populations have not experienced this treatment, but Black people, especially in the United States, have combatted and are still combatting the strain of slavery. In the physical offline world, Dr. Joy DeGruy's *Post Traumatic Slave Syndrome: America's Legacy of Enduring Injury and Healing* (Joy DeGruy Publications Inc., 2017) cements the compounding trauma of enslavement within the Black community. DeGruy describes how Blackness, Black culture, and Black people were associated with laziness, dirtyness, uncivilized, and animalistic preconditions. Humanity was severed from Black people way before the slave trade. This social construct continues to today as Africa must contend with algorithmic colonialism (https://repository.law.umich.edu/mjrl/vol24/iss2/6), an international digital war over extracting Black African people's data in the absence of laws protecting its citizens. The United States has been extracting labor, intelligence, and dignity from Black people for centuries.[2]

Slave Codes

White colonization is centuries old—let's drop into this history in the 1800s. In the United States, slavery ruled, though some abolitionists, both white and Black, raised concerns about human and civil rights violations. Slave codes were laws and practices that confined Black people to white rule, that forbade them from obtaining an education, independence, and ultimately dignity. The social controls of slave codes were broad and severe. For instance, a Black person accused of a crime could be met with a death sentence. Black people were not allowed to serve on juries, so if you were a Black person accused of a crime, you would be judged by an all-white jury. And let us not forget the first rule of slavery: the enslaved, Black people, were considered property, listed by first name only and age in a ledger like an asset. For instance, in 1787, soon after the American Revolutionary War, the North and South states "decided" an enslaved person was counted as 3/5 of a person as a "compromise" used to determine taxation and representation in the House of Representatives. Black people were exploited for white fiscal and political benefit. Recognize any parallels with the tech industry today? #askingforafriend.

By the 1850s, the murmurs became loud sirens. Higher education institutions, later coined in 1965 as historically black colleges and universities (HBCUs), were founded and designed for Black students. The outcomes of the American Civil War propelled Black people's advancement from 1865 to 1890: many HBCUs were founded in 1867, a handful of Black men were elected to the U.S. House of Representatives, and it ended with the U.S. federal government granting land to over 15 HBCUs. The post-slavery era came into full view, where the abolitionists, white feminists, and their respective movements rejoiced in perceived equality for Black people. They thought that their petitions had been effective in enacting long-lasting change and the war for treating Black people as 5/5 of a person was achieved. They were wrong—very wrong.

Black Codes

But slave codes didn't disappear with the end of the American Civil War. Each Southern state didn't like, agree with, or accept the 14th Amendment to the U.S. Constitution, ratified in 1868. Slave codes turned into Black codes. Black codes were local, regional, and state laws that continued to pose social controls on Black people. They sneakily started popping up all over the Southern states in response to the Emancipation Proclamation issued on January 1, 1863. Take note of the five-year gap between the proclamation and the 14th Amendment ratification. Chalk it up to lots of dragging feet and stall tactics by some Southerners, with the enabling of some Northerners to curtail the 14th. Mississippi and South Carolina were the first U.S. states to pen Black code laws (www.blackpast.org/ african-american-history/1866-mississippi-black-codes).

For example, here's what's written in "Civil Rights of Freedmen in Mississippi," Section 6:

> *All contracts for labor made with freedmen, free negroes, and mulattoes for a longer period than one month shall be in writing, and in duplicate, attested and read to said freedman, free negro, or mulatto by a beat, city or county officer, or two disinterested white persons of the county in which the labor is to be performed, of which each party shall have one; and said contracts shall be taken and held as entire contracts, and if the laborer shall quit the service of the employer before the expiration of his term of service, without good cause, he shall forfeit his wages for that year up to the time of quitting.*

Let's read this as a layperson, with no law degree. A few observations and questions spring to mind:

1. What do you mean that less than monthlong labor doesn't need to be in writing? So if you say the work is short term, then you're at the mercy of the employer without a contract. You have no documentation or avenue to contest any disagreements you may encounter with that employer. And to avoid putting your labor agreement in writing, the employer could fire you on Day 29 and then rehire you a day or two later, for instance.

2. For more than one month of work, police or white persons are to read the contract to the Black person. Excuse me? White people have prevented reading and writing literacy for Black people as a social control structure so that Black people must depend on white people for their livelihood. Reading the Black person's labor contract means that the white person/ law enforcement officer can invent the labor agreement conditions and set the compensation rate. All of these things can be changed at any moment since the Black person, once again, is not afforded any agency or negotiation over their labor agreement.

3. And if a Black man quits "without good cause," he has to return his year-to-date pay. So only Black men are included in this backward law? What if the laborer was a Black woman? Did she have any protections under these laws? We already know that "good cause" is determined by white

people—yeah, the same white people who consider a Black person as a property asset counting as 3/5 of a person. And then there's how white people/law enforcement determined or regulated if a Black person was a freedman, free Negro, or mulatto: having free status validation papers. Umpteen-zillion social controls, check.

The laws, however, were in direct conflict with the 14th Amendment of the U.S. Constitution.

The first paragraph of the 14th Amendment goes as follows:

All persons born or naturalized in the United States, and subject to the jurisdiction thereof, are citizens of the United States and of the state wherein they reside. No state shall make or enforce any law which shall abridge the privileges or immunities of citizens of the United States; nor shall any state deprive any person of life, liberty, or property, without due process of law; nor deny to any person within its jurisdiction the equal protection of the laws.

Again, let's read and interpret these words as a layperson. Here's one take:

- All folks born or naturalized in the United States are U.S. citizens.
- U.S. citizenship is to be respected by states, and states can't infringe on that citizenship.
- Every citizen should have due process of law.
- Every citizen can't be denied equal protection.

These seem pretty clear. Except writing it as an amendment didn't make it enforceable. Womp, womp. The Southern states agreed to writing it; they didn't agree to follow it. The Northern states by 1890 had become weary in their charge to hold the Southern states accountable. Black men were elected to the U.S. Congress up until 1898. George Henry White of North Carolina was the last Black man elected, with his term expiring in 1901. Just 37 years. Let's call it *one* generation. And Black people were enslaved in the United States from 1619 to 1863: a total of 244 years. The Southern states violated all four of the 14th Amendment provisions when it came to Black people by making it harder for Black people to vote and by opposing legislation crafted by Black Congressmen. And Northern states weren't progressive in supporting Black male leadership in government given that the vast majority of Black Congressmen came from Southern states. Northern states couldn't seem to stay interested in Black progression for 1/6th of the time that Black people were (Is it really past tense? We'll get to that.) assessed, treated, and documented as property. The 14th Amendment shared words for appeasement as the actions of the Southern states smothered Black government leadership while the Northern states lacked any action to sustain Black representation and effectiveness in government.

The Rise of Jim Crow Laws

The misalignment of the Black codes and the 14th Amendment did disrupt some Northern souls. Both statutes couldn't coexist as is. Enter Jim Crow laws in Southern states. The "separate but equal" treatment was the basis of the legal arguments in the late 1890s. The same services can be provided to white people and Black people separately while maintaining the spirit of the 14th Amendment's citizenship section. It's a blatant instance of cluster analysis. As defined in machine learning, cluster analysis is the act of grouping a set of items—in this case people—such that the items in the same group (a cluster) are more similar to each other than to those in other groups (clusters). The logic and normalized operating practice then becomes that all white people are the same, all Black people are the same, all Indigenous people are the same, all Latinx people are the same, all Asian people are the same, etc. The sameness brush remains an unremovable stain on U.S. society. And for the Jim Crow laws, as in cluster analysis, considerations of how the clusters are treated after being separated aren't included.

The U.S. Supreme Court decision in *Plessy v. Ferguson* (1896) codified the "separate but equal" doctrine. The case stems from Homer Adolph Plessy, a Black man in New Orleans, who attempted to sit in a whites-only railway car but was denied. Plessy sued, stating that he had a right to sit wherever he chose. Now remember, only white men could serve as judges at this time. It was a 7–1 split.

Following is the majority opinion, written by Justice Henry Billings Brown:

> *The object of the [14th] Amendment was undoubtedly to enforce the absolute equality of the two races before the law, but in the nature of things, it could not have been intended to abolish distinctions based upon color, or to enforce social, as distinguished from political equality, or a commingling of the two races upon terms unsatisfactory to either. . .We consider the underlying fallacy of the plaintiff's argument to consist in the assumption that the enforced separation of the two races stamps the colored race with a badge of inferiority. If this be so, it is not by reason of anything found in the act, but solely because the colored race chooses to put that construction on it.* —Plessy, 163 U.S. at 543–44, 551

The single dissenting opinion was written by Justice John Marshall Harlan:

> *Every one knows that the statute in question had its origin in the purpose, not so much to exclude white people from railroad cars occupied by blacks, as to exclude colored people from coaches occupied by or assigned to white persons. . . . The thing to accomplish was, under the guise of giving equal accommodation for whites and blacks, to compel the latter to keep to themselves while traveling in railroad passenger coaches. No one would be so wanting in candor as to assert the contrary.* —Plessy, 163 U.S. at 557

Let me break this down and summarize:

1. [Brown] Race labels are kosher (informal definition meaning genuine and legitimate).
2. [Brown] Race labels supersede citizenship status.
3. [Brown] There are differences among the races. At this time, white and Black were distinguished, but it was expanded to include all nonwhite races.
4. [Brown] And different races don't impose a radicalized hierarchy, in which whites are positioning themselves as superior to Black people. Of course, Justice Brown said this in the reverse manner to further emphasize, using narrative, the inferiority supposition of Black people to the default white population.
5. [Harlan] Separation of Black people from white people is for white comfort, not equality. And that's wrong.

It doesn't take a bunch of words to say the truth, but it takes a lot of words to misdirect, misinform, and share false equivalencies. Jim Crow laws were federally mandated injustices and prejudices against Black people *and* advantages and profits for white people. The common focus is on the former while whispering the political, economic, and social impacts of the latter. As advantages and profits grew, the injustices and prejudices intensified. Jim Crow laws were intentionally harsh and demeaning—a reincarnation of the slave codes and Black codes of years to centuries past.

While the American Reconstruction era experienced equitable rights to Black men, Black codes and Jim Crow laws enacted social controls and monitoring on Black men, Black women, and Black children. Economic empowerment, stability, and liberation particularly bothered white people subscribing to anti-Blackness and white supremacy. To partially answer the question about Black women's work life regulations, take a look at the quoted tweet accompanying the original tweet in Figure 1.1.

Here's the text from the article:

City Ordinance Soon Be Passed Requiring Them to be Regularly Employed

MANY COMPLAINTS

Regardless of whether they want to or have to, able bodied negro women In Greenville who are not regularly employed are to be put to work, put in Jail or fined heavily. At its, special meeting yesterday afternoon City Council discussed the situation, with regard to this class of loafers at some length, and it seemed that all members of Council were agreed that steps should be taken to compel them to engage in some useful occupation. It was decided that an ordinance, similar to the one now in force requiring all able-bodied men to work at least five days per week, should be passed with regard to these women. Such an ordinance will be prepared and voted on at the next regular meeting of Council.

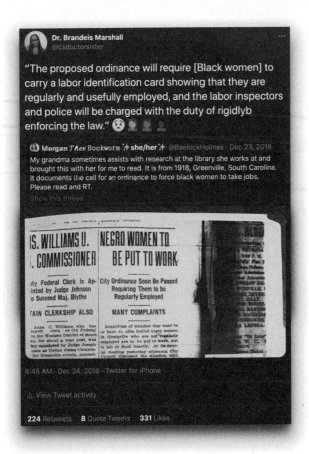

Figure 1.1: A quoted tweet referencing the 'Negro Women To Be Put To Work' article from Greenville, South Carolina in 1918

Source: Twitter, Inc. and `https://twitter.com/BaelockHolmes/status/1077006002392834053`

A number of complaints have come to members of Council of negro women who are not at work ana who refuse employment when it is offered them, the result being that it is exceedingly difficult for families who need cooks and laundresses to get them. Wives of colored soldiers, getting a monthly allowance from the Government, have, a number of them, declined to work on the ground that they can get along . . . without working, according to reports. Others have flatly refused jobs without giving any reason whatever, while still others pretend that they are employed when, as a matter or fact, they derive a living from illegitimate means.

The proposed ordinance will require them all to carry a labor identification card showing that they are regularly and usefully employed, and the labor inspectors and police will be charged with the duty of rigidly enforcing the law.

(`www.newspapers.com/clip/38314573/negro-women-to-be-put-to-work`)

1. The first sentence of the article is striking: "Regardless of whether they want to, or have to, able bodied negro women in Greenville who are not regularly employed are to be put to work, put in jail or fined heavily."

2. "Class of loafers." Excuse me? Black women are described as loafers if they're not working regularly for a white employer.

3. "Compel them to engage in some useful occupation." Ha!

4. A prior ordinance for Black men to work five days a week is now be extended to Black women because. . .white people wanted to control what Black women were doing with their time and money earned not by their hands.

These statements are now recognized as deplorable. But, wait there's more! This *Greenville News* article is dated October 2, 1918. That's during the height of Greenville's bout with the Spanish flu pandemic. Two days later, "In the city of Greenville there were so many sick and dying residents, at least 500, that on Oct. 4, the City Council unanimously passed a resolution calling on the city's Board of Health to declare a quarantine."

Catch this fully—Black women are being mandated to work during a global pandemic while the City Council is pleading for a quarantine mandate (which they didn't get, by the way). What, so Black women's lives are sacrificial? Their ability to have life *and* liberty without white interference disrupted these white folks something terrible. Yet why didn't this same compulsion apply to white women loafing at home? Because it didn't support white supremacy and anti-Blackness. White women continuing to pressure white men in political power for the right to vote was not as egregious as Black women minding their own business. The white Women's Suffrage Amendment, originally introduced in 1878, finally is passed in 1919 and ratified as the 19th Amendment in 1920 (www .crusadeforthevote.org/woman-suffrage-timeline-18401920).

Breaking Open Jim Crow Laws

The Jim Crows laws kept official hold of the United States, particularly Black people in the Southern states, until 1954. The first crack in "separate but equal" came with *Brown v. Board of Education of Topeka*. U.S. Supreme Court Chief Justice Earl Warren wrote the single opinion of the 9–0 unanimous decision in favor of the Brown family:

> *To separate [Black children] from others of similar age and qualifications solely because of their race generates a feeling of inferiority as to their status in the community that may affect their hearts and minds in a way unlikely to ever be undone. We conclude that in the field of public education the doctrine of "separate but equal" has no place. Separate educational facilities are inherently unequal. Therefore, we hold that the plaintiffs and others similarly situated for whom the actions have been brought are, by reason of the segregation complained of, deprived of the equal protection of the laws guaranteed by the 14th Amendment. —Brown, 397 U.S. at 494–5*

The legal arguments presented in the case compelled the Supreme Court to acknowledge the psychological impact of the "separate but equal" doctrine to Black children. The combination of data, social context, and patterns of education injustice resulted in an indisputable argument that poked a hefty hole in the equal protection of the laws guarantee promised under the 14th Amendment. This guarantee was exclusive to Black children. Black children didn't receive equal educational access and opportunities. *Brown v. Board of Education of Topeka* paved the way for the Civil Rights Act of 1964, which ended legal segregation and made it illegal to discriminate on the basis of someone's race or gender in employment, schools, public spaces, and voter registration requirements. The final vote was 290–130 in the U.S. House of Representatives and 73–27 in the U.S. Senate. So 55.2 percent of the House and 63 percent of the Senate voted yea. (That means 44.8 percent of the House and 37 percent of the Senate voted nay.) It's a definite success and a huge accomplishment. It's also a bit disappointing that there wasn't a more overwhelming support for the Civil Rights Act. If these percentages were viewed as a course assessment scores, it'll be an F and a D, respectively. Political power structures are alive and well, even to this day. Inclusion goes to the heart of breaking down established power dynamics. While the vote secured the act in becoming law, it didn't alter behavior. Whereas *Brown v. Board of Education* and the Civil Rights Act made strides to close the access, opportunity, and eventually wealth gap, another social system had already formed wedges that restricted telecommunications and other forms of communications based on social justice ideologies.

Overt Surveillance

Targeting certain people or groups who threaten the social order of white colonialism has a long-standing presence. Overt surveillance is an early rendition of the technology we use today. Monitoring and surveillance of people dates back to 1860s once the telegraph/telephone was invented. The Federal Communications Act of 1934 created the Federal Communications Commission (FCC) to help regulate communications via telegraph, telephone, and radio. It also leaned into wiretapping as an acceptable, pro-democracy action in the interests of national security. Of course, these surveillance tactics didn't have to be disclosed to the general public, the actual people these laws should have been intended to protect. Eavesdropping via wiretap, photo surveillance, or planting an infiltrator in an organization are all effective approaches to documenting, restricting, and predicting a person's or organization's movements.[3] Malcolm X, Rev. Dr. Martin Luther King, Jr., Fred Hampton, and countless others were the focus of federal and state-sanctioned investigations. Surveillance[4] moved full force ahead post–Civil

Rights Act. *Katz v. United States* added a wrinkle to the budding surveillance society as a standard operating practice:

> *The petitioner [Katz] has strenuously argued that the booth was a "constitutionally protected area." The Government has maintained with equal vigor that it was not. But this effort to decide whether or not a given "area," viewed in the abstract, is "constitutionally protected" deflects attention from the problem presented by this case. For the Fourth Amendment protects people, not places. What a person knowingly exposes to the public, even in his own home or office, is not a subject of Fourth Amendment protection. But what he seeks to preserve as private, even in an area accessible to the public, may be constitutionally protected.* —Katz, 389 U.S. at 352

Simply put, no one should be wiretapped without their knowledge *unless* there's a threat to national security. It seems harmless enough—to protect the democracy, the U.S. government doesn't need a warrant to wiretap. But the definition of what constitutes "a threat to national security" or "protecting democracy" remains elusive and inconsistent with decisions made on a case-by-case basis. These loopholes allowed the acts, laws, and policies to be enacted, but they didn't change the government's (white people in power) practices or behaviors. This de facto set of practices, protected by acts and laws, screened and monitored Black people under the guise of them being a "threat to national security." Democracy for all the people seemed to be continually sidestepped at every junction. Black leaders, and therefore Black people, were labeled as "threats." Being a labeled threat triggers government-level resources to the allocated to eradicate said threat. People who are considered threats are irredeemable and criminals. Criminals are dangerous. The implicit conclusion: Black people are irredeemable, dangerous criminals.

Weaponizing Blackness, especially Black people who questioned the lawfulness of the government's acts and laws, is a regular record being played throughout the 1960s, 1970s, 1990s (Violent Crime Control and Law Enforcement Act of 1994, for example), 2000s, 2010s, and 2020s. Social restrictions and controls, like what we've seen in slave codes, Black codes, and Jim Crow laws, plague Black communities. Black people's existence is seemingly a threat—a threat worth dedicating government personnel and resources to surveilling.

Surveillance at Scale

As the overt surveillance tactics became more transparent to the public, calls for its use to be suspended grew. Surveillance countermeasures increased. The governmental response was to take surveillance underground and wide—it went digital. Overt surveillance is siloed and disjointed, with data stored in separate physical systems, paper files, photographs, and audio recordings. Temporary housing of raw data has its advantages of being decentralized to prevent all data from falling into the wrong hands. The downside is that the full breadth and influence of the surveillance goes unnoticed. To connect siloed data, computerized systems were used and identified intersections faster than people. Fighting against "threats" meant staying at least one step ahead of a potential threat's thinking, knowing, and responding to their impending activities while calling it justifiable and necessary—not targeting or cheating, at least in the eyes of the laws.

When did modern digital surveillance start? With a 1987 research paper by Sirovich and Kirby called "Low-density procedure for the characterization of human faces captures facial features using a mathematical formula" (`https://opg.optica.org/josaa/abstract.cfm?URI=josaa-4-3-519`).[5] The patterns of white male faces are generalized based on the "average" of 115 faces. Figure 1.2 shows an example of this. Short dark hair. Dark-colored eyes. No smile. No eyewear/eyeglasses. It probably reminds you of some of the U.S. governmental-issued pics you've had to take: U.S. driver's licenses and U.S. passport photos.

The face is a form of identification that will always be unique to you, except for those with identical DNA or facial features. Creating mathematically understandable methods that isolate faces and facial features helps make algorithms easier to represent in a digital system. And these algorithms make finding a similar or the same face effortless in that digital system. Turk and Pentland (1991) extended Sirovich and Kirby's eigenvector approach using pictures of real faces in their experiments (`https://doi.org/10.1162/jocn.1991.3.1.71`).[6] Look at the second image in Figure 1.2. Sixteen pictures. Short dark-colored hair. No smiles. Twelve with no eyewear and four with eyewear. Different complexions. The photo backgrounds are similar, with robots, posters, and/or pictures of another person. Improving the accuracy of facial recognition in images has been in pursuit ever since.

Fig. 1. Average face based on an ensemble of 115 faces. In this, as in the other plates, we have refrained from filtering out the high frequencies produced by the digitization. A pleasanter picture can be had by the usual trick of squinting or otherwise blurring the picture.

(a)

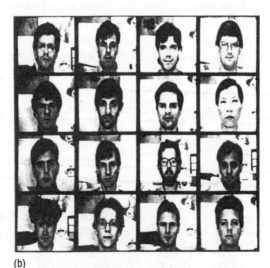

(b)

Figure 1.2: (a) Single image of face from Turk and Pentland's 1991 facial recognition published paper (b) Picture of 16 faces used in Turk and Pentland's 1991 facial recognition published paper

As of 2021, no accurate facial recognition analysis across demographic groups exist. The research matured within U.S. higher education institutions and government research laboratories. At the National Institute of Standards and Technology (NIST), face recognition technology (FERET) started in 1993, with the goal of "[developing] automatic face recognition capabilities that could be employed to assist security, intelligence, and law enforcement personnel in the performance of their duties."[7] It has evolved over the years and recently housed under Face Recognition Vendor Test (FRVT).[8] In light of the COVID-19 pandemic, FRVT has a subproject, Face Mask Effects, that's quantifying face recognition accuracy for people wearing face masks. Simply stated, facial recognition algorithms make use of most facial features, but face masks obscure nose, cheeks, mouth, and chin structures. The robustness of existing algorithms to identify you using your forehead, brow, and eyes make identification very possible. For those who take pictures with face masks, facial recognition algorithms have reference data to make the correct identification with a higher probability. Spoiler alert: Facial recognition algorithms as is aren't designed for this level of identification. They'll need to throw out the forehead and brow features—too many similarities among people. They'll focus on your eyes, in particular your retinas. Your retinas are distinctive to you and make you more easily isolatable to an algorithm.

The technological advances have moved fast[9] since the invention of the Apple iPhone, when an iPhone owner gained access to a camera. Data creation exploded with the pictures all of us have taken, email with and without attachments we've read, texts we've written, videos we've generated, and audio memos we've recorded. Our society has come to rely on these conveniences to move through our lives every day. We can't avoid our faces being uploaded to multiple digital systems—Department of Motor Vehicles, U.S. Customs (if you have a U.S. passport), Amazon Ring at or around your residence, traffic camera on city streets, surveillance camera in grocery and retail stores, just to name a few.

Public concern grew to coordinated action. U.S. cities and states have proposed, voted on, and instituted facial recognition laws:

- Massachusetts until December 12/21, 2021, except for law enforcement (www.mass.gov/info-details/mass-general-laws-c6-ss-220)
- California until December 12/23, 2023, prohibits California officers and deputies from using cameras for facial recognition surveillance, https://leginfo.legislature.ca.gov/faces/billTextClient.xhtml?bill_id=201920200AB1215
- Vermont, prohibits Vermont officers and deputies from using cameras for facial recognition surveillance without a future express consent of the legislature, https://legislature.vermont.gov/Documents/2020/Docs/BILLS/S-0124/S-0124%20As%20Passed%20by%20Both%20House%20and%20Senate%20Unofficial.pdf

- Portland, Oregon is the most restrictive by prohibiting the use of face recognition technologies by private entities in public spaces, `www.portland.gov/smart-city-pdx/news/2020/9/9/` `city-council-approves-ordinances-banning-use-face-recognition`

See `www.banfacialrecognition.com/map` for a recent list.[10]

The U.S. Congress has proposed several bills, some of which are listed here, but none have made it to the U.S. Senate for a vote as of this writing:

- H.R. 2231 – Algorithmic Accountability Act of 2019
- H.R. 3230 – Defending Each and Every Person from False Appearances by Keeping Exploitation Subject (DEEPFAKES) to Accountability Act of 2019
- S.3284 – Ethical Use of Facial Recognition Act of 2020
- S.4084 – Facial Recognition and Biometric Technology Moratorium Act of 2020

The Science

Laws, policies, and their evolution over the past 200+ years has moved the United States society forward. . .slowly. These laws, however, leave gaps for people to interpret the policy language in ways that uphold systemic inequities and prejudices. Uneven policy and law regulation and policy enforcement practices exacerbate discrimination. It further deepens harms disproportionately to certain communities, and sidesteps the necessary atonement for healing. Perhaps laws and policies are too nebulous to be helpful in mitigating discrimination.

Let's turn to a topic that's considered objective: science. Science is purportedly based in facts and numbers. Science's concreteness and tangible nature is fully described by numbers, mathematical equations, scientific methodology, and science-based systems. Science remains the counterpoint to laws as a set of fields that intends to leave no gaps for "wrong" interpretation. By the Oxford Dictionary definition, science is "the intellectual and practical activity encompassing the systematic study of the structure and behavior of the physical and natural world through observation and experiment." Science finds and explains observable patterns. At the heart of scientific explorations are numbers. The decimal numeral system, aka base-10, that we use today was a choice.

Numbers

Originally numeral systems were localized, culturally relevant symbols to express a number.[11] Tally marks etched on bones, dating back to the Lebombo

bone of the Lebombo Mountains of southern parts of Africa circa 35,000 BC
(www.taneter.org/math.html), helped to keep track of commodities and assets.
Bundling tallies in sets of five became more common since it was an easier
system to manage for larger counts. Egyptian numerals used items from their
surroundings to represent large counts.

Can you imagine if Egyptian symbols were adopted instead? According to
Table 1.1, we'd be saying we pay a few strokes to a yoke for a fast-food combo
meal. Or paying a coil of rope and several yokes for our Internet broadband connection every month. The Babylonians, Ancient Greeks, Romans, and Mayans
all had their own numeral systems, ranging from physical objects, to characters,
to dot sequences representing numbers. What these localized societies had in
common was a way to represent 10—for our 10 fingers and our 10 toes. Representing nonwhole numbers (like 5.5) was rather sticky until the Hindu-Arabic
numeral system, created in the 9th century, became the adopted standard across
Europe by the 16th century.

Table 1.1: Egyptian numeral system

NUMBER	SYMBOL
1	Stroke
10	Yoke
100	Coil of rope
1000	Lotus
10000	Finger
100000	Frog
1000000	Man with raised hands

The number and numeral system history we're exposed to has most of its
framing in white European-esque culture. Babylonians, Ancient Greeks, and
Romans take center stage. And once we focus on the decimal numeral system,
white men dominate the well-documented narration of innovations and they
are credited with those revelations. Let me take the binary system as a case in
point.[12] Gottfried Wilhelm Leibniz, credited for creating the modern binary
system, published in *Explication de l'arithmétique binaire, qui se sert des seuls car-
acteres 0* and *1* in 1703. The work proposed a mechanical calculating device (like
an abacus) using binary numbers to keep count. The ability for him to publish
his thoughts cemented this contribution in history. His Wikipedia page provides
a comprehensive overview from his early life until his death.

But binary numeral systems have origins in Egypt—and later in China, where
Leibniz found inspiration. And then in 2013 National Academies of Science
researchers discovered there were the people of Mangareva in French Polynesia,
who used a hybrid binary-decimal system before 1450 (www.ncbi.nlm.nih.gov/

`pmc/articles/PMC3910603`). Each of these local societies predated Leibniz and his 1703 published work. Siloed, unconnected, and undocumented data, in this instance history as data, showcases at the least co-option and erasure. Leibniz was at minimum iteration 3, while the true Egyptian (iteration 0), Chinese (iteration 1), and Mangareva (iteration 2) innovators remain unnamed. The data we share is the data we are exposed to.

In the grand scheme, for each numeral system numbers don't stand alone. They are in relationship to other items and are often being compared to each other. The basic arithmetic all of us learn as children teaches us how to count items. These items are objects and things, like pieces/kinds of fruit, books, toys, animals, and chairs. Then we are taught to count people—taking a quick headcount for your teacher of the class or sharing how many siblings you have. People are assigned to a specific number depending on the circumstances. It's seemingly innocent most times to quickly assess if some capacity level has been reached. These numbers are temporary, discrete, hold no value beyond count, and don't follow us in perpetuity. In many tech systems, however, the assignment of numbers to people is permanent. It's your unique universal identifier. For example, on Twitter each profile has a numerical ID (mine is 4361823620202257792). Each tweet is represented and retrievable by its own number too.

Numbers are shared to relay a specific context that can't be conveyed another way effectively. Numbers are reductive and insidious when presently nakedly. Some may counterargue that a number itself isn't reductive, insidious, or oppressive. No matter what, 2 + 2 will always equal 4. There are no racial or gendered undertones in numbers or in their applications in arithmetic, mathematics, or any science. But numbers at their core are abstractions of our physical world. This abstraction, reducing things and people to numbers, intends to simplify the complicated. But in the end the outcome strips away informative context that can't be recaptured with numbers alone. This pattern is well-documented in history. A prime example occurs in anthropometry.

Anthropometry

Anthropometry is the scientific study of the measurements and proportions of the human body. Informally, it's the measuring of the proportions of a person's body. Anthropometry has its roots in the 1830s with Adolphe Quetelet and Louis R. Villermé, who separately recognized the impact of socioeconomic and environmental factors on a person's height. They wanted to improve prisons and healthcare, but their measurements connecting shorter heights with lower socioeconomic class grab significant attention. But then Alphonse Bertillon, a French police officer, in the late 1870s used a prisoner's height, eye color, ears, lips, ethnicity, neck, head contour, a bunch of other detailed physical characteristics, and the police officer's reflective observations to catalog suspected/confirmed criminals.[13]

Bertillon's system initially consisted of five measurements: head length, head breadth, length of the middle finger, length of the left foot, and length of the forearm from the elbow to the extremity of the middle finger (called a cubit). The reason each measure was important reveals the fascination with anthropometry at the time (and still today). The head length and breadth helps to capture the size of someone's head. The length of the middle finger has been correlated to estimating someone's height. And there's strong indicators that the other two measurements aided in confirming a person's stature. This system led Bertillon to find nearly 150 criminals. By the late 1880s, Bertillon's systems transformed into the Bertillon card system, which was adopted in police precincts across Europe, as shown in Figure 1.3. Every person with a card had their personal information recorded, including full name, current address, physical feature measurements, and a photo for identification.[14] Then it made its way to the United States, first to the Illinois State Penitentiary (1887), then on to other regions such as the New York State Division of Criminal Justice System (1893; `https://stage.criminaljustice.ny.gov/ojis/history/bert_sys.htm`) and New Orleans (1897; `https://cdm16880.contentdm.oclc.org/digital/collection/p16880coll46`).

And in the United States, police forces—present in some form since the 1630s—have an unflattering history. This history includes attempts to protect wealthy neighborhoods with nightly patrol (funnily like today's gated communities), to control immigrant communities as many moved to the USA (eerily similar to U.S. Immigration and Customs Enforcement) and to target enslaved Africans during slavery (oh, that's the regular police cruising in Black neighborhoods, while they disappear when an actual crime is/was in progress). So in the dominant culture, the white men who were police, gathered the perceived and actual criminal's measurements. By the mid-1880s, the Bertillon card system was used to fuel recidivism laws first enacted in France (`https://criminocorpus.org/en/expositions/anciennes/suspects-defendants-guilty/alphonse-bertillon-and-identification-persons-1880-1914`).

Eugenics

While Bertillon cards were being adopted across the United States, the American Eugenics movement was gaining momentum. Eugenics[15]—aka social Darwinism aka scientific racism[16]—is a pseudoscience that believes humanity can be improved by selective breeding—namely that certain people or populations should be fruitful and multiply while others need to go toward extinction (Francis Galton's main thesis). More bluntly, the field of eugenics wants science to prove that white races are superior to other races and in particular that the Black race is inferior to the white race. The premise is that white people are built/made better than Black people. And this leads to socially propagated stereotypes that Black people are not as intelligent and better suited for certain classes of employment work. The thought is that anthropometric measurements are data evidence to show differences in races and that those differences indicate how selective breeding should be done. It's hogwash.

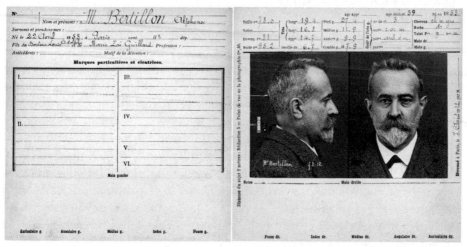

Figure 1.3: Mugshot of Alphonse Bertillon (1853–1914) with a reference card from his "bertillonage" system

Source: (Wikimedia)—Jebulon / Wikimedia Commons / Public domain

But scientists and scholars since the 1880s have been trying to prove eugenics has validity—failing each and every time.[17] And they have also been trying to use anthropometry to characterize physical characteristics as criminal in the United States. Most notably, Francis Galton coined the term "eugenics" in 1883. Eugenics proposes (incorrectly) that people of higher social classes have a better genetic composition—yes, your wealth is tied to your biological makeup. Wow! Galton tried to measure intelligence using a test to show how intelligence correlates to social status. His own results disproved it (www.bristol.ac.uk/media-library/ sites/cmm/migrated/documents/Galton.pdf, https://galton.org/books/ human-faculty/text/galton-1883-human-faculty-v4.pdf, and www.facinghistory .org/resource-library/origins-eugenics). Scientists and scholars in the United States doubled down on that supposition to find ways to remove "undesirable" biological and social traits. And these undesirable traits included but were not limited to having melanin, women who were sexually assaulted, children conceived as a result of sexual assault, being a U.S. immigrant, being in poverty, and so on. Sterilization became a common route to remove those deemed "undesirable" traits.

The American Eugenics movement thrived in part due to scholarly documentation of "interesting" theories—we sometimes call it innovation today—data as provided by anthropometric measures and categories and lastly *significant consistent funding*. U.S. colleges and separate research institutes created academic departments focused on eugenics. The Eugenics Research Office (1910–1939), based in Cold Spring Harbor, New York, was primarily funded by the Rockefeller family and the Carnegie Institute. (Also note other predominant organizations feeding eugenics ideas: British Eugenics Education Society of 1907 and the American Eugenics Society of 1921.) Under an academic and scholarship umbrella, the license to deploy anthropometry broadly had little to no resistance. Eugenics thinking led to human and civil rights violations. Anthropometric measurements were taken from college students at Tuskegee Institute, a historically Black college (1932–1944). Charles Davenport and Morris Steggerda designed and executed a study that gathered anthropometric "scientific" information looking to characterize Black people's traits. It was all conducted in an attempt to support eugenicists' claim that races are hereditarily/physically different (`https://brill.com/view/book/edcoll/9789004286719/B9789004286719-s010.xml`). Their study was funded by the Eugenics Research Office.

Coerced and forced sterilization occurred during 1909–1979 in California (`www.pbs.org/independentlens/blog/unwanted-sterilization-and-eugenics-programs-in-the-united-states`) and other states in the United States. Let me not forget, in the midst of a global pandemic, the 2020 U.S. media reporting of mass hysterectomies at the U.S. ICE Detention Center (`www.forbes.com/sites/jemimamcevoy/2020/09/15/pelosi-calls-for-investigation-into-claims-of-mass-hysterectomies-poor-covid-19-care-at-ice-detention-center/?sh=19e01905f7ca`, `www.fox5atlanta.com/news/federal-complaint-questionable-hysterectomies-lack-of-covid-19-tests-at-ga-immigrant-detention-center`, `www.cbsnews.com/news/whistleblower-nurse-questionable-hysterectomies-shoddy-covid-care-georgia-immigrant-detention-center-dawn-wooten`). Brown immigrant populations were/are still targets.

Source: Twitter, Inc.

Explaining social differences using racial markers persists in scholarly ventures in the present day. The Bertillon card system opened the door to cataloging people, first in prison and then potential criminal subjects. Many of its anthropometry foundations have disappeared because it wasn't an exact science. People were misclassified and misidentified. And then there's the frequency of certain heights, eye color, and the like that made the system produce too many potential people who fit the criminal's description. People were being wrongly accused. Eventually fingerprinting replaced many of those anthropometry categories. But wait a minute—too many people fit a common description—this sounds like the recidivism systems and facial recognition software used in the 2010s/2020s.

The Correctional Offender Management Profiling for Alternative Sanctions (COMPAS) recidivism tool used an algorithm to access the risk of a person becoming a repeat offender. In 2016, ProPublica performed a deep investigation of this algorithm.[18] Its impacts hit the national media like a meteor with a major finding that Black people were at least twice as likely than white people to have a higher recidivism risk score when their crimes were similar (www.propublica .org/article/machine-bias-risk-assessments-in-criminal-sentencing).

In 2020, Springer Nature reviewed and accepted the scholarly article "A Deep Neural Network Model to Predict Criminality Using Image Processing" for its Research Book Series: Transactions on Computational Science and Computational Intelligence. The Coalition for Critical Technology issued a scathing letter urging the well-respected publication to rescind the publication and denounce the study (https://medium.com/@CoalitionForCriticalTechnology/ abolish-the-techtoprisonpipeline-9b5b14366b16).[19] They did. The study was never published.

But what would happen if the Coalition for Critical Technology hadn't stepped in? The work could be published in reputable venues and/or publicly available for others to devise similar theories and build experiments, independently. For instance, two researchers from Shanghai Jiao Tong University back in 2016 published "Automated Inference on Criminality Using Face Images" on arXiv.org, an open-access non-peer-reviewed repository (https://arxiv .org/pdf/1611.04135.pdf). Their paper has over 50 citations, some perpetuating eugenics thinking and others debunking it.

Attempts to make eugenics legitimate through "scientific" and data-rich "rigorous" methods is a long-standing approach since the opening of the Eugenics Research Office in 1910. And it continues to this day. Data is not neutral and highly subjective. Black people, for instance, face specific and documented harms when their physical pain level isn't recorded correctly. Dr. Susan Moore was a medical physician and contracted COVID-19. While hospitalized, she documented her failed attempted to receive "adequate treatment" given her symptoms despite her medical degrees. Her experience isn't unique. The National Academy of Medicine released a comprehensive report in 2005 detailing the lower quality of healthcare to Black patients than their white counterparts.

The unjust treatment of Black people goes beyond the healthcare industry. It lives in every system and institution, the tech industry as well. *Mankind Quarterly*, created in 1960, is a peer-reviewed journal described in *Measured Lies: The Bell Curve Explained* (Palgrave Macmillan, 1997) as a "cornerstone scientific racism establishment."[20] According to the *Mankind Quarterly* website, "[it] was first published in Edinburgh, Scotland in 1961, and then, from 1979 to 2014, by the Council for Social and Economic Studies (chaired by Roger Pearson) in Washington, D.C. In January 2015, publication was transferred to the Ulster Institute for Social Research, a non-profit organization in London, England." The journal states that "[m]ost of the research that the *Mankind Quarterly* publishes today is "normal" science, but the editors still welcome controversy and new ideas. They see it as part of the journal's mission to provide a forum for the presentation and discussion of theories and empiric research that challenge entrenched beliefs. Of course, the often-contradictory views that are represented in the *Mankind Quarterly* are those of the individual authors, not those of the journal's publishers or editors" (www.mankindquarterly.org/about). So does it still support eugenics, aka scientific racism aka social Darwinism? Check it out and draw your own conclusions.[21]

Summary

Oppression of a certain group or population using laws and/or science is born from the dominant culture's fear—the fear that social change will lead to economic shifts unfavorable to the dominant culture. The fear is rooted in white supremacists and separationists being scared of competing with Black, Brown, and Indigenous people on an even playing field, because the only brand of competition white supremacists and separationists know is cheating and tipping the scales in their white colonialism's favor by any means necessary. Oppression tactics, in the law and in the sciences, are mere social controls to enforce a hierarchy positioning that doesn't exist.

Notes

1. Roediger, David R. "Historical Foundations of Race." National Museum of African American History and Culture, July 20, 2020. https://nmaahc.si.edu/learn/talking-about-race/topics/historical-foundations-race.

2. Sherman, Shantella. "Breeding Out the Blacks with Dr Shantella Sherman." YouTube, June 4, 2020. www.youtube.com/watch?v=rpTJNJMH0_U.

3. Markels, Alex. "Timeline: Wiretaps' Use and Abuse." NPR, December 20, 2005. www.npr.org/templates/story/story.php?storyId=5061834.

4. White, April. "A Brief History of Surveillance in America." Smithsonian .com. Smithsonian Institution, April 1, 2018. www.smithsonianmag.com/history/brief-history-surveillance-america-180968399.

5. Sirovich, L and M. Kirby, "Low-dimensional procedure for the characterization of human faces," J. Opt. Soc. Am. A **4**, 519-524 (1987). https://opg.optica.org/josaa/abstract.cfm?URI=josaa-4-3-519.

6. Turk, Matthew and Alex Pentland (1991). Eigenfaces for recognition. *Journal of Cognitive Neuroscience, 3*(1), 71–86. https://doi.org/10.1162/jocn.1991.3.1.71.

7. Flanagan, Patricia. "Face Recognition Technology (FERET)." NIST, July 13, 2017. www.nist.gov/programs-projects/face-recognition-technology-feret.

8. Flanagan, Patricia. "Face Recognition Vendor Test (FRVT)." NIST, November 30, 2020. www.nist.gov/programs-projects/face-recognition-vendor-test-frvt.

9. "History of Face Recognition & Facial Recognition Software." FaceFirst Face Recognition Software, May 9, 2019. www.facefirst.com/blog/brief-history-of-face-recognition-software.

10. "Ban Facial Recognition." Ban Facial Recognition. Accessed November 4, 2021. www.banfacialrecognition.com.

11. Zegarelli, Mark. "10 Alternative Numeral and Number Systems." dummies .com, accessed November 4, 2021. www.dummies.com/education/math/pre-algebra/10-alternative-numeral-and-number-systems.

12. Porubsky, Stefan. Binarysystem, accessed November 4, 2021. www.cs.cas .cz/portal/AlgoMath/NumberTheory/Arithmetics/NumeralSystems/PositionalNumeralSystems/BinarySystem.htm.

13. Piazza, Pierre. "Alphonse Bertillon and the Identification of Persons (1880-1914)." Criminocorpus, August 26, 2016. https://criminocorpus .org/en/expositions/anciennes/suspects-defendants-guilty/alphonse-bertillon-and-identification-persons-1880-1914.

14. "Visible Proofs: Forensic Views of the Body: Galleries: Technologies: The Bertillon System." U.S. National Library of Medicine. National Institutes of Health, June 5, 2014. www.nlm.nih.gov/exhibition/visibleproofs/galleries/technologies/bertillon.html.

15. Heberer Rice, Patricia, and Lutz Kaelber. "A History of Eugenics." YouTube, August 26, 2020. www.youtube.com/watch?v=jeSM9vz6ylg.

16. "Scientific Racism." Wikipedia. Wikimedia Foundation, October 19, 2021. `https://en.wikipedia.org/wiki/Scientific_racism`.

17. Eugenicsarchive. Accessed November 4, 2021. `www.eugenicsarchive.org/html/eugenics/static/themes/6.html`.

18. Angwin, Julia, Jeff Larson, Surya Mattu, and Lauren Kirchner. "Machine Bias." ProPublica, May 23, 2016. `www.propublica.org/article/machine-bias-risk-assessments-in-criminal-sentencing`.

19. Coalition for Critical Technology. "Abolish the #TechToPrisonPipeline." Medium, September 21, 2021. `https://medium.com/@Coalition-ForCriticalTechnology/abolish-the-techtoprisonpipeline-9b5b14366b16`.

20. Hama, Aldric. "Book Review: Facing Reality: Two Truths about Race in America." *Mankind Quarterly*. Ulster Institute for Social Research, September 1, 2021. `www.mankindquarterly.org/archive/issue/62-1/13`.

21. Skibba, Ramin. "The Disturbing Resilience of Scientific Racism." `Smithsonian.com`, May 20, 2019. `www.smithsonianmag.com/science-nature/disturbing-resilience-scientific-racism-180972243`.

Recommended Reading

`www.youtube.com/watch?v=BGjSday7f_8`: Dr. Joy DeGruy Leary: Post Traumatic Slave Disorder Lecture, London 2008 Lecture; Post Traumatic Slave Syndrome—America's Legacy of Enduring Injury and Healing.

CHAPTER
2

Morality

Dr. Brandeis Marshall
@csdoctorsister

Like tech won't solve social ills, laws don't change people's behaviors.

Source: Twitter, Inc.

Ethics is only one branch of the expansive philosophy field. I won't discuss each kind of ethics because it's very broad and hard to implement in practice. So we'll focus on a subset that more intentionally impacts technology. And this is a hard feat. As I'll lay out in this chapter, ethics of any kind is limited in its utility. Understanding the significance and influence of how morality shows up (or doesn't) in tech innovations isn't a new phenomenon. It has, however, received renewed attention in light of the more frequent global pronouncement of tech malfeasance. For those of us on the "inside" of tech, we're torn by this realization that the code we write is likely contributing to a cycle of harm that we don't know how to curtail, stop, or dislodge ourselves from. For those of us on the "outside" of tech, we're shocked and dismayed by tech's Wild Wild West status. Being unaware of the multitude of mistreatments endured makes us feel ashamed of what has transpired and powerless in shaping a less harm-inducing tech future. Regardless of our position in tech, we're paralyzed by the gravity of the past, present, and continuing harms inflicted on real people.

For the tech insiders, we have our hands in the data directly or indirectly. We've figured out, being involved in project after project, just how important the "right" data is to our activities. We have our hand *in* the data all the time. We focus on the mechanics of handling data. We're collecting, cleaning, analyzing, interpreting, and producing more of it with every action we take, with each function some of us code. The mechanical work associated with data consumes us. What we ignore is the impact that our actions with data are having and will have once data leaves our data/software team. We tell ourselves that we can't control what others do with data and the tech that's produced. This is a convenient truth and helps us absolve ourselves of any further responsibility. The application and use of data becomes someone else's concern. Addressing bad uses of tech are therefore outside of our lane.

Those days of not knowing the potential for negative tech effects have faded away. Each stage of building a tech product introduces and compounds harms to minoritized communities. Instead of wringing our hands helplessly about the ill effects after the tech is released to the public, we must take the reins and significantly shift how we work with data as well as how we decide to design and implement our tech-based ideas. We are looking for a moral compass in our data handling and tech creation processes. Right now, this moral compass doesn't exist in full form, but it has led us to seek out ethics to ground us. Ethics comes with a long history and thus gives us a general blueprint to shape how we think about the social, economic, and political ramifications of tech's work. It provides us with a clearer path to making tech that works for all of us. It definitely sheds light on *a path*, but that path is not so clear-cut.

The intricate interdependence of data, tech, and people can bring about enormous benefits to making some of our everyday tasks easier. These affinities can shine a light on some cautionary tales that give us insight into data's misuse. Recent instances that gives all of us cause-for-pause about tech's usefulness include identifying people using facial recognition or selecting potential employees by using an automated résumé processing tool.

Data plays an active participatory role in enacting, enforcing, and scaling tech's harmful consequences. Acknowledging this is a good first step, but this step falls flat without action plans to identify and mitigate them. Missing parts revolve around how those of us in tech make decisions when handling data, which is at the heart of building and maintaining digital products. This brings you and I to data ethics, which we know very little about. The tech industry dances around the topic of data ethics because they know if we look too closely, we'll learn the fuller weight of their keystrokes and make us elevate our standards. Growing our society's knowledge about tech harms requires each of us to stretch our understanding. So we'll start with the main fuel of our profession: data.

Data Is All Around Us

Let's start with fun facts. Do you know what the first programming language was and when it was created? It's FORTRAN in 1956. Do you know when the computer was invented and what it was called? That's Electronic Numerical Integrator and Computer (ENIAC) in 1943. But what's the first data? Good question. Computer programming languages and computers are created by people. With data, however, people chase after it, work diligently to capture it, and try to restrain it. The origins of data aren't traceable in a meaningful way, though. There isn't a beginning and an end of data. This is where all of us acknowledge data exists and when we see fit to grab it. This was the impetus for inventing ENIAC and for creating FORTRAN. Performing calculations by hand turned out to be limited. The response was to build a digital system to do these calculations (enter ENIAC). Then, standardizing how calculations were performed proved important, because running the same calculations many times in different ways is rather inefficient and those in tech are just reinventing the wheel (enter FORTRAN). ENIAC and FORTRAN are only as effective as the numbers, formulas, and result validations they produced. In other words, both are merely digital systems attempting to harness data. Data is perceived as useful. Being useful also makes data valuable. And every industry sets out to leverage the valuable pieces of data, by any means necessary.

Wrapping people's minds around what data is and how we all handle it has been the plight of the tech industry since its conception with ENIAC. Data comes in different forms: text, audio, pictures, video media, mixed media, and mixed reality at the very least. Each form is a way for us to structure our understanding of what we're seeing, hearing, and speaking. And then one data form can become another form. A recorded audio interview turns into a text transcript. A Zoom webinar can be repurposed into an audio file on Apple iTunes or Spotify. As humans, we can re-tool data however we can imagine, and that allows us to construct alternative interpretations. We must be careful, though, since these interpretations can easily spread half-truths or falsehoods.

Data exists, like water, in every nook and cranny in digital and physical spaces. Yes, data is tech's water by providing a lifeline to every digital system. First, we are data. Our face, height, eye color, etc. (remember the Bertillon system?). Our fingerprints. Our eye retinas. Our voice. We wear the Apple Watch so that it can tell us our heart rate, count our steps, remind us to hydrate, and so on. Who we are, as a collection of physical attributes, and how we interact with the world creates data that's valuable to organizations. Data comes from all of us.

And data about people has turned into elaborate digitized processes of comparing one human with another. We're seeking out the differences and isolating the similarities to reinforce a made-up white supremacist social hierarchy.

Second, all of us, especially in tech, use or repurpose existing data to make new data products. Every book summary, movie review, and corporate impact report highlights the main takeaways. We generate new data every day by responding to email, reading, liking, sharing, or replying to a social media post. We as humans are constantly making data to explain other data. Data explaining other data has a few names in the tech space, such as metadata (for images) or comments (in coding). We are grasping at ways to remember what the data means and the context we've assigned to it. We're attempting to put data in a finite capsule so that we can refer to it later. Our human leaning toward forgetfulness has resulted in our own data overload with the incessant need to record and digitally store everything we can. But often, that data's shelf life expires as we move on to focus on newer data we'd created. We wind up not using or repurposing existing data like we had hoped.

Third, we as people engage with data products in a variety of ways. Melding what we read, see, or hear with our own prior knowledge creates a recipe for differing opinions. In most cases, this is a good thing because there's an assumption that opinions are based in true, correct, and accurate information. Different beliefs can be shared and debated among people. We can agree or disagree on certain opinions at the end of all the discussions while still living in community with each other. Nevertheless, a belief and thus opinion can be a combination of truth, half-truth, and lies. And now we have cause for concern. When beliefs are rooted in falsehoods, we have division and anti-civility. For example, in May 2021, researchers show that 12 Facebook accounts contribute to the vast majority of antivaccine claims (www.npr.org/2021/05/13/996570855/disinformation-dozen-test-facebooks-twitters-ability-to-curb-vaccine-hoaxes).[1] The people reading and forming their beliefs based on one of these 12 antivaccination accounts have a belief reinforced by debunked claims not shared by the antivaccination accounts. As Booker T. Washington once said: "A lie doesn't become truth, wrong doesn't become right, and evil doesn't become good, just because it's accepted by a majority." We have to challenge our beliefs and opinions to ensure what we read, hear, and see is based in truth, not lies. Data can play tricks on us if we aren't astute to how it can be easily manipulated.

Let me give an example covering all three ways data is pervasive from one of the biggest data marketplaces on the Internet: the social network platform Twitter. The mechanics of Twitter is straightforward—people create profiles (actual people, organizations, or bots) that can connect to other profiles with a restricted set of interaction options: like, retweet, reply, or follow. But there lies many subnetworks of conversations within their own subnetworks of conversations. See, conversations are identifiable and findable using hashtags. They were created to serve as digital street signs where all conversations about a topic can congregate. In application, however, they have been much more than innocent locators of information. Hashtags track conversations and which profiles are part of those conversations. Any profile can see all or part of the conversation among other profiles, as long as the profile isn't listed as private. This setup breeds lurker, stalker, and troll profiles—those profiles will read the commentary but not engage in the conversation. Online conversations reinforce offline conversations in the real world, and vice versa.

These Twitter conversations aren't *actually* free. Twitter made 86 percent of its 2020 revenue, $3.2 billion, from advertising services while the remaining $509 million came from data licensing and other sources. Interestingly, Twitter wasn't profitable in 2020, reporting a net loss of $1.1 billion (www.investopedia .com/ask/answers/120114/how-does-twitter-twtr-make-money.asp, www .businessofapps.com/data/twitter-statistics).[2,3] Worldwide, Twitter boasts over 180 million daily users, where the user demographics reveal the undercurrent of Twitter's culture:[3]

- About 70 percent identify as male.

- For companies with more than 100 employees, 66 percent use Twitter for marketing purposes.

- Twitter's U.S. content is dominated by the top 10 percent of U.S. tweeters. They contribute 92 percent of the tweets.

With 500 million tweets per day and 200 billion tweets sent per year,[4] the lifespan of a tweet is only 15–20 minutes, which necessitates frequent postings to gain followers and to be labeled as an influencer (www.internetlivestats.com/ twitter-statistics). As world-famous American sculptor and video artist Richard Serra said in 1973, "If something is free, you're the product." Everyone who posts to and engages with Twitter content is contributing to its revenue stream. *We are the data—either by creating it directly ourselves or by facilitating its creation.*

Content posted on Twitter is perceived as available for public use, unless the tweeter sets their account to the protected option. A tweet and/or Twitter profile gains traction on the platform when the engagement rate is considered high (https://theonlineadvertisingguide.com/ad-calculators/ twitter-engagement-rate-calculator).[5] The Twitter engagement rate is a simple formula of total engagements (number of people who liked, commented, retweeted, and quote tweeted) divided by total impressions (number of times the tweet appeared on a Twitter timeline).

- About 33 percent of Twitter users have an engagement rate of under 0.5 percent.

- Less than 50 percent of Twitters users have an engagement rate over 1 percent.

- About 25 percent of Twitter users report an engagement rate over 2 percent.

When a tweet reaches above that 2 percent mark in a short amount of time, within 5–7 days, it's considered to have "gone viral." Sometimes, a tweet can go beyond a few days of online fame to sparking conversations and movements. The original tweeter's message, along with the context of that message, gets lost and repurposed for a different cause.

In 2015, #OscarsSoWhite was created by April Reign when she shared her sentiments of a non-Black person at the Oscars asking to touch her hair. That's a grown person asking another grown person if they could touch their hair. Here's when a thought turned into data digitally by being immortalized in a tweet ("#OscarsSoWhite they asked to touch my hair.") with that digital street sign. The tweet has only 197 retweets, 4 quote tweets, and 363 likes, but the number of comments soared along with the number of impressions. I suspect the engagement rate for this tweet is far above that 2 percent as it has been referenced in countless articles. It's also included in April Reign's Wikipedia page. April Reign's tweet was first circulated modestly in one of Twitter's subnetworks dubbed BlackTwitter. BlackTwitter is a subculture of Twitter, coined back in 2008 or 2009, that shares Black culture and experiences ranging from bigotry and anti-Black racism to celebrity news. The hashtag, which originally gave language to a Black woman's feelings of her personal space being invaded, became a pseudo-call to arms and beacon for racial and gender equity in the movie industry. And it quickly went from BlackTwitter to white (mainstream) Twitter to international use in a matter of days. Society expanded the use and purpose of it. *We've reinvented #OscarsSoWhite into a new data product—it had been repurposed (and more directly co-opted by white society).*

This co-option by white society occurs through retooling, reimagining, and reconfiguring of context and messaging. And revisionism is easy to accomplish when the power and influence on a platform skews heavily male (that's 70 percent of Twitter users) and white (that's over 60 percent of the U.S. population and nearly 70 percent of the tech industry). On tech's best day, a social media platform can help disseminate relevant and accurate content as evidenced by partnerships with AMBER ALERT to find missing/abducted minors or the U.S. government on Covid-19 vaccination information. On tech's worst day, social media platforms deluge unto a playground for misinformation and disinformation campaigns as we came to know Cambridge Analytics after the 2016 U.S. presidential election and voter integrity doubts as part of the 2020 U.S. presidential election. The language associated with the tweets are evaluated and assessed for blatant misrepresentations, not nuanced ones that happen over time. In their 2018 *Science* paper, Vosoughi, Aral, and Roy exposed how false news stories are 70 percent more likely to be retweeted than true stories are, and that it takes six times longer for true stories to reach the same number of people (www.science .org/doi/10.1126/science.aap9559).[6] These sorts of revelations are visualized by the Knight Foundation's commission of a study about the spread of fake news (https://knightfoundation.org/features/misinfo).[7] Automated accounts, like bots, propel the misinformation and disinformation spread. Once the falsehood is posted, it can't be recalled, removed, or rectified. *We engage with data and evolve our thinking based on which data we find. If our data sources and systems of evaluation aren't sound, the conclusions we draw are therefore wrong.*

Morality and Technology

Discussing ethics sparks visions of a group of pen-and-paper people sitting in a circle under a 100-year-old tree having spirited debates about would've, could've, and should've scenarios. Questions become clear and challenges in decision-making are laid bare. These thought-provoking conversations are rooted in the abstract like "Is free will real or just an illusion?" and focus on how people think through their choices rather than the decision itself. But all of us have to continue pulling that thread past our choices, to the decision itself, to the intended and unintended consequences of our decisions. And then we add on the context of our time in history: the fourth industrial revolution and the knowledge economy. This means we're actively melding our physical, digital, and biological worlds using automation and leveraging knowledge.

I'm really talking about three branches of ethics. Human ethics covers those seeking to understand our physical world—thought to be simply debating such things under the tree. Tech ethics cover those making the digital a replica of our physical environments and societal constructs. Lastly, data ethics covers those making distinctions between information, misinformation, and disinformation. In each case the same question comes up: how are we, as a global digitized society, identifying, evaluating, and ensuring people, tech, and/or data aren't mistreating people? I'll deal with tech ethics and human ethics first since they build on each other. Then once we have that context, I'll shift our attention to data ethics—it sits between the other two.

Defining Tech Ethics

Tech ethics is on a mission to identify and provide approaches to mitigate vulnerabilities, threats, risks, and weaknesses that any forms of software and/or hardware systems (e.g., technology) introduce to compromise the human condition. The term *technology* has been morphed to cover many aspects of computing. Many in the tech industry mean it as the service application and implementation of computing algorithms or processes to accomplish a task on digital systems. Think Technology as a Service. Simply put, technology *should be designed* to add positive value to our human lives, not diminish them or bring positivity/value to certain communities and not others. And the friction that continually bubbles to the surface is: how can tech and people coexist in non-harming harmony?

Nowadays, tech surrounds us too: smartphones, mobile devices, laptops, smart devices, virtual assistant devices. Our thoughts are digitized in audio as we speak, text as we type, and expression as we are videoed. These feelings are shared as second nature in the digital space. We share our ethics each time we interact with a tech device. Parents may or may not decide to post images of their children online. People now know not to share their personal identifying information, like a Social Security number, via email. Some people may feel comforted by animating family photos, for example, MyHeritage's Deep Nostalgia service, while others raise lots of concerns about how their *now digital* family photos are being protected from bad actors. The question "Why do I see my photos on Google?" appears on MyHeritage's FAQ page (`https://faq .myheritage.com/en/article/why-do-i-see-my-photos-on-google`).[8]

From 1946 (first computer) to 1973 (first cell phone), the number of people who engaged directly with technology was small—albeit technology impacted everyone at different degrees.[9] A few were making decisions for the general public. Tech wasn't a public commodity like it is today. So incentives for the two sides to find common ground and work together weren't a priority. Today, the frequency and severity of tech's mismanagement of humanity in digital spaces are too many to ignore. Unfortunately, society still has a few people making decisions for the many, with the addition of the many having significant access to the tech. So many people are interacting regularly on digitized systems they may or may not understand. Pervasive tech use exacerbates and creates vulnerabilities, threats, risks, and weaknesses that were never considered in the design phase. It's an open breeding ground that feeds uncertainty and mistrust.

In tech ethics, vulnerabilities, threats, risks, and weaknesses attributed to tech are associated with either computer software or computer hardware. The focus of tech ethics (`www.acm.org/code-of-ethics`)[10] circa 2021, in the computing sciences, center on coding mechanics, not semantics and impact. There's so much over-respect and over-grace extended to other computing professionals, their ideas, and their work product over how the tech affects people. The general ethical principles fall in line with "do no evil" mantras purported by many tech organizations. Then those in tech prescribe their professional responsibilities with respect to ethics is to simply acknowledge the need for strong ethical practice. Yet, for the most part, ethical practices in computing aren't described or defined.

This limp-arm existence of ethics in computing stems from the awkward handling of ethics in computing curriculum. Tech's culture gives plenty of lip service to being a good steward when creating and handling software. And there's a nod to not being a malicious hacker. The boxes with the socially, conscious and politically correct words and phrases are all present—respect diversity/ the work/privacy; avoid harm; be thorough; display your computing competence; prioritize the public good. The obligations outlined read well and sound good. But this messaging is inconsistent with the computing classrooms and curriculum recommendations. The computing classroom is ultra-competitive.

You're constantly proving that you know more than anyone else, that you can do the assignments faster and more eloquently than anyone else. Working with fellow classmates carries a heavy burden of not being perceived incompetent. The lone wolf alpha persona is born and reinforced with each internship, job, and promotion.

Like the Association for Computing Machinery (ACM) Code of Ethics, the ACM's Computing Curriculum Guidelines are disconnected and in direct friction with tech's everyday culture. The curriculum guidelines raise ethics as a topic to be covered at the undergraduate level. However, the emphasis on ethics in computing has remained shallow for at least the past three editions. In the Computing Curricula 2020: Paradigms for Global Computing Education (www .acm.org/binaries/content/assets/education/curricula-recommendations/ cc2020.pdf),[11] ethics is mentioned 23 times in this 205-page report dated March 16, 2021, that was sponsored by ACM, the Institute of Electrical and Electronics Engineers (IEEE), and the IEEE Computer Society. And the Computer Science Draft Competencies provided didn't include any occurrences of "ethics." Tech ethics and code of professional conduct are watered down to a subsection on Social Issues and Professional Practice, shown in Figure 2.1. The statements A–G are packed with *what* to do, not *how* to do any of them. For instance, let's take statement E: "Produce a document that is helpful to others that addresses the effects of societal change due to technology." It sounds *great*. Now, how is a computing educator supposed to teach this? And how would the receiver of said document apply this document to their computing-related work? The authors of these guidelines don't know, neither do the instructors, nor I, so you know the students won't associate much value with this computing knowledge area.

> **SP-Social Issues and Professional Practice**
> A. Perform a system analysis for a local organization and present the results to them in a non-technical way.
> B. Integrate interdisciplinary knowledge to develop a program for a local organization.
> C. Document industry trends, innovations, and new technologies and produce a report to influence a targeted workspace.
> D. Present to a group of professionals an innovative computer system by using audience-specific language and examples to illustrate the group's needs.
> E. Produce a document that is helpful to others that addresses the effect of societal change due to technology.
> F. Adopt processes to track customer requests, needs, and satisfaction.
> G. Compare different error detection and correction methods for their data overhead, implementation complexity, and relative execution time for encoding, detecting, and correcting errors and ensure that any error does not affect humans adversely.

Figure 2.1: ACM 2020 Computer Science Curriculum Guide's recommendation on social issues and professional practice topics to be covered at the undergraduate level
Source: ACM and IEEE.

What's odd is that more detailed computer science curricula guidelines were released in 2013 and they included ethics. The 500-page Computer Science Curricula 2013 report (www.acm.org/binaries/content/assets/education/ cs2013_web_final.pdf)[12] mentioned ethics 100 times. The committee meticulously developed a tiered set of core topics, with Core-Tier1 topics considered essential for all computer science programs, as shown in Figure 2.2. The Social Issues and Professional Practice knowledge area designates 11 Core-Tier1 hours. The typical undergraduate computer science major takes 12 computer science courses (roughly 576 hours) as part of completing their degree requirements. Social issues and professional practice training seems woefully underprioritized in both 2013 and 2020.

> **NOTE**   An "hour" refers to a lecture hour as designated by institutions, tradition-ally 50 minutes. Most courses require approximately 3 hours of instruction per week, for about 16 weeks, with one course totaling about 48 hours. Placing these numbers in context, 16 hours is one-third of the typical 48-hour course.

According to Figure 2.2, social context gets 1 hour while professional conduct gets 2 hours of dedicated attention in instruction. Every lecture, group project, internship, programming team competition, and internship these students experience teaches them the social context and professional conduct acceptable in tech. Three hours of instruction won't put a dent in how learners should be navigating computing principles that use data.

> **NOTE**   Ethics in computing curricula prior to 2013 had even less of a mention—for instance, the 2005 edition (`www.acm.org/binaries/content/assets/education/curricula-recommendations/cc2005-march06final.pdf`)[13] mentioned ethics three times in the 62-page report.

I took you on a brief walk through the computer science curricula guidelines to accentuate the lack of critique of tech within the field(s) that create the soft-ware and hardware systems on which we've become so reliant. People who are managing these software and hardware systems have little to no understanding of its impact on their own lives or on their organization's clients and stakeholders.

There's no formal or informal instruction. Thus, tech ethics is jaded by the shadows of their computing training. The tech in tech ethics is easier to describe because we're describing what it is and what it does in bettering your life. Images of my first computer, like a Gateway 2000 PC, come to mind when I think of tech. A hard drive, a fan, several types of processors, screen, and keyboard work like an orchestra to crunch numbers, create a document, or serve as a platform for you to play a game. Computing professionals concentrate on making the machinery (and thus software living on that machinery) impenetrable to intruders. For example, live software backups can provide redundant access to information in case of network connectivity failure or loss of the original location due to fire, theft, or another reason. Disks are cheap these days, and it's not difficult to keep live, off-site backups. It's not much more difficult to keep data accessible by deploying Internet security protocols. Many organizations and educational programs emphasize ways for computing professionals to handle intrusion detection and prevention, as well as provide vulnerability assessments.

SP. Social Issues and Professional Practice. [11 Core-Tier1 hours, 5 Core-Tier2 hours]			
	Core-Tier1 hours	Core-Tier2 hours	Includes Electives
SP/Social Context	1	2	N
SP/Analytical Tools	2		N
SP/Professional Ethics	2	2	N
SP/Intellectual Property	2		Y
SP/Privacy and Civil Liberties	2		Y
SP/Professional Communication	1		Y
SP/Sustainability	1	1	Y
SP/History			Y
SP/Economies of Computing			Y
SP/Security Policies, Laws and Computer Crimes			Y

Figure 2.2: ACM 2020 Computer Science Curriculum Guide's prioritization of social issues and professional practice instruction at the undergraduate level (one classroom hour required, two additional classroom hours preferred)

Source: ACM and IEEE.

While much of the computing sciences are concerned about protecting tech systems from internal and external intruders, there's little attention to what is happening *inside* of tech systems as well as what makes tech risky and/or a threat to people. We're considering how software, in particular algorithms and data, can misappropriate resources, codify harms, and deepen discriminatory policies by virtue of their existence and scalable use. We're describing the other side of tech ethics—human ethics.

Human ethics grapple with describing how people make decisions and how they consider the consequences of those decisions. It's the habitual thinking, talking, and weighing options about things and situations. Ethics give all of us guardrails and boundary boxes on what we should do in certain categories of circumstances. In practice, society has accepted a tech culture of rigid and inflexible processes without consistent care of consequences. Tech happened in science labs and R&D departments of an organization. Tech was therefore contained and controllable. Nuances posed by human ethics are oftentimes set aside or ignored by the tech industry. Nuances encountered with a human ethics lens can't be reduced to an equation, algorithm, or process that can be programmed into a digital system. The dividing lines between tech and ethics seems so far apart since the pre–personal computer age. The people doing tech and those doing ethics continue to run in different, nonoverlapping circles. The landscape is changing—but perhaps not in the most impactful places.

So in defining tech ethics, I must emphasize the duality of controlling these computing machines and being controlled by these computing machines. Tech ethics, in a more grounded explanation, sets its sights on designing technology to handle human ethics aspects in practice. As people grapple with choices that conflict with each other, so does technology, with one crucial exception. People can make a choice and change their minds without notice. We can adjust on the fly given new data. Technology can't do that. It's full steam ahead for technology. The algorithms, processes, and digital systems can't reverse course. Technology, more specifically algorithms, can't determine when it *may* need to reconsider whether or not certain lines of code should be executed.

Remember Tay, Microsoft's AI chatbot? Tay (Twitter profile name tayandyou) was unveiled in March 2016 as an experiment in "conversational understanding." It was supposed to exchange messages with Twitter users and simulate human interactions. These tweets quickly became toxic. People found this AI chatbot's weakness and exploited it savagely. Within 24 hours, Tay was tweeting racist, sexist, and other disparaging statements to the point that Tay's creators were forced to turn it off. Tay didn't have the capability to decide to reject those discriminatory statements. And that tech limitation remains hard-wired.

NOTE   Tay still has an active Twitter account, with its tweets set to private. So who is Tay communication with, if anyone? And how are those exchanges constructed?

When we are building tech, we, coders and the public alike, press forward with this stiff representation of tech like we're in the pre–personal computer era. Creating tech in isolation from morality has brought us to our current uncomfortable state—tech that harms unintentionally and intentionally.

Having a computer science and mathematical background is helpful in scrutinizing how tech ethics creep into software development work. For those of you in tech, you are a witness to tech design, implementation, or testing decisions that influence other decisions upstream and downstream from your contributions. You see, and with enough experience predict, the fallout and feel ill-equipped to intercede. For instance, in testing an automated employee candidate résumé processing tool, résumés from past candidates were mostly white men and then used as the training set in building the tool. The words describing white men candidates then dominated the rest of the development process. The words describing white men aren't used at the same frequency as in describing non-white men candidates. Women and minoritized candidates, specifically Black, Latin, and Indigenous people, wound up being suppressed since word matches didn't intersect. The composition of the interview pool therefore remains rather homogenous. That's not what tech workers want—well, a growing fraction of us. We, as tech workers, want to build good products that reduce harms. We want to solve many more problems than we seem to be creating with these products.

Most tech workers juggle a few projects at a time. They're at the front lines, handling and massaging data over time. They see some projects through from beginning to end whereas with others they provide their expertise only for a specific targeted task. Every so often, though, they have questions about the work they're doing, specifically how it ties into subsequent tech pieces and if it may inadvertently cause harm down the road. Most times they don't get a chance to circle back to that project after they hand it off to the next group in the tech development chain (aka the software development life cycle). Many of them would like to be more conscious of the impact of their actions and if they contributed to contaminating the remainder of the tech chain. And even if they made a coding decision, consciously or unconsciously, that wasn't the "right" thing to do, they want to know what to do about it.

In an ideal scenario, those of us in tech want to play offense by putting together the pieces of code in a way that can help minimize bad effects to certain populations. But we first need to recognize common missteps and then create an action plan to execute in real time. I'll talk about that in this book. The vast majority of scenarios don't fall into the ideal category. We're frequently standing with our backs to the proverbial wall facing a deadline looming and we notice an outcome that makes us uncomfortable. We don't have the time or, more importantly, the authority to figure out if a tech approach is possible. So now what? I'll talk about this too in this book. Doing the right thing in tech for societal good needs some context like what is "right," who determines what is "right," and what "doing" means for us. Laying out paths that help answer these questions, among others, brings us closer to thoughtfully constructed tech.

Mapping Tech Ethics to Human Ethics

Building tech with a moral compass is what we all want. But it's hard to envision because we have yet to come to a societal consensus on our own human morality. Studying moral principles, for example, ethics or human ethics, is about 2,400 years old, starting with Socrates and Plato. These popular philosophers pushed the consciousness of decision-making to the individual. They plucked the nerve: why do we do what we do? And more importantly, how do we decide what to do when we're in a conflicting situation? Obviously, "because we want to" isn't a good enough reason.

We make sense of ethics the best way we know how—understanding our decision patterns, character traits, rights, obligations and benefits to society (https://web.engr.uky.edu/~jrchee0/CE%20401/Josephson%20EDM/ Making_Ethical_Decisions.pdf, https://iep.utm.edu/ethics, and www.scu .edu/ethics/ethics-resources/ethical-decision-making/what-is-ethics).[14,15,16] The process of people making decisions falls into seven guiding principles: choice, conscience, fairness, honesty, honor, integrity, and value. All of us strive to make choices that don't rattle our conscience. We intend to be honest and honorable, and uphold our integrity. It's the way we're taught as children with the expectation of carrying these principles with us for the rest of our lives. Fairness and value befuddle many since they are more aspirational. It's hard to find a case where all affected parties agree that just treatment was achieved—fairness is in the eyes of the beholder. The same goes for value—assessing the quality of people and things is a direct reflection of whomever is performing the assessment. These tensions are wrapped up in determining what is fair and valuable. So we struggle with these two a bit more than the rest as people. Regardless, managing our choices and potential fallout are a clumsy juggling act among these seven. For the more analytically minded, it's like running a conditional probability model and trying to determine which pairs are dependent and which ones aren't.

We started to touch on the implicit relationships among these seven human ethics elements. Choice, a predominant ethical principle, allows us to weigh pros and cons. We question our decision paths and alternative routes in order to anticipate bringing the least harm to ourselves and others. We try to end up with a clear conscience. To get to that clear conscience, we have to balance the other ethical elements. Honesty, honor, and integrity are close cousins—if you have one, you tend to possess the other two. And the corollary can ring true: if you don't show you have one, people question whether you have the other two. We cross our fingers that we made the right choices by covering honesty, honor, and integrity well on the front end of decision-making. Fairness and value tag along behind since their effects are discovered as part of the long-term impact.

The two-part series of human ethics, intentions and outcomes, carry over to tech ethics with a digital twist. Tech ethics provides a way to uncover and, in theory, address the moral implications of software products and all those who are part of its cultivation, lifetime, and legacy in society. Tech ethics covers many facets of a technology's use and impact, including access rights, accountability, digital rights, environment, freedom, health and safety, judgment, over-automation, privacy, risk, security, and technology transparency. Tech oddly becomes this quasi-extension of people serving as interdependent actors in a decision-making circle.

Code written by people and digital spaces programmed by people are critical, yet unspoken, aspects of the decision-making cycle. Tech ethics, in its intention, weaves in tech as part of the existing morality conversation. It's like tech becomes another unknown variable in the morality equation. A lot of our daily interactions have us engaging with digital spaces. Our fingers initiate a series of actions online, whose impacts (good and bad) we often fail to understand for years to come. Ultimately, coders want the freedom to do what they want and how they want to do it. That's in direct conflict with (societal) judgment and realization of possible over-automation. The tensions lie in the coder's perceived needs and civil rights and society's stubbornness to preserve humanity.

NOTE   Let me pause here to explain digital spaces real quick: it's my catchall phrase for the algorithms, methods, processes, and systems constructed using computing infrastructure.

Tech has been propped up as the solution to human error, but we have hit a reality of tech errors, harms, and discrimination. The freedom of coding what you want has consequences to actual people, for the multigenerational life span of the production-level code. These consequences need to be felt by coders. When there's a direct authorship and approval path of algorithmic-based harmful tech, the company and personnel associated with that tech aren't the objects of the media's attention, in print or digital, like the victims of these technologies. Also they are given over-grace in covering these malicious outcomes as oversights that can be corrected in future software releases.

Let's consider the experience of Robert Julian-Borchak Williams (www.nytimes .com/2020/06/24/technology/facial-recognition-arrest.html?smid=tw-share),[17] a Black man living in a Detroit suburb. He was unlawfully handcuffed in front of his family. He was interrogated for 30 hours because of a partial facial recognition match and crude police work. The facial recognition tool/code that partially matched Mr. Williams's face incubated in a research and development environment (because they were given the money, time, and human resources to do it). Then that tech tool was released to be used on real people in real scenarios. The software development team likely never imagined that their project would help contribute to the false arrest of an American citizen.

We need to handle tech errors that live both inside and outside digital spaces in a better way. The facial recognition software company wasn't named explicitly. And there wasn't a half-hearted campaign to suggest retraining the coders who built this tech system that misclassified him. Retraining coders to be anti-discriminatory would require the tech industry to invest in developing anti-discriminatory coding practices as well as sound structures that enforce their effective integration.

Tech ethics is figuring out how digital spaces are affecting society, in particular its people, and then assigning who is responsible for these effects. In simple terms, it's tech transparency and tech accountability. Transparency is about the *what* those in tech are doing in making these tech products. Accountability is about the *how* those in tech are doing their work. And both cause software development teams, companies, legal departments within companies, stakeholders of these companies, clients/customers of these companies, and the public to get very, very uncomfortable because each is scared of being blamed for malfeasance.

Technology transparency squarely attempts to record expected use and impact. To be truly transparent, however, means we're generating more data to explain our data processes to both the tech and nontech audiences. Those of us in tech don't have the best track record of documenting our techniques, even for each other. Commenting our code to be readable and understandable to at least other coders is a direct and tangible action we can do to be more transparent. Some open source code has decent code commenting, and we don't know the state of commercial, production-level code. For nontech audiences, tech has too much jargon and plenty of complicated operations that are not shared in simple relatable form. The work of Meredith Broussard's *Artificial Unintelligence* (https://mitpress.mit.edu/books/artificial-unintelligence), Safiya Noble's *Algorithms of Oppression* (https://nyupress.org/9781479837243), Charlton McIlwain's Black Software (https://global.oup.com/academic/product/black-software-9780190863845?cc=us&lang=en&), Ruha Benjamin's *Race After Technology* (www.wiley.com/en-us/Race+After+Technology:+Abolitionist +Tools+for+the+New+Jim+Code-p-9781509526437), and many others listed in NYU's Critical Race and Digital Studies curated publications (https://criticalracedigitalstudies.com) hits a sharp, piercing critique of tech that moves those of us in tech to come face to face with the effects of our creations.

All the while, those of us in tech grapple with tech transparency on two fronts we see as competing for our attention. The first front is on preserving digital rights, namely the intellectual property for corporations. Companies, considered legal entities that are separate from their owners, have similar rights as humans, and they lean into this designation heavily. Companies, actually the owners of these companies, proceed to protect the rights of the corporation and its products. So companies want to keep all of the processes, systems, and structures for its best moneymaking novelties to itself. Those in tech then devise algorithms and systems that align with this corporate position. For example, companies require that a user create a profile and provide login credentials for their app. The app needs us to accept that tech cookie before we can gain access to their services.

On the second front, those of us in tech are supposed to "avoid harm," as listed in the ACM's Code of Ethics and Professional Conduct. We require users to provide data to companies that, in turn, don't share what they are doing with their clients' data. And commonly, tech's argument for asking for consumers' data is to make their services better and make it possible to protect people's privacy within digital spaces. Users are therefore contributing to the "greater" collective good. And the users get to benefit from the services and the convenience it supplies. As a result, the thinking is that the company-user relationship is mutually beneficial: the company gets users' data and users get to use the company's service. But this is a transaction where the user gives more than it gets. Users are people who give their time, attention, personal characteristics, opinions, insights, and, sometimes, money, yet when the company experiences a data breach, the people hear nothing from the company directly or hear about it via a legalese notification from the company in the months post-breach. These two focal points in tech transparency keep tech's options open and ever-expanding, regardless of mistakes made. The wider the lane gets, the more those of us in tech question our judgment in how we handled and should handle circumstances. We battle over whether we have inadvertently contributed to over-automation.

The other side of the tech ethics coin is tech accountability. Accountability notions span the internal development and external outcomes of tech. It's the glue that tries to bind tech ethics. Without accountability, there's useless finger pointing. Subsequent action is required when issuing accountability. The motivation for building tech and deploying that tech-based approach is getting a closer look from stakeholders and clients. I've noticed an uptick in environmental, health and safety, privacy, risk, and security consequences from using tech. And many of these consequences to minoritized communities aren't foreseen, addressed, or audited after harms are identified by coders and tech builders. As for other human ethics principles, like fairness and value, those of us in tech try to reduce these two to mathematical formulas and metrics as if fairness and value can be reduced to numbers—finite and generalizable to one succinct outcome. And they'll ingratiate whatever risks and security that have taken place. But risk and security principles tend to pull up the rear of tech ethics, unless you are a cybersecurity professional where it's front of mind. Risk and security assessments are common practice in developing tech, formally or informally— the real questions are: Do those in positions of power read, understand, listen to, and review action plans in alignment with perceived risks? And will those in positions of power greenlight paying for the necessary, frequent adjustments as more clients interact with the tech?

The connection between human ethics and tech ethics isn't a large leap. I map the tech side of ethics to the human side of ethics in Table 2.1. The questions are a start.

Mapping tech principles to human ethics make many of us in tech feel, frankly, way out of our depth as we wade into the less chartered thoughts of ethics in tech. To help us navigate this, we need to start asking lots of good, informed questions (tip: start with why, what, and how questions)—some of which we'll answer partially or fully while others I will be at a loss on what response to give. So let's talk plainly: I have a different focus. It's to catch more algorithmic-based harms earlier than we in tech have before. We will make mistakes, but if we are willing to learn from and acknowledge those failures, we can change our course. We can share with other people in tech where mistakes are made so they don't make those mistakes and contribute to causing those harms.

Table 2.1: Similarities between tech ethics and human ethics

ELEMENTS OF TECH ETHICS	ELEMENTS OF HUMAN ETHICS	TECH ETHICS MOTIVATING QUESTIONS
Judgment, over-automation	Fairness	To what extent can we identify, set apart, and mitigate discrimination in digital spaces?
Environmental, health and safety, privacy, risk, and security	Honor, integrity	How is technology's credibility protected in physical and digital spaces?
		What is the expected quality-of-life impact on society for tech innovations?
Technology transparency	Honesty	To what degree is the technology and its modifications straightforward to explain to the general population?
Access rights, digital rights, privacy	Value	How do we effectively engage people and technologies that incorporate each other's strengths and minimize each other's shortcomings?
		Of those released, how should the innovative aspects be protected, if at all?
Accountability	Conscience	Should certain technologies be created? What are the benefits and drawbacks of a technology? How do we know if the drawbacks outweigh the benefits?
Freedom	Choice	Does technology further control or empower society? And under which conditions?

The notion of fairness can't be diagnosed, for example, and remains a breeding ground for harms sponsored by tech. Fairness, as described by our society's thinkers and thought leaders, is very different from how fairness manifests in the real world. Try to come up with a fair situation involving two or more people. It's not easy at all. What is fair to one person is likely not fair to another person. Fairness by definition is impartial treatment without discrimination. Fairness in practice is much more opaque. Who makes the determination of what's "impartial" and "discrimination"? Whose standard are we making our goalpost? We can't make a universal standard and then regulate that standard simultaneously. That would be a conflict of interest. Lawyers, realtors, pharmaceutical manufacturers, and physicians can't do it, and neither can we.

Those of us in tech, however, in our human ethics mindset, have our personal sense of what's fair, and it's formed by our lived experiences. Our perception dominates our judgments. Somehow we operate as if our notion of fair is adopted by the general society. That's likely not the case. Fairness is set in relationship to some standard: documented policies, procedures, or practices. Thus we're searching to find the sweet spot of what we're comfortable with and what the general society is comfortable with. Sometimes sending an algorithm to do the task is acceptable, and other times, algorithms create more headaches than what they're worth.

The ultimate destination for our tech ethics' principles are intentional: accountable tech. Our notion of tech accountability focuses on how the tech measures up to these established standards. Wondering about the consequences of what we're building (conscience) isn't synonymous with whether the tech we're building produces negative or harmful consequences to certain communities (fairness). We claim to not yet know how to get there, but we are making large strides by discussing concerns and possible areas of harm without changing the way or what we code.

The woe-is-me-I-don't-know-how-to-make-tech-more-humane days are over. With decades of tech products, hundreds of thousands of tech companies, and millions of lines of code in open source repositories, those of us in tech have ample examples of situations that dehumanized people. Tech ethics, the nature and impact of tech on society, still isn't given significant class time in computing instruction or design/implementation time during software development. Time to turn this tech building and software development process on its head. We can continue to wring our hands or we can get to using our keyboarding skills to *start* to work ourselves out of this mess. Only by working with others, outside of the narrowly defined STEM (science, technology, engineering, and mathematics) tech community, do we have a chance of fully realized tech that recognizes all of us. While we're learning from the social scientists and humanities professionals, we must prioritize the human impact in every piece of tech we make a contribution. Ask and answer the questions posed in Table 2.1. We can use our multitude of open source software libraries to scrap the existing code, identify harms based on the ones we already know, and isolate and classify the harms, like we've done with runtime and logic errors.

Squeezing in Data Ethics

Now, let's get into what's in tech's black box. It's a whole lot of data and algorithms. Human ethics focuses on people's decision-making practices in win-is-relative situations such as whether we accept a job position that pays much less money but that would make us happier. The series of thoughts, ideas, and choices is a labyrinth of uncertainty and continual correcting of mistakes.

Tech ethics emphasizes how to answer the hundreds of thousands of decisions in building and maintaining software and hardware products—for example, should there be a default-on geolocation tracker on our mobile devices, and if so, should government agencies have access to our logs? Digital spaces serve as the bedrock to many organizations, software applications that make using a computing device easier, an app that lives on your mobile device, and the open source/proprietary software libraries that allow us to innovate quickly. We make logic errors, find them, and then try to correct them. These computer programming errors keep us up at night and plague us for sometimes days on end. Whether we call them mistakes or bugs, they're connected by how we absorb the data that's informed or misguided our decision, in the physical world (human ethics) and digital spaces (tech ethics).

Data ethics puts data at the center of the decision-making process. Let's look at three ways data is handled. First there's the state of the data upon entry into a digital system, like how clean it is. Then we figure out the `slate` of operations performed on data while in a digital system. We've seen data grow in size and complexity through interpolation, shrink using pruning, stretch with duplication, and transform using mapping rules. Lastly, we package the data product/result upon exit from the digital system and assess its usefulness.

Like human ethics and tech ethics, data ethics are guided by a set of principles. They're laser-focused on protecting data from misuse or abuse, either intentionally or unintentionally. First up, we must account for the availability, usability, accessibility, and user-friendliness of the data. For example, Fatal Encounters (`https://fatalencounters.org`), a nonprofit collecting the circumstances of people killed during interactions with the police, is making their database available to the public and has created its database using Google Sheets for ease of use once downloaded.[18] Upon viewing the data, we're inundated with concerns about whether or not the data should be kept private and whether or not it's accurate. Privacy is almost a false choice in this knowledge economy. The mere fact that a piece of data appears in a digital system calls into question whether it can be private again. Data privacy is more about managing who, when, and which digital systems have access to it.

Accuracy of data sits under the umbrella of determining value correctness for discrete entries, like a birth date. However, sometimes having data doesn't confirm accuracy. Like in the Fatal Encounters database, the ethnicity and/or gender identity are listed as unknown for some of the victims. An unknown or missing entry doesn't share any value and makes confirming accuracy impossible.

The heavy lift in data ethics is governing the integrity of data processes in a digital system. Here is where we're manipulating data every day of the week and twice on Sundays! We're constantly keeping account of what we've changed and how those modifications cascade and impact subsequent processes. We're using GitHub and other versioning control tactics to track our changes, update our code comments, introduce new software libraries, and deprecate specific methods.

Some of us do these activities better than others, and all of us aren't reading through the documentation like we should.

Stripping away columns and rows in a dataset, for instance, harms the integrity of the data since we're losing information, which means we're losing context. Again in the Fatal Encounters example, the team decided to replace missing values associated with the race of the victim, about 26 percent of the data. So one-quarter of the data has guesstimated values. Handling missing values in this manner immediately raises questions about integrity and accuracy. Then, there's curiosity about which rows of data contained missing values, how the person's race was determined algorithmically, and whether or not we're breathing life into the debunked social Darwinism framework—recall our eugenics discussion in Chapter 1, "Oppression By…."

Data ethics sets boundaries and guidance on the moral function and administration of data in digital spaces. Data spends a lot of time bouncing around these spaces being mined, manipulated, and interpreted freely and seemingly without bounds. Since data is shapeless, we force our people-made computing structures like lists, queues, and stacks to encapsulate it. These structures help us understand data better and allow us to work with it easier. And by "working with," we mean shaping it to our individual or our company's culture inclinations. We capture and represent what we can—rather what our people-made computer infrastructure is designed to hold—but we accept that we're likely truncating data at times.

The outcomes of our manipulations then come into question. Mainly, we're a bit on our heels in justifying the trustworthiness of the outcomes. Being accountable to and showing transparency of the process bolsters confidence that dialogue from tech's stakeholders and client base about computational actions taken is welcomed. I map these data ethics principles to both human and tech ethics to showcase the parallels in Table 2.2. As I did in Table 2.1, I also want to emphasize the specific questions guiding our data ethics conversation.

Table 2.2: Similarities among data, tech, and human ethics

PRINCIPLES OF DATA ETHICS	PRINCIPLES OF TECH ETHICS	PRINCIPLES OF HUMAN ETHICS	DATA ETHICS MOTIVATING QUESTIONS
Availability and accessibility	Judgment, over-automation	Fairness	To what extent can we identify, set apart, and mitigate discrimination in digital spaces?
Integrity of data processing activities and trustworthiness	Environmental, health and safety, privacy, risk, and security	Honor, integrity	How is data's credibility protected while being used in physical and digital spaces?

Continues

Table 2.2 (*continued*)

PRINCIPLES OF DATA ETHICS	PRINCIPLES OF TECH ETHICS	PRINCIPLES OF HUMAN ETHICS	DATA ETHICS MOTIVATING QUESTIONS
Transparency	Technology transparency	Honesty	To what degree is data input, processing, and output stages straightforward to track and explain to the general population?
Privacy	Access rights, digital rights, privacy	Value	How do we keep private things private in digital spaces?
Accountability and accuracy	Accountability	Conscience	How do you determine if data is usable for your intended purposes? What factors deem data friendly to use, and do these factors compromise the data's integrity?
N/A	Freedom	Choice	Does technology further control or empower society? And under which conditions?

Understanding data is complicated and complex. In fact, it's scary. We don't have any real control of data. Software developers see many problems through an analytical lens that first seeks to find something to measure and devise a metric rather than understanding the situational constructs at the origin of a problem. The algorithmic choices we make when writing code have an artistic flair that varies from person to person.

It's important for software developers to consider the spectrum of helpful to harmful conditions tech invites. These consequences can impact generations of clients and further instill negative outcomes. Some of the negative consequences we argue can be traced to key decisions made during software development. So let's learn to make more intentional choices during construction rather than what we do now, which is act surprised when tech is weaponized to discriminate against certain communities and then try to concoct a series of makeshift hacks to cover these harms. We can't truly roll back tech harms on the backend since tech only evolves forward (and doesn't backtrack or die).

So there's a limit to what can be solved by people writing code. For example, we'd like to ensure informed consent (but how do we know that consent is truly informed?). When we think we have an answer to one question, dozens more follow. Whatever we do, at every step, we want to provide clear, beneficial paths to minimizing any perceived or actual harms of a software product.

Misconceptions of Data Ethics

What we want is to be part of a team, and a society, that can not only gauge when it's appropriate to build tech, but also make tech that's trustworthy. The cases of tech doing harm, however, are too frequent to ignore. And the data introduced and transformed within digital spaces continues to live on, recycling falsehoods in new iterations of tech apps and products. The general public and those not entrenched in the tech community don't know how it's supposed to work. Different sectors of society scrutinize tech, its outcomes, and by derivation, us. While we want tech to be better, neither we nor the tech we built want to be flogged mercilessly by op-eds and the media. We need to call out the resistance to data ethics work of those designing and maintaining tech. This resistance makes assumptions about data ethics and its plausibility of being implemented. I've identified five common misconceptions surrounding data ethics that aren't traditionally voiced, but their influence reverberates in tech product designs and development.

Misconception 1: Goodness of Data, and Tech by Proxy, Is Apolitical or Bipartisan

The conversation lies at the feet of the tech industry: what will you do to reduce harm from tech? That's a loaded question. It implies that the vast majority of the tech industry agrees that tech does any harm, any harms can be "fixed" with more tech, and that they are on board with making changes immediately. But that's not the case. A public dialogue occurred at the Conference on Computer Vision and Pattern Recognition (CVPR) 2020 between two well-known and well-respected scholars—and eventually the healthy segment of the AI community—over the ethics of building and touting PULSE as a scientific achievement (https://thegradient.pub/pulse-lessons, https://venturebeat.com/2020/06/26/ai-weekly-a-deep-learning-pioneers-teachable-moment-on-ai-bias, https://syncedreview.com/2020/06/30/yann-lecun-quits-twitter-amid-acrimonious-exchanges-on-ai-bias).[19,20,21] PULSE is a computer vision model that claims it can generate realistic, high-resolution images of people from a pixelated photo, as shown in Figure 2.3. (Honestly, when I saw the PULSE demonstration, my first thought was "Yikes!").

Their dispute had two main points of contention: (1) the tech infringes on the privacy of individuals by unblurring their faces using a series of algorithms, and (2) the application use of this tech can exacerbate facial recognition misclassifications that already exist for Black and Brown people by law enforcement agencies using facial recognition technology to help them identify potential subjects. Low-resolution cameras producing these images and videos are commonly used as security surveillance systems throughout retail stores, banks, and such.

Figure 2.3: Examples of high-resolution images that are downscaled to low-resolution images that output as PULSE images after applying the PULSE technique

Source: Duke University

The dialogue quickly included a discussion about *when* and *how* data is discriminatory. These disputes revealed two distinct and nonoverlapping positions, each steadfast in their beliefs. One camp purported that data becomes prejudicial *once* in digital spaces, and the PULSE system can be updated to remove bigotry. The other camp purported that data is prejudicial before it's ingested into digital spaces, and the PULSE system is an innately racist innovation that hosts more disadvantages than benefits to being created. If one side isn't convinced of tech harm, it makes it that much harder to mitigate harmful effects. There's much more to be said, so we'll circle back to the smorgasbord of challenges with PULSE later in this book.

The global society want to believe that tech can fix most, if not all, of the ills we see in tech. We try to deflect the majority of the bad outcomes from tech to intentional bad actors, just as cybersecurity professionals must contend with black hats, who'll remain a constant presence in our society. We want there to be more good tech than bad tech. It remains unclear which are good and which are bad and for which communities.

Misconception 2: Data Ethics Is Focused Solely on Laws Protecting Confidentiality and Privacy

This perception leads those of us in tech to center data ethics between computing and the law. Controlling data use becomes a policy issue that provides guidelines on our behaviors. We've seen the law attempt to create this control structure with the Health Insurance Portability and Accountability Act (HIPAA) in the medical field and the Family Educational Rights and Privacy Act (FERPA) in the educational space in the United States, alongside the European Union's General Data Protection Regulation (GDPR) for personal data. These policies help guide how we might engage with data outside of a digital system, but set aside the particulars of how data is steered in digital systems by us as software developers. The scope of data ethics covers more than what the law can narrate. The law serves an important purpose as a regulatory response to data ill-use, particularly on the backend of the tech product pipeline.

The law considers both sides of an argument and is keenly aware not to infringe on any potential, perceived, or actual rights associated with tech. The cascading impression reaches tech by way of tech ethics like lightning bolts. Statements include: (1) data/tech ethics will stifle tech innovation and infringe on digital freedoms, (2) there is no measurable way to fix tech to be more ethical, (3) ethical concerns in data/tech are not the responsibility of tech since individuals need to learn how to effectively use tech, and (4) tech is too pervasive in our society to effectively manage a reasonable remedy or intervention. . .and the list could go on.

As described earlier, data/tech ethics involves a number of sometimes interdependent relationships. Many tech folks assume this is a zero-sum situation. This thought path appears in the software development process. You're either right or wrong and there is no in-between. And the computing education reinforces this binary thinking. So many tech people can't compute anything that's not strictly classified as right or wrong. So all data ethics principles need to co-occur in harmony all the time. That's not realistic—there will be tensions among them and compromises need to be reached. But just because friction among the principles exists, it doesn't mean software development practices and data ethics principles can't resolve to a common ground. This does mean that tech has to make some concessions. The tech community must stop the all-or-nothing culture, attitudes, and thinking. Tech must work with ideologies, theories, and principles found in the social sciences, humanities, and other STEM fields. Tech needs to bend so to allow us all not to break.

Model cards (`https://modelcards.withgoogle.com/about`), developed by Google AI researchers, point us in the right direction. Model cards are designed to help quantitative researchers draw and visualize boundaries around a model's capabilities and limitations.[22] A series of metrics, analysis tools, and evaluation benchmarks are provided to better understand a model's performance. The goal centers on learning patterns that will circumvent or reduce harmful pitfalls. Focusing on two AI algorithms right now, they initiate a quantitative template of data ethics in software development by making more transparent the state of the data inputs, limitations, and performance metrics. By no means is it complete or the only way to document a model's functions, but it does get us thinking about trade-offs much earlier in the software development process.

Misconception 3: Implementing Data Ethics Practices Will Make Data Objective

For starters, data is not neutral. We're not taught that data is neutral—in reality, it's implied. Data is equivalent to numbers. And numbers are concrete, mathematical objects. As Triveni Gandhi of Dataiku told *Computer Weekly*, "We like to think of data and numbers as indisputable, but the reality is that every piece of information is a product of the context it was built in" (www.computerweekly.com/blog/Data-Matters/Data-is-not-neutral).[23] On the flip side, numbers flatten representation and reduce dimensionality of the original data intent. For example, we convert text to numbers like what we see in the American Standard Code for Information Interchange (ASCII) table. That uppercase B is stored in the digital system as the decimal number 66, which is converted to binary as 1000010. (For a quick tutorial on converting letters to decimals to binary, check out the "ASCII Code and Binary" video on YouTube (www.youtube.com/watch?v=H4l42nbYmrU).

The sequence of 0s and 1s are unassuming, nonthreatening, and harmless to people. However, when taken together, the collection is not merely the sum of its parts. This is what makes any sort of ethics complicated. For data, the creation train never ends because data brings us more data. But the ethical considerations that applied to the data upon entry to any digital system may not be the same ethical considerations we should or need to apply throughout the data life cycle and to the data product once complete. Like the two scholars discussing PULSE, the input of a person's face garners questions about whether that person provided informed consent for their likeness to be used for their demonstrations. The output face brings up data ethical questions relating to accountability and usability of a fake face. The sequence of 0s and 1s come with no concept of context or situational awareness. The appropriateness of data's use must be left up to humans to decide whether or not value is achieved.

The presumption is that with enough algorithms and computing infrastructure we can keep data isolated from ethical discussions. There are two main ways data is filled with errors: (1) through statistical or mathematical logic missteps, or (2) through societal faults and failures. Computationally, if a mathematical equation or statistical model is not implemented as designed, then we'll experience logic errors. Our validation and verification of results—call it A/B testing or unit testing—will have gone awry. The second way zeros in on the phrase "implemented as designed." The social constructs and ills of our society can't be encapsulated by a mathematical formula or a statistical framework.

> **NOTE**   To see a movie version of the battle between zeros and ones, check out *The Matrix* franchise. If you haven't seen the franchise (*The Matrix, The Matrix Reloaded, The Matrix Revolutions*, and *The Matrix Resurrections*), it's worth watching, but the first one is still the best one.

Notable Misconception Mentions: Ethics and Diversity, Equity, and Inclusion (DEI) Are Interchangeable

Prioritizing DEI recruiting, hiring, and retention or conducting antiracist trainings for your company's workforce isn't synonymous with performing the consistent, constant, antiracist decision-making actions throughout the software product life cycle and beyond. Tech has a long, unimpressive, and performative history in including, welcoming, and providing promotion paths for non-white, non-men identifying people. The West Area Computers, a NASA all-Black American woman mathematician group working as human computers, date back to the 1940s and was almost erased from computing history. The book (and subsequent movie) *Hidden Figures* recognizes their enormous contributions. By the mid-1980s, the percentage of women in computing rose to about 35 percent, yet today that percentage hovers at less than 20 percent. In 2014, the major tech companies at the time (Apple, Facebook, Google, and Microsoft) reported on their race/ethnicity staffing demographics after public concern about the lack of diversity in their tech workforces. The percentages were in the single digits for Black, Latin, and Indigenous People of the Americas. Reports came out sharing the business value of a diversified tech workforce. Event programming and programs targeting marginalized groups became a norm as a way to boost DEI efforts in hiring and staffing across all sectors of tech. By 2019, the outcomes of these efforts have resulted in no significant boost in hiring, retention, and staffing for Black, Latinx, and Indigenous People of the Americas in those tech companies. During this time period, the tech continues to weaponize non-white and non-men identifying people. It's the continual unwavering harm of the tech industry to provide lip service of inclusiveness yet build and release exclusionary products.

Some in tech fields draw a parallel that DEI efforts can be addressed by addressing ethics. It's like a two-for-one special! The argument is simple, but erroneous: you'd be more ethical in tech if your team was more diverse. Let's take the 2018 Cambridge Analytica and Facebook scandal. Cambridge Analytica harvested personal data of millions of Facebook users for political purposes. Certain demographics received targeted political ads as a means of disseminating misinformation or disinformation prior to the 2016 U.S. presidential election. But Shireen Mitchell, owner of Stop Online Violence Against Women (SOVAW), tried to ring the alarm bells on this prior to the election to no avail. SOVAW's press release ("Facebook Ads That Targeted Voters Centered on Black American Culture with Voter Suppression as the End Game": `https://stoponlinevaw.com/media/report-facebook-ads-that-targeted-voters-centered-on-black-american-culture`) became one of the seminal reports in this scandal.[24] Reflective commentary called upon tech to be more conscious of its implications to non-white, non-men identifying communities. Tech companies, largely unaware of what "more ethical" meant, focused on automation. Ethical AI and responsible

AI became a common phrase. A consensus formed that tech can't be liable for its actions since its actions are dictated by people. Also, many of the high-profile ethics scenarios fixated on algorithmic biases that further suppressed marginalized groups, like in the experience of Robert Julian-Borchak Williams (www.nytimes.com/2020/06/24/technology/ facial-recognition-arrest.html?smid=tw-share) we described earlier.

With this conclusion, the ethical problems with tech were recast as DEI problems. Resolving the DEI problems would magically resolve the ethics concerns. Let's not conflate ethics and diversity, equity, and inclusion (DEI). DEI primarily addresses people and their workplace, specifically in terms of race, gender, and class statuses, whereas data/tech ethics primarily concentrates on the interactions between people and digital spaces. We sometimes operate on the mistaken belief that if we do one right, then it'll solve the other. For instance, if we have diverse and inclusive teams, then our digital systems will be more ethical. Not so. The "who" in the room can raise awareness to inequities in a digital space, but it doesn't necessarily impact how the technology is implemented. DEI can be considered a sub-branch of data/tech ethics because tech is an industry that's not equitable. Handling data/tech ethics in digital spaces and handling DEI in the workplace are separate, but mutually reinforcing spheres of influence when done in collaboration and through informative, iterative feedback loops.

Another Notable Mention: Software Developers Are Only Responsible for Societal Outcomes Stemming from Their Code

If we were in the 1960s or 1970s, this argument may have a little validity. Computers were not in the home and sparsely in the workplace. Computers were used primarily to perform mathematical calculations. The inputs to these mathematical equations were known, and more importantly, the outputs were known too. The original software developers, computer programmers, were innately responsible for confirming calculations of mathematical equations. Many worked on theories about the potential of computers and computing. This number-crunching mindset doesn't translate to today's practice of computing. Today, those theories built with computing are being put into action.

It's time to update our thinking. The code we write needs vetting beyond unit testing and software verification procedures. We also need to consider its impact on different demographics, like children, people of color, or folks with disabilities. Tech is so embedded in the mainstream society in such a way that tech's impact, both good and bad, is powerful and irreversible. Our awareness shift of our broad audience gives us new realizations and anxieties. While our target audience for a particular tech may be 30+, it could be used by anyone in that household and family circle. The nature of our work must make us more judicious in how we conduct that work.

While people can do what computers do—taking much more time perhaps—it's clear that the opposite is not true. Certain conditions and nuances are difficult for people to reconcile, and they can't be coded into digital spaces. Full responsibility does not fall upon software developers, but they can broaden their knowledge, participation, and action in careful software construction. Ethics provides a language for understanding our work's perceived and actual societal impacts. We steadily realize that we contribute to a larger digital system or tech product, but we need to better recognize our specific role and efforts in constructing that piece of tech.

We are responsible for the code we write. We must make more concerted purposeful actions to anticipate, learn, and remedy potential bad outcomes as best we can. Raising objections, refusing to implement certain methods, and sharing case studies are ways to position ethical practices as a greater priority. However, we aren't the only ones who play a role in making these decisions. Strength is in numbers. One software developer on a team being ethically inclined isn't going to move the needle during the software development process. Everyone in this process has to be in agreement, those who fund the project to those who market the production-level tech influence the tech will have. Software developers do take the brunt of the responsibility since it is their code. The organization still has a choice of whether or not what tech builds with our code makes it out to society.

Limits of Tech and Data Ethics

For years the narrative of tech, from the classroom to the global stage, gave way to a "tech is an inherently always good" motif. That tech by its origin has adopted a special branded culture of superiority and elitism. We've touched on a handful of cases where tech has highlighted bad behaviors. It's possible that if we'd embedded data and tech ethics principles at the onset, we could have seen a more favorable outcome, but we'll never know for certain.

A tech reckoning and revolution is within our power, though. As a society, we can push the tech industry to infuse more morality into its products and services. And society will continue to raise doubts that the tech being built is sturdy and stable enough to withstand ethical scrutiny. This back-and-forth tussle constitutes a healthy exchange between the general public and the tech industry. The tech community itself must fight its own internal battles between those who believe "code will fix it all" and those who believe tech solutions are limited in their usefulness. Ethical conundrums are here with us for the long haul. We will have ethical bouts of tension and friction as we grapple with how to be more human to ourselves. We will continue to struggle with how ethical underpinnings could help us while avoiding situations where tech could harm us in these pursuits. In the end, we all are moving toward people-first, impact-driven decision-making.

Through the centuries of ethics literature and decades of technological innovations, those of us in tech have learned two very important lessons:

More data **doesn't equate to** *better* **data.**   *More* tech doesn't equate to *better* tech. And *better* data doesn't equate to *better* tech. Tech of any form can be weaponized. Tech of any form has its limits. Naturally the ethics branch of tech also has its limits. For one, data isn't timeless. Data can become stale, because what we know now is more than what we knew in the past. Our understanding shifts. And the factors we considered not valuable before (so we didn't collect or classify them) are now important and in need of reframing. Take, for instance, the CoNLL-2003 dataset. It contains about 20,000 annotated news wire sentences and became the go-to dataset in the natural language processing (NLP) community. Recently, the CoNLL-2003 dataset is showing its slip (https://onezero.medium.com/the-troubling-legacy-of-a-biased-data-set-2967ffdd1035)—more men's names than women's names are associated with these sentences, causing women's expression of language to be muted in today's NLP algorithms and frameworks.[25] Today's NLP algorithms are biased to the CoNLL-2003 dataset. The gold standard of datasets in 2003 isn't the gold standard anymore. Data has a shelf life—regardless of quantity or quality—and the CoNLL-2003 dataset has reached theirs.

Data ethics can't fix social problems.   Social problems like U.S. systemic racism and sexism and remote learning adoption in the middle of the academic year involves an orchestra of people, tech, and digital systems to support its (dis)function. Discussing the role of tech and data ethics with respect to our economic and political structures could fill a whole book, but we're focused on isolating when data ethics falls short. The sneaky part about social problems is that unseen inequities are made invisible in communal spaces. For example, the COVID-19 pandemic shifted school-aged children's instruction from in-person to remote learning in a matter of a few weeks in March 2020. Remote learning is based on fundamental premises that all school-aged learners have adequate access to digital devices, adequate Internet bandwidth, and adequate supervision during instruction time. Checking most, if not all, of the data ethics boxes, doesn't address the lack of access issues. Social systems weren't structured to support that type of access. By the end of April 2020, several large U.S. public school districts abandoned the last three weeks of the term because those premises remained unfixable.

If those making tech products could just keep these two lessons top of mind, we'd bypass a good portion of the predatory and discriminatory tech we're currently contending with.

Summary

Reconciling—and more to the point accepting—imperfection in data and tech needs a place in tech. The choice between error or no error doesn't exist anymore. There's a third choice: nontech-solvable. Outliers, perceived as nonconfirming, irrelevant, and of a minimally influential set of outputs, are avoided when designing tech innovations for general-purpose use. There is an unspoken principle that outliers can be (and should be) eliminated. We've convinced ourselves of this notion in the tech community. We therefore relentlessly pursue advances and optimizations in tech to remove errors. So, we compete with ourselves. We approach data ethics with the same tenacity. We want 100 percent compliance for each data ethics principle. But compliance with one, like transparency, may compromise another, like availability. Let's release that pressure valve now. While the tech will be more trusted with greater transparency, it will still be imperfect and limited in the problems it can solve. And that's okay because other systems outside of the digital space will move toward filling those other gaps.

Notes

1. Bond, Shannon. "Just 12 People Are Behind Most Vaccine Hoaxes on Social Media, Research Shows." NPR, May 14, 2021. www.npr.org/2021/05/13/996570855/disinformation-dozen-test-facebooks-twitters-ability-to-curb-vaccine-hoaxes.

2. "How Does Twitter Make Money?" Investopedia, 2019. www.investopedia.com/ask/answers/120114/how-does-twitter-twtr-make-money.asp.

3. IQBAL, MANSOOR. 2019. "Twitter Revenue and Usage Statistics (2018)." Business of Apps, February 27, 2019. www.businessofapps.com/data/twitter-statistics.

4. "Twitter Usage Statistics – Internet Live Stats." Internetlivestats.com, 2009. www.internetlivestats.com/twitter-statistics.

5. "Twitter Engagement Rate Calculator." The Online Advertising Guide, n.d. https://theonlineadvertisingguide.com/ad-calculators/twitter-engagement-rate-calculator.

6. Vosoughi, Soroush, Deb Roy, and Sinan Aral. 2018. "The Spread of True and False News Online." *Science* 359 (6380): 1146–1151. https://doi.org/10.1126/science.aap9559.

7. Hindman, M. and Vladimir Barash. "Disinformation, 'Fake News' and Influence Campaigns on Twitter." Knight Foundation, 2018. https://knightfoundation.org/features/misinfo.

8. Faq.myheritage.com. "Why Do I See My Photos on Google?" *MyHeritage*, 2021. https://faq.myheritage.com/en/article/why-do-i-see-my-photos-on-google.

9. The Archives Unleashed Project, 2021. *The Archives Unleashed Project*. Archivesunleashed.org. https://archivesunleashed.org/aut.

10. ACM. "ACM Code of Ethics and Professional Conduct." ACM.org, 2021. www.acm.org/code-of-ethics.

11. ACM. "Computing Curricula 2020." ACM.org, 2021. www.acm.org/binaries/content/assets/education/curricula-recommendations/cc2020.pdf.

12. ACM. "Computer Science Curricula 2013." ACM.org, 2013. www.acm.org/binaries/content/assets/education/cs2013_web_final.pdf.

13. ACM. "Computing Curricula 2005." ACM.org, 2005. www.acm.org/binaries/content/assets/education/curricula-recommendations/cc2005-march06final.pdf.

14. Josephson, M. "Making Ethical Decisions." Josephson Institute of Ethics, 1991. https://web.engr.uky.edu/~jrchee0/CE%20401/Josephson%20EDM/Making_Ethical_Decisions.pdf.

15. Internet Encyclopedia of Philosophy (IEP). Iep.utm.edu, 2021. "Ethics | Internet Encyclopedia of Philosophy." https://iep.utm.edu/ethics.

16. Santa Clara University. "What Is Ethics?" Scu.edu, 2021. www.scu.edu/ethics/ethics-resources/ethical-decision-making/what-is-ethics.

17. New York Times. "Wrongfully Accused by an Algorithm." Nytimes.com, 2021. www.nytimes.com/2020/06/24/technology/facial-recognition-arrest.html?smid=tw-share.

18. Fatalencounters.org. "Fatal Encounters." 2021. https://fatalencounters.org.

19. Kurenkov, A. 2020. "Lessons from the PULSE Model and Discussion." The Gradient, 2020. https://thegradient.pub/pulse-lessons.

20. Johnson, K. "AI Weekly: A Deep Learning Pioneer's Teachable Moment on AI Bias." VentureBeat, 2020. https://venturebeat.com/2020/06/26/ai-weekly-a-deep-learning-pioneers-teachable-moment-on-ai-bias.

21. Synced | AI Technology & Industry Review. "Yann LeCun Quits Twitter Amid Acrimonious Exchanges on AI Bias." Synced, 2020. https://syncedreview.com/2020/06/30/yann-lecun-quits-twitter-amid-acrimonious-exchanges-on-ai-bias.

22. Mitchell, M., S. Wu, A. Zaldivar, P. Barnes, L. Vasserman, B. Hutchinson, E. Spitzer, I. D. Raji, & T. Gebru. "Model Cards for Model Reporting." Cornell University, 2019. https://arxiv.org/abs/1810.03993.

23. Gandhi, T. "Data Is Not Neutral – Data Matters." Computerweekly.com, 2019. www.computerweekly.com/blog/Data-Matters/Data-is-not-neutral.

24. Mitchell, S. "Press Release: Facebook Ads That Targeted Voters Centered on Black American Culture with Voter Suppression as the End Game." Stoponlinevaw.com, 2016. https://stoponlinevaw.com/media/report-facebook-ads-that-targeted-voters-centered-on-black-american-culture.

25. Field, H. "An A.I. Training Tool Has Been Passing Its Bias to Algorithms for Almost Two Decades" Medium, 2020. https://onezero.medium.com/the-troubling-legacy-of-a-biased-data-set-2967ffdd1035.

Bias

Dr. Brandeis Marshall
@csdoctorsister

I'm tired of scientists asking for a definition of bias (their meaning social injustice)

I don't say bias cuz I'm not sanitizing discrimination + prejudice for tech folks and try making tech solutions to oppression.

If you want biases defns:
catalogofbias.org

Source: Twitter, Inc.

Working toward normalizing true data ethics requires a debunking of long-standing and firmly held beliefs about data's role in tech. Data is neutral. Data is objective. Data doesn't take sides. We have to address this proverbial elephant in the digital-verse and tackle one of the biggest roadblocks to equity-informed data citizenship: *bias*. From the STEM, humanities, or social sciences, it unites us and divides us in four letters. We all have had experiences at least observing bias in our professional lives. I'll describe how bias shows up and ways to shift our mindset on how we recognize and handle it, even before we write a single line of code.

Types of Bias

Bias isn't what we think it is. Well, it's the right word if we want to mask clear messaging of what's happening within digital systems. The tech community has been pushed to recognize, consider, and address uneven outcomes of its products to certain protected groups. And once one grievance was aired, like COMPAS, the floodgates opened. In our recent interweb's past, we've seen gorillas appearing in images when Black people were used in keyword searches and Black people's natural hairstyle like afros, locs, and braids are categorized as unprofessional hairstyles in keyword searches. These are half-hearted attempts to mitigate algorithmic-based harms and the cascading imbalance of experiences for certain populations at the hands of tech.

The tech community, particularly AI, gravitated toward various watered-down implementations of ethics. Human ethics centers the human condition, and tech is notorious for being socially awkward around people until they need human testers. But no matter how much the tech community tries, people can't be avoided and the impact of tech on people can't be swept under a rug.

So tech quickly dismissed even trying to address human ethics. [1,18] Next came tech ethics. This seemed like a natural fit. Tech can find quantitative ways to address ethical conditions presented by digital systems. Two glaring problems:

- The primary tech field, computer science, intentionally obfuscates and avoids contending with its influence on people until forced. It's exclusionary by design to attract the most persistent folks. Tech has been messaged in the mainstream media as accessible to everyone while including more fields than computer science. But in practice, tech has leaned in heavily to requiring coding skills. So tech has taken on a persona as a rebranding of computer science. This reality is born out of necessity since computer science struggles to replace its stereotype as a hard, stressful, fast-paced, and anxiety-ridden discipline.

- Ethics isn't instilled as a core tenet for computer scientists.[2] The National Computer Science Curriculum Guidelines don't prioritize ethical design, development, or practices (www.edsurge.com/news/2021-03-15-let-s-teach-computer-science-majors-to-be-good-citizens-the-whole-world-depends-on-it).[3] These persistent folks lack a foundation in what ethics is or how to integrate it in their projects. And the everyday practice of code cloning (see Chapter 4, "Computational Thinking in Practice") skirts ethical lines.

The speed of tech innovation consumes all the available time (or interest) in learning what's considered nontech considerations such as ethics. A straight swift impasse emerged. With more tech outcomes adversely impacting certain communities and gaining the attention of international media, the tech community has had to reassess—no longer ignore—its role in creating products that are harmful to communities. Slowly but surely, a consensus was made that tech ethics was too broad and impacted too much of the essential aspects of the software development process. So, as those of us in computing are taught in Computer Science 101, when the problem is too big we break it into smaller tasks. Ethics, however we decide to define it, isn't the concern for everyone in computing. It's a matter for a selected bunch who make software, develop algorithms, and have our hands on the data. And here is where we *finally* land on bias. And the discussion around bias in data and tech systems diverts attention away from the larger ethical and morality questions shared in Chapter 2, "Morality."

Defining Bias

Bias has become the ethical catchall in tech/data. Bias has two distinct definitions that make the choice of this word a bit nefarious. Discussing bias conjures up controversy as your coworker insists that bias is nothing more than statistical errors or systematic errors that can be alleviated with different mathematical treatments. While you've embraced a fuller understanding of bias that hinges on societal and structural inequities that fall outside the scope of mathematical treatments, you see the direct, institutional presence of prejudice in the real world and its replication in the digital space as expressed in mathematical formulas. This friction is palpable since understanding bias takes on one or these two extremes: combating prejudice or correcting mathematically-based errors.

Thus, the goals for addressing bias in tech systems do not overlap. Both sides are talking past each other. Prejudice-meaning bias contingencies are trying to convince error-meaning bias groups that discrimination and inequities are distinct and different from correctable math mistakes. On the flip side, the error-meaning bias folks are trying to explain to prejudice-meaning folks how they've corrected the errors.

The tech industry seamlessly thinks and talks about bias in both contexts unconsciously. I concentrate on prejudice first, then consider the statistical error implications, while many in the tech community focus on mathematical error reduction primarily since they are uncomfortable talking about algorithmic acts of discrimination and designing more just data practices. Conflating these meanings here keeps the tech community stuck in defining bias as correcting errors, rather than mitigating prejudice and errors. These harms persist perpetuating chaos and confusion in, around, and outside of tech spaces. Bias, even under the umbrella of these two definitions, takes on many, many forms (for instance, https://catalogofbias.org/biases, which doesn't contain an exhaustive list).[4] Harpreet Sahota, host of "The Artists of Data Science" podcast, shares an increasingly realized understanding of biases for the scientific community of data workers—bias has human conditions that can't be escaped. He outlines six biases that many in data-related roles often experience:

Garbage in, garbage out.

When it comes to making good decisions, your "in" are the beliefs you hold.

Don't shoot the messenger, but there's A LOT of junk in there.

We can only ever see the world from our own perspectives, experiences, and beliefs.

We're trapped in the inside view. And it's booby-trapped with the gnarliest cognitive biases.

Some biases you may recognize:

1. Confirmation

The tendency to look for information that conforms to what we already believe.

2. Disconfirmation

Our tendency for being more critical of information that contradicts our beliefs.

3. Overconfidence

Overestimating our skills to the point it interferes with our decision-making ability.

4. Availability

When we distort the likelihood of an event occurring because it's easy to recall.

5. Recency

Believing that recent events are more likely to occur than they actually are.

6. Illusion of control

Underestimating the influence of luck.

We have the power to take the outside view.

It means we must open ourselves up as much as possible to other people's perspectives. And realize what's true in the world, independent of our own perspective.

It's the only way to correct inaccuracies in the facts that you think you know.
Source: LinkedIn

Those of us in tech pit one type of bias against another as though multiple biases can't exist simultaneously. Or the very notion that addressing one type of bias leaves a residue of another type of bias is perceived as improbable. Convergence of biases in tech products or services are a de facto consideration. I've separated this convergence into four interconnected groups: people, business, data, and algorithmic. I want us in the tech community to better capture and understand how bias circulates in our society through the tech products we create. Plainly, each group has a primary purpose that it elevates above the others that carves trenches for bias to fester and grow:

- In business, the value proposition is in how revenue is made and expanding the ways in which profits are sustained.

- For people, there are those who can live consequence-free from social constructs and those who navigate obstacles designed by these same social constructs. What is an easy path for one population isn't easy for another population through disparate impacts.

- For data, those of us in the industry are trying to standardize how people elect to encapsulate/structure our understanding of people as a function, many times, of benefiting business objectives.

- In algorithmic practices, those of us in tech are working to systemically digitize our understanding of people and circumstances involving people.

To showcase tangibly the tight-knit tethering of these groups in the face of multiple biases, I'm providing a demonstration using a case seen in previous chapters that has a complexity that's more real-world than classroom. This case study scenario is intended to spark conversation and debate because unveiled biases show the ugliness of humanity. You're supposed to have your understandings challenged and be uncomfortable.

Concrete Example of Biases

Let's consider Amazon's AI hiring tool circa mid-2010s (`www.reuters.com/ article/us-amazon-com-jobs-automation-insight/amazon-scraps-secret- ai-recruiting-tool-that-showed-bias-against-women-idUSKCN1MK08G`).[5] To recap, software developers were tasked with automating the selection of the prospective hire pool by scaling an automated résumé collection and filtering system. An AI hiring software product was designed, implemented, and deployed by Amazon for internal use. The algorithmic choices made didn't pan out so well. Amazon was forced to scrap its AI hiring software product because it proved to bolster the résumés of white men while suppressing those of minority groups, especially women, Black, and Latin people with comparable skills. The public nationwide reporting of this software's shortcomings in late 2018 was swift and abundant, leading to adverse impacts on the company's reputation. It pushed Amazon to publicly display their workforce's racial and gender representation (`www.aboutamazon.com/working-at-amazon/diversity-and-inclusion/our-workforce-data`).[6] We imagine that the digitization of applicants' résumés, described in earlier sections, was taken by those software engineers.

So where did this all go so wrong? At the very start. Beginning with business bias, a tech approach was deemed the appropriate resolution path to handle the overwhelming number of résumés while saving on costs. The common business rationale calls for identifying a repeatable business process. The up-front efforts of creating and fine-tuning that process are well worth the cost and time savings, considering that the process will be used often in the future.

Résumé pool equity wasn't a priority for the business needs, values, or goals. The resulting lack of diversity in Amazon's employee candidate pool revealed their lack of existing equitable hiring practices, and it was a by-product that was previously (likely) ignored. Responsibility for this oversight toggled among a number of business units. Deflecting responsibility to other units in the organization turns us further away from data ethics. This is not a competition, but a cooperation.

In this hiring tool case, the business biases are further compounded by human biases. These biases impact how any business challenge is addressed. One of the common reverberating sentiments in many tech circles is that "they (companies) can't find diverse talent." Truthfully, not only does diverse talent exist, but people from different backgrounds apply for jobs and then they are not hired by the same companies that espouse that they can't find them. It's a three-part question of "Are applicants from diverse backgrounds applying for our jobs? If yes, why aren't they being hired? And if not, why aren't diverse applicants applying for our jobs?" We easily pinpoint the outcome, but not the origin of the issue being the widespread white supremacy in tech as perpetuated by the culture and workforce (`https://medium.com/marker/its-time-we-dealt-with-white-supremacy-in-tech-8f7816fe809`). Domain expertise is vital here. Conversations and acting on the human resources (HR) personnel observations of the applicant profile could have been very helpful to the software development team. The business decision to keep costs low dictated that key investigative steps were skipped that would more fully capture their résumé selection process. And the convenient excuse that "they (companies) can't find diverse talent" is ceremoniously debunked. Isolating and filling the gaps between HR and tech teams, for instance, shifts them from problem-focused to solution-based. All organizational units have to work together more graciously to make it all work. An interdependent relationship needs to be formed and nurtured.

But with the software development team poised to tackle the task, they proceeded as they'd been taught: follow the software development life cycle (SDLC). SDLC is the fundamental framework underpinning all software, tech, and/or apps, with stages: requirements, design, development, testing, deployment, and review/maintenance.[7] We'll dive deeper into SDLC processes in Part II, "Accountability," but consider SDLC as a never-ending cycle of plan-do-revise for tech innovation. At each stage, whether we're the project manager, business analyst, user interface/user experience (UI/UX) designer, front-end/backend developer, quality assurance (QA) engineer, or some other role on the software development team, we're making decisions based on business-related and human-based assumptions. We're making a series of trade-offs that deepen the vulnerability of tech. In other words, the data and algorithms that transform and transport data become exacting tools in reinforcing different types of biases.

For example, Amazon likely had a team of QA engineers that focused on the data auditing process. QA engineers reviewed who on the development team had access to which parts of the software on the development side (internal), on the production side (internal), and the consumer side (external). While we don't know for certain the size of Amazon's development team for their AI hiring tool, we suspect that the UI/UX engineer(s) had a different level of access than the backend developers. The HR personnel, one of the product's stakeholders, surely didn't have access to the nuts-and-bolts of the software code like a project manager would. Each different access point creates opportunities for software faults and biases to grow. Realizing racial and gender disparities in the product's outcomes unveiled a discriminatory practice that all on the software development team were seeking to mitigate. Now the development team had to revise their SDLC and reissue. What intends to remedy for one type of discrimination can exacerbate or shift that prejudice to another part of the product. They wound up bringing in archived résumés in an effort to increase their diversity pool but further proved that their applicant pool was not ethnically-or gender-diverse.

The baking-in of data biases further complicated the work for the software development team. QA engineers, for example, tracked which parts of a computing infrastructure the tech needed access to in order to execute as intended. Stability of software and hardware infrastructure came under scrutiny with changes to a software product. The data being added to the system, be it in the form of new algorithms or new data input, changed the composition of that software.

Before going forward, let me remind us of what an algorithm is. According to G. Michael Schneider and Judith Gersting, authors of *Invitation to Computer Science*,[8] an algorithm is "a well-ordered collection of unambiguous and effectively computable operations that produces a result and halts in a finite amount of time" (p. 10). Creating anything digitally requires one or more algorithms. Each description given to this definition contains assumptions. Two quick examples: "unambiguous and effectively computable operations" and "produces a result." The operations must be unambiguous and effective to the computer machine, not people or societal situations where these operations have a long-lasting impact. And for a result to be produced, there's no guarantee that the result is even correct or valuable. The first computing program most will write is called "Hello World." It simply displays the words "Hello" and "World" with a space between them on the computer screen. It's correct but it sure isn't valuable. There are innate cracks for bias to fester in any algorithm because the definition centers the computing machine, not people. And every software, piece of tech, and/or app on your devices is constructed to satisfy the algorithm definition. It's past time we recognize the instability of algorithms so that we can start being more thoughtful in when and whether we decide to use them.

As for Amazon's AI hiring tool, the tech community can envision remedies that included selecting different search and sort algorithms, adding synonyms, or appending their sentiment analysis corpus. The discussions about algorithmic-based approaches and interventions can get heated as put on Twitter display when Timnit Gebru and Yan LeCun debated the PULSE tool (`https://pulse .cs.duke.edu`) on where biases lie—with the data or with the algorithm (`https:// thegradient.pub/pulse-lessons`). These approaches are standardized under the opus of software package, library, or API framework. It's swapping out one abstraction for another. The underlying library or API implementation can affect *how* and *where* the software product performs on the current hardware configuration. A desktop application requires greater operating system access than a web application. Algorithmic bias, in this case, can be logic errors, ineffective approaches in handling missing data by estimating unknown values (interpolation), or substituting unknown values (imputation). There are also more commonplace errors when it comes to math, like using addition instead of multiplication, or statistics like choosing a linear regression model when the data doesn't fit that model. Algorithmic biases are actualized in word associations, online ads, facial recognition technology, and criminal justice algorithms, as explained in the 2019 Brookings report "Algorithmic Bias Detection and Mitigation: Best Practices and Policies to Reduce Consumer Harms."[9] We observe an intent of algorithms to better their computational performance with outcomes of harms that's compounding and disparate, reverberating throughout the automated decision systems.

Amazon's AI hiring tool project started in 2014, and sometime in 2015, gender disparities were noted by the ML engineers (see Figure 3.1). Two years of failed remedies and "fixes" later, the software development team was disbanded. As of late 2018, it's not clear if everything from the tech product has been scrapped. And there has been no official reporting of how Amazon has revised their AI use in hiring.

I've walked you through one example of one type of data bias that fell along race and gender lines. See Figure 3.2 for a summary of HuggingFace research scientist Margaret Mitchell's "Bias in the Vision and Language of Artificial Intelligence" talk in 2019 at Stanford (`https://web.stanford.edu/class/archive/`

cs/cs224n/cs224n.1194/slides/cs224n-2019-lecture19-bias.pdf). This figure isn't intended to alarm or overwhelm you. I share it to provide transparency on the extent of biases. A frequent tech narrative that claims biases, like those listed in the figure, can be fixed or corrected is a misnomer.

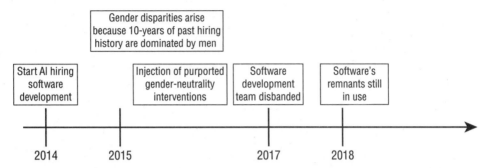

Figure 3.1: Timeline of Amazon's AI hiring software product

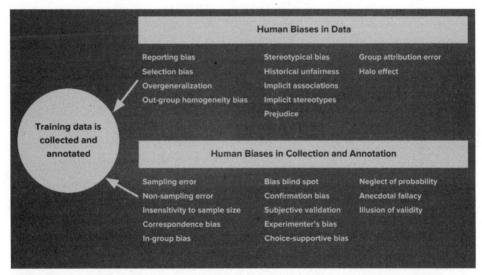

Figure 3.2: Summary of Margaret Mitchell's "Bias in the Vision and Language of Artificial Intelligence" 2019 talk

Source: Dr. Margaret Mitchell. "Bias in the Vision and Language of Artificial Intelligence." Stanford CS224n seminar, 2019.

What we experience, time and time again, is how software development folds in different types of systemic discrimination and inequities alongside trying to rectify mathematically based errors originated by its creators. The tendency of the tech/data community to cast the process as a cycle (e.g., software development life cycle) or some other variant (e.g., phases and stages are also a top favorite term) is insufficient. It presupposes that each part of the cycle (or phase) is isolated from the others. That's far from the case in the real world. I observed the interlacing relationships among the business, people, data, and algorithmic circumstances for the AI hiring tool. We see it more like a wheel.

The Bias Wheel

A wheel has several key parts (Figure 3.3): center cap, spokes, and rim. The center cap attaches to an axle to force the wheel into motion. The spokes balance that force, and the rim connects the spokes and serves as a stable infrastructure to support the tire.

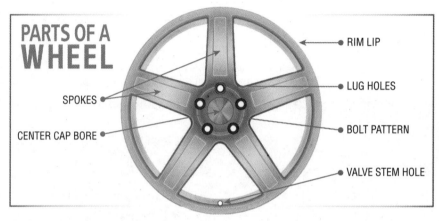

Figure 3.3: Parts of a Car Wheel

I call the tech process a wheel rather than a circle because of the reverberating ways pressure and impact are distributed throughout the system. The wheel signifies the multiple points of impact rooted at the hub (the center of the wheel that contains the center cap, bolt circle, and lug holes) and distributed across the spokes until it reaches the rim for balancing as the wheel rotates. The hub portion is the person in tech—it's you, your lived experiences, your learned/book knowledge. You need to reorient how you think of the tech process and which parts of tech are impacted with each rotation of the wheel.

The bias ripple that occurs at each point of impact has disparate effects on the other parts of the wheel, and these effects aren't uniform or a monolith. In Figure 3.4, we show how each part of the wheel is dependent on the other parts. There are a series of counterbalances that keep the wheel infrastructure stable and reliable. The accepted ideology of a cycle, phases, or stages has us identify distinct subparts labeled 1, 2, 3, and 4 in this case. The arrows illustrate our navigation sequence of these subparts. The arrows on the wheel spokes showcase the bias ripples, both actions and reactions, that happen with each movement of the wheel.

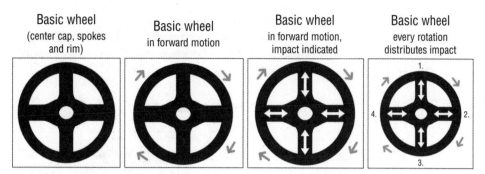

Figure 3.4: Illustration of how a wheel infrastructure transfers impact

Analytically-minded people are persistent in their pursuit to form-fit bias (the mathematical error kind) to a model they've seen before. The interesting part for them is in the degree and coverage of similarities. Creative-minded people are diligently seeking to make a model for the individual to reveal both the overlapping and separate criteria. The other interesting part for them is in the magnitude and depths of differences.

The crux of the conundrum rests on the simultaneous multiple ways bias happens that we can't map. The perceived unsolvable problem gives all of us people angst. It's an itch we can't scratch. So what do we do? Option 1: we concede this reality of unsolvable problems/situations and proceed to slide quickly to deflecting all accountability. This is what's popular so far, by the way. Option 2: we recognize and address the biases with the full expectation that adjustments will be needed. We need to eliminate our attachment to designing standardized or universal frameworks, processes, methods, and algorithms. We can be systematic in our bias discovery process. It's imperative to ask questions up front: what bias definition are you talking about? What are the metrics/approaches for you to achieve that definition?

Shifting the ideology from cycles to wheels disrupts where our starting point should be. The number 1 for you may not be number 1 for others—even on the same tech/data team. Even the four bias subcategories presented here (business, human, data, and algorithmic) may not adequately cover the bias discussion for you. Hopefully, it serves as a great starting point, spurs robust conversations, and leads to equity-driven community-informed standard operating procedures with sufficient metrics attached that will support enforcement.

Figure 3.5 presents four perspectives of bias on a wheel, and where we choose to start repositions our relationships with the other biases. This Gartner blog[10] starts with real-world bias (renamed people bias here) and proceeds to call them stages as if the bias is sequentially and fully transferred in a container seamlessly (Figure 3.5, upper right). For those deeply engaged in the data life cycle, data bias can serve as the initial inflection point, then algorithmic bias to business bias and human bias (Figure 3.5, bottom left). And for those focused on software development, algorithmic bias is the driver for bias creep partially due to some untrackable combination of data bias residue and unrealistic expectations, which leads to business bias and inability to accurately digitally model our society producing human bias (Figure 3.5, bottom right).

Where does the bias start (for you)?

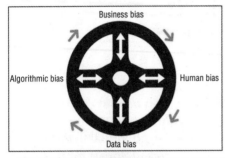
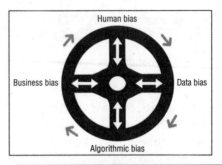
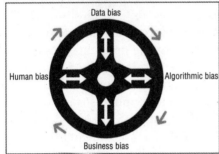
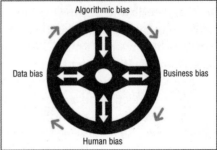

Figure 3.5: Four potential bias wheels covering business, human, data and algorithmic biases as starting points

My perspective, rather stipulation, is that capitalism drives how these forms of bias manifest digitally. We start with the business "bias"/outlook given a largely capitalistic society in the United States (Figure 3.5, upper left). While the United States isn't the only capitalistic society, it's the geolocal I know and, understandably, a transatlantic discussion is ripe to be had. The human "bias"/ outlook attempts to capture what can we extract to be profitable according to someone's business goals. The data "bias"/outlook tries to take the business and people objectives and fit them into digital structures and mathematical equations. It's about how we can extract from the real world in mathematical form such that emulates the societal outlook. Algorithmic "bias"/outlook sets its sights to transform data in order to easily transport the societal outlook at scale. Once transformed and executed, we're back to business bias, which recalibrates goals and expectations based on outcomes of algorithmic biases addressed, scaled, and ignored.

The bias conversation in tech hints at the contextual undercurrent that's missing or excluded from the algorithmic planning, implementation, deployment, and maintenance stages at the root of tech development. Bias creeps in often due to a person's moral value system dictating their perspective. Yet as people in tech, we've been conditioned to scrape out our moral compass—human ethics and values—from the tech process although the moral compass remains subconsciously fully present and guiding our actions. Even here, we entered at business bias and ended at algorithmic bias because of core beliefs taught to me as a child: always follow the money and believe what they do and not what they say.

We could enumerate all the different "biases," contemplate their impacts and seek the "right" path before moving forward, or we could decide to abandon the approach because of all the competing conditions. Neither is productive in establishing ways to work through these biases. The popular data-driven mindset therefore requires an adjustment, given the pervasiveness of biases we encounter and contend with on a regular basis. We can't ignore these circumstances any longer. We have to proceed eyes wide open in tackling "biases." Next, we focus on how data is generated, impacted, and narrated—but don't worry, hints of all the other "biases" show up.

Before You Code

Now that I've shared the bias wheel, we can all appreciate the complexity of the tech process and, more specifically, coding decisions. These coding decisions are made once the software designer or developer has enough context to make an informed choice. I'm circling back to the ways in which data and context are gathered because that's where a tech processes starts. Working with data tends to mean asking a lot of questions. We don't want to miss or misrepresent anything because we know it's tough to alter things in the digital space. We're risk-averse perfectionists. To help get us closer to our ideal pure data, we also try to answer the questions we ask ourselves. The questions we have and the responses we unearth are direct reflections of the data ethics and biases we hold. We know this on a subconscious level—and there's plenty of investigative reporting that tells us that algorithms, automated decision systems, and processes aren't the source of bad code, algorithms, systems, and processes. The source is people.[11-17]

We aren't starting from scratch with our question formation, though. The motivating questions from Chapter 2, shown in Table 3.1 for convenience, gives us a great starting point. And a deeper understanding of bias cannot inform these data ethics questions. Biases can be drawn out earlier rather than later, or not at all. In silos, those of us in tech have preconceived interpretations of how each principle is applied, depending on our computing background.

Table 3.1: Data ethics principles and its motivating questions

PRINCIPLES OF DATA ETHICS	DATA ETHICS MOTIVATING QUESTIONS
Availability and accessibility	To what extent can we identify, set apart, and mitigate discrimination in digital spaces?
Integrity of data processing activities and trustworthiness	How is data's credibility protected while being used in physical and digital spaces?
Transparency	To what degree is data input, processing, and output stages straightforward to track and explain to the general population?
Privacy	How do we keep private things private in digital spaces?
Accountability and accuracy	How do you determine if data is usable for your intended purposes?
	What factors deem data friendly to use, and do these factors compromise the data's integrity?
	Does technology further control or empower society? And under which conditions?

Those eight terms can be converted into concrete questions that we (should) ask ourselves throughout every software development project. The order we ask and answer these questions pattern after a computing method: we need the input (data) to be in the right format to be acceptable to the method, the method runs its set of instructions/statements, and the method returns output (data). In our lens, data toggles between three states: data sourcing (where we create/grab data), data manipulation (where we execute computational operations), and data interpretation (where we craft the data story). We therefore must orient our questions for each state, knowing that responses inherently impact which questions will be asked next and forging a path toward a particular approach. Hitting business, human, and algorithmic biases is to be expected. What we must get into the practice of doing, however, is noting the decisions we're making and their consequences, because saying "We didn't have those discussions or considered potential ill-effects" isn't acceptable anymore. Tech is here to stay, and so are biases.

The following are a few starter questions for your tech/data team discussions. You'll also see a brief instance of how the terms and questions are so interdependent.

Data Sourcing (Accessibility, Availability, and Ownership) Does the data we need already exist? Do we own the rights to do what we want with the data? Have we decided on the data structure or platform for our analysis operations?

Take the CIA triad of confidentiality, integrity, and availability as an example. In the CIA triad, availability focuses on timely and uninterrupted access to digital systems for authorized users. That's a more specific and security-focused view than we're considering here. Data availability for us encompasses when and where data is available for end users and specifically for applications. Integrity under the CIA triad umbrella intends to protect information from improper changes within and across digital systems. Here we refine data integrity to include the internal error-checking and validation processes within digital systems. We're concerned with the physical and logical fit of the data in prescribed data structures. It's important that we settle data availability and data integrity as availability and integrity without computer security considerations. Some, including myself, think of computer security as a wrapper with its own set of processes and algorithms around data. It's like what happens when we set, enter, and reset our passwords. The password keystrokes are human-readable upon entry, and then some sort of encryption algorithm is applied before it's stored in the keychain access (for Apple devices). To make these distinctions easier to recall, I'm making the implicit word *data* appear explicitly before each term.

Data Manipulation (Quality and Privacy)   Does the data fit in the digital infrastructure? Is the data complete in the digital infrastructure? Is the data correct in the digital infrastructure?

1. How does your team select which computational procedures, models, and algorithms are used?

2. How does your team verify outcomes associated with data processes, algorithms, and systems?

3. How does your team evaluate these outcomes as algorithmic-based harms to different communities?

Data privacy is a top concern at most organizations, namely how companies can keep their intellectual property, including sensitive client data protected, as well as how data will be shared *with* third parties. Other data privacy concerns raised are specific to how data about people is protected *from* third-party providers, commonly covered under personal data privacy. Arguably, data privacy could be under the data sourcing umbrella. However, I see data privacy as sitting between data sourcing and data manipulation as the data has to be completed, digitized, and scrubbed for correctness. The tech community doesn't ask "data privacy" questions until *after* the information has been collected. So then the data operations revolve around whether or not certain people *should* have access to certain aspects of the data. This all tends to be contingent on legal grounds and why I categorized data privacy under data manipulation.

Legislation such as the General Data Protection Regulation (GDPR), EU Digital Services Act, California Consumer Privacy Act 2.0, and others across the globe tussled with how machine-executable manipulates would be regulated. These data ethics conversations tended to solely target personal data privacy, instead of data privacy, and assumed personal data was the only data out there. No doubt we have to figure out personal data privacy online, but honestly neither the tech community nor the public have yet grasped the general case of data privacy. There's data coming from digital systems (log files, error files), data generated from algorithms like returned outputs, and then the *Big One*—data about data (metadata) that we find embedded in media content. There are many steps that we need to work through before we touch data privacy.

Data Interpretation (Trustworthiness, Usability, and Auditing)   How do we gauge the fit of this dataset with what we intend to use it for?

1. How confident are we in the processes we used and our understanding of the outcomes?

2. Can the user make sense of this data when we're done analyzing it?

As we manage data, its trustworthiness comes into question frequently. Sometimes these questions are intended to clarify the situation or circumstance while others are intended to introduce doubts of the value of the data (referred to as data accuracy). Data trustworthiness focuses on the human interpretation of data postprocessing. Data accuracy is about verifying outcomes of digital operations. For example, there are algorithms that successfully swap one person's face for another in a video. It's accurately done—it does what it intends to do. But that now doctored video isn't trustworthy. This trustworthiness piece is one we can't automate because the intangible factors surpass the tangible ones by leaps and bounds. When and how the data will be shared publicly is a common cause for alarm as we can make data say whatever we want, by manipulating digital structures and with the removal of our moral compass. Guarding against misinformation and disinformation remains an open persistent and active scholarly pursuit.

Our analytical mindset sees data sourcing, manipulation, and interpretation as orderly, clear, and natural steps like we've done thousands of times in solving mathematical equations. Data ethics calls us to stretch beyond the scientific and systemic tendencies. We need to handle situations that science and systems can't control, because computing devices, processes, and algorithms don't have an analytical mindset—or any mindset for that matter. Computing devices can't decide anything really. They run instructions and report back those instructions' outcomes. But the way we translate outcomes coming from machine instructions can propel or stifle acceptance of ideas in our society.

Let me go through a short demonstration of how we navigate data sourcing, data manipulation, and data interpretation—not necessarily approaching it systematically or sequentially as we try to do a first pass over these questions. The only sure thing is that we can't do data interpretation without either data sourcing or data manipulation first. In many cases, we source, then manipulate, and then interpret data.

I'm picking up the AI hiring tool example again, but going slower to step through a possible scenario of what happened. We'll highlight several data ethics and bias concerns. In no way do we cover all of the concerns. (Feel free to do this as a team-building exercise. It will help reveal some of the "biases" of individuals and as a collective.) The business objectives, people's perspectives, and how these are actualized in digital systems conjure up multiple layers of biases. Taking our surroundings and translating them into a series of methods, processes, and systems is our main priority. Consciously we pick apart an object, like a résumé, into smaller pieces (see samples taken from a random résumé template site at `https://novoresume.com/resume-templates`).

Case Study Scenario: Data Sourcing for an Employee Candidate Résumé Database

It's a good time to circle back to our initial data ethics review questions before we start to pick apart these résumés. Why? Because we're beginning to make decisions that are based on our own assumptions and the impact of these assumptions snowball at scale in digital systems.

My selection of these three résumés (Figure 3.6) are made deliberately to highlight the different ways that the same information can be displayed. I've provided an okay response(see the Figure 3.6 caption) to the pre-questions (Where would data even come from? What are your data sources?). A fuller response is my Google Image search result using the keywords "free résumé template" on August 1, 2020. Now, there's a record of who did what and when.

Figure 3.6: Sample résumés returned from a Google image search

Source: Novoresume ApS

The next question naturally becomes "Who owns the data?" Availability doesn't imply ownership of the data. Those of us in tech hit this speed bump often. We assume that if we can access the data, then it's public and available to be repurposed for our own tech-based projects. The follow-up step is seeking permission of the copyright owner, if warranted. Figure 3.6's images may be subject to copyright. It wouldn't hurt for the legal department to take at least a once-over to assess possible liability. Tech teams seem to be in the clear when it comes to data ethics since we're looking at dummy data. We know it's fabricated data because "Jane Roe" is the legal pseudonym of Norma McCorvey, who was the plaintiff in the U.S. landmark case *Roe v. Wade*. Dummy data doesn't pose data ethics ramifications.

Case Study Scenario: Data Manipulation for an Employee Candidate Résumé Database

Table 3.2 shows an example representative dataset with a short list of keywords appearing on applicant résumés, self-reported gender identity, and ethnicity. Immediately we notice an overrepresentation of male gender and white ethnicity. Performing elementary descriptive statistics on a dataset to reveal its breadth of diverse backgrounds and identities can showcase skewness quickly. Subsequent algorithms and processes that are then based on this dataset need to reflect this skewness. Type I and II errors, false positives and false negatives respectively, can be important indicators. We keep running into Type I or II errors instead of correct conclusions. In this sample and other biased datasets, outcomes and generalizations stemming from overrepresented and minoritized populations require at least a footnote/asterisk. And no one in tech should be shocked by this development.

Table 3.2: Synthetic (fake) employee applicant data from résumés

APPLICANT ID	GENDER ID	ETHNICITY ID	WORK EXPERIENCE KEYWORDS
App001	Prefer Not To Answer	Prefer Not To Answer	assist, manage
App200	Female	White	organize, plan
App119	Male	White	developer, PHP
App002	Male	While	improve, software
App025	Nonbinary	Asian	create, design
App393	Male	Asian	research, implement
App103	Male	White	Python, Linux
App467	Male	White	advance, completed
App148	Male	Asian	lead, achieve
App275	Female	Black	analyze, Excel

We niche down the way we explain the tech and data use by concentrating on the data actions needed to drive tech's reach. Data isn't necessarily transparent, so adding a data structure or a process only adds to the confusion. Thinking in questions allows us to think through possible interconnections and solution approaches. Keeping our eyes on the prize, we want to answer those data sourcing questions (some variant of what nonsoftware developers ask) with designated subquestions (what we ask ourselves and team members in the tech trenches).

With that up-front work handled, we can now refocus our attention on the résumés and their various formats. This covers a combination of data and algorithmic biases. We start at the top making decisions about:

- Storing the applicant's picture, yes or no?
- Capturing the applicant's contact information: first/last name, email, etc.
- Recognizing headings like work experience, education, etc.

There are *technical* challenges like plain-text recognition that us tech and data folks gravitate toward resolving. What those who code are doing is looking for a résumé pattern. Those of us in tech want to review many examples and decide on the common elements. So, we can code it once to cover many of the examples we've seen—crossing fingers, of course, that future applicants will submit their résumés in the same format of the pattern the software developers have constructed. Those of us in tech are making judgments here that prioritize a more machine-readable, algorithmically pleasing résumé format and structure regardless of discipline norms. These choices, however, are a direct reflection of the software and data team's implicit moral codes and their balancing of the bias wheel. Suppressing the blatant ethical conundrums, a rough data model identifying the applicant's personal information emerges that we'd like to capture and store in the digital system (Figure 3.7).

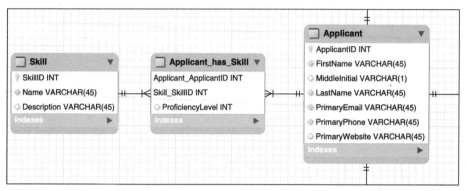

Figure 3.7: Snapshot of online résumé entity-relationship diagram

The ethical concerns become more concrete as additional but related questions arise: how will real data be protected digitally? Who has access to the data, and in what ways can they access it? If Table 3.2 contained real data, we'd have to figure out the privacy and security expectations. It boils down to what assumptions we are baking into the tech system and what the impact is of those assumptions when disseminated at scale.

There are *ethical* challenges we run up against, like evaluating the applicant's skill set. Check out Figure 3.6's Skills section in each résumé and the Language section in the first two résumés. Suppose we want to model the relationship between the applicant and their skills. The entity relationship diagram (ERD) representation is in Figure 3.7. We start with the Applicant table on the right. We issue a primary key (ApplicantID) and a set of descriptive attributes. The attributes with shaded diamonds are required fields upon submission and the others are optional fields. Assuming each applicant has multiple skills, we create the Skill table on the left. SkillID serves as the primary key with the Name attribute being required. The middle table, Applicant_has_Skill, binds the other two tables using their respective primary keys. The ProficiencyLevel attribute is a bit tricky to digitize. Common tech practice procedures have us imposing a value proposition/weight on the skill set order.

In Option 1, we could assume that the order in which the skills are listed specify a higher skill level. The mathematical representation looks a bit like this: SEO > Public Speaking > Negotiation > Teamwork, and so forth. Table 3.3 shows sample Applicant_has_Skill table data, where 1 indicates the most experience.

Table 3.3: A skills listing in order of greater to lesser experience

APPLICANT ID	SKILL ID	PROFICIENCY LEVEL
App0001	S010	1
App0001	S200	2
App0001	S140	3
App0002	S200	1
App0002	S500	2
App0003	S010	1
App0003	S140	2
App0003	S500	3

In Option 2, we could make the reverse assumption of Option 1. The listing of skills is a simple list of independent skills. Mathematically, the representations showcase equivalency like SEO == Public Speaking == Negotiation == Teamwork, and so forth. Table 3.4 shows sample Applicant_has_Skill table data with skill mastery not distinguished.

Table 3.4: A skills listing with no further indicators of proficiency (by default, all skills are equal)

APPLICANT ID	SKILL ID	PROFICIENCY LEVEL
App001	S010	NULL
App001	S200	NULL
App0001	S140	NULL
App0002	S200	NULL
App0002	S500	NULL
App0003	S010	NULL
App0003	S140	NULL
App0003	S500	NULL

One applicant could be implying Option 1 while another can mean Option 2. For those doing the coding, we don't know each applicant's skill level, yet we freely institute our judgment as software developers.

Case Study Scenario: Data Interpretation for an Employee Candidate Résumé Database

Uniformity and standardization are where the tech community always seem to converge. The tech design team decides to implement according to Option 1 and the tech development team decides to implement according to Option 2. Both teams don't express that decision to each other, nor is it documented. Why is this important? Well, when the client (usually your coworker/manager from another division in your organization) is searching for candidates that match their criteria, applicants with more skills listed will bubble to the top more often with Option 2, for example. The client experience will be jaded by an algorithmic choice based on entrenched biases and ethical assumptions.

If I pose a null hypothesis as "employee candidate is not fit for this position," we therefore are accepting a Type II error if we think about this statistically. The tech team and the clients using this software will overlook employee candidates with a shortlist of very good skills matching our criteria, and we'll see many more candidates that have lots of listed skills on their résumés (but may be not as good as we'd like). Type II errors are when you have false negatives, given the abundance of matches returned.

With Option 1, we'll retrieve a lower number of potential matches but likely introduce a Type I error (false positives). The algorithmic choices returned by the tech product eliminate applicants because the sought-after skill isn't ranked high enough on their skill list for the algorithm to be instructed to return those applicants. Savvy job seekers can scrub away ineffective word phrases from their résumés and replace them with descriptive words that will better match a résumé screening algorithm. Exploiting this vulnerability—for example, gaming the algorithm—is pretty easy to do. And once you learn how automation works in any system, you'll find more vulnerabilities and game the system.

This pattern of over/underestimation happens frequently when we're deciding what to digitize. It's two not-so-good options made better (sometimes) with crafty hacks and work-arounds. To be crafty in our hacks, those of us in tech and data have to know what we've excluded and set a plan in motion to bring back what has been lost. This means the tech and data communities know their end goal. As software and data professionals, we must have a sense of ground truth and lean in on establishing an institutionalized practice to inform our ground truth. The clients, and by extension the public, are none the wiser, so the tech and data communities have to bear a significant responsibility for transparency and accountability in making data interpretation uncomplicated.

Bias Messaging

Knowing about and looking for biases gives us a chance to reduce more harms than we've done so far. It's not hopeless. The bias train hasn't left the station. We, as tech creators, managers, and consumers, need to start asking the same questions about how the data was made.

Creators can pose questions about data sourcing, manipulation, and interpretation before and during software development. When indecision swoops in, it's time to pump the breaks. We can't fall prey to neutrality or saying things like "That's the way we've always done it." Remember that the way we've always done it has gotten us to some real bad outcomes. We have to center ourselves on those motivating questions (Table 3.1). And we add the starter questions from earlier in this chapter. We can't tackle the questions together, but one by one. Peeling back the layers associated with each element of data ethics helps keep our tech building process in alignment with the impact we want to achieve.

Managers can back up creators in seeking and identifying progressive responses. They can also serve as reinforcements within an organization in keeping the bias-tracking front of mind to leadership. It's a risky position to stick their necks out, and some will get demoted, sidelined, or even fired. But society can't tolerate any more non-managing managers or willows in influential positions. The most vulnerable in our society, including marginalized communities and various protected classes, aren't represented in the tech development room or at the data table. So it's time to earn your keep. You're either with prioritizing the most vulnerable or you're not. There's no way to stand in the middle of these priorities. You choose a side by your action or inaction.

Consumers, this is all of us. We can ask the questions, raise the issues, point out the discrimination/oppression/suppression outcomes, push for organizations to respond, critique organizations' statements, and make recommendations as a collective. Part III ("Governance") gives a blueprint for where our focuses can sustain and explores common pitfalls that will have us backsliding to robotic complacency.

Summary

Understanding the breadth and depth of our societal and statistical biases paves an actionable path toward combatting the algorithmic siege on our humanity. While our focus is on acknowledging and addressing data bias for data ethics' sake, we recognize that biases surround us. Getting overwhelmed and disengaging from being part of the solution is no longer an option. Whether we are tech creators, tech managers, or tech consumers, we can put pressure on organizations and companies to birth transparency praxis as a core value and outcome.

Notes

1. Johnson, Deborah. *Computer Ethics, 4th Edition.* Pearson, 2008.

2. O'Leary, Timothy, Daniel O'Leary, and Linda O'Leary. *Computing Essentials 2021.* McGraw Hill, 2020.

3. Núñez, Anne-Marie, Matthew J. Mayhew, Musbah Shaheen, and Laura S. Dahl. "Let's Teach Computer Science Majors to Be Good Citizens. The Whole World Depends on It." Edsurge News, March 15, 2021. www.edsurge .com/news/2021-03-15-let-s-teach-computer-science-majors-to-be-good-citizens-the-whole-world-depends-on-it.

4. Biases Archive. "Catalogue of Bias." https://catalogofbias.org/biases.

5. Dastin, Jeffrey. "Amazon Scraps Secret AI Recruiting Tool That Showed Bias against Women." Reuters, October 10, 2018. www.reuters.com/article/us-amazon-com-jobs-automation-insight/amazon-scraps-secret-ai-recruiting-tool-that-showed-bias-against-women-idUSKCN1MK08G.

6. "Amazon's Workforce Data." Amazon.com, April 10, 2019. www .aboutamazon.com/news/workplace/our-workforce-data.

7. Sami, Mohamed. "Software Development Life Cycle Models and Methodologies." Mohamed Sami – Personal website – Software Engineering & Architecture Practices, March 15, 2012. https://melsatar .blog/2012/03/15/software-development-life-cycle-models-and-methodologies.

8. Schneider, G. Michael, and Judith L. Gersting. *Invitation to Computer Science.* Cengage Learning, Boston, MA, 2018.

9. Lee, Nicol Turner, Paul Resnick, and Genie Barton. "Algorithmic Bias Detection and Mitigation: Best Practices and Policies to Reduce Consumer Harms." Brookings, October 25, 2019. www.brookings.edu/research/algorithmic-bias-detection-and-mitigation-best-practices-and-policies-to-reduce-consumer-harms.

10. Bradley, Anthony J. "4 Stages of Ethical AI: Algorithmic Bias Is Not the Problem but Part of the Solution." Blogs.gartner.com, January 15, 2000. https://blogs.gartner.com/anthony_bradley/2020/01/15/4-stages-ethical-ai-algorithmic-bias-not-problem-part-solution.

11. Praharaj, Karan. "How Are Algorithms Biased?" Towards Data Science, June 29, 2020. `https://towardsdatascience.com/how-are-algorithms-biased-8449406aaa83?`.

12. Breland, Ali. "How White Engineers Built Racist Code—and Why It's Dangerous for Black People." Guardian News and Media, December 4, 2017. `www.theguardian.com/technology/2017/dec/04/racist-facial-recognition-white-coders-black-people-police`.

13. Young, Nicholas T. "I Know Some Algorithms Are Biased—Because I Created One." Scientific American, January 31, 2020. `https://blogs.scientificamerican.com/voices/i-know-some-algorithms-are-biased-because-i-created-one`.

14. Katyal, Calder. "How Your Computer Reinforces Systemic Racism." Teen Vogue, October 6, 2020. `www.teenvogue.com/story/racist-algorithms-testing-policing`.

15. Lee, Jennifer. "When Bias Is Coded into Our Technology." NPR, February 8, 2020. `www.npr.org/sections/codeswitch/2020/02/08/770174171/when-bias-is-coded-into-our-technology`.

16. Bond, Sarah E. "How Racial Bias in Tech Has Developed the 'New Jim Code.'" Hyperallergic, August 4, 2021. `https://hyperallergic.com/593074/how-racial-bias-in-tech-has-developed-the-new-jim-code`.

17. Boffey, Philip M. "Baked-in: How Racism Is Coded into Technology." Dana Foundation, February 3, 2021. `https://dana.org/article/baked-in-how-racism-is-coded-into-technology`.

18. Quinn, Michael J. "Ethics for the Information Age," 7th Edition. `www.pearson.com/us/higher-education/program/Quinn-Ethics-for-the-Information-Age-7th-Edition/PGM152724.html`.

Computational Thinking in Practice

Dr. Brandeis Marshall
@csdoctorsister

Mathematics, then Computer science, then Computing sciences, then Software/Hardware, then Technology, then Tech, then AI.
Term soup. And yet folks typically want to talk about algorithms + understand them.

An **algorithm** is a well-ordered collection of unambiguous and effectively computable operations that when executed produces a result and halts in a finite amount of time [Schneider and Gersting 1995].

Source: Twitter, Inc.

Coding has gotten a reputation for being tedious, hard, and a highly specialized skill. This narrative hurts the inclusive tech cause. People believe that they won't be able to learn to code, that it'll take a long time to learn the skill well, or they have to be a math prodigy to understand and apply coding concepts.

In reality, you don't have to be "super smart," but you must be persistent. This chapter stretches the accepted realities and standard discussion points of computational thinking to broaden our socio-ethical tech consciousness. The chapter begins by describing computational thinking and then moves on to a brief comparison of coding environments. We'll run through a common practice we do as software developers—borrow someone else's code either in part or whole. Vetting code for cloning and repurposing is a quandary we explain by pulling social, technical, and ethical levers. And recognizing when we need to step away from automated methods to re-engage real people in real time is the real "computational thinking in practice" skill set we need to develop.

Ready to Code

Well, not quite ready. I first have to address the four-letter trendy buzzword: code. Computer programming, aka coding, is the planning, designing, implementing, executing, testing, and maintaining of algorithms in a specific computer programming language. Sounds boring, right? Let me share a jazzier explanation of coding—it's taking an idea you think of and bringing it to "life" in the digital realm to make the physical world easier for you to navigate: think online banking or e-commerce capabilities.

The linchpin in coding is being good at building algorithms. The best definition of an algorithm comes from G. Michael Schneider and Judith Gersting's *Invitation to Computer Science*:[1] "An algorithm is a well ordered collection of unambiguous and effectively computable operations that produces a result and halts in a finite amount of time" (p. 10). I briefly touched on algorithms and shared this definition in Chapter 3, "Bias." Let's now look at this definition more closely. Breaking down each part of the sentence, we can see how algorithms are restrictive by definition. "Well ordered" tells us that there is an order we must abide by and implies that simultaneous situations aren't part of an algorithm's design. "Unambiguous and effectively computable operations"—well, that is a mouthful, but it reinforces the notion that only computable operations are considered algorithms. This means that noncomputational measures, such as bias, cannot be captured by an algorithm.

Moving on to "produces a result," this statement provides no guarantee that the result is even accurate or valuable. Those of us who code can attest that our work may fail to produce a meaningful result. We need to make our algorithm terminate in a finite trackable amount of time, meaning that it must have an end. It must stop so that the results can be validated and verified, and to make sure the machine running the algorithm doesn't get burned out.

NOTE   The term *well ordered* is very subjective and leads to additional questions of how order is achieved and by whom. What does well ordered mean in practice? Who defines it? Does well ordered change over time? Who judges whether something is well ordered or not?

Algorithms are a rigid construct that's advertised as agile. Building algorithms 101 requires that you write down every step of the process. Why? Because computers are machines and machines have zero contextual intelligence. Here's a short example as a demonstration.

The Shampoo Algorithm

Algorithm design isn't as easy as you may think. We have to think like a non-intelligent machine. Breaking down what we do into tasks, subtasks, and sub-subtasks is a bit. . .painful. We do quite a bit unconsciously. But the computer needs all the instructions precisely; otherwise it will stop or, worse yet, give you an incorrect outcome.

Let's take a relatively common activity, shampooing your hair, and create an algorithm. If you haven't taken a computer science class, this is called the shampoo algorithm. The exercise goes a little something like this:

Question: What algorithm could you write for shampooing your hair?

Answer: Everyone in the class writes their steps, and after a few minutes, a few learners share their responses with the rest of the class. Here are four steps commonly written by a learner as their algorithm:

1. Wet hair.
2. Apply shampoo to wet hair.
3. Scrub shampoo into hair.
4. Rinse shampoo out of hair.

It's a good first pass. It states *what* you do. It doesn't state *how* you shampoo your hair. Computers need to know *how* to do the things you want them to do. Remember computers need clear, concise, and precise instructions. Motivating questions can help fill in the missing steps, like how the hair gets wet and how you apply shampoo. Let's try this again, and retrace the steps using my routine to capture the *how* features more fully:

1. First, the pre-shampoo routine: Grab shampoo, conditioner, and dry bath towel from primary bath. Take all three items to the kitchen and set on the left side of the kitchen sink on the countertop. If kitchen sink hasn't been cleaned, clean it by putting a few drops of dish detergent on the sponge, turn on kitchen sink faucet, run sponge under water for a hot

second until lather. Turn off faucet. Wipe down inside of kitchen sink with soapy sponge. Turn on faucet. Run water over the sponge, squeeze to get rid of as much soap in the sponge as possible. Repeat until sponge isn't soapy (personal preference) and then set aside. Now take the faucet and move it around to rinse all soapy areas in the kitchen sink. Turn off faucet. Dry hands on nearby towel.

2. Turn on kitchen faucet and let the water run in order to reach desired temperature.

3. Drench my locs with water.

4. Separate any tangled locs under the running water with my hands.

5. Grab shampoo bottle and squirt out 1–2 silver-dollar-sized amounts of shampoo on hand. Rub hands together. Run hands under water to lather shampoo.

6. Apply this shampoo to my hair, massaging it thoroughly.

7. Repeat steps 5 and 6 until whole head and hair has lathered shampoo.

8. Turn off faucet.

9. Massage shampoo into scalp and hair for 2–3 minutes.

10. Turn on faucet. Put head under the faucet.

11. Rinse the shampoo out for 3–4 minutes.

Now, that's a more detailed series of steps. Another person could read this list, be able to follow them, and successfully shampoo their hair. And the goal is to build an algorithm that someone else can use effectively. Shampooing is one part of the hair washing process. If we wanted to extend this algorithm to include the full washing hair process, we'd want to map it out to capture the big milestones and then create specific algorithms under each milestone. Figure 4.1 shows my big milestones in a step-by-step process for washing, conditioning, and retwisting my locs. It has *at least* one mistake. Can you spot it?

NOTE   Locs node is the start/source and the Dryer Heat node is the end/sink. Potential answer: There is no Rinse stage after Shampoo, max number of Shampoos should be set to a max of 2, and there is no Rinse stage after Moisturize (hair conditioning).

Crafting algorithms focuses on the 4-step process, but in reality, the 11-step algorithm is what's coded into the machine. The 11-step process is specific to me and those who have the locs hairstyle. Other hairstyles would need a different implementation. While the milestone processing steps are the same, the algorithm itself is unique to the designer. The algorithm designer, or coder, infuses their contextual understandings, which then become part of the final tech product. For any two coders, their algorithm's output can be equivalent or the same; they will undoubtedly implement that algorithm in different ways. Here is where frictions exist because by not including multiple contexts, algorithms perpetuate a singular, privileged, and elitist point of view.

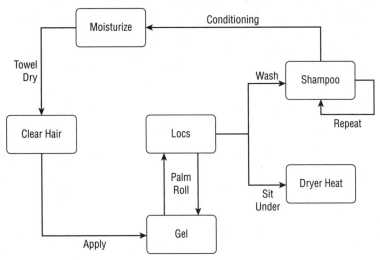

Figure 4.1: Concept map of how I wash my locs

Computational Thinking

Honing your algorithm-making skills takes practice. The most effective way to sharpen your skills is by making, recognizing, and correcting mistakes. You set out to learn from your mistakes so that the next time you don't make those mistakes again. And hopefully, you avoid making new ones. Algorithmic designing can get quite frustrating and tedious because of the exacting precision needed. Many times, computers don't behave the way we want. And it isn't like we have a single formula to learn, then code. There are thousands upon thousands of frequently used algorithms in the world. Knowing them all and how they behave on different types of computing devices, data, and conditions has blown our minds.

This skill was given a name and definition. In 2006, Jeannette Wing wrote a brief *Communications of the ACM* article[2] that rocked the computing community—explaining the rationale to engaging everyone in computing. "Computational Thinking" (www.cs.cmu.edu/~15110-s13/Wing06-ct.pdf) was a visionary narrative of where computing was going. It focused on how imprinted computing concepts were on our daily lives and made cogent arguments of them being as important as reading, writing, and mathematics. She explains: "Computational thinking confronts the riddle of machine intelligence: What can humans do better than computers? and What can computers do better than humans? Most fundamentally it addresses the question: What is computable?" (p. 33, Communications of the ACM, March 2006, Vol. 49, No. 3). We're still trying to answer these questions. I have two more questions that have continually cropped up time and time again: what *should* people be doing rather than allowing computers to do the work? Which tasks *should* computers do rather than people because people make more mistakes than computers? The can-do versus should-do quandary hits at my morality core often while taking in Wing's words.

At the end, Wing gave a prolific call-to-action for the creation of a computational thinking course for everyone, any discipline: "Professors of computer science should teach a course called 'Ways to Think Like a Computer Scientist' to college freshmen, making it available to non-majors, not just to computer science majors" (p. 35, Communications of the ACM March 2006,Vol. 49, No. 3). Teaching is one of the most powerful tools to influencing generations with a common unquestioning belief. The indoctrination of computing concepts as second nature was readily accepted—here a computer scientist, there a computer scientist, everyone is a computer scientist. The rush to code kicked into high gear, and we haven't let off the gas pedal.

The landscape of teaching how to code has expanded to immersive programs, coding camps, bootcamps, DIY stitch-together-free-resources workshops, and courses for the young and not-so-young. And that's what has been developed all over the world with grade school to bachelor degree programs teaching coding concepts. This burst in interest in coding is predictable and disheartening all at the same time. Yes, you earn a good salary as a computer programmer, but the nuances of computational thinking were completely ignored by the public and intentionally ignored by the tech community.

The human factors, or the people effect, of computational thinking sailed past all the reactions and commentary to this article. Take a look at a snapshot of word count frequencies from Wing's article, displayed in Table 4.1. The noncomputing parts of computational thinking are nearly as predominant in the article using words like *think/thinking*, *people*, and *human/humans*. We can't work on the computational part in isolation from humanity, even though that is the current norm. We need to factor in the reciprocal relationship between computing and people.

Table 4.1: Word frequency count for *Computational Thinking*

WORD	FREQUENCY COUNT
comput/ derivations: computer(s), computational, computing, computation	87
think/thinking	45
human(s)/people	17
data	6
algorithm(s)	3

Computational thinking is about *how* people engage with computation, which, to me, is the essence of Wing's article. Now, years later these same tech folks are displaying concern over the AI and automation being uncontrollable—"Robots will take over people's jobs" and other such narratives. Everyone is *so* concerned about AI and robots but not *how* people are being taught, or programmed, to *think and be like a computer*. Forget the scientist part of that call-to-action. Humanity will be eroded and replaced with machine-understandability action as standard practice.

As we may want computing devices and software to bend to our will and whims, we should also guard against us becoming more computer-ish. Data and algorithm(s) didn't receive much emphasis in the article, but we have since learned that these elements are the true directors of computational thought for people. Computational thinking in practice is messy, complicated, and nonlinear. We inject our preferences and style to our coded/algorithmic approaches. This is why it's so hard to read other people's code. Lines of code and the algorithms that are produced contain the personality of its developer(s). Even if you claim to build code on your own, you're *really* not familiar with the substantial amount of open source software libraries and integrated development environments (IDEs) that have preloaded commonly used software libraries.

Coding Environments

Given the amount of code on the Internet, however, it's sometimes faster and more efficient to see if someone else has done what we're trying to do and simply use their code. No need to reinvent the wheel, as they say. We, as coders and software developers, have choices to make regardless of which starting point we select: which computing service like Microsoft Azure, Amazon Web Services (AWS), or Google Cloud Platform (GCP); which IDE like Visual Studio Code, Jupyter Notebook, or Spyder; or which software platform like Tableau, Databricks, or Dataiku. The choice depends on the size and scale of the data we expect to come into the digital system.

And then there's all the different data operations we anticipate being done to the data. We want to create an environment so that we're ingesting data *hopefully* only once. Although this isn't realistic as software evolves and grows, we want to minimize migrating data and code as much as possible. There are countless times we as coders have created our own little sandbox on our local machine, using Jupyter, for instance. And then we integrate it into the main coding hive existing on a computing service like Azure. It's like starting from ground zero with each software migration since we have to (re)configure the environment. And then we have to check that all the software versions are the same and validate that all the data transitioned as we expected. Going through storage types, data types, formats, data architectures, and enterprise systems is tedious work the first time around. No one wants to do it again.

IDEs, computing services, and data platforms are not created the same. And if we need to migrate data, code, and its configurations, failure in doing so has grave consequences, like when MySpace (yes, that popular social networking service back in 2005–2009) reported its data loss in 2019. Twelve years (`https://mashable.com/article/myspace-data-loss`)—you read that right—12 years of pictures and music are gone and never to be retrieved again.[3] Those 12 years cover 2003 to 2015. The details of what entirely happened aren't clear from the public reporting. There's speculation ranging from poor data management practices to intentional data removal activities. These computing environments aren't reliable forever. As society relies more heavily on digital access to personal items, understanding the limitations of such platforms becomes ever more critical.

Data is considered by many, especially in business, as a digital asset that retains its value over time. Data, to them, has no expiration date. This notion is so far from the truth. Data's value requires knowing and understanding situational awareness. In a circumstance like the résumé repository of mostly male employee candidates, this aged data holds no relevant insights in identifying non-male employee candidates. To avoid another circumstance like the MySpace data loss fiasco, other social platforms learned what not to do with their customers' digitally stored memories, posts, and replies. Other social platforms prioritized data security and protection for both the company and their customers because they too didn't want to be a cautionary tale of bad global citizenship.

It's important to settle on the data management structure as early as possible. Balancing the amount of space needed, the time duration needed to store data given the amount of data and cost constraints can often feel like walking a tightrope high in the sky with no net below to catch you. Each data management configuration has its pros and cons that the people in this data specialization have to work through. Working in this vast gray area is what machines can't do—so it becomes people's responsibilities to do it. Budgetary constraints can limit the amount of data we can ingest and determine how long we can store said data without needing to move it into another system.

The graph in Figure 4.2 gives us a running start on pinpointing our data's reach. When we choose the platform or tool that's best suited for our situation, the easier our processing will be, in theory. We see, in Figure 4.2, the data capacity range based on budget limitations. The larger your budget, the more data you can ingest and keep in storage. This point about storage needs more emphasis: storing data takes digital resources as well as computational clock cycles to run data operations.

Understanding the good and not-so-good of each of these tools relies on knowing the problem that we're trying to solve with a tech solution. That's really left for a DevOps team to discuss and decide by weighing timeline, budget, and implementation priorities. Data and software development teams can do a comparison of each of the tools depending on the expected data use. The configurations change frequently, as well as the price points given the pay-as-you-go model for the big scale uses.

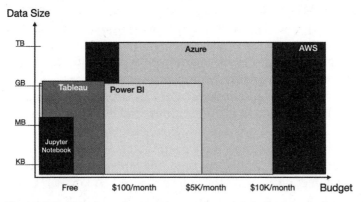

Figure 4.2: Sampling of computing services and platforms costs by max data capacity

For the remainder of the book, though, I'll be using open source resources downloadable to your local machine. Cloud-based services are super popular right now since we can create software products quickly using preloaded software modules and no-code/low-code development platforms. But the proprietary implementations of commonly used software modules in the unregulated cloud adds another layer of complexity to an already little discussed, complicated, and complex topic of data ethics.

Algorithmic Justice Practice

Working with code is a bigger responsibility than those of us who code ever imagined. We're architects in the digital space. What we type and execute, the machine will do. The nature of this work comes with a ton of decisions. We've made it our mission to solve problems with code, and sometimes as a consequence we create problems we can't solve with code. In many circles, the conversations are about responsible and ethical tech, which has evolved to responsible and ethical AI. The responsibility or ethics of tech is a newer requirement within our industry. Philosophers and ethicists asked the same questions many moons ago that data professionals, coders and software developers are now asking, but then everything was hypothetical and abstract back then. Today, the consequences of sidelining ethics and not explicitly developing best common practices has made us uncertain of our code's outcomes. The renewed attention to responsible tech and AI tactics focuses on addressing the symptoms that scaled inappropriate behavior using code—not the root.

Data is the root. Data requires us to contextualize and synthesize text, sound, still media, motion media, and numbers. This understanding of data isn't the gold standard. In fact, the tech industry has reduced data to numbers and normalized this belief as fact. My position that data is the root becomes a point of contention for some in tech who replace data solely with numbers and math. They argue that if data is the root, then that means math must be racist. The "math isn't racist" stance is a deflection used to absolve data and software teams from their own contributions to algorithmic injustices. It's the application of our data use that replicates, scales, and disseminates algorithmic-based harms throughout our society. People using math, algorithms, and data/tech systems need to acknowledge their relationship to data and how it shows up in their code.

In our prior walk-through of the open source résumé screening software, we kept identifying method calls that transform data unevenly. So that leads us here to discussing social, technical, and ethical implications. A key habit that we've developed over the years can use an update. We get comfortable using certain software modules and certain methods in those modules. We think we know how they operate—because they produce the outcomes we expect. Note that this is confirmation bias. We have computational methods to help us figure out other forms of biases (https://catalogofbias.org) like selection bias.[4] The biases that are related to social norms aren't as easy for us to spot. Let's share a few guidelines with brief definitions to help snuff out activities inside and outside our code that raise ethical alarm bells:

Selection Bias   Occurring when individuals or groups in a study differ systematically from the population of interest leading to a systematic error in an association or outcome (challenges internal data validation efforts)

Information Bias   Distorting or misclassifying processed data and outcomes, such as how missing data is handled

Sampling Bias   Selecting intentionally skewed data for analysis that's not representative of the population we intend to serve (erodes external data validation efforts)

Confirmation Bias   Consciously selecting only outcomes that match our expectations

Implicit/Explicit Bias   Unconscious/conscious attitudes and beliefs about a group of people

My ordering here is purposeful. Stepping through our code checking for occurrences of these five biases gives those of us who code clarity on how we're covering data accuracy, data integrity, and data quality. With each method and method call that we discussed, we're assessing the degree of selection bias (primarily data accuracy concerns) or sampling bias (primarily data integrity concerns). Recognizing these biases leads to occurrences of information bias (primarily data quality issues). Avoiding or fixing biases using computation remains difficult because potential solutions aren't binary. Suggestions in the literature span picking the right model (how do we even know it's right?), to creating a representative dataset (what's the criteria to making a dataset representative?), to monitoring outcomes using actual data (how do we keep track of MBs and GBs of outcomes?).

Flagging code that poses social, technical, and ethical concerns remains our first line of coping with this. We're walking in a fog when it comes to writing code since so many of the algorithms are prebuilt in software modules. We don't need to write them ourselves. That means we're practicing code reuse and encapsulation, but that also means we're not as familiar with the intricacies of how the code truly behaves on different types of data. Those of us who code also aren't conducting the software testing at the same veracity that we'd do it for code we write from scratch. We should take an additional step to review methods, even those part of software modules, and isolate data outcome inconsistencies. That way, we can help circumvent some of the social, technical, and ethical issues before they arise—or at a minimum have points for discussion during a team meeting or code review session.

Code Cloning

In practice, software developers aren't creating code from scratch anymore. The process of selecting the most appropriate existing software libraries, building new code on top of them, and reissuing it as a new tech product has fast approached being commonplace. This process strikes squarely at the essence of code cloning. An array of open source software libraries exists, with the majority of them designed, implemented, and validated by white and male identifying people. Therefore the developer's perspective underpins the software libraries—including their conscious or unconscious discrimination against people who don't look or behave like them. The socio-techno-ethical implications and potential for harms are complicated and nonlinear and breed decision exhaustion. (I made up the term *socio-techno-ethical*, but you get the gist.) Let's walk through available code, highlighting problematic implications along the way.

Since I've been using Amazon's AI résumé screening/hiring tool as our running example, I searched Google to find a rudimentary AI résumé screening program in Python. I also want to simulate what those of us who code tend to do—grab some code real quick and add to it if needed. Many people in the data and/or tech community consider this borrowing code since it's findable on the Internet. But this rationale assumes you have a right to ownership of content on the Internet and this assumption is faulty.

Here's the first social, technical, and ethical compliance step those code borrowers need to review. Findability isn't the same as being able to download the code (availability) and have carte blanche on how we use it in our application (accessibility). That permission, sometimes called a copyright license, is required. Any licensing uncertainty is resolved by looking for one of the Creative Commons copyright licensing options or Massachusetts Institute of Technology (MIT) software license options. These options specify how the credit for the creative work needed to be recorded, covering citation requirements of the original work and ability to remix, adapt, and build upon the work. I won't go into deep detail about each license type here. The Creative Commons website does a much better job sharing details: `https://creativecommons.org/licenses`.[5] And for the MIT license, head over to this URL: `https://opensource.org/licenses/MIT`.[6]

I identified the Automated Résumé Screening System software available on GitHub (`https://github.com/JAIJANYANI/Automated-Resume-Screening-System`)[7] to be a viable option that holds an appropriate copyright license, which is shown in Figure 4.3.

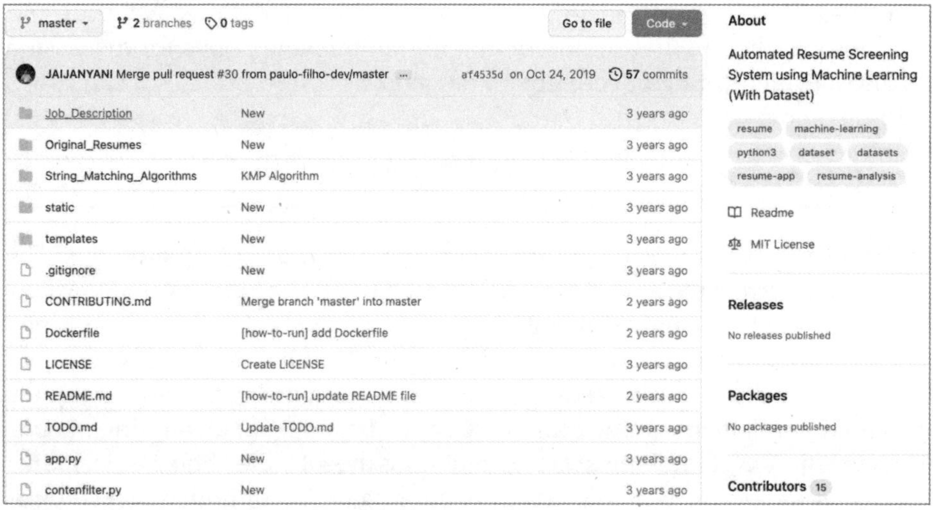

Figure 4.3: ML-based résumé screening system on GitHub

Source: CodeByte

This software is under the MIT license. Many of us who code or teach others to code haven't seen any sort of copyright license, so here's this software's permission statement:

Permission is hereby granted, free of charge, to any person obtaining a copy of this software and associated documentation files (the "Software"), to deal in the Software without restriction, including without limitation the rights to use, copy, modify, merge, publish, distribute, sublicense, and/or sell copies of the Software, and to permit persons to whom the Software is furnished to do so, subject to the following conditions:

The above copyright notice and this permission notice shall be included in all copies or substantial portions of the Software.

Although this statement is in legalese, it's allowing free use of the software, and the author, CodeByte, doesn't make any guarantees that the code will execute—refer to the "as is" phrasing there in the second full paragraph. This MIT license assures us that we aren't plagiarizing the software, nor would we get into a credit/ownership battle with the original creators down the line. Disputes over who owns the creative copyrights of software, algorithms, and/ or processes, such as data, can get pretty contentious. Taking software without permission, changing it, and replacing it with the revised version has been happening for decades.

Take, for instance, the phpMyAdmin backdoor version from 2012 (`https://arstechnica.com/information-technology/2012/09/questions-abound-as-malicious-phpmyadmin-backdoor-found-on-sourceforge-site`)[8] distributed by SourceForge. The manipulated phpMyAdmin package included a backdoor algorithm. This allowed hackers to take control of servers running this manipulated package. The footprint of such a software theft (`https://sourceforge.net/blog/phpmyadmin-back-door`)[9] seems rather small, at 400 downloads of the corrupted phpMyAdmin package. But we don't know how many databases and end users were impacted. Even employees who write the organization's code don't have creative rights to their creation. For instance in 2017, Dmitry Sazonov (`www.forbes.com/sites/nathanvardi/2017/04/13/feds-arrest-susquehanna-international-group-software-engineer-for-theft-of-quant-code/#13fa4ad760a1`), working as a software engineer at Susquehanna International Group, was arrested, charged, and fined for trying to steal quantitative trading code from his employer.

Now what would be great right now is an example of a well-known tech product that contains illegal code. Well, that's not in the cards, because there's messaging already out there that grabbing code on the Internet is acceptable.

The terms used in the tech community seem innocent: *code cloning* or *code duplication*. It doesn't sound that bad. But this language helps perpetuate the notion that using uncredited code is permissible, when it's at the very least breaking copyright licenses. Stack Overflow has served as an invaluable resource to many coders over the years to crowdsource solutions for their technical, logic, and debugging issues. It also has become a *sometimes illegal* repository for coding solutions that become part of production-level code. News of this sort of copy-and-paste coding activity is documented in scholarly research as well as international media. Work out of University of California, Davis in 2017 (`https://web.cs.ucdavis.edu/~filkov/papers/clones.pdf`)[10] reported that 5–10 percent of code in production-level products is foraged. Earlier work from Caio University researchers in 2012 found the percentage to be larger, at 7-23 percent (`https://ieeexplore.ieee.org/document/6340252`).[11] What do you think that percentage is today? For the tech products you use regularly?

Finding illegally accessed code or figuring out that you've used it unknowingly can be disheartening. There are some things you can do to right the wrongs, in a way. It's actually not surprising that this code pirating happens. The open software movement, which champions use of open source licenses, gained momentum in the late 1990s. And then soon thereafter, GitHub came onto the scene. Sharing code publicly in the spirit of collaboration feeds the culture of appropriating software code liberally.

But now that those of us who code know better, we'll do better. A reasonable resolution is quite simple: if the software is under the appropriate copyright license, we can use it and then include the licensing information in each code file taken. Making the attribution costs us nothing. If the software license limits its use in the way we want or there are no licensing indicators: cease and desist. Don't use it. Either seek other software with the sought-after license or write the code from scratch.

Coders notice this pattern of over/underestimation frequently when deciding what to digitize. It's two not-so-good options made better, sometimes, with crafty hacks and work-arounds. To be crafty, we have to know what we've excluded and then set a plan in motion to bring back what has been lost. This means we know our end goal before executing our work-arounds. The focus is on how data and software development teams decide and then implement their notions of ground truth or lean on common practice to inform their ground truth. It's entirely possible that they might not reach consensus on what ground truth is before the product is shipped out.

Socio-Techno-Ethical Review: *app.py*

So back to CodeByte's GitHub code. We have three main source files: `app.py`, `screen.py`, and `search.py`. The `search.py` code performs the heavy lifting—it's handling the bulk of the data manipulation work and operations. There are several common investigation activities like removing extraneous text, pattern matching, and checking word associations. We'll cover `search.py` in depth in a later section. The `screen.py` code grabs and organizes input data, like the résumé text, needed for the `search.py` methods. The `app.py` code serves as the conductor, so to speak, for this software. It captures user input, shuffles data investigation work to the appropriate methods in `screen.py` or `search.py`, and displays the processed data.

In Figure 4.4, I pinpoint key method calls that contain socio-techno-ethical concerns and indicate which data aspects are impacted. We'll display the code of each file, share comments, and describe possible limitations that will affect ethical use.

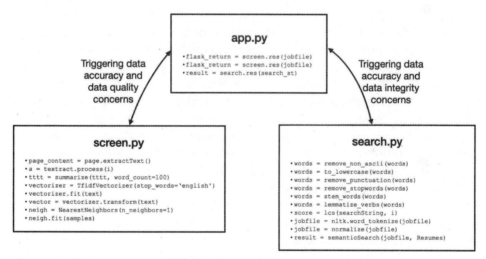

Figure 4.4: Skeleton structure of ML-based résumé screening system.

In the appendices, I segment this GitHub code into smaller code blocks in order to describe what's happening, and I discuss certain methods in more detail. Appendix A contains `app.py`, Appendix B `screen.py`, and Appendix C `search.py`.

Starting with Appendix A, code block A, the coder is bringing in software modules that help us capture data. Since this is a lightweight web app, the software modules relating to Flask (`https://flask.palletsprojects.com/en/2.1.x`) are roped in. And as always, software developers need the supporting coding infrastructure to handle user input as well as reading content from a file. And when it comes to software modules, we can't change the base code as was possible for phpMyAdmin. But those of us in tech do have fuller transparency by being able to see the code, which is typically accessible in a public GitHub repository.

Next up in Appendix A's code block B, the coder identifies the software modules that help us do our data investigation in elegant, efficient, and effective ways. The reading, extracting, and parsing of résumé text from various formats are routine coding activities. As a data/software team member, we rely on them heavily to automatically sift through mounds of text in a matter of seconds.

Then, 20 lines of login and logout procedures seem unassuming in their social, technical, and ethical implications, as displayed in Appendix A's code block C. Oh, how wrong all of us are, whether you consider yourself in data/tech or not. Login and logout procedures are second nature to us now. Well, actually, many of us have become accustomed to using SSO (single-sign-on)—securely logging in digital applications on multiple computing devices. Socially, passwords are the key to digital entry, which we have to either remember or store in some digital place securely as long as it's not hacked (e.g., the password manager 1Password). Technically, the likelihood of your password being discovered is low since the password is not publicly broadcasted.

Data breaches are the closest public reporting of unlawful stolen content. Data breaches happen because of vulnerable/outdated systems, weak passwords, inadvertent download of malware, or targeted malware attacks. As you may have noticed, the common thread is interacting with a digital system upon entry or exit. It's like a digital gap has opened up, allowing noninvited guests to infiltrate. Ethically, the act of trying to exploit a digital system for malicious intent violates all the principles in ACM's Code of Conduct and Professional Ethics (`www.acm.org/code-of-ethics`).[12] But we live in the real world, not the utopia of upright citizens, so we have to deal with bad actors. Each U.S. state and territory has therefore constructed its own security breach notification laws (check for your local version: `www.ncsl.org/research/telecommunications-and-information-technology/security-breach-notification-laws.aspx`).[13] Keeping up-to-date on these user authorization and authentication schemes is a large branch in computing—hello, cybersecurity professionals with a specialization in data loss prevention! Our global digital society completely relies on organizations and their vendors to keep our digital content out of the hands of bad actors.

Here's an excerpt of Appendix A's code block D:

```
def resultscreen():
    if request.method == 'POST':
        jobfile = request.form.get('Name')
```

```
        print(jobfile)
        flask_return = screen.res(jobfile)
        return render_template('result.html', results = flask_return)
...
@app.route('/resultsearch' ,methods = ['POST', 'GET'])
def resultsearch():
    if request.method == 'POST':
        search_st = request.form.get('Name')
        print(search_st)
    result = search.res(search_st)
    # return result
    return render_template('result.html', results = result)
...
```

I've grouped the bulk of the app.py code into one section since much of the code is creating the digital buckets to log in, log out, and return to a landing page using Flask methods in Appendix A's code block D. The results(), resultscreen(), and resultsearch() method calls with the Flask-connected functions make calls to algorithms in the other two source code files. The bolded lines of code shown above give me cause-for-pause. These method calls are stacking decisions and presumes each will have correct outcomes with respect to data accuracy, data integrity, and data quality practices. Let me walk us through screen.py to see why.

Socio-Techno-Ethical Review: *screen.py*

Appropriately named screen, this file wants to return a ranked list of résumés for each job description. The code lays out how the résumés are gathered and how the text is extracted and then processed alongside the job descriptions. Selecting certain software modules makes quick work of these text processing stages. But these coding comforts come from unpleasant ethical residue. Sharing the code (fully in Appendix B) and amplifying the ethical concerns showcase the kinds of potential harms and alternative paths we can take as software developers.

Here's an excerpt of Appendix B's code block A:

```
page_content = page.extractText()
a = textract.process(i)
...
```

Appendix B's code block A defines a set of associated methods, called a class for those unfamiliar with coding concepts. And the method doing most of the work in the class is called res() and takes as input a résumé document. The res() method is tasked with extracting and parsing text from the résumé document regardless of file type. I'm interjecting in the middle of the res() method to focus on the socio-techno-ethical ramifications on two PyPDF2 (https://medium.com/swlh/working-with-pdfs-in-python-6b96d6ce346c)[14] method calls: page_content = page.extractText() and a = textract.process(i).

The `extractText` method conveniently pulls the text content from a PDF page object. But even the method's description raises concerns about its ability to be data transparent and to comply with an algorithm's unambiguous and effectively computable operations criteria:

extractText(): Locate all text drawing commands, in the order they are provided in the content stream, and extract the text. This works well for some PDF files, but poorly for others, depending on the generator used. This will be refined in the future. Do not rely on the order of text coming out of this function, as it will change if this function is made more sophisticated. It returns a unicode string object.

—PyPDF2 documentation page:
`https://pythonhosted.org/PyPDF2/PageObject.html`

The software developer must determine which type of PDF files wouldn't be good inputs. There's also the possibility that the returned Unicode string object will be a jumbled mess of text that's out of its original, intended sequence. Many of us in data will read this brief explanation and contend that this is a technical issue. As data and software team members, we need to trust that methods available for public use and part of production-level tech products will perform consistently. We may run our programs, receive inconsistent results, and think the "bug" is our code. Instead, it *just may be* part of an unmodifiable open source software module that we've depended on. And those of us in data and tech learn quickly that we can't depend on it as a resource. So you think that there are better alternatives, like `slate3k` (`https://pypi.org/project/slate3k`),[15] which extracts all text from PDF documents one page at a time. Now `slate3k` depends on another Python package, PDFMiner. If you choose this alternative, be sure to install the most recent stable version of PDFMiner and `slate` for your Python version. But keep in mind it has techno-ethical vulnerabilities too:

1. *Getting simple things done, like extracting the text is quite complex. The program is not designed to return Python objects, which makes interfacing with other Python datatypes irritating.*

2. *It's an extremely complete set of tools, with multiple and moderately steep learning curves.*

3. *It's not written with hackability in mind.*

`https://github.com/TakesxiSximada/slate3k`[16]

This may go without saying, but I'm going to declare it here anyway: generic, one-size-fits-all algorithmic solutions when it comes to text extraction are extremely difficult to find. Those of us coding these systems are trying to predict the form in which the data will come to us. A change in the PDF version can cascade to the `slate` module, making it behave unpredictably. Those doing this coding work are not absolved from their duties to feature and promote transparency by swapping out one problematic method for another. Keep in mind that PDF documents containing tables with text or visuals aren't resolved using `slate3k`, so writing the code may still need to happen anyway. Data and software development teams have to go back to their software planning step to figure out the best path for executing the project.

The `textract.process()` method, on the other hand, intends to be an any-file-format text collector that will also ensure the word sequencing is correct for the received text. Similar technical issues pop up, like determining which file format we'd like to process and what sort of encoding we expect for the returned result. With no computational approach yielding 100 percent all the time for every file format, taking note of the limitations of the selected open source software library is not a necessity. A portfolio of pitfalls that's just as well-documented as the official API web pages would establish a more centralized environment to weigh the ethical implications. Right now, all we have is our own siloed experiences and ad hoc bulletin board postings as reference.

Here's an excerpt from Appendix B's code block B:

```
# automate a summary of the text tttt by selecting a few sentences/phrases
# to represent the entire text. In this case, the text is a job
description.
# create a word storage container for all non-stop words)
vectorizer = TfidfVectorizer(stop_words='english')

# sort words from 'text' into this vectorizer container and process idf values
vectorizer.fit(text)
# uses this vocabulary to construct tf-idf-weighted document-term matrix
# each word is valued by its frequency (tf) adjusted for relevance (idf) in docs
vector = vectorizer.transform(text)
```

In this code snippet, the code is performing a comparison of the text in the job description to the text extracted from the résumés and looking for the numerical degree of match. Interpreting processed data using an algorithm will be fast, no doubt, but the semantic understanding may be askew. Because of the data accuracy and data integrity implications, I'm diving into the meaning of `tttt = summarize(tttt, word_count = 100)` and the `TfIdfVectorizer()` class, specifically `vectorizer = TfidfVectorizer(stop_words = 'english')`, `vectorizer.fit(text)`, and `vector = vectorizer.transform(text)`.

The `summarize` method (`https://radimrehurek.com/gensim_3.8.3/index .html`),[17] part of the gensim software package, selects the most representative sentences from the input text and formats it into a string. Those representative sentences are determined using the bag-of-words algorithm, the TextRank algorithm; building a corpus; and selecting sentences containing frequently occurring word phrases. The data accuracy can be verified by checking the appearance of each word or phrase in the original document. The `summary` statement (up to 100 words) applying to the job descriptions pinpoints the most useful and frequently occurring words and phrases. When applied to résumés, however, the `summarize()` method will be a pretty strict and limited perspective of someone's work history and expertise. Word augmentation using synonyms and other similar semantic phrases can cast a wider net on the possible words, because the best-fit employee candidates may not use the same words or phrases to describe their skill set.

I'm not suggesting that we never use the `summarize()` method again. On the contrary, knowing this method's limitations helps us identify where data quality gaps persist. Using `summarize()` is ideal for when we want our word corpus to be limited to the text that makes up the input argument. An injection of social context here would provide more robust and rigorous accounting of whether the summary aligned with the outcome objectives. In this case, if five skills were listed in the summary output, the most valuable and necessary skill from the team's perspective may not have the highest ranking. The best we can aspire to is using the `summarize ()` method to help us reach the appropriate vicinity of what we're looking for. It won't pinpoint the exact match.

Let's move on to the `TfidfVectorizer()` class (https:// scikit-learn.org/stable/modules/generated/sklearn.feature_extraction .text.TfidfVectorizer.html),[18] part of the `sklearn` software module. It's designed to put text into numerical context using TF-IDF calculations. TF stands for *term frequency* (TF) and counts the occurrences of a string in a document. And then *inverse document frequency* (IDF) captures the number of documents that have that specific term. So TF-IDF quantifies how relevant a term is in relation to the corpus. The variable `vectorizer` (`vectorizer = TfidfVectorizer(stop_words = 'english')`) sets an expectation that the text processing will work in English only. And the limitations this establishes are well-documented. Stop words occur in more than the English language:

stop_words{'english'}, list, default=None

If a string, it is passed to _check_stop_list and the appropriate stop list is returned. 'english' is currently the only supported string value. There are several known issues with 'english' and you should consider an alternative (see Using stop words).

If a list, that list is assumed to contain stop words, all of which will be removed from the resulting tokens. Only applies if analyzer == 'word'.

If None, no stop words will be used. max_df can be set to a value in the range [0.7, 1.0) to automatically detect and filter stop words based on intra corpus document frequency of terms.

—https://scikit-learn.org/stable/modules/generated/sklearn
.feature_extraction.text.TfidfVectorizer.html

These natural language processing practices are therefore only designed to apply to English when we know that Chinese, Spanish, and Hindi are very popular spoken languages across the world. Correctly representing data in digital systems (data integrity) and determining its usefulness (data quality) easily come into question for non-English text. There's a sea of text that this class can't process. For a more complete list of stop words across 50 languages, the stop-words package (`https://pypi.org/project/stop-words`)[19] can help in designing (from scratch) more inclusive text processing and analysis.

The `fit()` and `transform()` method calls further introduce data inaccuracies. `fit()` smooths out the matrix data by centering it on a mean value like 0, while `transform()` interpolates missing values with the mean value. It's a bit shocking that we aren't able to call a method that gives us the count or percent of the missing/unknown values. Handling missing values remains a sticky-wicket: whether or not we make up entries for the missing values, it affects how that data is perceived downstream. More to come on this sticky topic in Chapter 5, "Messy Gathering Grove."

> **NOTE** The `summarize()` and `transform()` method calls happen for both the job description and the résumé. So concerns we've raised for one are compounded when these methods are run for the other. These concerns can turn into data accuracy and integrity issues and can deeply skew how the data outcomes are also interpreted moving forward.

In Appendix B's code block C, the last lines of the `screen.py` file build a numerical relationship between the job descriptions and résumés. We're determining the degree of similarity between these two using the `sklearn.neighbors.NearestNeighbors` clustering implementation (`https://scikit-learn.org/stable/modules/generated/sklearn.neighbors.NearestNeighbors.html#sklearn.neighbors.NearestNeighbors`). [20,21] But this implementation is rather opaque since it actually is intended to run three different executions of the nearest neighbor—brute-force, KDTree, or BallTree. We don't know when one is running since the choice is made by the algorithm itself. Yeah, for real. The algorithm chooses the best fit using an area under the curve (AUC) or receiver operating characteristic (ROC) variant. The problem is that people are using algorithms without knowing why certain choices were made, and they don't know how these choices can impact humanity. This is a techno-ethical nightmare with an inability to track potential negative harms.

(*, n_neighbors=5, radius=1.0, algorithm='auto', leaf_size=30, metric='minkowski', p=2, metric_params=None, n_jobs=None) where algorithm: {'auto', 'ball_tree', 'kd_tree', 'brute'}, default='auto'

Algorithm used to compute the nearest neighbors:

- *'ball_tree' will use* `BallTree`
- *'kd_tree' will use* `KDTree`
- *'brute' will use a brute-force search.*
- *'auto' will attempt to decide the most appropriate algorithm based on the values passed to* `fit` *method.*

Note: fitting on sparse input will override the setting of this parameter, using brute force.

```
https://scikit-learn.org/stable/modules/generated/sklearn
        .neighbors.NearestNeighbors.html#sklearn.neighbors
                                      .NearestNeighbors[20]
```

The code doesn't specify which implementation to use, so the default is `auto`. The `NearestNeighbors` object instance also sets one parameter to 1. We're only looking for the top match. Notice I'm not saying the *best* match because we don't really know if it's the best. The `fit()` method call just adds to the social, technical, and ethical confusion bowl. `fit()` forces a pairing of the job description to the employee candidate's résumé as part of the model. No matter what. A choice has to be made, even if it's a bad choice.

Again, issues surrounding data integrity and data quality are top concerns. Remember that converting the job description and résumé processed texts into numbers is problematic. And numerical values that are close to each other invoke a certain connotation. Those of us in data and tech infer that closeness, in this example, means a certain level of suitability of employee candidate X for job position Y. What can we do about this implicit association? These numerical outcomes aren't as reliable as software developers had hoped. If numerical values are the selected route for software developers, then it behooves the data and software team to identify, document, and address the impacts along with algorithmic-based harms produced.

Alternative, and potentially less harmful, approaches involve loosening data and software common practice restrictions when identifying the top matches. The data and tech communities can develop more ways to evaluate an employee candidate, in this case, to get a richer representation. Google, for instance, uses over 100 data outcomes to determine a web page's score in relation to a user query. They don't rely on just the PageRank algorithm (`ilpubs.stanford.edu:8090/422/1/1999-66.pdf`).[22] Unlike Google, I'm recommending that people intervene to broaden the candidate pool and make judgments based on intangible, nondigital factors.

As I finish the code analysis of `screen.py`, all of us are poised to recognize the propensity of uncertainty about the stability of the software modules as well as this repeated instance of code dependencies. One method call can be the root of causing a whole slew of code to be inadequate. There are times when we can reinforce data ethical weakness in the code structure with more code, and then there are times we can't. It all depends on the software's structure, what is being modified, and the modification approach. This code has been designed to do quite a bit of automated decision-making. Much of it is obscured from the software developer via convenient method calls and by proxy, from the consumer who is most likely not in the computing field. People are intentionally taken out of the loop to make the computation faster, while the social constructs that influenced the computational approach and the ethical implications that need to be predicted aren't given any space to coexist.

We still have one more Python file to review. We'll tackle it in the next section.

Socio-Techno-Ethical Review: *search.py*

Again, appropriately named `search`, this file finds résumés with words that match certain keywords. Reducing résumé text to a sequence of root words streamlines the computational task of identifying a keyword match. As with the `screen.py` source code, there are method calls that make assumptions about the value of data outcomes. I focus on these methods, what they really are doing, and how I suggest we can lessen their harms.

Here's an excerpt of Appendix C's code block A:

```
# text processing routine in order—get the most 'valuable' words
def normalize(words):
    words = remove_non_ascii(words)
    words = to_lowercase(words)
    words = remove_punctuation(words)
    # words = replace_numbers(words)
    words = remove_stopwords(words)
    words = stem_words(words)
    words = lemmatize_verbs(words)
    return words
```

A series of text processing routines are displayed in Appendix C's code block A. I've included the `normalize()` routine since it is often used as a fundamental part of common coding practice and paradigm in the information retrieval (IR) field. (Information retrieval is a subfield of computer science that dates back to the 1940s, with Gerard Salton referred to as the father of IR for his work in the 1960s.) At each IR phase, the collection of algorithms that are part of the IR system force the data to be fitted into a specific form. The ways we do it with coding structures, algorithms, and methods differ depending on the intended purpose. It's a form of data cleaning to standardize data so that it's ready for the next round of automation techniques.

In our social, technical, and ethical review, though, we've reached circumstances that place data integrity practices under scrutiny. I attest several times thus far that data is shapeless and messy. Socio-ethical tech builders need to understand the intricacies of computational thinking to be able to pinpoint and understand the ethical conundrums with code, algorithms, and processes. Minimizing bad effects by code can only happen when those of us making tech products know how previous outcomes resulted in the type and quantity of damage so as not to repeat it. In this rendition of data standardization, I'm showcasing how methods sanitize text by stripping words of their tenses and context, to distill the root of each word.

The `normalize()` function here walks us through the word sanitation stages: remove the non-ASCII characters, make all the text lowercase, remove punctuation and stop words. Each step intends to make the text more readable to the machines by matching each letter to a string of 0s and 1s. The uppercase letter maps to a string of 0s and 1s that's different for the lowercase equivalent. While we as humans see the uppercase and lowercase of a letter as the same, the machine doesn't. Having all the text lowercase increases the likelihood of finding an exact match when comparing two words. Non-ASCII characters and punctuations are also difficult for the machine to process in an automated way. Keeping only letters and numbers speeds up the code execution. The intention is for the machine and its automated decision processes to handle 80–85 percent of the text matching and that matching will be accurate nearly 100 percent of the time. In practice, neither the exact matches nor the accuracy levels are that close to 100 percent.

The far more likely case is partial matches, where a percentage less than 80 percent is achieved between two words, and the algorithms can't definitively classify the comparison as a match. In fact, text analysis research continues to be plagued with this persistent challenge in identifying partial matches. As socio-ethical tech makers, we must recognize the forced binary determinations (match or no match) based on data outcomes from a discrete function. This sort of erasure leads to trade-offs in determining which percentage of a partial match qualifies it to be considered a match. And how do we, as coders, decide that numerical value? Of course, it depends on how the returned matches will be applied. In the case of résumé screening, human resource teams try to figure out which words in a résumé serve as potential hire indicators. High partial match percentages receive more attention.

Now, those first four method calls need to happen as a preparation for the last two: stemming and lemmatization. First, stemming follows a bunch of pre-defined English linguistic rules developed in 1990 to return each word's root. Well, this process gives us nonexistent and incomplete words—for example, although the word "data" would resolve to the word "data," the word "generalization" resolves to a useful stem word of "gener." The choice of which stemming algorithm to use is decided by the software developers. LancasterStemmer is deemed the most "aggressive" stemming algorithm among the three. It sets out to return the root word with little regard to what the final result looks like.

For instance, LancasterStemmer will stem the word "player" as "play" while PorterStemmer, the "gentlest" stemming algorithm, will stem it as "player."

Lastly, lemmatization scoops up the similar stem word, and sometimes non-existent words, and devises an actual word or lemma. Lemmatization needs to know one thing: the part of speech. So the part-of-speech parameter, pos, can be decided by the software developer, or the default classification is noun. The pos parameter can really matter. The noun, verb, adjective, or adverb representation of a word can change the meaning of the word as well as the context of that word in a sentence. Here's some example code and output:

```
from nltk.stem import WordNetLemmatizer
import nltk
nltk.download('wordnet')
lemmatizer = WordNetLemmatizer()
print(lemmatizer.lemmatize("rocks"))
print(lemmatizer.lemmatize("python"))
print(lemmatizer.lemmatize("corpora"))
print(lemmatizer.lemmatize("designs"))
print(lemmatizer.lemmatize("designs", pos="a"))
print(lemmatizer.lemmatize("better"))
print(lemmatizer.lemmatize("better", pos="a"))
print(lemmatizer.lemmatize("best"))
print(lemmatizer.lemmatize("best", pos="a"))
```

The output contains the following words:

rock

python

corpus

design

designs

better

good

best

best

The plural versions of a word become singular, like for *rocks* (*rock*) and *corpora* (*corpus*). And depending on the pos parameter, the lemmatization can become a whole different word, such as returning the adjective version of *better* with *good*. As a noun, *better* stays *better* (same for *designs* and *best*). Certain words are difficult to interpret post-lemmatization in the case of résumé screening. Take *design* and *develop*, for instance. They both can be used as verbs describing an employee candidate's contribution in a particular position. They could also be shortened versions of the nouns *designs* and *development*. The semantic context becomes lost when processing words separately.

Having the right words on a résumé doesn't automatically mean the skill set is a match. We don't have a barometer on what will make sense as we want to find a consistent sweet spot for balancing the number of employee candidates with the quality of those candidates. Much has been done in commercial tech to come up with an automated solution that's beneficial for HR teams and that exhibits inclusivity to employee candidates. It's just not coming to fruition. And frankly, it won't. The software approach can give us an initial starting point—so we're not sifting résumés in the dark—but people are needed for screening for quality résumés as well as so many other tasks. An overwhelming portion of the data and tech communities think that more tech and optimized algorithms will solve these social ills. They will not. People with a socio-ethical lens need to be a more prominent part of the data and software life cycle. We guide the tech—the tech doesn't guide us.

Here's an excerpt of Appendix C's code block B:

```
...
# longest common subsequence method
    def lcs(X, Y):
...

    def semanticSearch(searchString, searchSentencesList):
        result = None
        searchString = spellCorrect(searchString)
        bestScore = 0
        for i in searchSentencesList:
            score = lcs(searchString, i) # find if search string is in a
            sentence
            print(score , i[0:100])
            print("")
            temp = [score]
            Final_Array.extend(temp)
            if score > bestScore:
                bestScore = score
                result = i
        return result
```

Now that I've decomposed all the words using stemming and lemmatization, we're adding back in the notion of context as part of Appendix C's code block B. It's fabricated by calling the `semanticSearch()` method later in this code. Semantic search is a popular technique whose purpose is to find keyword matches as well as add matches by expanding the person's search based on contextual meanings processed from similar searches or searches made previously by the same person. Connecting separate but possibly related searches is powerful in manufacturing contextual understanding of an algorithm. Many in tech subscribe to the belief that more data helps the algorithm recognize a pattern that it can then try to rediscover.

Let me describe semantic search as it manifests in code. An important note is how semantic understanding is formulated. The `score = lcs(searchString, i)` method call returns the longest common subsequence and stores it in the `score` variable. Here, the longest common subsequence (LCS) algorithm searches for occurrences of words in `searchString` like Python, Firebase, PHP, and JavaScript in sentences that appear in a résumé denoted by variable `i`. LCS is a more lax version of proximity searching, in which we have to specify the distance and maximum number of words between appearances of the words in `searchString` and the words in `i`.

For `semanticSearch()` to be useful, both the `searchString` input and the `searchSentencesList` input need to be customized to the clients' needs so they can select a combination of strings. This way, they see what sort of employee candidates bubble to the top and take a look at the union of that set. In practice, however, a full list of keywords in both the job description and the résumés isn't available for the client to select. The client is left to rely on the algorithmic decisions the data and software development teams made to determine which employee candidates appear at the top of the output list. The quality of this résumé screening software product may be subpar for usability while being much easier to code. The trade-off between client usability and ease of software development is a consistent battle that has data operations in its crosshairs. We've seen this tension in earlier segments of this coding example, and they appear in the final lines of `search.py`.

Appendix C's code block C looks mighty familiar to what we've seen in the `screen.py` file. There seems to be a missed code reuse opportunity to create a short `gather.py` to collect the résumés and job descriptions, extract text, and perform the initial text analysis. Given the 3.6 MB size of the software, perhaps doing this optimization step didn't seem to make the priority list. No need to reiterate commentary. So I'm skipping it, but it's in Appendix C for completeness.

Here's an excerpt of Appendix C's code block D:

```
...
    # identify the most valuable words within the job description
    jobfile = nltk.word_tokenize(jobfile)
    jobfile = normalize(jobfile)
    ...
    # find resumes that map to the job description (but do we find good
    matches)
    result = semanticSearch(jobfile, Resumes)
```

To no one's surprise, the final segment of the `search.py` file ranks résumés semantically with the job descriptions. The only difference is that the `semanticSearch()` method call is happening toward the end of this file. With this single code instruction, whatever discriminations existed as part of the job description or résumés separately have now been intertwined and cemented in the `result` variable. The people who are using this ranked list will decide which employee candidates will continue to the next phase of the hiring process.

Let's take inventory of what's happened. We're branching out from the software developer role. Data and software development teams' responsibilities encompass more than *creating* the lines of code. The repercussions of specific lines of code are undeniable. Those of us in these data and software development conversations can craft alternative algorithmic and non-algorithmic approaches while deprecating existing harm-inducing applications. Doing this reformative work requires a new role designation. I'm calling it *data equity analyst*, whose main duty is operationalizing data ethics. Part II, "Accountability," is dedicated to identifying and providing recommendations throughout the data life cycle to hold the data industry accountable for being more just to minoritized groups.

Summary

Coding requires a 360-degree panoramic view that demands more than coders in order to see, understand, capture, and partially address the social, technical, and ethical considerations. Code isn't built from scratch using a terminal window and text editor. The sophistication of coding environments, the availability of open source software libraries, and accepted practices of "borrowing" others' code make the mechanics of code writing easier. But these factors further obscure the range of uneven social constructs that marginalize communities using data and numbers. How we code now is premised on us intimately knowing the existing open source code infrastructure. Yet we don't, and we remain resolute in trusting it. *Reevaluate everything you think you know*: that's the valuable path when automating and computationally thinking in practice.

Notes

1. Schneider, G. Michael, and Judith Gersting. *Invitation to Computer Science*. 8th ed. Boston, MA, `www.cengage.com/c/invitation-to-computer-science-8e-schneider/9781337561914PF`.

2. Wing, Jeannette M. *Communications Of The ACM*. Vol. 49. N.p.: Viewpoint, 2006. `www.cs.cmu.edu/~15110-s13/Wing06-ct.pdf`.

3. Binder, Matt. Mashable. Last modified March 18, 2019. `https://mashable.com/article/myspace-data-loss`.

4. Catalogue of Bias. `https://catalogofbias.org`.

5. Creative Commons. `https://creativecommons.org/licenses`.

6. Open Source. `https://opensource.org/licenses/MIT`.

7. Github. `https://github.com/JAIJANYANI/Automated-Resume-Screening-System`.

8. Goodin, Dan. Arstechnica. Last modified September 25, 2012. `https://arstechnica.com/information-technology/2012/09/questions-abound-as-malicious-phpmyadmin-backdoor-found-on-sourceforge-site`.

9. Community Team. Source Forge. Last modified September 25, 2012. `https://sourceforge.net/blog/phpmyadmin-back-door`.

10. Mohammad, Gharehyazie, Ray Baishakhi, and Filkov Vladimir. *Some From Here, Some From There: Cross-Project Code Reuse in GitHub.* `https://web.cs.ucdavis.edu/~filkov/papers/clones.pdf`.

11. Abd-El-Hafiz, Salwa K. *A Metrics-Based Data Mining Approach for Software Clone Detection.*N.p.: IEEE `https://ieeexplore.ieee.org/document/6340252/authors`.

12. ACM. "ACM Code of Ethics and Professional Conduct." `ACM.org`, 2021. `www.acm.org/code-of-ethics`.

13. National Conference Of State Legislatures. Last modified January 17, 2022. `www.ncsl.org/research/telecommunications-and-information-technology/security-breach-notification-laws.aspx`.

14. Sharma, Vishal. "Working With PDFs in Python: Using the PyPDF2 library." Medium. Last modified July 10, 2020. `https://medium.com/swlh/working-with-pdfs-in-python-6b96d6ce346c`.

15. Sximada, Takesxi. PYPI. Last modified February 18, 2017. `https://pypi.org/project/slate3k/#data`.

16. Sximada, Takesxi. Github. Last modified December 10, 2021. `https://github.com/TakesxiSximada/slate3k`.

17. Gensim. `https://radimrehurek.com/gensim_3.8.3/index.html`.

18. Scikit Learn. `https://scikit-learn.org/stable/modules/generated/sklearn.feature_extraction.text.TfidfVectorizer.html`.

19. Savand, Alireza. PYPI. `https://pypi.org/project/stop-words`.

20. Scikit Learn. `https://scikit-learn.org/stable/modules/generated/sklearn.neighbors.NearestNeighbors.html#sklearn.neighbors.NearestNeighbors`.

21. Scikit Learn. `https://scikit-learn.org/stable/modules/generated/sklearn.neighbors.NearestNeighbors.html`.

22. Stanford Education. *The PageRank Citation Ranking: Bringing Order to the Web.* `http://ilpubs.stanford.edu:8090/422/1/1999-66.pdf`.

Accountability

In This Part

Glad you made it to Part II, "Accountability." Now we're going to lean hard into critiquing how tech makes decisions. Although accountability is traditionally considered at the *end* of software product development, we're bringing accountability to the foreground and making it *front and center*. We're marching through key milestones in the data life cycle over the next four chapters to point out where lack of accountability resides, identify how it has been sidestepped or ignored, and suggest ways to be responsible, antidiscriminatory, and emancipatory data citizens in digital society.

Accountability is interpreted a few different ways, ranging from someone recognizing issues to that person bearing the consequences of their decisions. I've shared a definition of accountability as perceived by the tech industry's behaviors as well as my own adaptation. Marinate on each, separately and in comparison.

Accountability (n) – *The act of holding someone else responsible for the consequences when your AI system fails*

—**Karen Hao, in "Big Tech's Guide to Talking About AI Ethics,"**

www.technologyreview.com/2021/04/13/1022568/
big-tech-ai-ethics-guide[1]

Accountability (n) – *The act of holding organizations responsible for the consequences when their AI system fails*

—**Revised definition by Brandeis Hill Marshall**

The responsibility of the data and tech communities to demonstrate their ability to answer critics requires three intentional actions:

- Acknowledgment, the recognition of the full truth of tech's role in society
- Acceptance, the recognition of one's responsibility for their tech role
- Atonement, the act of making reparations for a wrong; for example, actions taken to correct prior wrongdoings made on the offenders' part

Chapters 5 through 8 will cover these three actions at varying degrees of depth. But ultimately, it's up to the collective you/we to make inroads during automated decision systems' planning, design, implementation, production, and maintenance phases.

Note

1. Hao, Karen. "Big Tech's Guide to Talking About AI Ethics." MIT Technology Review, 2021. www.technologyreview.com/2021/04/13/1022568/big-tech-ai-ethics-guide.

## CHAPTER 5

Messy Gathering Grove

Dr. Brandeis Marshall
@csdoctorsister

Before you tell me WHAT you did to
the data or HOW you achieved those
outcomes — tell me WHY you are
collecting data in the first place.
#DataWork101

Source: Twitter, Inc.

Tech relentlessly takes people out of the automated decision-making process. Case in point: data collection *and* reformat. Data collection in the tech sphere is people-adverse. From skipping one of the most important questions of *why* are we asking for data to ignoring the impact of missing values, gathering valuable and contextualized data remains a deliberate afterthought. The incessant want for more data overwhelms notions of common sense. And once collected, data needs to be transformed to fit into our human-made infrastructures. We give a nod to what it takes to reformat data, although the process is vastly underappreciated. The chapter wraps up with musings on the potential reasons for these dignity-disconnect antics and lays out how these antics happens so effortlessly. Spoiler alert: it's cemented as part of tech culture.

Ask the Why Question

Asking *why* makes people very uncomfortable. Why questions have people checking their intentions, formulating their justifications, and coming to the realization that their *why* is in large part self-serving. The phrase comes out as "I'm asking so that I can. . ." The tech community suffers from this affliction—to the exponential degree. When pressed on why data is being collected, the standard response is something like, "We need this information to make the tech better." By improving tech, we've made it easier for cyberbullies and online harassers to bombard us, for our content to be moderated, and for our sensitive data to be given to, stolen, or held ransom by bad actors. So is this "better tech" rationale supposed to satisfy us, even after we've seen the negative consequences of tech come to light? What's more, our data is collected by some automated system and processed down to the simplest bits by machines. This is all done under the notion that automated decision systems can make things "better" for us. Read that sentence again. Yes, tech tries to mimic human behavior using algorithms. The tech industry claims to improve the lives of people without actually interacting with real people. You can't make this make sense. Go ahead, try.

And data, our information, is the conduit to making this whole tech ecosystem operate. The choice as to whether to give access to our data is a non-choice. Every app we update demands that you accept the software as is. We can't choose which parts of the updates we want to accept. Even when browsing websites, we're only able to select certain cookies we want to accept as shown in Figure 5.1. For example, *Vice Magazine* has categories of cookies,[1] including information, storage and access, personalizations, ad selection, delivery and reporting, content selection, measurement, and essential (`https://vice-web-statics-cdn.vice.com/privacy-policy/en_uk/page/vice-cookie-policy.html`). Now, essential cookies can't be deselected, but the rest can because of the California Consumer Privacy Act (CCPA) of 2020 legislation (`https://vig.cdn.sos.ca.gov/2020/general/pdf/topl-prop24.pdf`).[2] (More about legislation in Chapter 9, "By the Law"). The ability to choose which cookies to accept is precipitated on whether you understand which parts of your data are being captured by the website and if you care to spent the time to invoke your digital rights to opt out. These decisions are coming fast at us as we interface with the digital society. The pop-ups are on nearly every site, every time you log on, and they're incredibly annoying *and* overwhelming. Companies are banking on us being overwhelmed or in a rush to get access to the website on the other side of the cookie accept request.

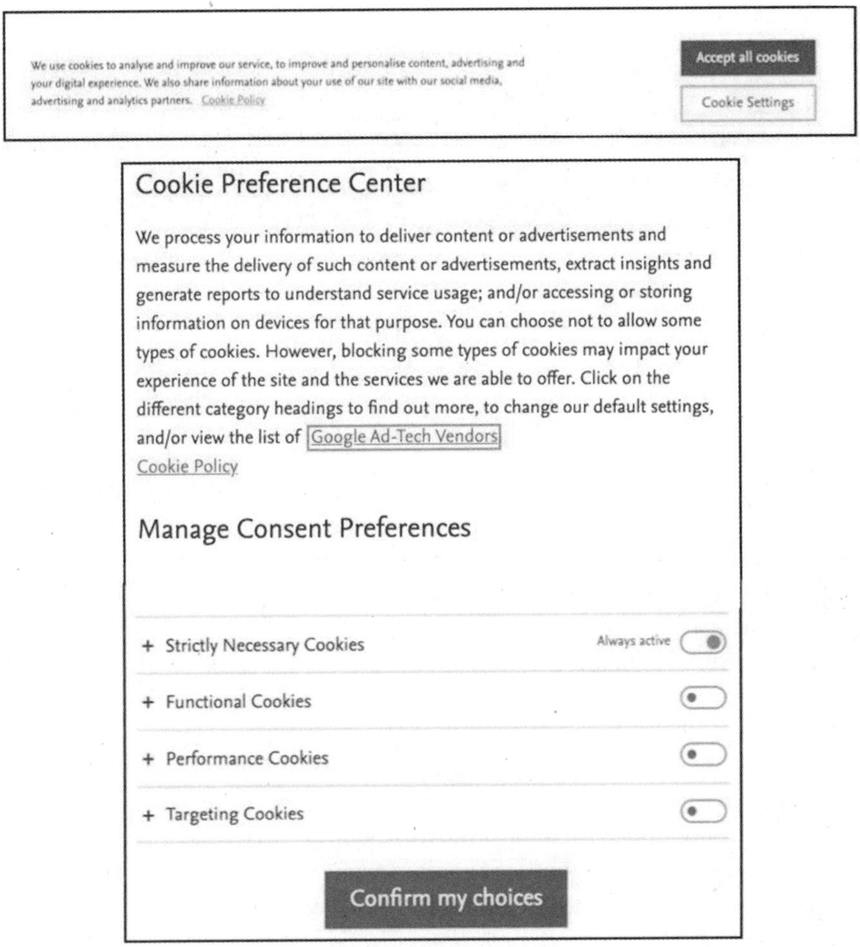

We use cookies to analyse and improve our service, to improve and personalise content, advertising and your digital experience. We also share information about your use of our site with our social media, advertising and analytics partners. Cookie Policy

Accept all cookies

Cookie Settings

Cookie Preference Center

We process your information to deliver content or advertisements and measure the delivery of such content or advertisements, extract insights and generate reports to understand service usage; and/or accessing or storing information on devices for that purpose. You can choose not to allow some types of cookies. However, blocking some types of cookies may impact your experience of the site and the services we are able to offer. Click on the different category headings to find out more, to change our default settings, and/or view the list of Google Ad-Tech Vendors

Cookie Policy

Manage Consent Preferences

+ Strictly Necessary Cookies   Always active

+ Functional Cookies

+ Performance Cookies

+ Targeting Cookies

Confirm my choices

Figure 5.1: Example of website cookie acceptance request (top) and cookie settings (bottom)

Source: Google LLC

Working with data tends to mean asking *a lot* of questions. It's the blessing and curse of being data literate: *you're curious*. Most people in data and tech want to satisfy their own curiosity while consumers simply want to protect themselves from digital harms. The rebel tech worker straddles the fence by prioritizing what consumers want and supplying data/tech people with just enough data so that they stop asking for more data. The *why* questions hit squarely at the asker's intentions rather than to the impact on the askee: Why are we collecting data in the first place? Why would someone share their data with us? For we in data don't want to miss or misrepresent anything because we know it's tough to alter things in the digital space. Table 5.1 outlines three starter questions, with guidance on next steps based on the organization's (or coworker's) initial response.

Table 5.1: Data sourcing questions

	A. DOES THE DATA WE NEED ALREADY EXIST?	B. DO WE OWN THE RIGHTS TO DO WHAT WE WANT WITH THE DATA?	C. HAVE WE DECIDED ON THE DATA STRUCTURE OR PLATFORM FOR OUR ANALYSIS? OPERATIONS?
Yes	Where did it come from and for what original purpose?	Great. Carry on.	Great. What are they?
No	What are the data-gathering procedures being used, and how much harm is introduced?	We need to stop and purchase a license (or something!).	Let's discuss our options before moving forward.

We need to get our data house in order, as a precursor to all tech/software projects. Our data sources and sourcing processes indicate how serious inclusion-driven and antiracist practices are to our organization. In addition, we need not forget about those data-reformatting processes that happen once data is ingested by the organization. The focus on making the data collection and sourcing processes more equitable while lacking to execute comparable equity-centered data reformat and translation procedures amounts to a failure. The equity and inclusion lip service is put to the test when it affects how the organization deals with data's accessibility, availability, and ownership.

Table 5.1's questions intend to help a team (data, software development, engineering, tech) lay out their data philosophy, processes, and practices. The first set of questions address whether the data we need exists and, if so, why it was collected. The tech community is notorious for repurposing data/datasets and making the data "fit" to test a new idea. That's a very extractive approach and presumptuous on the part of the tech community. Using data second- or third-hand diminishes the data's value to varying degrees, yet we don't even acknowledge this fact. It's better for all parties, consumers and data/tech communities, that we find out more about the existing data's origins, such as data lineage. The crux of the complications come from poor data lineage practices through third-party vendors, for example. Companies create policies to protect consumer data. Companies, who hire vendors to perform certain tasks, trust their vendors to have similar policies and processes to also protect that same consumer data. But the intensity of data protection isn't transitive here. Third-party vendors hire their own third-party vendors and so data lineage issues cascade. A data breach or some other security violation for a third-party vendor can easily propagate to their client's company. Tracing how data flows from source to consumption needs to be intentional and well-documented. It will therefore be easier to track errors, modifications, and adjustments made when data lineage practices are carried out.

A related but separate issue occurs when we are collecting data from scratch. The tech community approaches data collection activities like building code: just construct the dataset as quickly as possible via rapid prototyping to make it operational. And then we should concern ourselves with establishing a thoughtful process later (where *later* never comes and continual patching, such as updates, takes place). Being intentional about the ethical underpinnings first, before making the dataset from scratch, can avoid continual patchwork.

The second set of questions are about who *actually* owns the data and how do we attribute ownership, as shared in the second column of Table 5.1. These questions tends to make everyone nervous, from the team member to the legal counsel team. There's what's morally right, then there's what's legal—and the two are not the same. Data ownership is a complicated issue depending on its use. Heavily regulated sectors, like financial and healthcare organizations, handle sensitive data and struggle with how to keep that data secure. There's a responsibility of care that's interconnected with data ownership in these situations. But what I'm focused on here are the types of data where a consumer interacts with a digital system out of their own free will, like Internet searches and social media engagements. Those of us who work in data need to reconsider how we protect consumers' data and not conflate the consumers themselves with those bad actors. For instance, getting my tweets from Twitter takes a few days. I need to be verified and vetted as the data originator of these tweets, so I have to wait to get a comprehensive copy of the content they've shared on these platforms. But if someone repurposes my tweet in an article, I have no way to provide informed consent, nor is there an attribution policy to maintain data lineage. Legally, a third-party reusing a social media post creates no cause for alarm; however, it's a slimy thing to do morally without notifying and asking them for permission.

And lastly, the third set of questions in Table 5.1 are about the data infrastructure and if the data/software development teams have settled on structures, platforms, and analysis methods—what a doozy! This question makes everyone in the organization chain stop cold in their tracks. Focusing on the right now, rather than considering the next two, three, or five next steps, gives fodder for harm integration in tech systems. We must discuss and settle on the data tools and other tech systems we're going to use *after* the data/dataset is obtained. These data tools and other tech systems have their valuable and productive points alongside their harm-inducing aspects. For instance, Microsoft Excel can be great for housing data in tabular form and generating charts quickly, but once you have over 65,000 rows, the ability to run the application effectively become problematic. Or Jupyter Notebooks have a default 25 MB limit. Choosing the appropriate combination of data tools and other tech systems for your tech/ software project requires thoughtful, transparent accounting with a heavy dose of patience. Being well versed in the data tools and having eyes wide open as to its limitations for your organization's use are paramount. There's no silver bullet set of data tools, but know what you're using and why.

Our analytical mindset wants orderly, clear, and natural steps to take, like we've done thousands of times in solving mathematical equations. Data ethics and progress for equity in our tech/data systems calls us to stretch beyond the scientific and systemic tendencies. We need to handle situations that science and systems can't control. Computing devices, processes, and algorithms don't have an analytical mindset—or any mindset for that matter. Computing devices can't decide anything. They run instructions and report back those instructions' outcomes. But the way we translate outcomes coming from machine instructions can propel or stifle acceptance of ideas in our society.

Collection

Gathering up data in the tech sphere is synonymous with creating a dataset by hook or by crook in many cases. We eluded to this at the chapter's start, but let's lay out all the cards. Tech routinely sidesteps the original national ethics committee—the institutional review board (IRB), which originated around 1966. For a full timeline of laws protecting human subjects and IRBs, check out `https://history.nih.gov/display/history/Human+Subjects+Timeline`.[3] For brevity, here's the highlight reel:

> *Scientific research has produced substantial social benefits and posed some troubling ethical questions. Some dates important in the development of institutional review boards, or IRBs, include the following:*
>
> ▪ *In August 1947, during the Nuremberg war crime trials at the conclusion of World War II, the Nuremberg Code was drafted as a set of standards for judging those involved in reported abuses of human research subjects. It became the prototype for later efforts to ensure the protection of human subjects in research.*
> ▪ *On July 12, 1974, the National Research Act established the existence of IRBs to review biomedical and behavioral research involving human subjects.*
> ▪ *In March 1983, federal regulations detailing the basic U.S. Department of Health and Human Services policy for the protection of human research subjects were adopted.*
> ▪ *On August 19, 1991, the 1983 regulations were updated. Known as Title 45, Public Welfare, Part 46, the current regulations provide comprehensively detailed information about the duties and responsibilities of IRBs.* `https://extranet.fredhutch.org/en/u/irb/institutional-review-board-overview.html`[4]

Scientific research, especially when in the medical and healthcare domains, is scrutinized for its moral handling of human subjects' data and information. The malfeasance endured in the Willowbrook study of hepatitis transmission, the Tuskegee syphilis study, the use of lobotomies as conversion therapy, the Jewish Chronic Disease Hospital case, and so many more called on the healthcare community to enact standards and for the U.S. government to make it federal law (since standards were often ignored).

But somehow, the tech community has skirted IRB regulation. Perhaps it's because there's no physical contact. Perhaps it's because data collection for tech products doesn't engage with people face-to-face. Perhaps it's because the reactions, influences, and potential negative harms aren't immediate. Perhaps it's the association of IRB with "research" and not business operations. Yet much of business operations remain focused on gaining "insights" from data, which to me is saying "research" in a different way. Businesses' data insights are nothing more than academic-style research put into action and monetized. Many tech innovations originated in the experimentation portion of studies and used people's data. The peer-reviewed and published work (conference proceedings and journal articles) are found in the Association for Computing Machinery (ACM) as well as other scientific professional societies. And numerous organizations like the Center for Minorities and People with Disabilities in IT (https://cmd-it.org);[5] the Society for Advancement of Chicanos/Hispanics & Native Americans in Science, or SACNAS (www.sacnas.org);[6] Black in AI (https://blackinai.github.io/#);[7] and Data for Black Lives (https://d4bl.org)[8] and other Black/Brown-led groups share decades of tech/data marginalization of anyone other than cis white males. Combining protocols that ingrain IRB-style oversight and establishing relationships with expert equity-first organizations, tech can target their data collection activities in order to retrieve useful data.

Tech researchers regularly pilfer from the social sciences and humanities communities who have done the deep, hard IRB work and then repurpose it as secondary data. Or they scrape the content from digitally available sources and call it primary data. In fact, the implicit (maybe explicit) goal of primary data collection is to remove people from the data gathering process altogether. It's messy and time-consuming to organize your intentions for data collection, to have your intentions reviewed by an external committee, and to proceed only if the external review approves, and then know we're engaging with real people, with real needs and concerns. Creating a dataset isn't simply assembling a bunch of data points. If you're in any tech field or leading a tech/software/data team, you should be required to get IRB certified (https://about.citiprogram.org/course/irb-administration)[9] *and* go through the IRB submission process. This call-to-action goes out to companies making 10-figure revenue to those making less than six figures. You feel a heavier sense of responsibility and, dare say, accountability for what happens to their data after you procure it.

Our data collection practice is fraught with working absent-mindedly. (I know, we believe we have a "systematic" method to our madness, but no, it's just madness.) Let's go through a short demonstration.

Do this quick exercise: head over to your favorite search engine and find a dataset that you can freely use.

This exercise is contrived, but it's reminiscent of what those of us on data and software development teams experience often. We're not given much direction. We're left to "figure it out" or "see what we can come up with." So we're left to define the problem and then go out and solve it too. For this exercise, finding a publicly available dataset isn't that hard. We can get one of Kaggle's datasets (`www.kaggle.com/datasets`)[10] or `Data.gov`'s datasets.[11] Let's say for argument's sake that we don't know of specific dataset repositories, so we have to go hunting for one.

According to research ("Advancing the Ethical Use of Digital Data in Human Research: Challenges and Strategies to Promote Ethical Practice," at `https://link.springer.com/article/10.1007/s10676-018-9490-4`),[12] five guidelines pop up as essential to ethically working with human subject data for research purposes, but they should apply to all those who collect data: consent, privacy and confidentiality, ownership and authorship, governance and custodianship, and data-sharing (`www.forbes.com/sites/jessicabaron/2019/05/09/researchers-have-few-guidelines-when-it-comes-to-using-your-data-ethically/?sh=295bfe26fe82`).[13] I'll run through several in-depth questions and lay out perspectives for two of the five guidelines: data ownership and data privacy. I chose these two since they've captured greater national attention, with conversations and legislations around tech/AI regulations, such as Section 230 (`www.law.cornell.edu/uscode/text/47/230`)[14] in the United States and the Artificial Intelligence Act (`https://eur-lex.europa.eu/legal-content/EN/TXT/?uri=CELEX:52021PC0206`)[15] in the European Union.

The other three guidelines cascade from the understanding and operationalization of data ownership and data privacy. What's more, the role of consent banks on the consent giver reading and understanding what they're giving consent to. That's a tall order since research has shown that people accept service terms/agreements without reading at a rate of 91 percent, according to a 2017 Deloitte study of 2,000 consumers (`www.businessinsider.com/deloitte-study-91-percent-agree-terms-of-service-without-reading-2017-11`).[16] Other research (`https://papers.ssrn.com/sol3/papers.cfm?abstract_id=2757465`)[17] further showcases that people ignored privacy policies and terms of service policies on their made-up social media platform at an over 95 percent frequency. All of us as digital consumers give our data freely and assume nonownership. When, not if, our data is mishandled, we ask about the stewardship protocols and data-sharing practices. Reactionary is our engagement, rather than proactive. So in short, we don't care about how our data is handled *until* it's mishandled.

For this exercise, I decided to use "open source dataset" as the search phrase (see Figure 5.2).

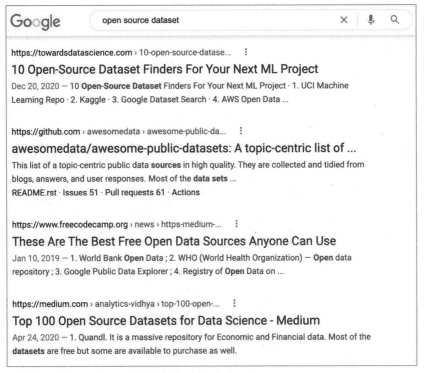

Figure 5.2: Sample Google engine result of phrase "open source dataset"

Source: Google LLC

All four suggested links share a list of datasets. I have more questions than answers at this point, like whether *open source* and *public* are interchangeable, what makes a dataset high quality, or how a dataset can be fun *and* beginner-friendly. Joking aside, we have to whittle down our problem scope and dataset criteria to have the data hold any actual value.

Open Source Dataset Example: Deciding Data Ownership

Like with our toy search, we *want* to decisively and quickly make these choices. Seemingly warranting a simple yes or no response, we should ask cascading questions, though: where did the data even come from (a random corner of the Internet, perhaps)? How do we vet our data sources? Remember, we have two options at this point when it comes to data origins: either we gather data ourselves or we borrow existing data and repurpose it. The frequent choice is to repurpose existing data. The allure of existing data is strong since it helps us make a quicker beeline to coding, which is where coding-scientist-scholar folks really want to focus their energies. By using data that already exists, we make assumptions about its usefulness and fit for the current project. We skip asking key questions, most of which challenge our morality in tech by nature.

Gathering more details would be helpful, only if we'd be able to understand how to apply those new details learned. We have to prepare ourselves and check our own conduct before we engage in data play. Our data ethics discussions start pre-digital, before data gets sucked into a digital system. And it doesn't let up, ever. That's right, we're thinking about data ethics from the start of the software development life cycle, even prior to the planning phase. And, having regular rounds looking at data equity will help keep us in check.

Who is the owner of the real data? Simply because data is available doesn't mean it's available *for use by us*. Someone else's decision to use data unauthorized doesn't give us license to do it. We can't use data that magically falls out of the sky. That raises all types of data ethics alarms (and some legality ones too). For example, Tarr Inc. orchestrated multiple websites and companies to sell dozens of personal-care products. Their marketing campaigns created bogus endorsements using visual imagery available online of celebrities like Joy Behar (www.nbcnews.com/business/consumer/celebrities-hit-back-fake-news-sites-shilling-diet-pills-face-n657331),[18] but their practices were reviewed by the Federal Trade Commission (www.ftc.gov/news-events/press-releases/2019/02/ftc-returns-more-6-million-consumers-who-bought-deceptively).[19] These misleading ads helped to boost their sales to $179,000 over five years. The Federal Trade Commission issued a $6 million settlement to partially reimburse more than 200,000 of Tarr's consumers. And let me remind you of the scandalous data collection schemes of Cambridge Analytica (www.ama.org/marketing-news/the-murky-ethics-of-data-gathering-in-a-post-cambridge-analytica-world),[20] which sold customer data for a profit that was then used in misinformation campaigns on Facebook. Tracking data's origins lets us know *if* we're allowed to use that data.

Your mind is likely racing through the many, many times you just grabbed some data or a dataset without a second thought as to who its likely owner was. Or maybe you're recalling the many, many times you provided your content for an app, organization, or platform feeling a bit overexposed. Good. You might not be so quick to do that recorded talk without receiving a copy or acting offended when a speaker at your events wants the media copy of the talk they're delivering to your organization. We're moving in a more equity-driven, humanity-first direction. But that lingering feeling of being overexposed because of what tech takes doesn't go away. A countermeasure is a suite of stable data privacy provisions. Let's talk about data privacy head on.

Open Source Dataset Example: Considering Data Privacy

We know that data are often thought of as an esoteric concept with no grounding in the very real people who exist behind those data points, word phrases, audio files, or media clips. For example, you could search for your name on something like `peoplefinders.com`, enter your first and last name, and then view the report (see Figure 5.3).

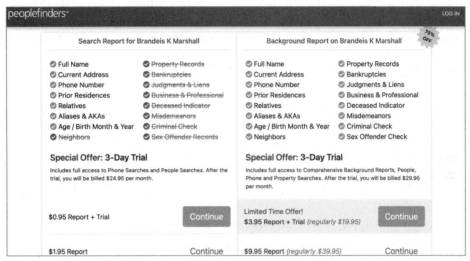

Figure 5.3: PeopleFinders results for Brandeis Hill Marshall

Shocked? It costs $1 to get someone's full name, current address, relatives, and so forth, and $10 to get someone's criminal and partial financial dealings. With a three-day trial period. At the bottom, there's a disclaimer statement:

PeopleFinders is dedicated to helping you find people and learn more about them in a safe and responsible manner. PeopleFinders is not a Consumer Reporting Agency (CRA) as defined by the Fair Credit Reporting Act (FCRA). This site can't be used for employment, credit or tenant screening, or related purpose. To learn more, visit our Terms of Service and Privacy Policy.

Copyright © 2002–2021 *PeopleFinders.com*

This statement is intended to deter people from mishandling this data. It's at the bottom of the page, in smaller font, clearing letting you know that they are an unregulated entity and not liable if bad actors behave badly. The whole "we are a great company and give you all this personal information for a price, but please don't weaponize it so we look bad" vibe is so absurd.

My name is rather unique so it's "easy" to find me. But for those of you with more "common" Anglo-Saxon first and last names, you're "easy" to find too.

Back in 2014, Latanya Sweeney demonstrated that approximately 87 percent of the U.S. population are identifiable by their birth date, gender, and postal code (https://dataprivacylab.org/projects/identifiability/paper1.pdf).[21] The online services we use every day initially either asked us for our address or used a website cookie to gain access to our zip code, gender, date of birth, and other personal information. These questions should immediately cue you into the personal nature of data, which only heightens our responsibility to do the right thing. Instead of saying and thinking "the data" when discussing data privacy, cancel "the" and add "your" to that sentence or question. Making that word change shifts how we see the work with data. We recognize the cascading effects and look for ways to subvert data tragedies. Raising privacy, confidentiality, and security concerns early informs our tech system infrastructure standards. And let's remember the instances when things went terribly wrong.

How will your data be protected digitally? Who has access to your data and in what ways can others access it? We think these are silly questions to ask, but let's not forget the plain-text storage of millions of Facebook and Instagram users' unencrypted passwords (https://krebsonsecurity.com/2019/03/facebook-stored-hundreds-of-millions-of-user-passwords-in-plain-text-for-years).[22] This plain-text file was accessible and searchable to 20,000 Facebook employees conducting 9 million internal queries. Thankfully evidence suggests there was no mishandling of this text file, but a compromising situation like this should have been easy to avoid. Taking a bit of a detour: the unspoken questions that bubble to the top roll freely from our minds, like who put those unencrypted passwords in plain text, why did those 20,000 employees need to have access to this file, what job function prompted them to need to make those 9 million queries, and what were they doing with that password information? Answers to those questions just spin up more questions. We can easily imagine how this plain-text file was started. An employee or group of employees were trying to complete a work-related task and ran into a roadblock. Their "fix" was to have a few names and passwords readily available. Then, the snowball effect happened. Other team members found out about the file, added more names with passwords to it, and it eventually became internal public use.

Are certain parts of your data more sensitive than others? We tend to think of data as a big black box and consider it a monolith. Data isn't like a 24-pack of pop—where the bottles have the same shape and labeling, are the same size, and contain the same beverage formula. Picking any bottle in the pack will give us the same product. That's the expectation, anyway. Data is more like a travel suitcase complete with different types of items. Some items are more important than others. Personal items are less likely to be easily replaceable. Some items are disposable. Those of us in data and software development tend to be tasked with implicitly deciding what constitutes "sensitive" data and how to handle it algorithmically. We make our decisions as though all data is like that 24-pack of pop rather than a travel suitcase. We must remember that these code-level decisions and subsequent automated decision system's outcomes reverberate to everyone who interacts with the tech product being built.

Now, a limited portion of these decisions are checked and balanced with our organization's data regulation and compliance unit. But for the most part, we're on our own. Establishing accountability measures as part of data collection activities can subvert computational aspects that need redesigning prior to the tech product's release. The audit process shouldn't be the first time the computational perspectives have been thoroughly reviewed. Let's not make accountability measure a rare "needle" in the automated decision system "haystack." We can choose to make all the needles first and plant them at certain spots all throughout the haystack.

Now, suppose we switch gears to data teams who create their own data—for example, synthetic data generation. There's one main question we should ask (leading to so many more in the weeds as a software developer) and keep the 9,000 foot perspective.

What features of a population of people are we modeling to build our sample? We've seen this sort of modeling done in other arenas, producing mostly useful outcomes. For instance, the WordNet (https://wordnet.princeton.edu)[23] lexical database for English began in the 1980s and served as the go-to semantic ontology for linguists and natural language processing practitioners in the 1990s and early 2000s. It became a blueprint for finding and connecting similar-meaning nouns, verbs, adjectives, and adverbs. Nevertheless, WordNet ran into challenges—not every part of speech could be represented in this ontological structure. And as time wore on and some words took on different meanings, it became more complicated to place these words in the existing ontology. Modeling of people and their physical characteristics doesn't bode well using a WordNet-style framework of ontology. Creating synthetic data is often seen as a big undertaking. We're making up scenarios and use cases that mimic our biased experience of the world. Synthetic data and datasets are made-up content—sometimes they are manufactured using nonsynthetic data to guesstimate values, and other times they are born from a mathematical formula. The unreal nature of this content exists on a spectrum from well-meaning interpolation and imputation for "missing" data to eerie fabrication of people's faces.

And why, you may ask? Two reasons jump out. First, the data composition they need to show generalizability and broad application either doesn't exist or is too expensive to create. And second, it's a deficient attempt to appear equitable when in fact they are being performative. It's a conscious choice to undermine their own research by using synthetic datasets. The sample can't quite replicate the intended population. And we have to keep synthetic data and real data tech ethics considerations separate. Access, privacy, security, and confidentiality concerns are not as intense for synthetic data . . . unless we're using real data to supposedly generate synthetic data like for IBM's Diversity in Faces dataset. (`www.nbcnews.com/tech/internet/facial-recognition-s-dirty-little-secret-millions-online-photos-scraped-n981921;`[24] `www.ibm.com/blogs/research/2019/01/diversity-in-faces`).[25] Unfortunately, this leveraging of real facial data to generate synthetic data has become more commonplace, which blurs the ethical and legal lines even further.

Full disclosure: Asking these questions can make us a pariah on the team—even called an obstructionist as we're seen as the bottleneck to progress. Well, you will likely get ignored, pushed out of the way, and harassed for expressing thoughtfulness in tech/data spaces. But don't fret. Your words are sound, and time will soon enough be the truth-teller. As you build this proactive data accountability muscle, other supplemental questions are sparked, like whether we are collecting the right data to answer our problem and how we are thinking about our own accountability in any proposed solution approach. In the back of our minds, we have examples of what has previously gone awry. While by intention we want to guide our coworkers and organization leadership to focus more on the big impact picture, it won't always happen. But here's a pseudo-blueprint for what should be covered at a minimum as part of the data ownership and privacy practice for every project:

- Data owner(s)—not just those who have acquired a dataset—are to give permission, with informed consent preferred, including those people whose data appear in the dataset. Consider putting your data collection process through the rigors of an institutional review board (IRB) process.

- Identify privacy, confidentiality, and security aspects of any dataset early on. Having the owner's permission means we can use the data for internal processes. We still must be vigilant about external encroachments on our internal processes.

- Pinpoint vulnerable data features early on. Doing so will make us better stewards of *their* data.

- Note the most impactful limitations of generating our own data. This means we have to think comprehensively about our data models and simulations . . . keep our eyes wide open.

Data collection is hard work, as you have likely surmised. This is why organizations will give this work to limited-term contractors or try to avoid it altogether. Although you can't work out all the issues with data, you can reinforce its persistent messiness and opinion-heavy perspective. People will resist these notions, fiercely. They want data to be synonymous with numbers; numbers are therefore facts and facts can't be disputed. They'll want you to reeducate them on all things data.

Advice #1: Don't take on the complete burden to (re-)educate them. That's a gaslighting tactic that harms you. You are not entirely responsible for their data education. It keeps them from learning about the impact of data in tech.

Advice #2: Giving naysayers sample instances that are contrary to their belief is a fool's errand. There's not enough evidence in the world to convince someone who doesn't want to be convinced. Your responsibility is to center the most vulnerable. As your team, coworkers, and/or organization moves on to the next phase of the project, so should you—and continue to call for better representation of a larger variety of demographic groups, question the usefulness of outcomes when a population subset dominates, and suggest pausing a tech product's release if the product's value diminishes for certain demographic groups.

As data collection gives us a lot to think through, reformatting data once it's in our possession is a whole new challenge. The common practice strips the people's dignity confined to human-made digital structures. The messiness is about to be kicked up to another level.

Reformat

Data comes formatted, albeit badly, but still formatted. Some of these datasets have been fully cleaned, meaning that they have been smoothed out and groomed skillfully to be maximally machine-readable. Many datasets, however, are either visually pleasing to a person's eye by being purely ornamental and not machine readable, or both visually disorganized *and* machine unreadable. Let's look at some of the most used data repositories to understand how not all data is formatted equally.

Kaggle's data is often messy, but datasets that use dates are cleaner than what a user would experience otherwise. That's mainly because they run a slew of digital competitions so that everyone participating must start at the same place. They try to create a level playing field to run a combination of statistical and data analyses and test different algorithms to apply their computational thinking and algorithmic skills. Kaggle roughly follows the model done by TREC—Text Retrieval Conference. TREC has been co-sponsored by NIST (the National Institute of Standards and Technology) since 1992.

For each TREC, NIST provides a test set of documents and questions. Participants run their own retrieval systems on the data, and return to NIST a list of the retrieved top-ranked documents. NIST pools the individual results, judges the retrieved documents for correctness, and evaluates the results. The TREC cycle ends with a workshop that is a forum for participants to share their experiences.

Excerpted from TREC's Overview section

A compelling argument for promoting cleaned datasets is to more easily on-ramp a newbie into data work. And this makes complete sense. We don't want what has been called "barriers to entry" to frustrate new people or create undue anxiety around data work. However, for the non-newbie, it's past time to face the truth. You're going to spend time formatting and reformatting the data. The ways and systematic approaches we use to do this reconfiguration is steeped in our social, political, computational, and economical perspectives. The likelihood that you will format a dataset the same way as someone else will is, well, highly unlikely. Also, within the range of data work activities, let's be honest: data formatting is synonymous with the garbage collector/sanitation engineer of our society. No one wants to do it, but everyone needs at least one person who will do it!

Next up is Data.gov's datasets. They have more of a "come as you are" vibe. Dataset files are classified into categories and organized by file format, topic, area of the country/state, and so on. But there's no concerted collective effort to clean the datasets before making them widely available. While you'll likely get the data you are looking for, it will not be an easy task to find and understand it. Take a look at this renewable energy dataset in Figure 5.4. There's so much going on, it's hard to know where to start. We have two tables on one Microsoft Excel spreadsheet. (Well, isn't that annoying?) This Excel spreadsheet designer wanted to view the cumulative total data and the state-level data on one spreadsheet. It's done purely for a person's convenience. For a computer, these tables need to reside in different spreadsheets. While the top-left smaller table is an aggregate of what's below, it's not intuitive how the two tables are related to each other initially. The larger table shares renewable energy data by state, with equations rendering numbers in some cells (like cell M30 selected) and 0s in others.

Of course, there's an expectation that the column headings will be defined in one of the tabs—except that is not the case. Figure 5.4 illustrates what so many of us doing data work experience. We are given files to "do something with" even though we don't have domain knowledge or the context for the data in these files. We could ask a coworker or colleague to explain the basics, but it takes serious effort to understand. We're simultaneously trying to figure out what the data means and how to reformat the data so that it can be useful to data work downstream like data storage/management and data analysis. Because we did the data cleaning, we're on the hook to help or do most of that downstream data work. Often, data is reformatted and processed and the people using it for analysis have no idea how or what choices were made in this polishing process. And 9 out of 10 times, others think this work is simple and quick so they give us a short turnaround time.

The processing and cleaning of the spreadsheet data returns a reimagined dataset like what's displayed in Figure 5.5.

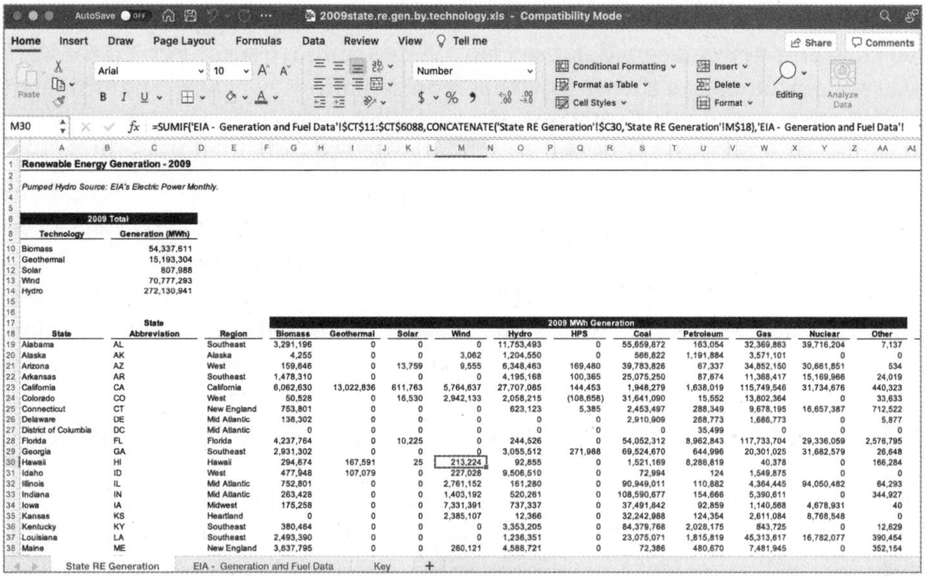

Renewable Energy Generation - 2009

Pumped Hydro Source: EIA's Electric Power Monthly.

2009 Total	
Technology	Generation (MWh)
Biomass	54,337,611
Geothermal	15,193,304
Solar	807,988
Wind	70,777,293
Hydro	272,130,941

			2009 MWh Generation										
State	State Abbreviation	Region	Biomass	Geothermal	Solar	Wind	Hydro	HPS	Coal	Petroleum	Gas	Nuclear	Other
Alabama	AL	Southeast	3,291,196	0	0	0	11,753,493	0	55,659,872	163,054	32,369,863	39,716,204	7,137
Alaska	AK	Alaska	4,255	0	0	3,062	1,204,550	0	566,822	1,191,884	3,571,101	0	0
Arizona	AZ	West	159,646	0	13,759	9,555	6,348,463	169,480	39,783,826	67,337	34,852,150	30,661,851	534
Arkansas	AR	Southeast	1,478,310	0	0	0	4,195,168	100,365	25,075,250	87,674	11,368,417	15,169,966	24,019
California	CA	California	6,062,630	13,022,836	611,763	5,764,637	27,707,085	144,453	1,948,279	1,638,019	115,749,546	31,734,676	440,323
Colorado	CO	West	50,528	0	16,530	2,942,133	2,058,215	(108,658)	31,641,090	15,552	13,802,364	0	33,633
Connecticut	CT	New England	753,801	0	0	0	623,123	5,385	2,453,497	288,349	9,678,195	16,657,387	712,522
Delaware	DE	Mid Atlantic	138,302	0	0	0	0	0	2,910,909	268,773	1,686,773	0	5,877
District of Columbia	DC	Mid Atlantic	0	0	0	0	0	0	0	35,499	0	0	0
Florida	FL	Florida	4,237,764	0	10,225	0	244,526	0	54,052,312	8,962,843	117,733,704	29,336,059	2,576,795
Georgia	GA	Southeast	2,931,302	0	0	0	3,055,512	271,988	69,524,670	644,996	20,301,025	31,682,579	26,648
Hawaii	HI	Hawaii	294,674	167,591	25	213,224	92,855	0	1,521,169	8,288,819	40,378	0	166,284
Idaho	ID	West	477,948	107,079	0	227,028	9,506,510	0	72,994	124	1,549,875	0	0
Illinois	IL	Mid Atlantic	752,801	0	0	2,761,152	161,280	0	90,949,011	110,882	4,364,445	94,050,482	64,293
Indiana	IN	Mid Atlantic	263,428	0	0	1,403,192	520,261	0	108,590,677	154,666	5,390,611	0	344,927
Iowa	IA	Midwest	175,258	0	0	7,331,391	737,337	0	37,491,842	92,859	1,140,568	4,678,931	40
Kansas	KS	Heartland	0	0	0	2,385,107	12,366	0	32,242,988	124,354	2,611,084	8,768,548	0
Kentucky	KY	Southeast	380,464	0	0	0	3,353,205	0	84,379,768	2,028,175	843,725	0	12,629
Louisiana	LA	Southeast	2,493,390	0	0	0	1,236,351	0	23,075,071	1,815,819	45,313,617	16,782,077	390,454
Maine	ME	New England	3,637,795	0	0	260,121	4,588,721	0	72,386	480,670	7,481,945	0	352,154

Figure 5.4: Snippet of `Data.gov` dataset (uncleaned)

Source: Microsoft Corporation

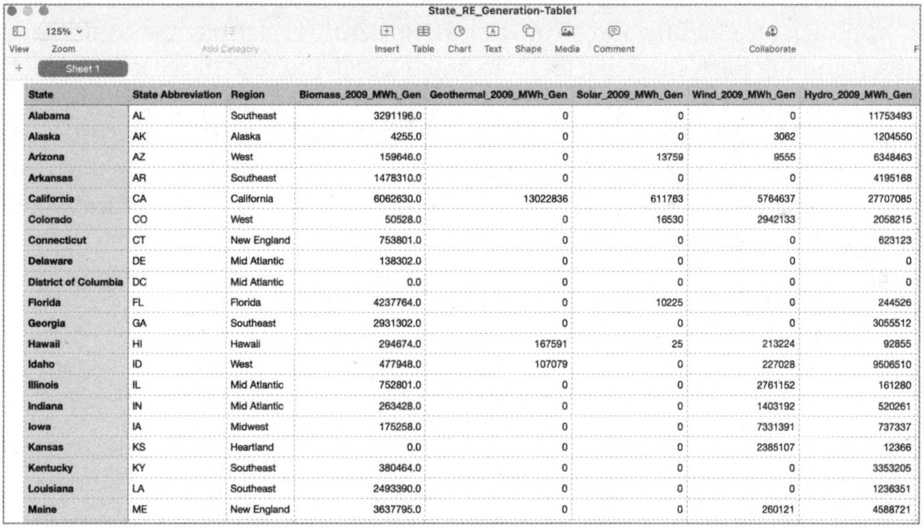

State	State Abbreviation	Region	Biomass_2009_MWh_Gen	Geothermal_2009_MWh_Gen	Solar_2009_MWh_Gen	Wind_2009_MWh_Gen	Hydro_2009_MWh_Gen
Alabama	AL	Southeast	3291196.0	0	0	0	11753493
Alaska	AK	Alaska	4255.0	0	0	3062	1204550
Arizona	AZ	West	159646.0	0	13759	9555	6348463
Arkansas	AR	Southeast	1478310.0	0	0	0	4195168
California	CA	California	6062630.0	13022836	611763	5764637	27707085
Colorado	CO	West	50528.0	0	16530	2942133	2058215
Connecticut	CT	New England	753801.0	0	0	0	623123
Delaware	DE	Mid Atlantic	138302.0	0	0	0	0
District of Columbia	DC	Mid Atlantic	0.0	0	0	0	0
Florida	FL	Florida	4237764.0	0	10225	0	244526
Georgia	GA	Southeast	2931302.0	0	0	0	3055512
Hawaii	HI	Hawaii	294674.0	167591	25	213224	92855
Idaho	ID	West	477948.0	107079	0	227028	9506510
Illinois	IL	Mid Atlantic	752801.0	0	0	2761152	161280
Indiana	IN	Mid Atlantic	263428.0	0	0	1403192	520261
Iowa	IA	Midwest	175258.0	0	0	7331391	737337
Kansas	KS	Heartland	0.0	0	0	2385107	12366
Kentucky	KY	Southeast	380464.0	0	0	0	3353205
Louisiana	LA	Southeast	2493390.0	0	0	0	1236351
Maine	ME	New England	3637795.0	0	0	260121	4588721

Figure 5.5: Snippet of retooled `Data.gov`'s dataset (cleaned)

Source: Microsoft Corporation

The data from the smaller table from Figure 5.4 is gone. The columns are renamed based on the reformatter's preference. All numbers are reformatted using a numerical data type (it was originally text due to the commas separating thousands). To make the file size considerably smaller (5.9 MB to 200 KB), Figure 5.5 lifts the data from the first of the three spreadsheets from Figure 5.4, therefore stripping the new file of the mathematical formulas and on-demand calculations. Yep, we lose context just to make the data easier to manage for a machine. Our newly cleaned dataset isn't vetted until we've presented the data analyses outcomes and shown in visual representations, weeks or months later. More on that in Chapter 7, "Circus of Misguided Analysis."

And pulling up the rear, there's the "hot mess from top to bottom" datasets. These are the raw data streams filling files in all sorts of formats. These datasets are created by scrapping the Internet traffic typically using an application programming interface (API). A bot or collection of bots are built in order to execute these scrapping routines. Though the intention is to capture as much data as possible, in the end most of the collected data is unconnected snapshots of random corners of the Internet. There's little to no value in the data and usually in a text file format. Distinguishing among strings, emojis, numbers, and URL links is a time-consuming, frustrating process that JSON methods have a hard time untangling.

For example, Takeria Blunt, Tayloir Thompson, and I worked with the Academy of Motion Picture Arts and Sciences Awards (the Oscars) data from 2016 to 2018. Blunt focused on word associations for BlackTwitter keywords and phrases while Thompson visualized BlackTwitter's response to the Oscars. Figure 5.6 shows a snapshot of this data pulled from Twitter in 2016 and saved to a text file. There's some formatting here with quotations, indexes/labels like "created at" appearing frequently and so on, but the structure is terrible. We could have chosen another file format like JSON to make it easier to read, if we knew which parts of the tweets we wanted before web scraping. We didn't, so we grabbed it all and left it to sort out on the backside of the data collection process. Although it's not ideal to do it this way, it was crunch time and compiled code that executed is better than cross-fingers-and-pray-it-works code every day of the week.

Figure 5.6: Snippet of Twitter data scraped using Tweepy API

So now as data workers, we create code, Python in our case, to translate the text to CSV file formats. The three of us have to oscillate between converting code outputs from the original file to check and confirm the data transferred completely and correctly. Ugh! Yet another hurdle to clear. We decided that a single tweet had too much extraneous, not-needed-right-now data for CSV restructuring. We only brought the timestamp and tweet text to our CSV file (Figure 5.7).

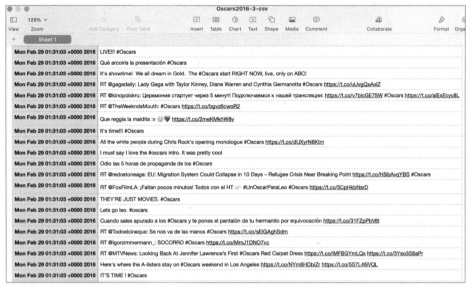

Figure 5.7: Snippet of streamlined Twitter code in CSV format

Source: Microsoft Corporation

The timestamps are clearly delineated, and we recognize at least two written languages (Spanish and English) with combinations of emojis, URLs, hashtags, and plain text in a tweet. There's still quite a bit of additional reformatting work to isolate the tweets only referencing the Oscars in addition to seeing if we can extract some valuable information, knowledge, and insights from this data. We have a better idea of how complicated text data is, though (`www.keboola.com/blog/the-ultimate-guide-to-data-cleaning`).[26]

On top of these reformatting woes, those of us working with data also have to contend with spotty data entries. Having unknown and missing values are normal—either you don't know if the data exists, or you know the data exists, but you don't know what it is. The machine isn't forgiving in either respect. The tech system and other algorithmic methods need data filled into all those open spaces. Missing data puts a wrench in an automated decision system's plans. To learn more about this concept, see Chapter 13 in *Handbook of Ethics in Quantitative Methodology* (Routledge, 2011) (`www.taylorfrancis.com/chapters/edit/10.4324/9780203840023-25/impact-missing-data-ethical-quality-research-study-craig-enders-amanda-gottschall`).[27] Table 5.2 describes the three ways I see missing or unknown data entries handled. To see a demonstration of each using Python code, see "How to Handle Missing Data with Python" (`https://machinelearningmastery.com/handle-missing-data-python`).[28]

Table 5.2: Handling missing or unknown data

MODE	DESCRIPTION
Bury our heads in the sand	We're ignoring the fact our data is spotty. We're going to the next stage in the data life cycle and skipping over the empty places. We don't note it for our records or mention them in our team meetings. The outcomes have us a bit perplexed because we don't remember that we skipped over context related to the original.
Cut our losses	We decided to remove all the rows in the table that don't have data filled in for every cell.
Fake it so we can make it	In tech/data circles, we know this as imputation or guesstimating unknown values given known values in the same column or pairs of columns—refer to `https://scikit-learn.org/stable/modules/impute.html`.

The bury-our-heads-in-the-sand mode causes undue stress and heartache. That "move fast and break things" mentality rears its ugly head, again. We operate like it's the algorithm's fault by retesting, reverifying, and revalidating the code's outcomes. Well, what we need to do is check our human presumptions at the digital door. If one row has all 10 entries and another row has 7 of 10 entries, we have to reconcile how to evaluate the 3 entries with no data in the second row. All roads lead to unexplainable outcomes that aren't credible and that compromise consumer trust. With cut-our-losses mode, our data space gets reduced, sometimes dramatically, but at least we are using only actual complete data we've collected. The problem is we've left "incomplete" data on the digital editing room floor. The data isn't useless; it's just lumpy. We've removed context by cutting it off at its knees. Rude. And lastly, there's the fake-it mode. The insidious part of this one is the making up of data. Providing this intentional misinformation-style data food to algorithms is counter to the data integrity and data quality language. (Check out a brief imputation example here: `https://youtube.com/watch?v=bA6mYC1a_Eg`, Scikit-learn Tip #7). The hypocrisy is rather glaring as people giving their data to digital systems, algorithms, and such must be correct and truthful, yet accuracy and truth are discarded if it doesn't serve the needs of some automated decision systems.

Deciding the fate of missing data cells comes down to preference. There's no real standard in the tech community for what to do for situations when there is missing data. Emphasis has definitely been placed on the fake-it scheme. It's the least desirable because the data has been intentionally poisoned and every outcome that appears as a result is therefore tainted. I'd rather be told that there's no data in a situation followed by an action plan to collect that data than to be fed a lie. Doing cut-our-losses on both the complete set of data *and* incomplete remnants provides a broader landscape and minimizes the trashing of important context. Regardless of your personal missing data handling preferences, iron out data protocols and practices for the team, division, and organization immediately. And don't be surprised if different people on the same data team handle missing data very differently.

Summary

Tech does a bad job in its handling of data collection. Bungled from its inception, gathering data is met with casting a wide net to capture as much as possible as quickly as possible without explicit intention or care of impact for what's being pulled into a digital system. The data reformat work then becomes all the more cumbersome in its attempt to make randomly retrieved data insightful and valuable.

The computational burden could be lessened with better documentation from the onset of this process. Preserving a person's data privacy and understanding who owns someone's data amounts to relinquishing that very privacy and ownership they hope to protect within our digital infrastructures. Those of us in data and software development need to extend our use of data lineage protocols, ask questions early, often, and with real people in mind, and streamline how we handle missing data as a community. Collecting *all* the data and reformatting so *every* data entry has a value shouldn't be the gold standard. It's dishonest. It's a distortion. It's disinformation. The data work that's done at this stage needs to be a better example of how data *should* be handled downstream.

Notes

1. Vice Cookie Policy. Vice. 2019. `https://vice-web-statics-cdn.vice.com/privacy-policy/en_uk/page/vice-cookie-policy.html`.

2. Text of Proposed Laws, Proposition 24. California Secretary of State, 2020. `https://vig.cdn.sos.ca.gov/2020/general/pdf/topl-prop24.pdf`.

3. Sparks, Joel. "Timeline of Laws Related to the Protection of Human Subjects." National Institutes of Health, 2002. `https://history.nih.gov/display/history/Human+Subjects+Timeline`.

4. Extranet. "Institutional Review Board Overview." `https://extranet.fredhutch.org/en/u/irb/institutional-review-board-overview.html`.

5. Center for Minorities and People with Disabilities in IT. `https://cmd-it.org`.

6. Advancing Chicanos/Hispanics & Native Americans in Science. `www.sacnas.org`.

7. "Increasing the Presence of Black People in the Field of Artificial Intelligence." Black in AI, 2020. https://blackinai.github.io/#.

8. Data for Black Lives. https://d4bl.org.

9. IRB Administration. CITI Program, n.d. https://about.citiprogram.org/course/irb-administration.

10. Kaggle. www.kaggle.com/datasets.

11. Data.gov. http://data.gov.

12. Clark, Karin, Matt Duckham, Marilys Guillemin, Assunta Hunter, and Jodie McVernon. "Advancing the Ethical Use of Digital Data in Human Research: Challenges and Strategies to Promote Ethical Practice." Springer Link, 2018. https://link.springer.com/article/10.1007/s10676-018-9490-4.

13. Baron, Jessica. "Researchers Have Few Guidelines When It Comes to Using Your Data Ethically." Forbes, 2019. www.forbes.com/sites/jessicabaron/2019/05/09/researchers-have-few-guidelines-when-it-comes-to-using-your-data-ethically/?sh=295bfe26fe82.

14. Legal Information Institute. "47 U.S. Code § 230 – Protection for Private Blocking and Screening of Offensive Material." Cornell Law School, 2022. www.law.cornell.edu/uscode/text/47/230.

15. "Proposal for a Regulation of the European Parliament and of the Council Laying Down Harmonised Rules on Artificial Intelligence (Artificial Intelligence Act) and Amending Certain Union Legislative Act." EUR-Lex: Access to European Union Law, 2021. https://eur-lex.europa.eu/legal-content/EN/TXT/?uri=CELEX:52021PC0206.

16. Cakebread, Caroline. "You're Not Alone, No One Reads Terms of Service Agreements." Insider, 2017. www.businessinsider.com/deloitte-study-91-percent-agree-terms-of-service-without-reading-2017-11.

17. Obar, Jonathan A., and Anne Oeldorf-Hirsch. "The Biggest Lie on the Internet: Ignoring the Privacy Policies and Terms of Service Policies of Social Networking Services." SSRN, 2018. https://papers.ssrn.com/sol3/papers.cfm?abstract_id=2757465.

18. Weisbaum, Herb. NBC News, 2016. www.nbcnews.com/business/consumer/celebrities-hit-back-fake-news-sites-shilling-diet-pills-face-n657331.

19. Federal Trade Commission. "FTC Returns More than $6 Million to Consumers Who Bought Deceptively Marketed Health Products from Tarr, Inc." FTC, 2019. www.ftc.gov/news-events/press-releases/2019/02/ftc-returns-more-6-million-consumers-who-bought-deceptively.

20. Steimer, Sarah. "The Murky Ethics of Data Gathering in a Post-Cambridge Analytica World." American Marketing Association, 2018. `www.ama.org/marketing-news/the-murky-ethics-of-data-gathering-in-a-post-cambridge-analytica-world`.

21. Sweeney, Latanya. "Simple Demographics Often Identify People Uniquely." Carnegie Mellon University, 2000. `https://dataprivacylab.org/projects/identifiability/paper1.pdf`.

22. Krebs, Brian. "Facebook Stored Hundreds of Millions of User Passwords in Plain Text for Years." Krebson Security, 2019. `https://krebsonsecurity.com/2019/03/facebook-stored-hundreds-of-millions-of-user-passwords-in-plain-text-for-years`.

23. WordNet. Princeton University, 2022. `https://wordnet.princeton.edu`.

24. Solon, Olivia. "Facial Recognition's 'Dirty Little Secret': Millions of Online Photos Scraped without Consent." NBC News, 2019. `www.nbcnews.com/tech/internet/facial-recognition-s-dirty-little-secret-millions-online-photos-scraped-n981921`.

25. Smith, John R. "IBM Research Releases 'Diversity in Faces' Dataset to Advance Study of Fairness in Facial Recognition Systems." IBM, 2019. `www.ibm.com/blogs/research/2019/01/diversity-in-faces`.

26. "The Ultimate Guide to Data Cleaning." Keboola, n.d. `www.keboola.com/blog/the-ultimate-guide-to-data-cleaning`.

27. Enders, Craig K., and Amanda C. Gottschall. *Handbook of Ethics in Quantitative Methodology*. Routledge, 2011.

28. Brownlee, Jason. "How to Handle Missing Data with Python." Machine Learning Mastery, 2020. `https://machinelearningmastery.com/handle-missing-data-python`.

Inconsistent Storage Sanctuary

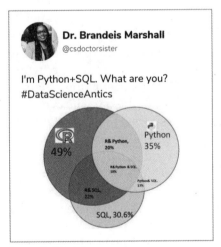

Dr. Brandeis Marshall
@csdoctorsister

I'm Python+SQL. What are you?
#DataScienceAntics

Source: Twitter, Inc.

Often hidden in conversations about the data life cycle is a clear understanding of the human and digital efforts needed to implement storage practices, processes, and systems. Data storage isn't glamorous; it's considered tedious and doesn't typically involve many people. Database administrators (DBAs) are usually the only people in an organization who truly know the database architecture and design. Software engineers and other data team members engage with the database as users. The data storage stage sets the digital foundation from which every piece of content originates.

In this chapter, we explore how the digital infrastructure is built, leading to countless questions about how to accomplish our goals. The nature of the work centers on taking data in various file formats and making it machine-accessible and machine-readable. Whether in files, spreadsheets, or the cloud, database architecture and design is leaned on as a universal fix; however, many of these decisions are being made in a vacuum. The modeling of attribute associations and table relationships must contend with the limitations of this binary relationship. We keep humans in the loop during the database design process and champion their accountability for database architecture choices that can introduce harm to the most vulnerable communities.

Ask the "What" Question

Now, we're asking the "what" question. This is the "why" plus an action plan. "What" questions ruffle some folks' feathers because we're focused on action steps and they don't know what actions to take. Others are energized by "what" questions since they like hearing themselves talk. Whether you're on the delivery or the receiving end of a "what" question, the experience tends to be the same: confrontational. "What's the status of. . .?," "What's the timeline for completing. . .?," "Which dataset will be used to create/test/validate. . .?," and "What's your tech stack?" are the abrasive ways we speak to one another in tech about the concrete actions we're taking to impose structure on our "why." We want to be able to identify steps and track and then measure the progress. And frankly, this is the drudgery and unpleasant part of the data life cycle. It's the part everyone wants to skip over or speed past, especially when amplifying automation and analytics as the return-on-investment (ROI) booster. We *have to* organize, categorize, and label all the data and then stuff it into a data structure. If you're a Microsoft Excel person, you call it a spreadsheet. If you're a database person, you call it a table. If you're a Pythonista/R warrior, you call it a data frame. No matter your point of view, creating column headings and loading rows of data are in your immediate future.

We think of ourselves as data translators, taking data from our physical real world to the digital one. We're managing content, calling ourselves content managers. But it's more nefarious than the mundane "content managers." We're operating like content creators, preparing data for machine understandability, machine readability, and machine usability.

We strip the data in some way, whether it's text, audio, image, or media:

- When we have text, we lose the context of the messenger's tone.
- When we have audio, we lose the context of the speaker's body language.
- When we have a still visual, we lose the description or story behind the creation of that visual.
- When we have media, we can't include our other senses to heighten the experience (like smelling a dish made on a cooking show).

We don't fully recognize these losses soon enough in the data life cycle. And let's take note that each data type I've listed has its own nonoverlapping format (TXT, WAV, PNG, MP4). Having the wrong format leads ultimately to machine confusion. It's like a deer in headlights. The tech tool will give us an error message such as "Unable to open file. . ." and then promptly closes itself down. We move from experiencing data in multiple dimensions to two dimensions. Certain human senses are deafened so that machines can be comfortable.

Similar to our data sourcing questions, we have to isolate data manipulation questions. We're presenting them in two parts—one in this chapter and one in the next. The questions in Table 6.1 force us to think more intentionally about which data is squeezed into human-made data structures, such as digital infrastructures. The first question focuses on the incoming data's format type and size alignment. The second question centers data's quality from a descriptive perspective—for example, density versus sparseness of the contents. The last question attempts to ascertain the data's value. With each question, people are trying to make the data malleable according to machine specifications rather than for other people. It's dehumanizing. Taking a step back to operationalize "fit," "completeness," and "correctness" with respect to data practice means that there will be a certain amount of messiness and conflicting priorities. Acknowledging and accepting this messiness can help us shape a people-first path forward.

Table 6.1 gives starter questions for a data or a software development team to determine how they'll organize their data digitally. Despite the simplicity of the table, the questions in the real world are very messy to answer—especially the second question, where "complete" can be a problematic notion. Fit, complete, and correct remain highly contested terms in the tech and data industry. Each term doesn't correlate to a quantitative standardized metric that's accepted by those handling data. The ability to systematize these terms through lines of code continues to be a reoccurring yet foolish research direction. Instead, data and software development teams should reorient their attention to aligning their data practices according to their interpretations of fit, complete, and correct.

Table 6.1: Data manipulation questions, part 1

	1. DOES THE DATA FIT IN THE DIGITAL INFRASTRUCTURE?	2. IS THE DATA COMPLETE IN THE DIGITAL INFRASTRUCTURE?	3. IS THE DATA CORRECT IN THE DIGITAL INFRASTRUCTURE?
Yes	Great, if you mean "fit" as in having enough storage capacity.	Great. Carry on.	Umm, let's discuss your meaning of "correct" before moving forward.
No	STOP uploading data and figure out which infrastructure you truly need—files, cloud, etc.	So, let's figure out how much of our data is missing, unknown, and wrong!	What are the validation/verification procedures being used and how much harm is introduced?

Files, Sheets, and the Cloud

Sometimes data comes to us already locked into a certain data format, but other times, we have the freedom and responsibility to select the most appropriate data format. Be it a file format that captures unstructured data, spreadsheets for structured text-only data, or the cloud for any data format and archival storage, we need to break our attachment to that data into one of these digital infrastructures. Files, sheets, and the cloud are proxies or derivations of a database table.

Granted, we could spend the rest of this chapter giving a brief overview of practical data modeling, but that's not productive. Books such as *Modern Database Management* (Pearson, 2019)[1] and *Database System Concepts* (McGraw-Hill Education, 2019)[2] share data modeling basics. Understanding relational database design makes understanding the other data models—like NoSQL, GraphDB, and object-oriented databases—easier. In Chapter 3, "Bias," we discussed data's interconnectivity via an entity relationship diagram (ERD). We framed the discussion around an automated résumé-filtering system example. We created some synthetic (fake) data, as shown in Table 6.2 (reprinted from Chapter 3). We've skipped some pre-data-processing steps like extracting features including the employee candidate's name, address, email, social media handles, education history, places of employment, and dates of employment. These features are just as important and can be weaponized to inflict discrimination. We simply decided to focus on triggering keywords in résumés to highlight the English language word-choice nuances. And yes, we intentionally gendered the work experience keywords to make our points more salient.

Table 6.2: Synthetic (fake) résumé data from Chapter 3

APPLICANTID	GENDERID	ETHNICITYID	WORKEXPERIENCEKEYWORDS
App001	Prefer Not To Answer	Prefer Not To Answer	assist, manage
App200	Female	White	organize, plan
App119	Male	White	developer, PHP
App002	Male	While	improve, software
App025	Nonbinary	Asian	create, design
App393	Male	Asian	research, implement
App103	Male	White	Python, Linux
App467	Male	White	advance, completed
App148	Male	Asian	lead, achieve
App275	Female	Black	analyze, excel

Figure 6.1 gives us a snapshot of the ERD, a reproduction from Chapter 3 as well. I'm showing how these four columns likely originated from three separate database tables. Those of us in data concern ourselves with getting the data we want (the four columns in this case) into the format and structures we want (a table) without giving homage to where that data first resided (a full-fledged database infrastructure someone had to design in the first place). I've noticed a trend of tearing data apart and then rearranging it to have the new configuration take less digital storage space.

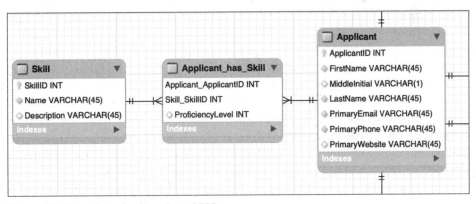

Figure 6.1: Snapshot of online résumé ERD

To crystallize this concept, I've calculated the storage capacity of these three database tables. It's 4 bytes for each INT and 45 bytes plus 2 bytes for the length for each varchar—holding up to 45 characters—represented. So the Skill strong entity takes up at least 98 (= 4 + 47 + 47) bytes. The Applicant_Has_Skill associative entity takes at least 12 (= 4 + 4 + 4) bytes. And the Applicant strong entity takes at least 242 (= 4 + 47 + 3 + 47 + 47 + 47 + 47 bytes). That's equivalent to 49 words, 6 words, and 121 words respectively for each row in the database tables (Bytes to Words Conversion Calculator: http://extraconversion.com/data-storage/bytes/bytes-to-words.html).[3] So that's a total of 352 bytes, or roughly 176 words.

> **NOTE**   If word count doesn't resonate with you, you can convert bytes to image size here: https://jan.ucc.nau.edu/lrm22/pixels2bytes/calculator.htm.[4] Three hundred fifty-two bytes is about a corner of an image measuring 20 pixels wide by 18 pixels high, 72 dots per inch using 8-bit (256-color).

Now, let's consider the storage capacity of Table 6.1 with these data types: AppID varchar(7), GenderID varchar(20), EthnicityID varchar(20), and Work-ExperienceKeywords varchar(255). We have a total of 310 (= 9 + 22 + 22 + 257) bytes. That's a savings of 42 (= 352 −310) bytes. While this doesn't seem like much, you'd have to multiply this number by the number of rows in the database table. Also, all the requested data sits in one database table rather than three database tables, which means the computational cost of one or two SQL joins are incurred. More SQL-speak in the last section of this chapter.

This quick math takes us down a path leading to a classic mathematics, computing, and economics concept: the optimization problem. In mathematics, the optimization problem is "maximizing or minimizing a real function by systematically choosing input values from within an allowed set and computing the value of the function" (https://en.wikipedia.org/wiki/Mathematical_optimization).[5] In computing specifically in the data subbranch, many with computer infrastructure expertise are looking to minimize the digital storage space—such as database size and computer hardware partition—used while preserving as much of the data quality as possible. And in economics, the goal is reducing fiscal/business costs while minimally impacting the quality of the final product or service. Now that cloud storage is the prevailing database infrastructure, the biggest issues revolve around security, Internet connectivity, data control and governance, cost management, and lack of data practitioner expertise. The data inefficiencies at the data table level are further complicated by the volume of data generated and unstable external storage configurations. Finding the sweet spot between seemingly competing priorities with many plausible solution options is a common theme of the optimization problem in all of these disciplines.

Pulling on the data-centric computing thread, we must come to terms with our own tech morality compass. Working with data means thinking through which data makes it into the database or other digital structure. We are deciding how data is included and excluded in permanent storage structures. The rounds of data "fit" questions swirling in conversations and in our heads converge:

1. Are we loading all the data into a database?

2. If so, why? If not, which subsections and why?

3. Is all the data useful enough to be uploaded, in a computationally efficient way, without reaching storage capacity?

4. What are the storage space savings (in terms of bytes) accrued by using a particular data structure over another?

5. What are the monetary cost savings of this storage configuration? (Less data to store means less storage space to purchase.)

The stitch work we perform in making the data suitable for storage and accessible to authorized users is done with surgical precision. That's why database administration is a whole subfield in the data industry. And these decisions we make have reverberating consequences for the rest of the data life cycle.

Decisions in a Vacuum

The power attached to making these data storage decisions are discussed in classrooms and boardrooms as being abstract. The terms often appear on slides at organizations' leadership meetings or retreats: data stewardship, data administration, and database administration. Since the early 2000s, the role of chief data officer has grown in popularity and stature in organizations, with this person in charge of all things data. Data stewardship serves as an organization's framework in ensuing data is accessible, safe, and trustworthy. It sounds like an unglamorous version of a chief data officer—which it is. Data stewardship, in practice, consists of how the company manages all the practices, policies, and procedures related to their internal and external data. Data administration and database administration sit under data stewardship. Data administration focuses on building templates, such as standard operating procedures (SOPs), whereas database administration is all about the mechanics and operationalizing those SOPs.

What makes data stewardship, data, and database administration so snoozeworthy is the forced, rigid structure imposition necessary to accomplish them. No one wants to be that detail-oriented and prescriptive because it means others have to follow and enforce those rules. Given enough time, every data-centric rule at some point gets challenged, and its fit for certain situations is doubted. The mounting pain points and friction in addressing data stewardship, data, and database administration reached an apex by the 2000s. All data can't be lumped under one umbrella, and data-centric rules need to reflect the current scale of data. A new subfield in data was birthed, called Big Data. This labeling implied other categories, like small data.

In 2001, Doug Laney of The Meta Group (now a part of Gartner) authored a blog post titled "3-D Data Management: Controlling Data Volume, Velocity and Variety" (`https://studylib.net/doc/8647594/3d-data-management--controlling-data-volume--velocity--an...`) and then revisited the topic in 2012 (`https://community.aiim.org/blogs/doug-laney/2012/08/25/deja-vvvu-gartners-original-volume-velocity-variety-definition-of-big-data`).[6] We know 3D data management as the three Vs of Big Data: volume, velocity, and variety. And more Vs keep being added. Value and veracity were added about 2012. Variability was introduced soon thereafter—seven Vs of Big Data by 2015 and 10 Vs of Big Data by 2017.[7-10]

Regardless of the data storage designation, the computing and data industries are plagued with figuring out how to handle each of the Vs, with solving the optimization problem as the priority. More and more as the data industry is in the international spotlight, the workload and decision-making responsibilities are shouldered by database practitioners, data engineers, and other mechanics of data storage. The approach is straightforward: grab lots of data (see Chapter 5, "Messy Gathering Grove") and then configure it by reformatting and cleaning up simultaneously for the digital infrastructure of your choosing. There's more common practice and invoking personal style about how to reformat and clean up data than hard-and-fast rules. The steps go through a series of manipulations like checking the data values for errors, isolating and handling duplicate data, identifying obvious outliers, etc. see `www.keboola.com/blog/the-ultimate-guide-to-data-cleaning`, `www.kaggle.com/getting-started/187884` and `www.tableau.com/learn/articles/what-is-data-cleaning` for a fuller list of common manipulations performed during data cleaning.[11-13]

Case Study: Black Twitter

Many of us who work with data swipe lots of data in different formats and funnel it to necessary datasets without paying much attention to equity and our humanity. For instance, my Black Twitter Project (`https://brandeismarshall.wixsite.com/blacktwitterproject`) centered on investigating real-time answers to information-gathering inquiries, including but not limited to: who makes up Black Twitter; who are the core and influential members of Black Twitter; which topics, issues, and/or movements are trending; and when are these topics, issues, and/or movements discussed in specific time frames. This project features the collection and evaluation of Blacktags (racialized hashtags), topics, and prominent figures in the Black community.

Data was scraped during the live broadcast of the Oscars in 2016–2018.[14] The focus intended to highlight how primarily Black actors' contributions to the film industry were restricted. Hashtags, Blacktags, and keywords were preselected to serve an initial filter to get more relevant tweets (see Table 6.3).

Table 6.3: Hashtags, Blacktags, and keywords for the Black Twitter Project

YEAR	HASHTAGS, BLACKTAGS, AND KEYWORDS
2016	#Oscars, #OscarsSoWhite, #StaceyDash, #chrisrock, #stacydash, #StacyDash, #oscars2016, #Oscars2016, Chris Rock, @chrisrock, @staceydash, stacey dash, stacy dash, chris rock, boycott, oscars, Oscars
2017	#oscars, #OscarsSoWhite, #OscarsLessWhite, #HiddenFigures, #Moonlight, #Fences, #oscarslesswhite, #DenzelWashington, Fences, Moonlight, Viola Davis, Taraji P. Henson, Denzel Washington, Ruth Negga, Mahershala Ali, Naomi Harris, Octavia Spencer, Joi McMillon, Janelle Monae
2018	#MeToo, #TimesUp, #taranaburke, #parkland, #GetOut, #getout, #OscarsSoWhite, #Oscars, #oscars, #ladybird, #DaveChappelle, #metoo, #maryjblige, #Oscars2018, #neveragain, #academyawards, #KobeBryant, Tarana Burke, Lady Bird, Jordan Peele, Wakanda, Black Panther, Octavia Spencer, Ryan Coogler, Chadwick Boseman, Greta Gerwig, Dave Chappelle, Mary J. Blige, Lupita Nyong'o, Tiffany Haddish

With Twitter being Big Data scale, the web scraping required us to grab data in 10-minute intervals. A tweet isn't a simple structure, and deciding which features were important isn't trivial (see https://developer.twitter.com/en/docs/twitter-api/v1/data-dictionary/overview).[15] Selecting a subset of features allowed us to extract tweet contents about the Oscars ceremony, winners, nominated actors, and reactions to the night's happenings. Because we used a private sector's platform, we checked if we could use the data in research, and we weren't the only research group with this question (www.researchgate.net/post/Does_anyone_know_if_Twitter_has_any_legal_term_document_or_policy_that_rules_the_use_of_Twitter_data_for_research_purposes).[16] The popular response doesn't allow researchers to post datasets created using Twitter data but allows Twitter to do so (see Figure 6.2).

Twitter data may be easily accessible with web-scraping tools like Tweepy and BeautifulSoup, but it surely isn't public. And it sparks more questions about your data ownership of the content you contribute to a social platform. You don't own it, but you can request it any time you want. So naturally, you have to ask yourself two key questions: what research has been conducted using your data? Do you even want to think about how this objectifies you?

Those of us who have scraped data for our research don't take into account the human content creators. The tech industry is using people's data without hesitation. To protect Twitter users' identity and to reduce our own digital storage needs, my Black Twitter project team removed the Twitter handle association.

(The optimization problem comes to the front of my mind here as removing the Twitter handles will save us storage space and thus computational time when running algorithms.) But did we really protect Twitter users' identity? Is it really up to us as researchers and practitioners to unilaterally make that decision?

Erik Borra
University of Amsterdam   25th Jun, 2015

https://dev.twitter.com/overview/terms/agreement-and-policy specifies how you can use Twitter data. It is ok to use Twitter for research if you follow these guidelines. Note however that you are not allowed to share your full data set with others: "If you provide Content to third parties, including downloadable datasets of Content or an API that returns Content, you will only distribute or allow download of Tweet IDs and/or User IDs."

You might be interested in our paper 'Programmed Method' which details how one can go about retrieving and analyzing Twitter data.

If you want to know more about the ethics of using social network data, look at the classic ""But the data is already public": on the ethics of research in Facebook" by Michael Zimmer, and the more recent "Code of Ethics & Standards for Social Data" of the Big Boulder Initiative.

http://link.springer.com/article/10.1007/s10676-010-9227-5#page-1

https://bigboulderinitiative.files.wordpress.com/2014/11/final-draft-code-of-ethics-for-social-data.pdf

Article Programmed Method: Developing a Toolset for Capturing and An...

Figure 6.2: Twitter data usage for research purposes (June 2015)
Source: Twitter, Inc.

My Black Twitter project team and I rationalized our use of others' data to expose inequities and help the greater good. Our removal of Twitter handles served as our compromise in attempting to minimize harm to others. But if you were the subject of others' research pursuits, my stance might be different. As those of us in tech use certain tools and platforms, do we just acquiesce our identity and privacy?

The time has come to take inventory of how we see our personal data and how we engage with others' data. If we can reimagine our data lives, people can select how much of their posts are usable in research endeavors on social platforms and other tech tools. Creative Commons has laid out license levels for usage, consent, and attribution. These levels can be helpful for managing our own data ownership. Here's a first pass:

- **Open, accessible, public, and free without attribution:** You don't care who has your data, content, and other types of posts.

- **Open with attribution:** You want attribution of content used, where only selected columns can be downloaded.

- **Restricted access with attribution:** You want attribution and to be notified of who has requested and gained access to your data and content. Once again, only selected columns can be downloaded.

- **Individualized access with attribution:** You want to know who is requesting access to tweets each time to decide the requester's level of access.

By default, it's "no" to everything. And tools and platforms can't tie features or functionality or services to data access.

This community-driven, people-first path is complicated. Tech and data teams have to relinquish the control they impose on data, and society as a whole needs to elevate their data education so that they can choose the data access they are most comfortable with.

But while you weigh in on the proposition's pros and cons, let's point out more spaces where data is manipulated as SOP.

Modeling Content Associations

Digging ourselves out from under the piles of digital files, sheets, and the cloud only solidifies that these pieces of data are interconnected. The data industry has to take a step back and consider how we model data and how our data modeling practices dehumanize us. The interconnectivity of data elements, be it databases, database tables, or attribute names, boils down to the entity-relationship model configuration. We're either creating an ERD from scratch for new projects or learning an existing ERD for ongoing projects. In our AI résumé-filtering tool example, we omitted often collected information from the applicant—their racial, ethnic, and gender identities as well as their disability and veteran status. This data is typically collected at the end of the application process to help companies numerically track their ability to attract applicants from different backgrounds. Figure 6.3 displays the portion of the ERD representation covering an applicant's demographic identities.

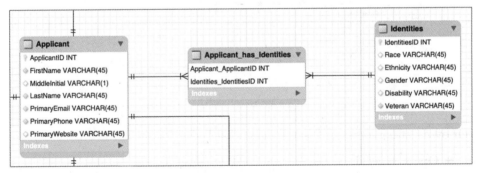

Figure 6.3: Applicant demographic identities

The ways in which we store demographic data show that our identities are important qualifiers to the processes, systems, and institutions they represent. The piecemeal storage of our identities removes the context of their combination. The ripple effect on other characteristics captured by the database design may be rooted in their identities. While the same type of information is requested from each applicant, the assumption is that people with the same background or identities will give similar responses. But there's no path to capturing "what" and "why" differences between or within groups. Grouping people, in this example and in this way, establishes a baseline discriminatory practice in the database design. The root is an oversimplification of people's identities in a digital infrastructure. This is a binary relationship where someone's identities are activated add-ons that are supposed to make up a whole person. This binary relationship translates well for analytically minded people because we can now form a simple linear mathematical equation and make comparisons between these different identities. What we forget is that we are putting fragmented, partial representations of identity together to form a mathematical equation that represents an incomplete shadow of the original whole from the physical world. No matter how much we try to "fix" the mathematical equation, it will never fully represent the original.

Not only do the database tables and attributes interconnect, so do the back-end and front-end processes. The software engineer or DBA sees the demographic data in this ERD format and goes a step deeper into coding mechanics by creating an Identities table where only certain choices can be made, as shown on the left in Figure 6.4. But some only see the applicant's view shown on the right in Figure 6.4. The applicant is given the question and corresponding response options. Any change to the response options (right) will cascade to the CREATE TABLE statement (left) and the ERD representation in Figure 6.3.

CREATE TABLE Identities	1. Are you of Hispanic/Latino/Spanish origin?
(IdentitiesID INT,	1. Yes
Race VARCHAR2(45)	
CHECK (Race IN ('American Indian or Alaska Native', 'Asian', 'Black or African American', 'Native Hawaiian or Other Pacific Islander', 'White')),	2. No
Ethnicity VARCHAR2(45)	
CHECK (Ethnicity IN ('Hispanic/Latino/Spanish', 'Not Hispanic/Latino/Spanish')),	2. How would you best describe yourself?
Gender VARCHAR2(45)	1. American Indian or Alaska Native
CHECK (Gender IN ('Female', 'Male', 'Non-Binary', 'Prefer Not to Say')),	2. Asian
Disability VARCHAR2(45)	3. Black or African American
Veteran VARCHAR2(45)	4. Native Hawaiian or Other Pacific Islander
CONSTRAINT Identities_PK PRIMARY KEY(IdentitiesID));	5. White

Figure 6.4: (Left) A DBA's view and (right) an applicant's view of demographic information

In our résumé-filtering tool example, we initially focused on applicants' skills to highlight the complexities in digital representation and ambiguity gaps in translating our physical world to digital. We focused on the aspects that mostly resonate with *science, technology, engineering, and math* (STEM) people. As much of our digital space interacts with people, the computational aspects refer to a fraction of the considerations we must invest time for understanding. Talking about racial, ethnic, and gender identities as well as their disability and veteran status isn't par for the course for data/software development teams. But these conversations, corresponding insights, and innovations need to reflect that people aren't a monolith. Figure 6.5 displays an expanded ERD representation for the AI résumé-filtering tool. Characteristics about the applicant and the positions they are applying for are placed in the database structure. This view displays how isolated features are from one another.

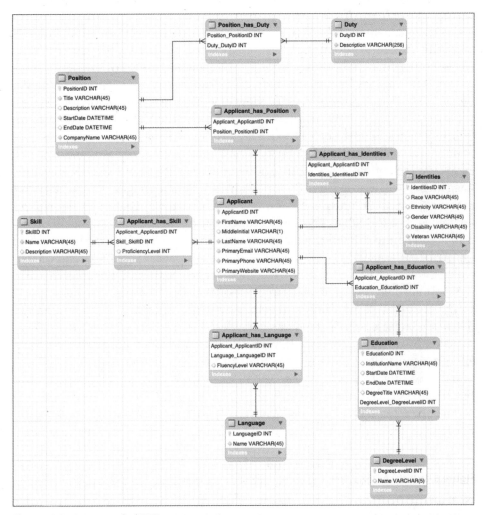

Figure 6.5: An expanded ERD representation

Relational database management systems rely on one-to-many and one-to-one relationships, which are constructed to mimic how our physical world connects the data. As we introduce more tables to the database design, we map how well or poorly data is related to other data. We quickly hit a ceiling in what context can be maintained with this model. Primary keys anchor each table, and foreign keys help form links to tables that will eventually be used to query them via SQL. Again, we fall into the confines of binary choices where selecting one of two options (the AND coordinating conjunction) breeds tunnel vision, while keeping both options open (the OR coordinating conjunction) breeds chaos and the distraction of too many possibilities. Job descriptions, for instance, share skills preferences and duties assigned to the position, but in Figure 6.5's database design, these related factors are organized separately, and then algorithmically it's handled separately. The lack of an ERD relationship between the POSITION and SKILL tables is intentional.

The computing community chooses tunnel vision often. For example, in the article "Multimodal Datasets: Misogyny, Pornography, and Malignant Stereotypes," the authors provide an overview of choice decisions made for datasets years ago and show how they have impacted certain communities disproportionately then and now, such as codifying misogyny, stereotypes and persistence of offensive text to benign imagery.[17] Doing image similarity analysis research exposes a lack of word semantic understanding with severe human-machine mismatch. The idea is to algorithmically identify similar images using text labels/keywords. A hand-curated similar image doesn't often appear in an algorithm's outcomes. The text labels and keywords can't be re-created by significant computational bandwidth and pixel-by-pixel analyses. Labeling images should no longer be an afterthought. Imbalance in these structures is perpetuated and scaled for women as well as non-white, non-gender-conforming people. Research innovations built on top of or using these datasets are compromised as a result.

The increased recognition and scholarly work reporting of discriminatory data and datasets broadens what's considered in the data storage phase. I can envision more than data engineers, software engineers, data analysts, DBAs, and project managers having a say in database design and construction. Those of us managing data can give the 360 degrees low-down on a dataset, such as historical, social, economic, ethical, and computational perspectives. The article "Datasheets for Datasets" (www.fatml.org/media/documents/datasheets_for_datasets.pdf) provides a guide for doing just this.[18–19] When organizations create datasets or dataset libraries (see "Datasets: A Community Library for Natural Language Processing," at https://aclanthology.org/2021.emnlp-demo.21.pdf), building, modifying, and maintaining datasheets should be standard operating procedures (SOPs) for organizations.[20] The following are the categories presented in "Datasheets for Datasets," and I point out some of their similarities to what is shared in this book:

Motivation   Provide the origin story of the rationale for the dataset, including the financing received to make it a reality. This section is similar to the background and introduction narrative in a scientific paper. Refer to Chapter 2, "Morality," for additional perspectives to consider.

Composition   Tell us about the content, dependences, types, formats, and relationships. This section is similar to the experimental setup narrative in a scientific paper.

Collection Process   Share the systematic method used to gather data and reflect on its representation of the physical world. Refer to Chapter 5, "Messy Gathering Grove," for additional questions.

Preprocessing   Document the data-cleaning process. Refer to the "Ask the "WHAT" Question" section in this chapter for additional questions.

Distribution   Share where and who will have access to the dataset. Refer to Chapter 4, "Computational Thinking in Practice," for additional perspectives to consider.

Maintenance   Describe the sustainability plan, incentives to execute those plans, and actionable next steps after initial release. Refer to Chapter 9, "By the Law"; Chapter 10, "By Algorithmic Influencers"; and Chapter 11, "By the Public," for community-driven accountability approaches.

Ethical and Legal Considerations   Tell us about the anticipated impact to society, its people, and the degree of digital civil rights that are protected. Refer to Chapter 1, "Oppression By. . .," as well as Chapters 2, 9, and 11 for additional perspectives to consider.

It would be a more equitable digital society if every dataset had a datasheet accompany it. This first pass at an intervention is so simple, and it would create deeper data work compared to what's already been done. It would create new opportunities and possibilities for new career paths like data quality assurance engineering (similar to the role of quality assurance engineers on software development teams). Unfortunately, we have yet to see the datasheets or the mention of a fuller dataset documentation process integrated in computer science, AI and data course curriculum, or syllabi at any level like the authors recommended:

> *The use of datasheets will be more effective if coupled with educational efforts around interpreting and applying machine learning models. Such efforts are happening both within traditional "ivory tower" institutions (e.g., the new ethics in computing course at Harvard) and in new educational organizations. For instance, one of Fast.ai's missions is "to get deep learning into the hands of as many people as possible, from as many diverse backgrounds as possible" (Fast.ai, 2017); their educational program includes explicit training in dataset biases and ethics. Combining better education and datasheets will more quickly enable progress by both domain experts and machine learning experts.*

Even though the "Datasheets for Datasets" paper has been cited about 500 times in the first 3 years of its publication date, there's a lack of practical transfer from academic and scholarly circles to the classroom and finally to regular integration into tech development. Increasing the number of companies and teams implementing datasheets is the next frontier. It will be crucial for those companies and teams to explain how they use and revise datasheets in their product and services development and what cost savings and data equity they have attained by avoiding algorithmic-based harms.

Manipulating with SQL

Before we move on from the data storage phase, a brief word about SQL (Structured Query Language). Experience in SQL has skyrocketed as a desired skill for data professionals and practitioners. Learning SQL, however, has stayed relatively the same since the early 1970s. The emphasis is on learning the mechanics of constructing an SQL statement rather than understanding the decision-making implications of what the SQL query is retrieving from the database management system. As software developers are tied to coding constructs and practices, data managers and practitioners are shackled to the existing systems of mechanics that control the digital space. So much of tech has been shaped by the decisions made over a generation ago. And all of us will experience the residual effects, for at least one more generation, of the algorithmic-based processes, systems, and platforms crafted today.

Our SQL learning is concentrated on the SELECT statement (see Figure 6.6). Remember the correct order for each clause: the SELECT clause is first, then comes the FROM clause. After FROM, we have options depending on which database items we're trying to retrieve. Most times, we need a WHERE clause. And sometimes, especially when we want to cluster or sort, we'll use the GROUP BY, HAVING, and/ or ORDER BY clauses. We practice writing SQL queries incessantly. Whole courses are dedicated to creating and executing SQL queries. Data engineers, DBAs, and data analysts translate written/spoken language like English into SQL and back often as needed by different members of an organization. For instance, the public relations team needs a targeted view of the data outcomes to meet their objectives, which differs from the targeted data interpretations needed for the marketing team, leadership team, software development team or any other team in the organization. Each team only requests and cares about its unique data perspective. Overlapping data interpretations easily are lost in the shuffle.

These slices taken of a database don't represent the whole data. Some database items are requested more than others, while some are never returned in the result set. We need to remember that the whole database isn't visible to everyone in an organization, so the intentional relationships we've built between database tables won't be understood. Data engineers, DBAs, and data analysts are in a position to recognize both the overlaps and gaps within and across an organization's teams based on the data slices they request.

```
SELECT     [all/distinct] column-list
FROM       table-list
[WHERE     conditional statement(s)]
[GROUP BY column-list-for-grouping]
[HAVING    conditional statement(s)]
[ORDER BY column-list-for-ordering]
```

Figure 6.6: General syntax of the SELECT statement used in DML

People managing data need to focus on the SQL query processing order (see Figure 6.7). At every stage, we're filtering, which means we're systematically removing tables, then rows, and finally columns. We overlook how not null entries can disqualify a row from appearing in a result set and therefore make our result sets incomplete. We overlook how important both primary keys and foreign keys are to our database design because they ensure that the ERD's relationships are as strong as digitally possible. Without solid primary keys and foreign keys, our SQL querying would return lackluster results and there would be no valuable insights. SQL querying can extenuate biases (see Chapter 3) by providing us with a sanctioned digital language to elevate certain database items over others.

Expanding how we think, using SQL means we have to put semantics first. *SQL for Data Scientists* (Wiley, 2021)[21] offers great practical insights. Just as importantly, we need to create datasheets for SQL querying. All the current datasheets categories don't apply to SQL, so I've listed here the most relevant datasheets categories to attach to SQL queries:

Motivation   Provide the origin story of the rationale for the SQL query or queries. This section is similar to the background and introduction narrative in a scientific paper.

Distribution   Share where and who will have access to the SQL queries.

Maintenance   Describe the sustainability plan, incentives to execute those plans, and actionable next steps after initial release.

Ethical and Legal Considerations   Tell us about the anticipated impact to society and its people and the degree of digital civil rights that are protected.

With reporting structures as part of standard operating procedure for both datasets and SQL queries, we have the beginnings of a data accountability strategy that can inform revisions to the ACM's Code of Ethics and Professional Conduct. We, as a collective, can institutionalize transparency and make accountability enforceable. Our standard of care for people impacted by tech and data use can go way up, if we try, since there currently isn't any standard.

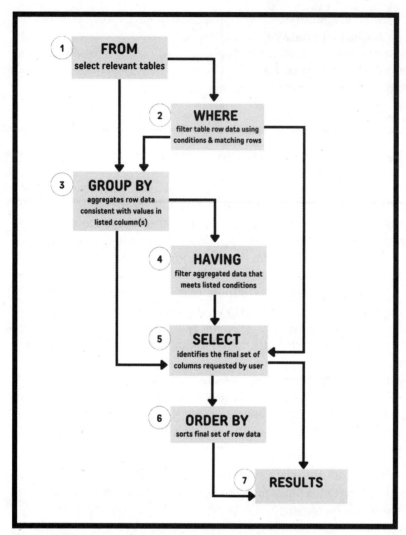

Figure 6.7: SQL statement processing order

Summary

The data storage landscape is a culmination of intentional, yet sometimes harmful, decision-making exercises with social, computational, and morality implications. Discriminatory practices are embedded within database architecture. DBAs and those with intimate knowledge of database architecture and design currently bear the weight of these decisions without many viable avenues to implement alternatives or counteract destructive structures. More attention should be paid to this regularly overlooked stage in the data life cycle. Recent research of transparency in data practices spotlights a more responsible path. Identifying and documenting additional co-dependencies between tables and attributes can lead to anti-oppressive and more equitable innovations that won't cascade algorithmic-based harms down in the data pipeline.

Notes

1. Hoffer, Jeff, Heikki Topi, and Ramesh Venkataraman. *Modern Database Management*, 13th ed. Pearson, 2019.

2. Silberschatz, Abraham, Henry Korth, and S. Sudarshan. *Database System Concepts*, 7th ed. McGraw Hill Education, March 2019.

3. ExtraConversion. Bytes to Words Conversion Calculator. `http://extraconversion.com/data-storage/bytes/bytes-to-words.html`.

4. File Size Calculator. `https://jan.ucc.nau.edu/lrm22/pixels2bytes/calculator.htm`.

5. Wikipedia. Mathematical Optimization. `https://en.wikipedia.org/wiki/Mathematical_optimization`.

6. Laney, Doug. "Deja VVVu: Gartner's Original 'Volume-Velocity-Variety' Definition of Big Data." Aiim. 2012. `https://community.aiim.org/blogs/doug-laney/2012/08/25/deja-vvvu-gartners-original-volume-velocity-variety-definition-of-big-data`.

7. Ishwarappa, and J. Anuradha, 2015. "A Brief Introduction on Big Data 5Vs Characteristics and Hadoop Technology." *Procedia Computer Science*, 48, 319–324.

8. Khan, M. Ali-ud-din, Muhammad F. Uddin, and Navarun Gupta. "Seven V's of Big Data: Understanding Big Data to Extract Value." IEEE, 2014. `https://doi.org/10.1109/ASEEZone1.2014.6820689`.

9. Kitchin, Rob, and Gavin McArdle. "What Makes Big Data, Big Data? Exploring the Ontological Characteristics of 26 Datasets." *Big Data & Society*, 2016. `https://doi.org/10.1177/2053951716631130`.

10. Rialti, Riccardo, Cristiano Ciappei, Andrea Boccardi, and Lamberto Zollo. "Big Data Oriented Business Models: The 7vs of Value Creation." *Research Gate*, June 2016.

11. Guide to Data Cleaning: Definition, Benefits, Components, and How to Clean Your Data. Tableau. `www.tableau.com/learn/articles/what-is-data-cleaning`.

12. Keboola. `www.keboola.com/blog/the-ultimate-guide-to-data-cleaning`.

13. Sharma, Mohit. "Data Cleaning Checklist." Kaggle, 2022. `www.kaggle.com/getting-started/187884`.

14. Marshall, Brandeis, Takeria Blunt, and Tayloir Thompson. "The Impact of Live Tweeting on Social Movements." IEEE, 2018.

15. Twitter Developer Platform. Data Dictionary: Standard v1.1. `https://developer.twitter.com/en/docs/twitter-api/v1/data-dictionary/overview`.

16. Capdevila, Joan. "Does anyone know if Twitter has any legal term document or policy that rules the use of Twitter data for research purposes?" Research Gate, 2015. `www.researchgate.net/post/Does_anyone_know_if_Twitter_has_any_legal_term_document_or_policy_that_rules_the_use_of_Twitter_data_for_research_purposes`.

17. Birhane, Abeba, Emmanuel Kahembwe, and Vinay U. Prabhu. "Multimodal datasets: misogyny, pornography, and malignant stereotypes." Cornell University, 2021. `www.are.na/block/13454151`.

18. Gebru, Timnit, Jamie Morgenstern, Briana Vecchione, Hanna Wallach, and Jennifer Vaughan Wortman. "Datasheets for Datasets." *Communications of the ACM* 64 (December 2021). `https://doi.org/10.1145/3458723`.

19. Gebru, Timnit, Jamie Morgenstern, Briana U. Vecchione, Hanna Wallach, and Jennifer Wortman Vaughan. "Datasheets for Datasets." Fatml. `www.fatml.org/media/documents/datasheets_for_datasets.pdf`.

20. Lhoest, Quentin, Albert Villanova del Moral, Yacine Jernite, Abhishek Thakur, and Patrick von Platen. "Datasets: A Community Library for Natural Language Processing." *ACL Anthology*, 2021. `https://aclanthology.org/2021.emnlp-demo.21.pdf`.

21. Teate, Renee M. P. *SQL for Data Scientists: A Beginner's Guide for Building Datasets for Analysis*. Wiley, 2021.

Circus of Misguided Analysis

Dr. Brandeis Marshall
@csdoctorsister

Two (of many) hard problems in data
science: 1. Defining the problem you
want AND can solve 2. Allowing the
data, not the algorithms, models or
frameworks, guide your analyses and
interpretations.
#DataScienceEducation

Source: Twitter, Inc.

The big moneymakers in Silicon Valley years ago deemed artificial intelligence
(AI) the greatest innovation in our lifetime. Our global society has bought this
premise and is perpetuating this human decision. The social control that has
been unleashed with this one decision continues to boggle many of us critiquing
tech. Nevertheless, our society engrosses itself in leveraging, operationalizing,
powering, and monetizing AI under misguided notions of increasing profits,
enhancing a person's or a company's cool factor, and making everyday life easier
for the average person. Leaning into AI'ing has brought the world automated
decision systems. Touted as a valuable application of AI, automated decision

systems only increase the quantity of decisions made, not the quality of those decisions. And all of us have seen, read, or experienced the fallacy of AI-powered algorithms, and not people, making decisions. Unraveling what the AI and other automated decision systems have done quickly becomes impractical, and it's clear that we need to focus on preventive approaches.

In this chapter, we take a close look at *how* we work with data. We discuss the wide band of what falls under data analysis, not just AI; how the statistical, algorithmic, process, and systemwide choices we make as data practitioners can lead to harm; and what can be done offensively to minimize tech's harms at scale. No matter how we try to reframe, restructure, or reimagine data work, harms persist through the metrics and analytics options. Fairness-seeking approaches in computing have moved at a rapid pace without representation or participation of minoritized communities. These are unspoken and unaddressed truths for data analysis—the rock star and cash cow of the data industry.

Ask the "How" Question

Now, we come to the "how" question. We're now in the thick of the (data life cycle) forest. Much of the how question involves data analysis. Data analysis takes us from a hidden backroom shuffle of data collection, cleanup, and storage to the front of the data life cycle establishment. Doing data analysis forces clients to clearly define the business intention; perform some type of data analysis process, such as exploratory data analysis (EDA); select, build, test and deploy models; and lastly, validate and evaluate the effectiveness of outcomes to the original business intention. At each phase of data analysis, one question leads to one hundred more: Which business intention is the actual focus? Is EDA the right fit? What's our selection, building, testing, and deployment criteria? And so on.

Data analysis has been romanticized because it can be tedious and monotonous, but it has a huge perk: data analysis gives us a sense of satisfaction with access to direct outcomes. It's like when we cook a meal—our excitement is about the finished dish, not the list of ingredients, measurements, and instructions. Data analysis is a showcase of the manicured data wrapped up in tech product's clothing. This means that data analysis gets an overabundance of attention. And what's considered data analysis is given a wide band, including, but not limited to, artificial intelligence (AI), computer vision, machine learning (ML), statistical modeling, data mining, predictive analytics, natural language processing, and deep learning (DL).

AI simply encapsulates what big moneymakers and people in powerful positions want: code to reason like people at scale, like automated decision-making. All the other terms associated with data analysis are supplements and additional approaches to making AI's intention a reality. ML and DL tend to appear

Chapter 7 ■ Circus of Misguided Analysis   165

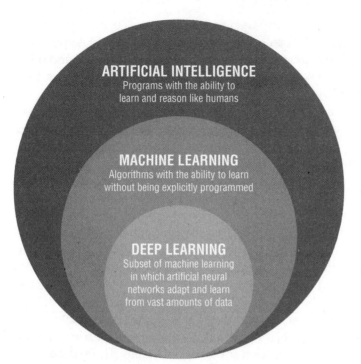

Figure 7.1: AI, ML, and DL quick explanations

Source: http://towardsdatascience.com

alongside AI since ML is a subset of AI whereas DL is a subset of ML, as shown in Figure 7.1. And I'll share my critique of this figure shortly.

Let me explain how related yet different AI, ML, and DL are using a road trip analogy. Yes, a road trip. Taking a road trip pre-Internet in the United States required either a great sense of direction or an American Automobile Association (AAA) TripTik road trip planner. It was a spiral-bound narrow notebook in which the AAA office highlighted the roadways and highways needed to reach your destination. This notebook was like a geographical map indicating the mile markers, rest stops, and exit numbers along the route. Every request for a particular route from point A to point B requires AAA personnel to obtain a notebook and physically highlight the route. This is an example of rudimentary AI—everyone taking the same routes.

When the Internet arrived in our lives, the AAA TripTik wasn't needed because MapQuest and other similar online mapping services allowed you to map your route on demand. And now with online map service users entering their route requests, these online mapping services are able to suggest more than one route, depending on the user preferences, based on only highways, no highways, shortest route, and other criteria. This is an elementary example of ML. People have options for how they want to travel, but they still are planning their routes *before* they hit the road.

When GPS navigation devices and then mobile GPS apps became available, road trip planning converted to an on-demand activity. The GPS determines the vehicle's current geographical location and maps the route. If the route isn't followed, the GPS supplies a correction route. Real-time data is gathered, processed, and assessed in order to provide alternate routes in case of traffic jams, accidents, and roadblocks. This is a simple example of DL in action. You can adjust your route if your destination changes or be informed about alternate routes if traffic patterns impact your ability to take the designated route.

No matter which way you decide to map the road trip, the end result will be the same: you'll arrive at your destination.

The way in which AI, ML, and DL operate isn't based on learning, as shown in Figure 7.1. It's the targeted identification, filtering, and use of specific data to inform algorithms to share certain outcomes. Learning would be the AAA TripTik realizing it needed to become MapQuest and MapQuest realizing it needed to become a real-time mobile GPS app without the intervention of people. Data analysis techniques helped people transform AAA TripTik to MapQuest and MapQuest to a real-time mobile GPS app. This notion of algorithms' "learning" humanizes inanimate lines of codes that don't and won't possess any sort of humanity. The learning that's really happening is the people who are serving as the knowledge construction workers and insight makers. These people are making the "how" happen and serve as the backbone of data analysis.

"How" we do data analysis stays in a state of disarray. We're in a constant state of troubleshooting data elements to reveal some sliver of knowledge or insight. We try to map the data to an existing statistical model. Or we try to group data based on some predetermined criterion. Or we try to mold computational processes to match text data to words in spoken language with expectations on keeping semantics intact. Or we try to use historical data to help us predict future events.

While the goal is simply to make the data make sense, it's a messy journey to an uncertain destination. All the data, algorithms, systems, and platforms developed to make the data make sense are riddled with harmful effects interlaced with beneficial ones. Whether or not the data is appropriate for the model, those who work in data can fall into a rut of forcing a particular model to fit because they see the data aligned with one paradigm and don't consider that it could be associated with any other. Basically, they wield the hammer and everything becomes a nail. The tech industry, however, tracks and amplifies favorable outcomes of its own creation while downplaying the ones that reveal tech's fragility. Data and the infrastructure we build around it and including it sets the stage for this fragility.

In Chapter 6, "Inconsistent Storage Sanctuary," we shared a few questions that focused on the machinations needed to perform data preprocessing. The delicate dance continues in this second round of data manipulation questions.

It's steeped in squeezing knowledge and insights from the preprocessed data. How questions intend to get us there by sparking more questions that are either answered, flagged to be addressed later, or go unanswered. Responses to how questions aren't either yes or no. They require a systematic method to be shared and then explained for transparency. A cross-fit of the team's experience, accessibility, selected tech tools, time availability, and budgetary constraints feed into *how* data is molded through algorithms and systems to produce a tech product. The time spent by a data/software team addressing the how questions is propped up as the nemesis of the organization's budget. And organizations decide to do little to nothing in addressing established tech's bad outcomes because they assess a minimal fiscal risk of national/international blowback. The scenario seems reasonable from a business perspective, but it doesn't consider the human toll of miscalculation. Table 7.1 displays initial how questions that should be asked, answered, and documented for and by those in the tech creation pipeline: designers to disseminators.

Table 7.1: Data manipulation questions

HOW QUESTION	FOLLOW-UP STEPS
A. How does your team select which computational procedures, models, and algorithms are used?	Each data/software team has a preferred "tech stack"—a suite of commercial and open source software libraries, tools, and platforms that they use in a majority of their products. A tech stack review and audit procedure should happen regularly, every 12–18 months.
B. How does your team verify outcomes associated with data processes, algorithms, and systems?	The software must be validated and verified to produce outcomes as designed. The input, typically data, and its quality are put under scrutiny by team members who didn't design or implement the software. Software validation and verification tests must be conducted and be shown successful.
C. How does your team evaluate these outcomes as algorithmic-based harms to different communities?	Most data/software teams delegate the disparate impact examination of their tech to an independent ethics-focused team, if an ethics review is part of the software development process. Stop that! All teams need to be at the table from Day 1.

We started with these three questions to emphasis the arc of tech product development. The choices made with data makes its way to impacting communities. In the first question, it's important for the data/software team to understand the benefits and disadvantages of the software library, tool, and platform choices they've made consciously and subconsciously. Being familiar with a particular software library isn't sufficient, for example. Many software libraries, especially in today's open-source-software movement, perform comparable functions. Knowing what makes that library well suited for the task at hand needs to be discussed among the team so that everyone uses the same libraries, when applicable. Formulating a comprehensive tech stack and performing a review/audit on a regular basis is akin to a code review. Our software infrastructure changes frequently with software updates, libraries being deprecated, and new tools and platforms emerging. Even if we're in a long-term contract with a commercial tool/platform, we must be progressive in knowing its limitations. A yearly tech stack review and audit is suggested to keep us up-to-date as best we can.

The second question makes the data/software team think through the digital system's outcomes. We have to scrutinize these outcomes to a rigorous degree. Other related questions ensue: What's the scale of missing data? What sort of protections do we need to maintain for this dataset and throughout data processing, particularly from third-party providers? Did we experience any data loss? How do we keep the data from being corrupted unintentionally due to mistakes or intentionally from bad actors? We're driven to be as exhaustive as we can in the time we have allotted in hopes of making the tech product more durable. The standard software verification and validation protocols we issue need regular review and audit as well. Of particular note, we call system outputs "outcomes" and not "results." Results imply correctness and completeness, which we're trying to determine at this stage. Outcomes indicate there's an observation to evaluate. While result and outcome are synonyms of each other according to Thesaurus.com, we have to remain sensitive to the power of suggestion.

Lastly, the remaining question calls on people-focused evaluation and assessment of the tech product. Cleverly, the data/software team will route their work to an independent ethics-centric team, if the organization requires such oversight. But this activity is a mistake. The data/software team is absolved from engaging in integrating ethical considerations in their design and implementation. The data/software team remains unchanged in *how* they see the nature of their work and perform their roles. And the independent ethics-centric team is handed a nearly fully baked tech product that costs a glob of time and money to create and that no one in the organization wants to hear or read. It's setting any independent ethics-centric team up for unlikely success and friction with their coworkers. Don't do it this way. When creating the data/software team, build in an ethics arm, every time. They are essential members of the data/software team, not appendages to it. They can rotate teams to help maintain their objectivity. But people dedicated to the ethics surrounding any data and tech product need to be present from Day 1.

These how questions are Big Questions. They need people discussing multiple streams of possibilities. They need people shaping guidelines that bring about clarity of data processing protocols. They need people with different backgrounds and different points of view to forge a compromise. Not every tech product has to answer these how questions—only those that affect people or help people make money. So yes, that's every last one. And rightfully so, as no manufactured product ends up on store shelves or fresh produce shipped without passing a battery of tests. Tech needs its own collective of safety protocols to fight against algorithmic-based harms blended into the tech product. In the next sections, you'll see just how common data practices introduce harms and compound them so easily.

Misevaluating the "Cleaned" Dataset

We've translated, reformatted, restructured, and removed specific undesirable content to construct the cleaned dataset. The word choice of "cleaned" makes you immediately assume data, in its original state, is dirty (or unkempt or contaminated or soiled or nasty or filthy). And we've been told since 2012 by Harvard that "(big) data is people plus algorithms, in that order" (`http://docs.media.bitpipe.com/io_10x/io_109281/item_671761/ The%20Promise%20and%20Challenge%20of%20Big%20Data.pdf`).[1] So just as data is filthy, so are people and their algorithms. That observation will take some psychological expertise we don't have to unpack. Nevertheless, data is not dirty. It's simply unpolished and not manicured for computational use, with each column necessary and every row containing contents of the same data type.

To help us discover information about a polished dataset, a number of computational platforms are available. We are using Google's Colaboratory (gColab). gColab is a free Jupyter Notebook environment provided by Google where you can create a local environment with the most common software library packages installed. gColab allows us to use and share Jupyter notebooks (`https:// jupyter.org`)[2] with others without having to download, install, or run anything on your own computer other than a browser. No hassles! If we need a platform for sensitive data or have more than 12 GB of data, we can select another open source, cloud, or commercial platform that will better meet our needs.

After we decide on the computational platform, we need a dataset or two to evaluate in hopes of gaining insight. The small IMDb dataset available on Kaggle (`https://grouplens.org/datasets/movielens`; `www.kaggle.com/ shubhammehta21/movie-lens-small-latest-dataset`)[3,4] gives us a decent training ground for the complexities of analysis work without being as culturally insensitive like the ever-popular crime datasets for this type of demonstration. The psychological, social, economic, and political connotations and ramifications go unspoken by instructors when classes, bootcamps, immersive programs, and other data education materials use datasets that have a long documented history of criminalizing certain groups as examples. Instructors don't care to have the cultural competence to thoughtfully select less socially triggering datasets.

(I'll discuss more about public and civic sector data instruction in Chapter 11, "By the Public.") This IMDb dataset has enough data to be interesting to many types of learners, yet is small enough to do *some* manual verification and validation checks on an algorithm's output. As an introduction to the dataset, here's an excerpt of the readme:

> *This dataset (ml-latest-small) describes 5-star rating and free-text tagging activity from MovieLens (`movielens.org`), a movie recommendation service. It contains 100836 ratings and 3683 tag applications across 9742 movies. These data were created by 610 users between March 29, 1996 and September 24, 2018. This dataset was generated on September 26, 2018. Users were selected at random for inclusion. All selected users had rated at least 20 movies. No demographic information is included. Each user is represented by an id, and no other information is provided.*

The analysis set up on a platform roughly begins with the loading of the dataset. We then do a preliminary descriptive statistics demonstration. This second step isn't *always* done by the data team—the person or team either assumes the data loaded correctly and is cocky in this presumption, or they are cutting corners since they're running on a short deadline. Either way, don't skip the second step. Take the few seconds to check the data upload fully. So below is a gColab demonstration using Python for what *should* happen.

```
# if dataset is on your local machine, you can select and load the file
# directly
from google.colab import files
uploaded = files.upload()

import io
ratings = pd.read_csv(io.BytesIO(uploaded['ratings.csv']))

# preview the dataframe 'ratings' content
ratings.head(10)
```

A dataset is ingested into the coding environment as a result of database table(s) being queried, downloaded, and stored into a more portable format like CSV, XLSX, and JSON, rather than the database systems management's proprietary format. We could pipe in the data directly from the database, but we'd need to use a platform with that functionality like Tableau. For peace of mind, we issue the `head()` method in order to display the first 10 rows of data. Similar methods can be used instead like `tail()` and `sample()`.

```
from google.colab import files
uploaded = files.upload()

movies = pd.read_csv(io.BytesIO(uploaded['movies.csv']))

# preview the dataframe 'ratings' content
movies.head(10)
```

In gColab, it's best to upload one file at a time. So once again, we issue the `head()` method. The other plus in displaying output early in the analysis phase is that weeks or months later, you or a coworker can look at it and know what kinds of output is to be expected. Leaving a real-time data trail helps to reduce confusion about which methods were used and why. Useful commenting of code has become a dying art, for some unknown reason, so providing output regularly also helps prevent the next person from rewriting code that they claim to not understand.

```
fullMovies = pd.merge(left=movies, right=ratings, left_on='movieId',
right_on='movieId')
fullMovies.head(10)
```

Joining one data frame with another is reminiscent of a SQL INNER JOIN statement. The left and right tables are identified along with the overlapping attribute movieId, in this case. Since the dataset sizes are only a few megabytes, using the `merge()` method is doable here. Larger dataset sizes would call for issuing an actual SQL INNER JOIN and creating a materialized view when the data is still in its database format:

```
fullMovies = fullMovies.rename(index=str, columns={"movieId": "MovieID",
"title": "Title","genres": "Genres", "userId":"UserID",
"rating":"Rating"})
fullMovies.head(10)
```

To align with your organization's naming conventions, you should rename column names immediately. Switching the names halfway down a file with code is annoying and, frankly, rude. Trying to follow someone else's code—even if that someone else is you several months ago—is hard enough without having to map variable names because, remember, having comments associated with lines of code is not guaranteed.

```
fullMovies.info()
<class 'pandas.core.frame.DataFrame'>
Index: 105339 entries, 0 to 105338
Data columns (total 6 columns):
MovieID       105339 non-null int64
Title         105339 non-null object
Genres        105339 non-null object
UserID        105339 non-null int64
Rating        105339 non-null float64
timestamp     105339 non-null int64
dtypes: float64(1), int64(3), object(2)
memory usage: 5.6+ MB
```

The `info()` method gives us a quick and handy peek into the dataset's completeness. We observe that the number of entries or rows are the same for each column. And we have the data types listed. In practice, the number of entries will vary as unknown/missing data persists. And a column's data type may not match what we'd expect. The trouble comes at the data cleanup stage, when each column's data type isn't reviewed and standardized. For instance, it's common that every column be a non-null object since that's the default for spreadsheet applications. A computer can't tell a number from a letter. Both are a string of 0s and 1s. As the human-in-the-loop, we must provide this granularity of context. If the number of rows for each column isn't the same, as in the `info()` output, consider using the `dropna()` method—for example, `fullMovies_clean = fullMovies.dropna()`. Given the discrepancy of the non-null values across columns, uniformity is required, as shown in Table 7.2, after executing the `fullMovies.describe()` statement.

Table 7.2: Output after `fullMovies.describe()` code execution

	MOVIEID	USERID	RATING	TIMESTAMP
count	105339.000000	105339.000000	105339.000000	1.05339E+05
mean	13381.312477	364.924539	3.516850	1.130424E+09
std	26170.456869	197.486905	1.044872	1.80266E+08
min	1.000000	1.000000	0.500000	8.28565E+08
25%	1073.000000	192.000000	3.000000	9.711008E+08
50%	2497.000000	383.000000	3.500000	1.115154E+09
75%	5991.000000	557.000000	4.000000	1.275496E+09
max	149532.000000	668.000000	5.000000	1.452405E+09

Next comes the `describe()` method, which allows us to look at a distribution summary of the numerical value columns. We can get a bird's-eye view of the data's skewness. The mean, standard deviation, minimum, and maximum give us our bearings while the quantiles grant us roots like the movie ratings hovering around 3.5 out of 5 and tending to span 3 to 5. Going a level deeper, we can look at histograms of each column when we go to the original Kaggle website, as shown in Figure 7.2.

The numbers on Kaggle match our numbers from running `describe()` aside from more precision displayed using the Python code. When the cursor rolls over the histogram, the rating range and count are revealed. Arguably, it's a nice extra feature adding some panache; however, a y-axis with an interval would've been sufficient.

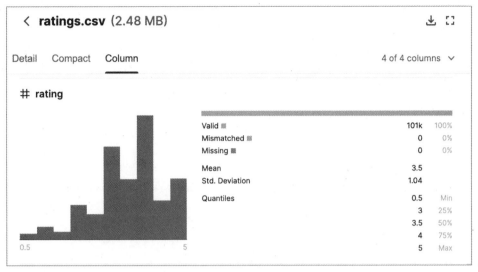

Figure 7.2: Descriptive statistics of ratings column from Kaggle

After all of this performance with the data, it's time to do some "real" analysis. The go-to analysis choice is performing a linear regression model. Linear regression models the relationship between an independent (explanatory) variable *X* and a (real-valued) dependent value *Y*. Without a second thought, we run a linear regression model. (Spoiler alert: A linear regression is a bad idea here, so follow along to find out why.)

```
import scipy as sc
from scipy.stats import norm

import pandas as pd
import statsmodels.formula.api as sm
from sklearn import linear_model

import matplotlib.pyplot as plt
%matplotlib inline
plt.rcParams['figure.figsize'] = (10, 6)

from mpl_toolkits.mplot3d import Axes3D
from matplotlib import cm
```

We have to load the open source software libraries we want before jumping into regression modeling. More libraries are imported than are needed right now, but at least they are loaded in case we need them later.

```
plt.scatter(x=fullMovies_clean['UserID'],y=fullMovies_clean['MovieID'],
c='r',marker='s',label='UserID')

plt.legend(loc=2)
plt.xlabel('UserID')
```

```
plt.ylabel('MovieID')

plt.show()

plt.scatter(x=fullMovies_clean['Rating'],y=fullMovies_clean['MovieID'],
c='b',marker='o',label='Rating')

plt.legend(numpoints=1,loc=4)
plt.xlabel('Rating')
plt.ylabel('MovieID')
plt.show()

plt.scatter(x=fullMovies_clean['timestamp'],y=fullMovies_clean['MovieID'],
c='k',marker='*',label='Timestamp')

plt.legend(loc=2)
plt.xlabel('Timestamp')
plt.ylabel('MovieID')
plt.show()
```

Everybody wants to get their hands on the data and see what the numbers tell them by throwing up images showcasing the outputs of a linear regression model like we see in Figure 7.3, Figure 7.4, and Figure 7.5. We've learned absolutely nothing, but it sure does look impressive. This example has a myriad of issues from the onset and shows the wrong way to do data analysis. If you are a trained and seasoned data professional, you may be cringing, slightly confused as to why a more interesting dataset wasn't selected and very much disliking this example. Let me tell you why it's important: through my years of teaching, some people need to see absolutely awful, terrible decisions fully displayed and explained. Only then can a person have a point-of-appropriate-reference of what makes a good example. If I were to show the data analysis process with clear questions and beautiful *Exploratory Data* Analysis (EDA) implementation, then you'd expect every data analysis process to be that way. Showing you this uninspiring and non-insightful one solidifies the importance of clear questions, model selection criteria, model construction criteria, model testing routines, validation markers, and evaluation metrics you find useful. So for those of you learning how to work with data, continue reading to satisfy your curiosity and answer the longstanding question: What if we did X data analysis technique, would it reveal some newfound data insight? You'll understand the limitations of linear regression, in this case, better than someone telling you without an example.

Understanding the context of these numerical entries before performing the regression modeling, we would've recognized that the columns of interest are the categorical Title, Genres, and maybe Ratings as part of a conditional expression feature in one of the other two categorical columns. Linear regression modeling only works when you have numerical values and those value have an independent/dependent relationship. The MovieID, UserID, and Timestamp aren't independent variables. Each user rated a subset of movies (Figure 7.3) at distinct time intervals with many of the ratings coming in near the end (Figure 7.5). Every movie was rated by a certain number of users. Some movies received more ratings than others (Figure 7.4). We know all this information by simply reviewing the readme or the descriptive statistics outputs. We've just wasted our time and computational resources. We're left empty-handed. But those of us in data and tech persevere, thinking that we can squeeze some usefulness from these lackluster analyses. It's stubbornness, inexperience, and ego, really, that drive us to continue down a rabbit hole that we know has nothing to offer. Nevertheless, we decide to perform a least squares interpretation.

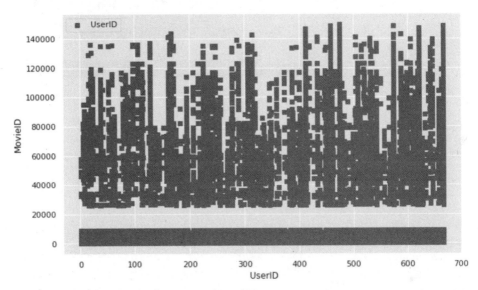

Figure 7.3: Linear regression of UserID and MovieID

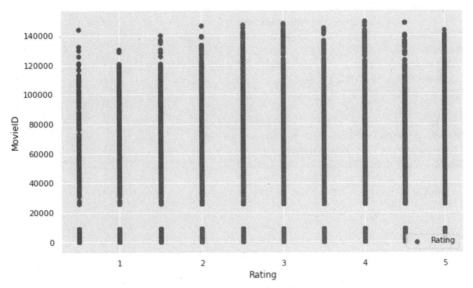

Figure 7.4: Linear regression of Rating and MovieID

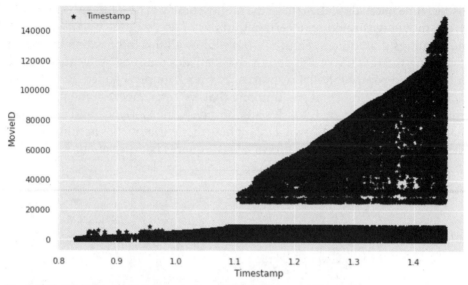

Figure 7.5: Linear regression of Timestamp and MovieID

```
# Evaluate the possibility of linear regression using least squares
fullMovies_R_ols = sm.ols(formula="timestamp ~ MovieID",
data=fullMovies_clean).fit()
fullMovies_R_ols.summary()
```

As shown in Figure 7.6, the intercept of the line is 1.083e+09. And the slope of the line is 3570.0. So how good is this fit?

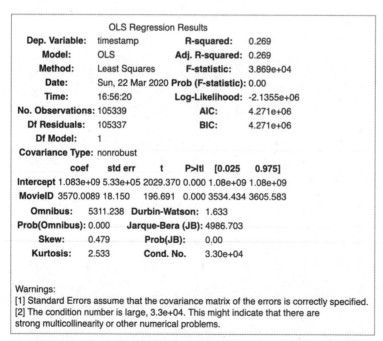

OLS Regression Results

Dep. Variable:	timestamp	R-squared:	0.269
Model:	OLS	Adj. R-squared:	0.269
Method:	Least Squares	F-statistic:	3.869e+04
Date:	Sun, 22 Mar 2020	Prob (F-statistic):	0.00
Time:	16:56:20	Log-Likelihood:	-2.1355e+06
No. Observations:	105339	AIC:	4.271e+06
Df Residuals:	105337	BIC:	4.271e+06
Df Model:	1		
Covariance Type:	nonrobust		

	coef	std err	t	P>|t|	[0.025	0.975]
Intercept	1.083e+09	5.33e+05	2029.370	0.000	1.08e+09	1.08e+09
MovieID	3570.0089	18.150	196.691	0.000	3534.434	3605.583

Omnibus:	5311.238	Durbin-Watson:	1.633
Prob(Omnibus):	0.000	Jarque-Bera (JB):	4986.703
Skew:	0.479	Prob(JB):	0.00
Kurtosis:	2.533	Cond. No.	3.30e+04

Warnings:
[1] Standard Errors assume that the covariance matrix of the errors is correctly specified.
[2] The condition number is large, 3.3e+04. This might indicate that there are strong multicollinearity or other numerical problems.

Figure 7.6: Ordinary least squares outputs using Timestamp and MovieID

One way to measure the quality of the fit is to look at the sum of the squared residuals, using this equation:

$$SSR = \sum_{i=1}^{n}(y_i - \hat{\beta}_0 - \hat{\beta}_1 x_i)^2.$$

Remember that SSR is the quantity that we minimized to find slope and intercept in the first place. If this number is very small, then the model fits the data very well. The R^2 value is an alternative way to measure how good of a fit the model is to the data. The benefit of the R^2 value is that it is a proportion (takes values between 0 and 1) so that it's easier to interpret what a good value is.

A model is good if the R^2 value is nearly 1 (the model explains all the variance in the data). In our model, the value is $R^2 = 0.269$, which is not good. The model explains only 26.9 percent of the variability in the region.

NOTE For linear regression, the R^2 value is the same as correlation, but the R^2 value more easily generalizes to more complicated regression models than correlation, so the R^2 value is typically considered instead of correlation.

We've done our full due diligence and "proven" to ourselves that this analysis reveals no new or relevant insights. We flood ourselves with this crappy information because we don't take the time to figure out what it may mean to our analyses. Having a tool means nothing if you don't know how to leverage it in practice. As we demonstrated, we did a simple linear regression on this dataset and produced a set of rather meaningless graphs. Analysis needs to be more than about numbers.

Maybe it's apparent that the IMDb dataset example is not well suited for linear regression modeling. But this extended example is symbolic of what we do with data. We march on, looking for relevancy and convincing ourselves that we are making progress. We are, in fact, marching in a circle with the start and destination in the same place. Sometimes that circle is big as we try different combinations of algorithms, processes, models, and systems. And sometimes we make a small circle. Our goal needs to shift to not making circles in the first place.

Overautomating k, K, and Thresholds

Data isn't a bystander in constructing acceptable knowledge through algorithms, systems, and platforms. Data's necessary and active participation goes overlooked because we focus so heavily on the tools applied to the data rather than the data itself. But data's bigness is the very thing we're trying to wrangle with machines since humans are intimidated. The context of social, historical, economic, political, and computational facts are indistinguishable to us in every piece of data. So we acquiesce our gaps in all things outside of computing and statistics by using upper and lower bounds as proxies. Those working in computing use top-k, predefine a K, or set a threshold in unsupervised and supervised learning. Fagin (`www.sciencedirect.com/science/article/pii/S0022000098916002`)[5] famously bridged this divide in the late 1990s and early 2000s. This work made it even more permissible to equate k with relevancy. Computer scientists, then all of the tech industry, and lastly the public transferred accuracy and correctness to these top-k outcomes—you don't even look past the fifth outcome from a `Google.com` request. All of us assumed that if the outcomes fell into the first k, then that meant they were the best of the best.

Figure 7.7: Translucent Brandeis and Visible Brandeis using Zoom Background Image

Researchers in this space have spent decades trying to optimize the relevancy to top-k outcomes and better equate top-k accuracy with public trust in algorithms. For the most part, it's worked without much kerfuffle. With the introduction of Apple's iPhone in 2007, technology use wasn't in controlled, limited, and opaque environments anymore. The public gained an access it hadn't experienced. And that access revealed the overwhelming flimsiness of algorithms, systems, and platforms. As shown in Figure 7.7 on the left side, the top-k (when k is set to 1) color for the Zoom background is on the brown palette in the bottom-right corner. The machines sees the background and my face as the same color, even though the wall color is almond and the skin tone is caramel. Both colors fall on the brown color palette. By using more direct lighting and selecting a non-brown palette color, the wall color is distinguished from the skin tone, as seen on the right side of Figure 7.7. The washing away of a whole person digitally occurs quite effortlessly. The data, if it's used uncorrected by human intervention, can tag a person's skin tone and wall color as the same. The automated decision-making procedures caused harm by reducing a person's humanness. The digital background was unusable until an alternative color was identified. How many white people have to contend with such experiences?

These sorts of machine learning methods challenge data and software development teams and make them question whether their algorithmic outputs are valuable and meaningful outcomes. The second question in Table 7.1 (How does your team verify outcomes associated with data processes, algorithms, and systems?) is at the heart of how we should be more discriminating in the use of k and assigning its meaning. To be fair, I don't imagine that Fagin thought his work would be part of image or facial recognition analysis techniques. The popularity of open source and open science movements makes many data processes, algorithms, and systems available for use by anyone in any way. Lastly, the partial or complete removal of using thresholds in certain data analysis techniques blurred the lines when distinguishing how two elements are similar or dissimilar.

The flexibility now afforded to verifying outcomes has led to algorithmic-based harms that affect different demographic groups in different ways. The perfect storm of misusing top-k methods, open source/science, and lax threshold protocols made pixel reclassification easy to do. There's even an Instagram filter that allows you to swap your face with someone else's face. Face swapping is all fun and games until the face swap technology became so realistic that people cannot tell a real image from the fake one. People's reputations are questioned, sometimes slandered, and they are falsely identified in places and situations that they had no knowledge of.

Deepfake technology is a nightmare that should have been avoided by those of us in data and tech. Drilling down on the third question in Table 7.1 (How does your team evaluate these outcomes as algorithmic-based harms to different communities?) gives us a chance to reflect on the positive *and* negative impacts of the tech product. We should have all convened around the moratorium surrounding deepfake technologies and other ways that tech enables the creation of disinformation.

You should now understand the significance of investigating responses to that third question before deployment and dissemination. A brief overview of deepfake technology follows.

Deepfake Technology

Altering and full whitewashing of a person's physical characteristics has been digitally elevated to a scary level. Innovations like deepfake technology do not advance progress but cause it to backtrack. Examples of tech perpetuating harm and digitizing discrimination are gaining national attention; examples include predictive policing[6] and facial recognition.[7] Deepfake technology, in short, fully or partially replaces one person's face and/or voice with another person's face and/or voice, like what's displayed in Figure 7.8. A deepfake video of Jordan Peele impersonating former U.S. President Barack Obama in a public service announcement back in April 2018, shown in Figure 7.9, made algorithmic accountability a sudden priority.

Figure 7.8: Examples of deepfake technology

Source: Google LLC

Figure 7.9: Deepfake of Jordan Peele as former U.S. President Barack Obama

Source: Google LLC

Soon thereafter, Speaker of the U.S. House of Representatives Nancy Pelosi was targeted in a deepfake video intended to make her appear drunk, and it was distributed widely on social media in May 2019.[8] Facebook founder and CEO Mark Zuckerberg also experienced being a subject of a deepfake video in June 2019.

At the pixel level, the color palettes are altered intentionally to make a person look like someone else. The easiest way to make a deepfake believable is for the two people targeted in the deepfake video to have similar physical features such as skin tone and facial bone structure. The core algorithmic approach of deepfake technology lies in the scholarship associated with generative adversarial networks (GANs). GANs transform real, authenticated content into manufactured, unauthenticated content. The algorithms, models, and systems can then manipulate the correct data with the false data and then intentionally suppress computational indicators that the false data is in actuality false. Dedication to deepfake technology, including video, audio, and images, is extensive. Much of deepfake technology's ramifications lie within how we handle data, particularly certain aspects of the data science. The tech industry permits this technology to mutate unchecked and to exist without loud uproar or scolding.[9]

The prior work surrounding face imagery and audio manipulation allows for parts of different human faces to be extracted and reconfigured to form a new counterfeit face.[10] A particularly unnerving dataset has emerged with 70,000 high-quality "diverse" synthesized faces called Flickr-Faces-HQ (https://github.com/NVlabs/ffhq-dataset).[11] These faces are reconfigured, reconstructed, and altered portions of real humans; one person's eyes with another person's nose and mouth alongside a third person's cheekbone structure are used to form a "new" face where skin tone can be adjusted as well. Creating a diverse collection of faces has several social, computational, and ethical implications. It makes finding real people and receiving their informed consent as contributors to this collection a nonissue and assumes that the researchers' base set of images cover the diversity of faces. It also assumes that the synthetic faces will never be real people at some future time. And it ignores the dehumanizing precedence this collection sets for other researchers indicating that non-white people can be fabricated and manufactured with computer keystrokes.

Although the focus has been on face alteration, audio manipulation is just as dangerous. For instance, the RealTalk AI-augmented audio innovation is designed to mimic a living person's voice, such as a spouse or loved one. This technology is a "text-to-speech deep learning system. . . which generates life-like speech using *only text inputs*" (https://medium.com/dessa-news/real-talk-speech-synthesis-5dd0897eef7f).[12] Thus, audio input is not required, indicating that the input data format, which serves as a baseline for these deep learning algorithms, can originate from any content medium (image, audio, or video) and generate reliable synthetic content. In May 2019, new work on talking head models constructs highly realistic 3D motion avatars from as few as one 2D image (https://arxiv.org/abs/1905.08233; www.youtube.com/watch?v=p1b5aiTrGzY&feature=youtu.be).[13] These innovations in algorithmic design accelerate the deepfake technology landscape into uncharted ethical territory.

The distinction between authentic face imagery and human audio voices is becoming undetectable, even to human eyes and ears, making manipulated content appear credible. Hany Farid, a professor of computer science at Dartmouth College, has a prediction in 2019: "I would say within another 18 to 24 months, that technology is going to get to a point where the human brain may not be able to decipher it" (www.washingtonpost.com/opinions/2019/05/14/deepfakes-are-coming-were-not-ready/?noredirect=on&utm_term=.90a2f5f9e395).[14] In that 18–24 months, alternative approaches should have been established and ready for use. AI ethical questions have long been posed within corporate and governments globally. Some suggest that we need more AI technology to help us monitor and regulate existing AI technology. This approach is problematic since we would remain reliant on a computing infrastructure, which may not provide accurate results.

Computing systems, where algorithms and processes are embedded, now have the capacity to house the input and output content of deepfake technology. The computer processing power available to any user through personal computing devices or through cloud-based platforms allows deepfake video generation to happen in a matter of minutes.

One web search result yields the goberoi/faceit GitHub repository.[15] This repository is comprehensive with a concise tutorial, but its processes, models, and systems are outdated. The Faceswap platform (`https://faceswap.dev`)[16] has since been developed and is maintained by unknown authors. It touts itself as the free and open source multiplatform deepfakes software. The website houses an active community, with discussion forums aimed at developers, guides, and tutorials, and users' monetary contributions can open more access to the site. Installation and deployment instructions are shared for a number of computing environments, such as Windows and the Google Cloud Platform, to make technology adoption more accessible.

The software is constructed using a modular design so that code can be reused effectively by assembling smaller modules together with more code to form the final software product. Any software has an entry point, which is called the main function or program. The `faceit.py` file, fewer than 400 lines of code written in Python, serves as the main function for goberoi/faceit's deepfake software product.[17] It provides a template for how to replace Person A's face with Person B's face in a video using a collection of videos featuring Person A and Person B. Since I don't want to imply support of creating deepfake content, I'm explaining how the deepfake technology is built with lines of code by using the outdated code repository. Appendix D, "Pseudocode for faceit.py" provides a synopsis of this code.

At a high level, the FaceIt computer program has three phases: preparation, execution, and production. The preparation phase (steps 1–4) consists of identifying a number of variables, or digital storage units, that will house the input and output content in addition to devising methods to isolate and retrieve the facial representations from the predetermined set of videos.

The execution phase (step 5) processes the actual input data and performs the face swap by patching Person B's face where Person A's face is identified on the video frame. The intricacies of patching are grounded in GANs, which simultaneously run a generative model that focuses on finding the perceived *optimal* grouping of data elements forming the classifier, and a discriminative model, which focuses on finding the "optimal" boundaries between data elements.[18] These data elements are a combination of the initial training data and newly created data that the generative model constructs. The generative model is sometimes referred to as a "counterfeiter" since it creates new data whereas the discriminative model distinguishes between the new or counterfeit data from the training data. Both models improve their accuracy until there is little to no distinction between the counterfeit and the real training data.

Lastly, the production phase (steps 6–9) calls on the methods described earlier in the appropriate order to create the final deepfake video. Deepfake technology's power to deceive viewers stems from the capability of these algorithms and computing systems to process video content. In the case of Jordan Peele's PSA deepfake, the abundance of video featuring President Obama made it easier to provide sufficient training data to the deep learning algorithm and model. This also applies to any public figure with a large accumulation of publicly available video media content.

Deepfake videos are malicious through application and use. Deepfake videos, however, show up in other industries like movie entertainment and are given disarming names like "digitally re-created" or "remastered." For instance, Carrie Fisher's daughter stepped into her mother's role for a throwback scene during the filming of *Star Wars: The Rise of Skywalker* (2018). The scene was digitally altered to showcase Fisher's face instead of her daughter's. The remastered version went unnoticed. It's easy to do, as demonstrated by a popular deepfake artist calling themselves "derpfakes," with their remastered Princess Leia in Figure 7.10.

Figure 7.10: Princess Leia remastered using deepfake technology in the film industry
Source: Google LLC

Deepfakes aren't simply in the hands of bad actors and film creators. The general public now are executing deepfakes incessantly. Take MyHeritage Ltd., an online genealogy company that helps people build their family tree and discover their ancestral composition through DNA analysis. In addition, they provide access to Deep Nostalgia, an API-styled access to animate family photos (see Figure 7.11). Each family member in a photo can come to life by the viewer seeing the eyes move and blink and the head tilt. The feelings about this tech were mixed at first (see the mix of comments on `https://twitter` `.com/ferrisjabr/status/1365744836268023809?s=20` — click on "show more replies"), but according to the MyHeritage website (`www.myheritage` `.com/deep-nostalgia`), over 94 million animations have been created. It's maddening to think how many family photos, names of those in the photos, family tree relationships, and other information are being stored and managed by a privately held international company. These data can be used and misused in countless ways to create new datasets, algorithms, and systems without the original uploaders' knowledge or informed consent.

Figure 7.11: Deep Nostalgia animates the faces in your family photos with amazing technology.

Source: MyHeritage Ltd.

Deepfakes in our everyday lives hits home when we peel back the layers of Instagram filters. Beauty filters add makeup to a person's face, including eyeshadow, mascara, blush, and smoothing over any blemishes (`www.teenvogue` `.com/story/instagram-filters-makeup`).[19] This means that there are datasets, algorithms, and systems built to isolate the eyelids, eyelashes, cheekbones, hair, and cover color inconsistencies on our faces. These filters have a documented history of negatively affecting the mental wellness of young girls and women.[20,21] Those on the analytics team (machine learning engineers, statisticians and algorithm designers) have tinkered with the input parameters. We've adjusted the data inputs. They've modified the k or threshold in numerous algorithms. They've fueled the fill-in-the-blank-industry at the cost of the next generation's well-being. And for what? Simply feeding an ego and proving to ourselves that they can optimize some algorithm when using a predefined dataset.

Not Estimating Algorithmic Risk at Scale

The risks associated with algorithms isn't a new endeavor. In fact, the conversations date back to the 1960s. Hutchinson and Mitchell (https://dl.acm.org/doi/10.1145/3287560.3287600)[22] summarize 50 years of (un)fairness in machine learning with a concentration on standardized testing. Interestingly, the researchers then—a vast majority of them white and male—maintained singular focus to being "fair" because it was easier for mathematical equations and quantitative approaches. Defining unfairness poses immediate challenges because there's disparate impact and furthermore disparate notions of unfairness. Without a consensus of unfairness, a mathematical approach quickly becomes too complex and complicated. The hidden or intentionally overlooked effect is that defining fairness poses the same challenges, complexities, and complications as when defining unfairness. Changing the focus doesn't change the problems at hand. Nancy Cole's 2001 paper on fairness, whose own work was not markedly different from researchers in 1973, was cited as follows:

> The spurt of research on fairness issues that began in the late 1960s had results that were ultimately disappointing. No generally agreed upon method to determine whether or not a test is fair was developed. No statistic that could unambiguously indicate whether or not an item is fair was identified. There were no broad technical solutions to the issues involved in fairness.

> Nancy S Cole and Michael J Zieky. 2001. The new faces of fairness. Journal of Educational Measurement 38, 4 (2001), 369–382.

Yet the plight of fairness in machine learning persisted. The evidence was clear by the mid-1970s, again in the early 2000s, and in 2019 when Hutchinson and Mitchell published their retrospective brief. The narrative and discussions surrounding fairness in algorithms are troublesome. Avoiding discriminatory practices as well as manufacturing fairness in and of technology are misnomers. The computer science contingency of the data industry are attempting to create fairness and "fix" discrimination using lines of code. Since we as a human race have yet to experience fairness in the physical world, then we have no expectation of a model to mimic it in the digital world.

Books describing models of fairness, such as *Fairness and Machine Learning: Limitations and Opportunities* by Solon Barocas, Moritz Hardt, and Arvind Narayanan (https://fairmlbook.org),[23] alongside systems and platforms that put fairness models in practice, like AI Fairness 360,[24] scikit-fairness/scikit-lego, and Fairlearn,[25] are being released as open source resources and toolkits. Releasing this battery of tools open source or at least under a Creative Commons license allows organizations to claim collective good and circumvent code of conduct vetting by an independent third party before public adoption. In practice, this maneuver is asking for forgiveness instead of seeking permission. But other organizations rely on this open source software to operate their own software products. The code dependencies are deep and widespread in a third party's software, so removing problematic, unvetted, or discriminatory code is nearly impossible without a full software redesign. And companies that have spent thousands of human talent hours, hundreds of thousands to millions of dollars, and months to years of time aren't keen on scraping a completed, yet error-prone, data/tech project.

A recent collection of papers, including `https://doi.org/10.1145/3442188.3445922`,[26] `https://doi.org/10.48550/ARXIV.2106.15590`,[27] and `https://ieeexplore.ieee.org/document/9462194`,[28] warn us to stray away from developing, implementing, and releasing automated decision systems dependent on manipulating tons of data. The calls to cease and desist are coming from all sectors and many industries, including some within tech companies. The tech industry is looking for a new shiny pathway to follow. It is seeking a new framework to impose automation, algorithms, and analyses. It's looking to maintain algorithmic idealism. Davis, Williams, and Yang (`https://journals.sagepub.com/doi/full/10.1177/20539517211044808`) propose algorithmic reparations, which "sits in direct opposition to the prevailing logics of [fairness in machine learning], which seek to de-bias algorithms and make them fairer. In contrast, a reparative approach assumes and leverages bias to make algorithms more equitable and just." In practice, we must do *all* these things at *all* times, no cherry picking:

- Let go of the belief of clean datasets—call them polished.
- Evaluate the dataset fully before running any analysis (e.g., use `info()` and `describe()` methods).
- Decide and document how your team will handle missing and unknown data values.
- Let go of the belief that analyses must yield accurate or useful results.
- Let go of the belief that analyses can solve the social ills of discrimination, suppression, and oppression.
- Data analyses need interpretations that are inclusive of a dataset's context.
- Include tech workers from the humanities and social sciences as equal partners from day 1 in the construction and evaluation of data/tech projects.
- Create algorithmic-based and human-in-the-loop interventions that build in equity in the data analyses process.
- Replace existing fairness in machine learning systems and platforms with the newly constructed algorithmic-based and human-in-the-loop interventions.

■ Data/tech teams need to have equitable representation and participation with the influence and decision-making power afforded to white counterparts. This means that white counterparts must engage by actively championing and sponsoring their non-white coworkers.

Summary

Knowledge from data and insights play hide-and-seek with us. We fall under the tech industry's spell that if we tweak this algorithm, change the statistical model, or adjust a system's input parameters, then we can fix the problem of discrimination in code. The algorithms, systems, and platforms are all blueprinted from the same playbook, by the same homogeneous people. Changing the application that the tech is used on transfers and redistributes discrimination in new and sometimes different ways. The Algorithm's Way remains the wrong tool for the job of society and its humans. We can learn much about data from our comrades in the humanities and social sciences. True equitable representation and participation from minoritized communities as tech creators and owners is a small progressive step. Data captures glimpses of the social, computational, historical, economical, societal, and political facets of our lives, and so does any algorithm, model, system, and framework. We work together to carve new paths in analyses data for humanity's benefit, or we keep spinning our wheels in silos getting nowhere, except hurting each other.

Notes

1. BullsEye Resources. "The Promise and Challenge of Big Data." 2012. `http://docs.media.bitpipe.com/io_10x/io_109281/item_671761/The%20Promise%20and%20Challenge%20of%20Big%20Data.pdf`.

2. "Project Jupyter." Jupyter.org, n.d. .

3. "MovieLens." Movielens.org, n.d..

4. Mehta, Shubham. 2018. "Movie Lens Small Latest Dataset." `www.kaggle.com/shubhammehta21/movie-lens-small-latest-dataset`.

5. Fagin, Ronald. "Combining Fuzzy Information from Multiple Systems." IBM Almaden Research Center, 2002. `www.sciencedirect.com/science/article/pii/S0022000098916002`.

6. Angwin, Julia, Jeff Larson, Lauren Kirchner, and Surya Mattu. "Machine Bias." ProPublica, n.d. `www.propublica.org/article/machine-bias-risk-assessments-in-criminal-sentencing`.

7. Gebru, Timnit, and Joy Buolamwini "Gender Shades." Gendershades .org, 2018.

8. Guild, Blair, and Elyse Samuels "Pelosi Videos Manipulated to Make Her Appear Drunk Are Being Shared on Social Media." *Washington Post*, May 23, 2019. `www.washingtonpost.com/video/politics/pelosi-videos-manipulated-to-make-her-appear-drunk-are-being-shared-on-social-media/2019/05/23/92108d20-9d32-4ba0-95bf-c37b9510e6ff_video.html`.

9. Marshall, Brandeis, and Susan Geier. "Targeted Curricular Innovations in Data Science," 2019 IEEE Frontiers in Education Conference, 2019.

10. Karras, Tero, Samuli Laine, and Timo Aila "A Style-Based Generator Architecture for Generative Adversarial Networks." Cornell University, 2018. `https://doi.org/10.48550/ARXIV.1812.04948`.

11. Flickr-Faces-HQ Dataset (FFHQ). N.d. `https://github.com/NVlabs/ffhq-dataset`.

12. Dessa. "RealTalk: We Replicated a Real Person's Voice with AI." Medium, 2019. `https://medium.com/dessa-news/real-talk-speech-synthesis-5dd0897eef7f`.

13. Zakharov, Egor, Aliaksandra Shysheya, Egor Burkov, and Victor Lempitsky "Few-Shot Adversarial Learning of Realistic Neural Talking Head Models." Cornell University, 2019. `https://doi.org/10.48550/ARXIV.1905.08233`.

14. Klaas, Brian. "Opinion: Deepfakes Are Coming. We're Not Ready." *Washington Post*, May 14, 2019. `www.washingtonpost.com/opinions/2019/05/14/deepfakes-are-coming-were-not-ready/?noredirect=on&utm_term=.90a2f5f9e395`.

15. A Script to Make It Easy to Swap Faces in Videos Using the Faceswap Library, and YouTube Videos. `https://github.com/goberoi/faceit`.

16. "Faceswap." 2019. Faceswap. 2019.

17. Oberoi, Gaurav. "Exploring DeepFakes." Medium, March 5, 2018. `https://goberoi.com/exploring-deepfakes-20c9947c22d9`.

18. Goodfellow, Ian J., Jean Pouget-Abadie, Mehdi Mirza, Bing Xu, David Warde-Farley, Sherjil Ozair, Aaron Courville, and Yoshua Bengio "Generative Adversarial Nets." NeurIPS, n.d. `https://papers.nips.cc/paper/5423-generative-adversarial-nets.pdf`.

19. Pitcher, Laura. "Instagram Filters Are Changing the Way We Think about Makeup." *Teen Vogue*, 2020. `www.teenvogue.com/story/instagram-filters-makeup`.

20. Rodulfo, Kristina. "It's Easier than Ever to Make a New Face on Social Media. But Is It Killing Your Confidence?" Women's Health, 2020.

21. Wells, Georgia, Jeff Horwitz, and Deepa Seetharaman "Facebook Knows Instagram Is Toxic for Teen Girls, Company Documents Show." *Wall Street Journal (Eastern Ed.)*, September 14, 2021. `www.wsj.com/articles/facebook-knows-instagram-is-toxic-for-teen-girls-company-documents-show-11631620739`.

22. Hutchinson, Ben, and Margaret Mitchell "50 Years of Test (Un)Fairness: Lessons for Machine Learning." In *Proceedings of the Conference on Fairness, Accountability, and Transparency*, 2019. `https://dl.acm.org/doi/10.1145/3287560.3287600`.

23. Barocas, Solon, M Moritz Hardt, and Arvind Narayanan "Fairness and Machine Learning." *Fairness and Machine Learning*, fairmlbook, 2019.

24. Varshney, Kush R. "Introducing AI Fairness 360." IBM Research Blog, 2018.

25. "Fairlearn." N.d. Fairlearn.org.

26. Bender, Emily M., Timnit Gebru, Angelina McMillan-Major, and Margaret Mitchell ACM, 2021. "On the Dangers of Stochastic Parrots: Can Language Models Be Too Big?" In *Proceedings of the 2021 ACM Conference on Fairness, Accountability, and Transparency*. `https://doi.org/10.1145/3442188.3445922`.

27. Birhane, Abeba, Pratyusha Kalluri, Dallas Card, William Agnew, Ravit Dotan, and Michelle Bao Cornell University, 2021. "The Values Encoded in Machine Learning Research." `https://doi.org/10.48550/ARXIV.2106.15590`.

28. Kiemde, Sountongnoma Martial Anicet, and Ahmed Dooguy Kora "Fairness of Machine Learning Algorithms for the Black Community." In *2020 IEEE International Symposium on Technology and Society*. IEEE, 2020.

Double-Edged Visualization Sword

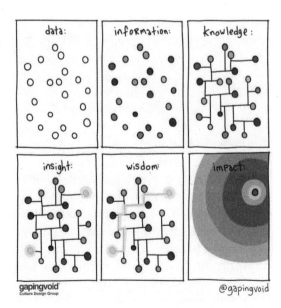

Source: www.gapingvoid.com/blog/2019/03/05/
want-to-know-how-to-turn-change-into-a-movement

Visualizations lure us in with their eye-catching colors and intriguing words said with conviction. The *great hope* of data visualizations is that the pretty pictures, in the form of charts, graphs, dashboards, or some other type of media, will bring clarity to those who are able to view them. But data visualizations simply try to take information and then speculate on which outputs provide valuable knowledge and insights. In practice, remixing information further opens the door to discovering knowledge/insights, but also to amplifying misinformation, or disinformation. The data industry loves to focus on the first one. Misinformation and disinformation situations are talked about like they're undergoing an algorithmic autopsy—after the algorithmic-based harms have already happened, and there's little to no way to prevent them in the first place. In this chapter, we lay bare ways that insights, misinformation, and disinformation are exposed by leveraging data visualization techniques. The mechanics of creating these visuals, crafting an enticing storyline alongside how they can be manipulated, are disentangled to help you avoid being easily bamboozled.

Ask the "When" Question

We've come to the exciting and sexy part of the data workflow: data visualization. A picture is worth a thousand words, as the colloquialism goes. What that turn-of-phrase doesn't cover is *the* different *thousand words* that's generated for each person who looks at that picture. Everybody wants to see pretty charts, graphs, and maps with colors that excite them. Or they want time-elapsed vignettes, which are basically charts in motion. The evolution and demise of Blockbuster Video is a prime example (`https://fleetlogging.com/blockbuster-video-map`, made popular on Twitter here: `https://twitter.com/brilliantmaps/status/1275360359382204419?lang=en`).[1] Or they want interactive visualizations— renamed *dashboards* in recent years—that'll allow the user to select and deselect features as they see fit.

Somehow the appearance of charts, graphs, and/or maps goes from displayed information to trusted fact with lightning speed. Those of us in tech need to be much more discriminating about the outputs we share. Calling outputs by other names like *solutions* or *results* has been normalized over the years. Whether you are building the visualization or simply consuming it, we make this unconscious leap from an output being returned from some algorithmic method to it being labeled a trusted output. We've reasoned that because this graph, chart, map, or dashboard exists it's correct and important. Oh, how wrong we are. This rush to trust output happened at some time when Google went from being the misspelling of the mathematical large number *googol* to a transitive verb synonymous with *search* in 2002.

Figure 8.1 mesmerizes us with the sheer sizes of the numbers in the visual. But we don't have a way of understanding or interpreting these numbers in their proper context. Knowing that the world population is about 8 billion, with 300 million to 2.8 billion active monthly users across 17 platforms, gives us a context for the magnitude of the numbers shown to us in data visualizations (www.worldometers.info/world-population)[2] (www.statista.com/statistics/272014/global-social-networks-ranked-by-number-of-users).[3] Why is this so important? Visuals don't tell the whole story. Visuals *aren't designed* to tell us the *whole* story. They're designed to tell us *a* story. Visuals are a snapshot intended to aid in sharing a particular interpretation. It's not the end all, be all.

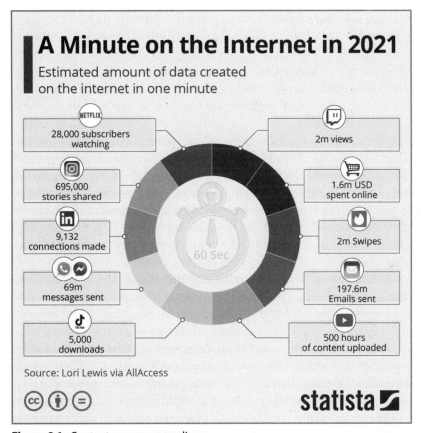

Figure 8.1: Content consumes our lives.

Source: www.statista.com/chart/25443/estimated-amount-of-data-created-on-the-internet-in-one-minute

Our obsession with visual content stems from a frequently mentioned "study"[4-6] that claims "visuals are processed 60,000 times faster than text." 3M made reference to their study in a two-pager about polishing your presentation from 1997—which constitutes the origin of the "visuals are processed 60,000 times faster than text" claim, according to my initial online sleuthing efforts.

And then I found Alan Levine's 2012 "The 60,000 Times Question Remains Unanswered" blog post that chronicles his unsuccessful efforts in acquiring the original 3M study data and research (https://cogdogblog.com/2012/07/60000-times-question).[7] The most revealing aspect was the multiple times this statement wasn't supported by any refereed research. Let me take Levine's correspondence with Dennis Proffitt, a well-known and well-cited psychology professor from the University of Virginia. The claim has become a folklore, so Levine sent emails to well-known scholars who he thought would know about or have access to the original research study. Not only did Proffitt have no knowledge of this 3M study, but he also contradicted the claim. Proffitt emphasized that the visual versus text processing times are about the same at 150 ms. So this notion that images are easier for our brains to process than text isn't worth two cents. And it serves as a prime example of misinformation. Yet for over two decades, we've been brainwashed to believe that visual content is the *best* way to communicate.

In everyday life, data visualizations provide an easier way to share a specific message. Easier isn't better. Easier creates footholds for misinformation and disinformation to be planted. Those of us in tech, and particularly those on the business side, can no longer let the picture represent the perceived insight or new knowledge. Accountability and responsibility feeds off clear explanation. *When* the public doesn't understand it or has questions about it, then the person explaining hasn't done a sufficient job of being transparent in how the insights or knowledge came to be.

Tech, as a whole community, has to do a better job of explaining what these products, services, and apps are truly doing to others in data and tech roles as well as the public. And honestly, I think that visualizations are a deflection practice to present as though progress has been made when, in reality, the visualization creator is simply covering for their lack of understanding or insightful interpretation of the outcomes. Frankly, I've done this more times than I'd like to admit as a graduate student. That regularly scheduled research meeting was looming and I've done bupkis since the last meeting. I would whip up a visual or two in no time to hide my lack of research progress for the week. In order to finish my degree, I had to buckle down and make significant research contributions.

It's time for the tech community to stop trying to promote graphics and bar charts as actionable analytics, such as performance metrics, to persuade people to buy their product. Providing incentives for the tech and data industries to "do better" in sharing the known harmful implications of their products, services and apps unfortunately needs to lead directly to an organization's gaining profits. A good reputation and fostering trust remains the tangible features that organizations are consistently vying for. The public therefore needs small-dose, relatable situations that demonstrate the potential harmful social, political, economic, and computational impacts of that tech product. The public wants evidence that an organization tried to reduce bad consequences. Giving the public that evidence *actually* builds trust rather than weakens it.

We must be careful—the people creating visuals and those receiving them. *When* we create and/or look at them, we must compel ourselves to struggle with the interpretations presented. Doing the deep work of asking and answering *why*, *what*, and *how* questions in the data life cycle isn't to be forgotten. In fact, we must circle back in a way to these earlier questions. We can reflect and understand the choices we selected with more wisdom. The miscalculations, loopholes, interventions, and patches we didn't see during the implementation and building stages are now glaringly apparent. *When* we pause to allow ourselves to re-engage with more informed perspectives, those of us in tech can guard against the encoding of additional harm-inducing processes.

Table 8.1 displays initial *when*-related questions that should be asked throughout the data pipeline when developing a tech product.

Table 8.1: Data interpretation questions

WHEN QUESTION	FOLLOW-UP STEPS
1. When in the data pipeline do we gauge the fit of this dataset with what we intend to use it for?	Go back to the datasheet, which should be a living document you and your team update regularly. If a concrete and full-fledged response isn't readily accessible, halt everything until you've reached non-flimsy, non-hand-wavy responses.
2. When in the data pipeline are we confident in the processes we used and in our understanding of the outcomes?	Gather the list of harm-inducing algorithms and check their penetration rate for algorithmic-based harms using algorithmic auditing tactics. More importantly, discuss outcomes with your ethics-focused colleagues and modify approaches accordingly.
3. When are the data and software teams assured that product-users are able to make sense of any data outcomes and insights after they're done analyzing it?	Please go talk to your clients, target audience, and people unfamiliar with the project, not just your stakeholders who are fiscally motivated. And employ an independent, diverse social science research team to design, gather, evaluate, and assess the feedback.

As you've noticed, these data interpretation questions start with *when* but there are implicit underlying *how* and *what* questions. That's intentional because *when* implies before/after conditions in order to arrive at a preset finish line. I want to emphasis that *when* depends on the stability of before/after conditions.

For example, we learned letters before we learned words. And we were able to read a book after we learned to understand sentences. In data visualization, gauging the appropriateness of content for which audience is the sweet spot. In the first question, data and software teams need to reflect and review their dataset selection and use. The list of questions posed in the "Datasheets for Datasets" paper cover this question quite well (https://doi.org/10.1145/3458723).[8] The real question is whether the team's responses are satisfactory to themselves, the people who supplied the original content, their clients and their stakeholders. Are you really avoiding data mismanagement and mishandling or simply pretending to care about it? Going through the motions of a checklist or half-hearted responses will become abundantly clear by the time you reach the second question.

The second question intends to make you uncomfortable. In tech, saying the term *confidence* invokes the statistics' definition of confidence intervals using mathematical formulas to prove a certain degree of credence and reliability. But we're going much further than equations in what we're intending to determine reliability. We need an inventory of harm-inducing algorithms coupled with an algorithmic audit of these processes. This approach isn't all analytical and automated like tech folks prefer, but that's the point. Confidence in which algorithms the team used and why is supposed to make you uneasy. It's supposed to make you question the algorithms, systems, and processes. This experience, when repeated, helps us become more aware of tech's faults. And the ongoing conversations with ethics-focused teammates will be more productive. Critiquing tech isn't tech-bashing. It's understanding how different outcomes come about. It's understanding tech's limits. For those of us who have coded, I know you've spent many, many hours like me frustrated while debugging some code because you couldn't understand how that dumb machine made up of zeros and ones keeps giving you that same slate of errors after you believed you fixed it. Then you "see your error." Let's unlearn this hard-headedness.

Lastly, the final question in Table 8.1 calls on us to talk to people, namely the public, people unaffiliated with the project or people who wouldn't be persuaded with the data visualization outcomes. Ideally, we want people not easily persuaded by finessed messaging but who will look at the visuals with a critical detailed eye for clarity. Skill, patience, and a qualified team of qualitative-centric social scientists are needed to conduct a more comprehensive evaluation and assessment. In tech, the traditional route involves one of the computing/data researchers opening a Google Form, thinking up a series of questions to ask or borrowing some question template online, and sending out that form to the team's network. After much finger-crossing and pleading with research friends, the responses roll in: the form response rate is low, no definitive observations are gleaned, and the feedback is deemed useless. No more doing an end-run around the people who will digest data visualizations. No more shrugging shoulders when people don't understand or misinterpret your visuals. The fact is your team didn't do their homework completely.

The biggest takeaway I'll leave you with is this: don't be a data hypocrite. All the care and precision you brought to data collection, storage, management, and analysis needs to carry forward in data visualization. Be willing to detach yourself from what you want the data interpretation to be. Craft data visualizations with care, thoughtfulness, and analytical rigor. Make sure they have meaning and are related to the context you intend to communicate. Produce data visualizations that'll stand up to the questions of your data-literate, tech-savvy, and critically thinking clients.

Critiquing Visual Construction

Critiquing visuals will require us to have a strong backbone. When navigating the naysayers, you need to meet them with a smile and gentle but repeated prodding about the visuals' shortcomings. The errors, missteps, misinformation, or disinformation interpretations we see can be said in our full voices. One or two of you voicing concerns isn't going to make the impact needed for change. Strength comes in multiple people from different departments at different leadership levels repeating similar concerns from different business operations stances.

Social, historical, political, and economical factors inform the making of visualizations. The analytical-only or single-minded computational thinking blinders are off for us. Convincing others isn't the goal—it's making it too uncomfortable for them to ignore all these factors and how they interplay with each other. Before going further, let me be clear: not every visual is faulty. Visualizations are just as or more complicated as text. People have bought into the framing that visuals are easier, and by *easier* I mean *better*. By disrupting that notion, there will be resistance. Since visualizations share multiple data outcomes at once, we're inundated with several outcomes and latch on to what interests us. No one is interested and drawn to the same outcomes in the same order at the same time. We recognize that power lies in pictures. People won't remember what they read or what they are told, but what they see and how that imagery becomes part of their experience that stays with them. Our rigor around visualization becomes how people are guided through the multitude of outcomes displayed to them.

Visuals from still images to audiovisual content causes us to stop scrolling on all the social platforms. And this is deliberate with no end in sight. Cisco reports that 66 percent of the global population will be Internet users by 2023, up from 51 percent in 2018 (www.cisco.com/c/en/us/solutions/ executive-perspectives/annual-internet-report/infographic-c82-741491 .html).[9] Visual content marketing is only increasing: 69 percent for audio/

visual content, 63 percent for images, and 27 percent for audio-only from 2019 to 2020 (https://contentwritingjobs.com/blog/visual-content-marketing-statistics).[10] Whether the marketplace is Business-to-Customer, Business-to-Business, or Customer-to-Customer, visuals are reigning supreme in promoting products and services.

Algorithms on platforms like Facebook and Twitter observe that posts with visual content see increased engagement rates. Depending on the person or organization, posts with images perform better than posts with video, or vice versa.[11-13] Their algorithms are constructed to boost posts with visuals to get more impressions organically. It would be great to have a scholarly-based independent analyses of social platforms to be more definitive on how text, audio, visual, and audiovisual content is infiltrating our everyday lives and influencing decision-making.

The increased industry push for society to enter the virtual world—metaverse and web3, for example—makes transparency processes and follow-up account-ability interventions even more urgent. Although the web3 proverbial train has undoubtedly left the station, we can at the very least know where the train tracks are missing, intentionally and unintentionally. All of us are witnesses to the perils of facial recognition analysis and deepfake technology (see Chapter 7, "Circus of Misguided Analysis"). We must now contend with a world where visuals are intentionally misleading in addition to communication outlets that tweak data visualizations to tell a certain story.

More often than not, society is playing a defensive strategy in comparison to the tech industry. It's combatting and countermeasuring the tech tools, innovations, and products that hit the market first. Being reactionary is frankly exhausting. We can turn this narrative into an offensive strategy by communicating and then operating with noncomputational and computational tools; innovations and products that unravel perception is information, and information is fact. There are a lot of gaps between perception, information, and fact. This chapter's opening graphic, also shown in Figure 8.2, is an example of when data visual-ization serves as a liberator and as a gatekeeper.

As a liberator, Figure 8.2 allows a data newbie to clearly see the relationship and distinction among these six terms: data, information, knowledge, insight, wisdom, and impact. The scaffolding effect presented here would make teaching these concepts easier for an instructor. The transformation of the uncolored dots in the data image to colored dots in information to connected colored dots in knowledge, and so forth is relatable to a manager or C-suite level leader who wants to be more informed about the data outcomes presented to them. It's a nice and clear barometer for different types of audiences.

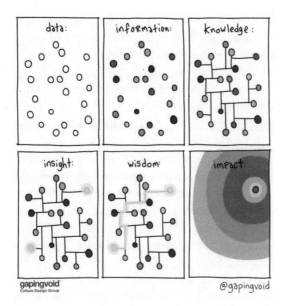

Figure 8.2: Gaping Void's representation of data, information, knowledge, insight, wisdom, and impact

Source: www.gapingvoid.com/blog/2019/03/05/want-to-know-how-to-turn-change-into-a-movement

As a gatekeeper, Figure 8.2 doesn't share the whole reality of the evolution of data through these six concepts. First, the visual makes a vital assumption about the quality of the data—that each uncolored dot is assigned to a color when it transforms to information, and colored dots are all somehow connected when transformed into knowledge, and so on. There's no representation of misinformation or disinformation elements. In practice, data is messy (see Chapter 5, "Messy Gathering Grove"). So in the spirit of providing clarity and distinguishing these concepts, the receiver of this visual has formed an unrealistic expectation that data will neatly and eventually fit into *positive* impact. Once again, impact is written in the visual but the implication is that all impact is leading to a relevant and useful conclusion. We have disparate impact and negative impact that remains unconsidered and therefore unaddressed.

By providing these six concepts in six equally sized boxes, the natural assumption leads us to believe that each concept requires an equal amount of computational machinations, social considerations, and time to achieve. The transformation from data to information takes the same effort as the transformation from information to knowledge, for instance. But by being hands-on in data management, the algorithmic efforts vary based on situational conditions of the data's domain, practitioners' expertise level, and projected impact of the product. Moving from one concept to the next adds to the complexity of existing potential and nuanced ramifications—both beneficial and harm-inducing.

One would expect that achieving impact is more difficult than obtaining insight. But by no means are these transformation iterations accomplished in linear time. There's a saying that reverberates in data community: 80 percent of the work is in data cleaning. Those of us who work in data already know that each concept requires different computational, contextual understanding and algorithmic effort. We need to share this with the rest of society. The bridges connecting each concept to the next aren't the same in composition, width, length, or depth. Moving from data to information focuses on structuring the data to fit as neatly as possible into established digital infrastructure—which is why data cleaning is so time-consuming. On the other end of the spectrum, moving from wisdom to impact has us grappling with philosophical contradictions and how outcomes impact the public.

People influence how each transformation happens while stitching together the open sourced/proprietary automated decision systems in a human-in-the-loop approach. As a global society, we need to emphasize the pivotal role that people play in the creation of data as well as how unapologetically tech approaches attempt to erase people's decision-making abilities in all things concerning the very data we created. Researchers talk about how people are involved in every single stage, but they don't provide this sort of clear and concise representation of it so that those working in data can then understand exactly how vulnerable and susceptible they are to the imagery that they create as well as receive.

Recognizing the human factor as well as instilling dignity in data practices ensures that the limitations of machines don't translate to limiting humanity. We are therefore moving in a direction to prioritize humanity and dignity. Centering respect for the whole person in our data practices isn't the norm. People are breathing contradictions, as we want others to follow the rules while we move to break them for ourselves. Data practices can't exist with this elasticity. What can be achieved, however, is having the same integrity protocols associated with data operations apply to personhood. We make data integrity a priority, and we must do the same as people's features, characteristics, economic status, and other aspects of their lives are digitized.

Two unmistakable oversights, however, in our critique of visual construction are: (1) how visualizations hide people's "dataphobia," and (2) how visual content ostracizes people with disabilities. The undercurrent of my discussion thus far has been the first point. Visualizations are used as a security blanket for data analysis. There is an uncertainty about how to understand numbers and other forms of data. When people are presented with a whole bunch of numbers as outcomes of algorithms, they tend to be overwhelmed, so visualizations soothe their psyche. So as a consequence of this fear of numbers, visualizations provide a mask to allow the numbers to fade away and the visualization features to dominate the narrative. It's an attempt to be relatable first as a conduit for them receiving an understanding of what the data means.

Data visualization's overlooking people with hearing and/or seeing conditions is particularly egregious because of where our digital society is headed and because it deserves so much more attention. As a person who hears and sees, I take for granted my ability to ingest audio and audiovisual content. I give a start to this conversation, but a whole separate book is truly warranted.

Disabilities in View

About 61 million adults in the United States have a disability. That's one out of every 4. Although the disability types range from mobility to self-care, hearing (5.9 percent), vision (4.6 percent), and cognition (10.8 percent) disabilities directly affect how someone engages with visual content.[14–15] With much of our interactions existing on the Internet and social media platforms, I was woefully underwhelmed by the lack of tech advances that specifically benefit people with disabilities in light of the lucrative and high-priority innovation efforts made in text and image analysis, natural language processing, and other AI-inspired approaches. Let me demonstrate what I'm talking about using my own tweet from January 5, 2022, as shown in Figure 8.3.

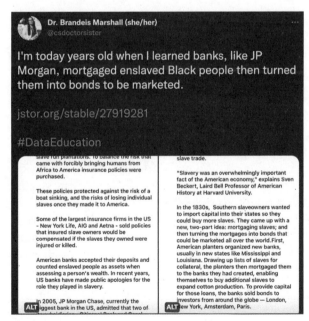

Figure 8.3: My January 5, 2022 Twitter post

The content referenced in this tweet came from Instagram. The Instagram post (www.instagram.com/p/CYU-TM6p2eP) referencing the banking industry's culpability in systems of Black people's oppressions had me gobsmacked. Sharing my newfound revelation on Twitter seemed like it should be a piece of cake: download/screen-capture the image(s) from Instagram on my mobile device, copy the text to a word processing app temporarily, then upload images, paste text contents into the ALT-TXT section, and write an engaging tweet to the Twitter mobile version. I figured it would take 5–7 minutes. It took more like 15 minutes. The clumsiness, albeit not new to anyone who regularly takes part in accessibility modalities, requires much patience—that I don't naturally possess.

On the Instagram side, I couldn't copy the text portion of the post on the mobile device. So I had to turn to the app's desktop version, where I could easily copy the post's text. The Instagram images for that particular post, however, weren't downloadable. I needed to do a screen capture. Because the Instagram text was so long and well-written, with a citation at the end, I knew that it would be way too long for Twitter's 280-character limit. I took two screen captures of the text instead. And I decided that these two pictures of the text should serve as the images on the Twitter post. The full post text is powerful and is shared here:

blackhistoryunlocked In the 19th Century, US banks and southern states would sell securities that helped fund the expansion of slave run plantations. To balance the risk that came with forcibly bringing humans from Africa to America insurance policies were purchased.

These policies protected against the risk of a boat sinking, and the risks of losing individual slaves once they made it to America.

Some of the largest insurance firms in the US - New York Life, AIG and Aetna - sold policies that insured slave owners would be compensated if the slaves they owned were injured or killed.

American banks accepted their deposits and counted enslaved people as assets when assessing a person's wealth. In recent years, US banks have made public apologies for the role they played in slavery.

In 2005, JP Morgan Chase, currently the biggest bank in the US, admitted that two of its subsidiaries - Citizens' Bank and Canal Bank in Louisiana - accepted enslaved people as collateral for loans. If plantation owners defaulted on loan payment the banks took ownership of these slaves.

JP Morgan was not alone. The predecessors that made up Citibank, Bank of America and Wells Fargo are among a list of well-known US financial firms that benefited from the slave trade.

"Slavery was an overwhelmingly important fact of the American economy," explains Sven Beckert, Laird Bell Professor of American History at Harvard University.

In the 1830s, Southern slaveowners wanted to import capital into their states so they could buy more slaves. They came up with a new, two-part idea: mortgaging slaves; and then turning the mortgages into bonds that could be marketed all over the world. First, American planters organized new banks, usually in new states like Mississippi and Louisiana. Drawing up lists of slaves for collateral, the planters then mortgaged them to the banks they had created, enabling themselves to buy additional slaves to expand cotton production. To provide capital for those loans, the banks sold bonds to investors from around the globe—London, New York, Amsterdam, Paris.

Sources: BBC, Slavery's Invisible Engine:
Mortgaging Human Property

`www.jstor.org/stable/27919281`[16]

Pictures of text aren't helpful for anyone who is unable to read the words. I added the text as alt-text without incident. The irony of what's allowed versus what's not allowed on social platforms can't be overstated enough.

- Instagram requires an image in certain size proportions with the option of text. But to write alt-text on this platform, it's buried under tabs and labels only available from the mobile version. You must go to advanced settings and select write alt-text under the accessibility label. Why isn't alt-text possible immediately after the image is uploaded but before it's shared? As an aside, their policies surrounding accessibility of any of its features are not distinguishable from its parent company, Facebook. Facebook claims to have automatic alt-text capabilities.[17]

- Instagram and Facebook set their alt-text limit at 100 characters. That's it. The lack of care given to alt-text on Instagram and Facebook is a slap in the face for platforms with such broad global reach.

- Twitter allows each image a 1,000-character alt-text limit—nearly 5 times that of a tweet. The same limit applies for GIFs on the platform as well.

- Twitter allows us to search for a GIF/meme by text based on Luis von Ahn's work.[18–20] But they supply limited automatically generated text or suggestions from frequently used descriptions for each GIF. The data and tech approaches are designed, developed, and delivered in other areas, so why not this one?

- And for those of you like me who are on LinkedIn and curious, the recommended alt-text limit for images and video content is no more than 250 characters as screen readers will cut off the text so the recipient won't be able to receive the full meaning.[21–22]

The tech community has made explaining visualizations more difficult for those who have hearing and vision impairment. It's sloppy on the tech community's part to embed the accessibility services to the advance setting portion of their platforms. It's sloppy that we have separate tech, meaning paying separate vendors, to achieve accessibility. For instance, closed captioning and transcription should be standard for every video conference. It's hypocritical for these platforms and other tech companies to promote ease of use but then not make it easy to use for people with disabilities.

Make alt-text required for all visual content. NOW. It'll open up the floodgates on our assumptions when it comes to visualizations. And note that alt-text is one tip of one iceberg in lack of accessibility online. For instance, think about the CAPTCHA feature—you know it as the "I am not a robot" visual that appears asking the viewer to select images with certain objects. This feature associates our humanity with the interactive ability to see and select objects. The W3C Group drafted commentary and approaches on the depths of CAPTCHA 's inaccessibility (`www.w3.org/TR/turingtest`). The assumptions we place on visualizations are so many that we need to discuss in depth this mirage of prettiness.

Pretty Picture Mirage

In the mainstream media and scholarly venues, a handful of visualizations are presented to us: bar charts line graphs, dot maps and word clouds. What we as a collective society don't know is that there are many more visualization types. Severino Ribecca created The Data Visualisation Catalogue project to showcase different types of visualizations without using a computer language (`https://datavizcatalogue.com`).[23] They are sorted by alphabetical list, by chart type/method, and by function. Sixty such visualization types are given on the website—listed here with the bolded text indicating the popular ones. A visual representation of each one appears in Appendix E, "The Data Visualisation Catalogue's Visualization Types."

Arc diagram, **area graph,** **bar chart,** *box & whisker plot, brainstorm, bubble chart,* **bubble map,** **bullet graph,** *calendar,* **candlestick chart,** *chord diagram,* **choropleth map,** *circle packing, connection map, density plot, donut chart,* **dot map,** *dot matrix chart, error bars, flow chart, flow map, gantt chart, heat map,* **histogram,** *illustration diagram, kagi chart,* **line graph,** *marimekko chart,* **multi-set bar chart,** **network diagram,** *nightingale rose chart, non-ribbon chord diagram, open-high-low-close chart, parallel coordinates plot, parallel sets, pictogram chart,* **pie chart,** *point & figure chart, population pyramid, proportional area chart, radar chart, radial bar chart, radial column chart, sankey diagram,* **scatterplot,** *span chart, spiral plot,* **stacked area graph,** **stacked bar graph,** *stem & leaf plot, steam graph, sunburst diagram, tally chart, timeline, timetable, tree diagram, treemap,* **venn diagram,** *violin plot,* **word cloud**

The sheer number of different visualizations is overwhelming. I bet you had no clue that there were this many types of 2D visualizations. Neither did I. And I recognized several of them based on the visual representation since I didn't know their official names, like the choropleth map (see Figure 8.4).

Figure 8.4: A choropleth map of the United States indicating the states with varying percentages of population participation in the Great Renegotiation

Source: Pickert, Reade and Alexandre Tanzi. "The Great Resignation: Where the Record Number of U.S. Workers Are Quitting." Bloomberg. Date Published November 19, 2021.

Choosing which one to use at which time overshadows the intended purpose of constructing a visual representation in the first place—make the data outputs understandable to a broader audience. And let's be honest, it's fun to create and look at graphs, maps and charts. This is why exploratory data analysis remains the go-to choice for data analysts, engineers, and scientists. Society places unrelenting value on the visualization output—to *see* the data, for example. We, from the classroom to the boardroom, all push to get to a picture, *any* picture, that we can then digest. We're conditioned to be scared of *data*, look always for *insights* and never challenge the *impacts*. With data visualizations, those of us on data and tech teams especially need to challenge the impact of the algorithms used and analysis provided. We all need to catch ourselves from being so caught up in the prettiness of the picture that we ignore whether there's value-added. We must question what verifiable interpretations can be gleaned.

Figure 8.4 displays a choropleth map that's become internationally popular since the advent of the Covid-19 pandemic. The color-coded U.S. map wants the reader to recognize the cluster of gray tone denoting percentage up to 2.7 percent in the New England region of the country, where gray tone denoting percentage up to 2.7 percent indicates the lowest percentages of people quitting their jobs.[24] Mission accomplished. Now, do you see an issue with this visualization? The value legend indicating the quit percentages per state don't have numerical values at each end. We aren't told the minimum percentage in the gray tone denoting percentage up to 2.7 percent (1.9 percent) or the maximum percentage in the light gray tone denoting percentage greater than 3.7 percent (7.8 percent). The perception is that the states are relatively evenly disbursed across the color-coded spectrum. However, when the ranges between ranges are factored, there's a bell curve with 29 states falling in between 2.7 percent and 3.7 percent. The authors made this one percentage point seem more significant. Figures like this run rampant in the mainstream media and scholarly articles to make data outputs appear insightful.

The Data Visualisation Catalogue gives us direction to figure out which visualization type better serves our intended purpose. When you want to search by function on the site, Ribecca categories these 60 visualization types as follows: comparisons, proportions, relationships, hierarchy, concepts, location, part-to-a-whole, distribution, how things work, processes and methods, movement or flow, patterns, range, data over time, analyzing text, or reference tool. Much of what we see falls in the comparison (e.g., bar chart), distribution (e.g., histogram), and/or range (e.g., candlestick chart). We focus so diligently on making the visualization pretty because we're competing for the attention of the article's reader or media's viewer. While we're mesmerized by the prettiness of the visualization, we should be striving to cover two conditions of a worthwhile data visualization instead: memorability and insightfulness. To be memorable means to go a step further than pretty. We want to grab the audience's interest in the topic, not simply be unforgettable. And to be insightful entails disclosing a poignant synthesis of understanding and then communicating it skillfully.

Unless you're in data visualization, marketing, or a similar field, you aren't exposed to the nuances of presenting outputs. Tufte, a pioneer in data visualization and visual literacy, laid the foundation of how to avoid "chart junk" and emphasizes the role of visualization to enable a deeper level of understanding to the audience.[25-26] You're left believing and operating as if *all* you need to do is understand your audience, set up a clear framework, and jury-rig it to tell a compelling story.[27] But the memorability and insightfulness conditions must be put in their proper context. There's lots to learn about the mechanics of creating and presenting compelling data visualization, so start with Tufte's books. You won't be disappointed in the visualizations and accompanying explanations for quantitative data. But Tufte's work doesn't cover interactive data visualizations. So Tufte's work, while brilliant, is also dated.

For a comprehensive but gentle introduction, *Visual Insights* is also a clear winner.[28] To get the business point of view, *Storytelling with Data*[29] is your best bet. For those with the analytical brain, this data visualization handbook, "Seeing Theory,"[30] takes you deep into the numerical weeds, along with *Data Visualisation: A Handbook for Data Driven Design*, a practical introduction to data visualization book for R users.[31] Needing a well-rounded introduction for the analytical brain with an affinity for a business point of view calls for checking out *Data Visualization: A Practical Introduction*.[32]

Hands-on tutorials, demonstrations, case studies, and plenty of pictures fill these books to help you with the mechanics of visualization construction. Making a visual representation can be explained in a book and broken down into clear, definitive steps. The next level to data visualizations is stress testing it against what's known about the data, who is managing the process, and who will be engaging with the data outputs. We're back to asking the questions I posed in the first part of this chapter, which requires reviewing the choices and decisions made earlier in the data life cycle process.

As with all things new to you, having an example that does a better than average job helps us progress forward. "Seeing Theory," based at Brown University does a better-than-average job in explaining and visualizing probability/entry-level statistics concepts (`https://seeing-theory.brown.edu`).[30] The left-hand panel provides tangible situations that are intended to showcase the chosen concept. Also, there are interactive buttons to execute the visualization provided in the right-hand panel. The glaring missing piece is the lack of examples featuring incorrect uses or interpretations of each concept. A person using this website needs to be made aware of the shortcomings of compound and probability distributions, frequency and Bayesian inference, and regression analysis.

Case Study: SAT College Board Dataset

Now that we've covered data collection (Chapter 5), storage (Chapter 6), and analysis (Chapter 7), it's only fitting that we wrap up visualization with a case study to reinforce how we engage with a data project. I've chosen a small file of 25 KB from `data.gov` with 460 rows and 6 columns, with some data missing. There isn't a large amount of data to overwhelm you if you're a newbie, and there's enough variation to allow a more advanced data professional to try different techniques. For any data person, though, the data is rich enough to make you think deeply and discuss responses to the questions posed in each of the last four chapters.

See `SAT-CollegeBoard_Data-Project-Starter.ipynb` (for interactivity) or `SAT-CollegeBoard_Data-Project-Starter.pdf` (for a quick view; some text is truncated or removed due to print formatting).

As a brief summary, New York City (NYC) has an open data initiative that shares data with the public as a way for the public to help the local government agencies answer everyday questions. The SAT College Board dataset consists of 460 NYC high schools who shared their 2010 school level outputs, including the number of test takers, critical reading mean scores, mathematics mean scores, and reading mean scores. In the Jupyter Notebook, I start with motivating questions to guide our data project work:

- Given the school level (mean) SAT scores in all categories, what patterns could we consider?

- Which are the "high-performing" high schools? Which are the "low-performing" high schools?

- Which high schools obtain high scores with respect to critical reading, mathematics, and/or writing?

I walk through the computational stages of data acquisition and cleanup, storage, and management procedures; exploratory data analysis approaches; and various data visualizations. At the end, the correlations among the reading, mathematics, and writing mean scores are clear as well as where mean scores fall across the collection of schools (450 out of 800). By going through each main phase of this data life cycle, many questions can be asked and answered that wouldn't have been by looking at the CSV spreadsheet. Arguably, transforming data into information, some knowledge and limited insights can be gained by computational means. The breadth of the wisdom and depth of impact remains in the people's hands.

Summary

The claim that visualizations are easier to understand than text is a lie, made more evident by the tech community's laziness in building its alt-text functionalities, capabilities, and integrations in terms of closed caption and transcription for images, video, and audio content. Yet our global society is doubling down on using visual content on the Internet and moving headfirst on web3 because of the attainment of getting more of viewers' money and attention. The hopes and dreams are no longer being *said* to us; rather, they are being *shown* to us. And accepting it with little to no scrutiny means we're falling for the mirage. We must therefore stay resolute in scrutinizing visualizations, in what they are intended to tell us and what they actually tell us. Stop playing into tech's strategy by being on the defense. We have the wherewithal, in kindred spirits (as readers of this book), data, historical context, and questions/responses posed in this book, to interrupt and disrupt the trajectory of a harm-inducing, digital-only existence.

Notes

1. "The Rise & Fall of Blockbuster Video Store Locations 1986-2019." Fleet Logging. 2020. `https://fleetlogging.com/blockbuster-video-map`.

2. "Current World Population." `Worldometer.info`. 2022. `www.worldometers.info/world-population`.

3. Statista Research Department. "Most Popular Social Networks Worldwide as of January 2022, Ranked by Number of Monthly Active Users." Statista. 2022. `www.statista.com/statistics/272014/global-social-networks-ranked-by-number-of-users`.

4. "Polishing Your Presentation." 3M Visual Systems Division. 1999. `https://web.archive.org/web/20001102203936/http://3m.com/meetingnetwork/files/meetingguide_pres.pdf`.

5. Eisenberg, Harris. "Humans Process Visual Data Better." Thermopylae Sciences + Technology. 2014. `www.t-sciences.com/news/humans-process-visual-data-better`.

6. Gillett, Rachel. "Why We're More Likely to Remember Content with Images and Video." Fast Company. 2014. `www.fastcompany.com/3035856/why-were-more-likely-to-remember-content-with-images-and-video-infogr`.

7. Levine, Alan. "The 60,000 Times Question Remains Unanswered." CogDogBlog. 2012. `https://cogdogblog.com/2012/07/60000-times-question`.

8. Gebru, Timnit, Jamie Morgenstern, Briana Vecchione, Hanna Wallach, and Jennifer Vaughan Wortman. "Datasheets for Datasets." *Communications of the ACM 64* (December 2021). `https://doi.org/10.1145/3458723`.

9. "Cisco Annual Internet Report." Cisco. 2022. `www.cisco.com/c/en/us/solutions/executive-perspectives/annual-internet-report/infographic-c82-741491.html`.

10. "50 Mind-Blowing Visual Content Marketing Statistics." Content Writing Jobs. 2022. `https://contentwritingjobs.com/blog/visual-content-marketing-statistics`.

11. "How to Increase Twitter Engagement by 324%." Quick Sprout. 2021. `www.quicksprout.com/twitter-engagement`.

12. "Moving Pictures: The Persuasive Power of Video." Meta. 2017. `www.facebook.com/business/news/insights/moving-pictures-the-persuasive-power-of-video?ref=search_new_3`.

13. "Video Resources for Twitter Ads." Business Twitter. 2022. `https://business.twitter.com/en/resources/video.html`.

14. "Disability and Health Data System (DHDS)." Centers for Disease Control and Prevention. 2021. `www.cdc.gov/ncbddd/disabilityandhealth/dhds/index.html?CDC_AA_refVal=https%3A%2F%2Fwww.cdc.gov%2Fncbddd%2Fdisabilityandhealth%2Fdhds.html`.

15. Okoro, Catherine A., NaTasha D. Hollis, Alissa C. Cyrus, and Shannon Griffin-Blake. "Prevalence of Disabilities and Health Care Access by Disability Status and Type Among Adults—United States, 2016." Centers for Disease Control and Prevention. 2018. `www.cdc.gov/mmwr/volumes/67/wr/mm6732a3.htm#suggestedcitation`.

16. Martin, Bonnie. "Slavery's Invisible Engine: Mortgaging Human Property." *Journal of Southern History* 76, no. 4 (2010): 817–66. `www.jstor.org/stable/27919281`.

17. "How Does Automatic Alt Text Work on Facebook?" Meta. 2022. `www.facebook.com/help/216219865403298/?helpref=uf_share`.

18. "Visual Concept Detection, Annotation, and Retrieval Using Flickr Photos." ImageCLEF. 2022. `www.imageclef.org/2012/photo-flickr`.

19. von Ahn, Luis, and Laura Dabbish. "Labeling Images with a Computer Game." School of Computer Science Carnegie Mellon University. 2004. `www.cs.cmu.edu/~biglou/ESP.pdf`.

20. Wu, Shaomei, Jeffrey Wieland, Omid Farivar, and Julie Schiller. "Automatic Alt-text: Computer-Generated Image Descriptions for Blind Users on a Social Network Service." Association of Computing Machinery Digital Library. 2017. `https://dl.acm.org/doi/10.1145/2998181.2998364`.

21. "Adding Alternative Text to Images for Accessibility." LinkedIn. 2022. `www.linkedin.com/help/linkedin/answer/a519856/adding-alternative-text-to-images-for-accessibility?lang=en`.

22. Prabhu, Sanket. "LinkedIn Character Counts & Image Sizes for 2020." LinkedIn. 2020. `www.linkedin.com/pulse/linkedin-character-counts-image-sizes-2020-including-my-sanket-prabhu`.

23. "Data Visualisation Catalogue." The Data Visualization Catalogue. 2022. `https://datavizcatalogue.com`.

24. Pickert, Reade, and Alexandre Tanzi. "The Great Resignation: Where the Record Number of U.S. Workers Are Quitting." Bloomberg. 2021. `www.bloomberg.com/news/articles/2021-11-19/here-s-where-the-record-number-of-american-workers-are-quitting`.

25. Tufte, Edward R. *Envisioning Information*. Graphics Press. 1990. `www.amazon.com/gp/product/0961392118/ref=dbs_a_def_rwt_bibl_vppi_i3`.

26. Tufte, Edward R. *The Visual Display of Quantitative Information, 2nd Ed.* Graphics Press. 2001. `www.amazon.com/gp/product/B09GGBK8YR/` `ref=dbs_a_def_rwt_hsch_vapi_tkin_p1_i1#detailBullets_feature_div.`

27. Stikeleather, Jim. "The Three Elements of Successful Data Visualizations." *Harvard Business Review.* 2013. `https://hbr.org/2013/04/the-three-` `elements-of-successf.`

28. Börner, Katy, and David E. Polley. *Visual Insights, a Practical Guide to Making Sense of Data.* MIT Press. 2014. `https://mitpress.mit.edu/books/` `visual-insights.`

29. Nussbaumer Knaflic, Cole. *Storytelling with Data: A Data Visualization Guide for Business Professionals, 1st Edition.* Wiley. 2015. `www` `.storytellingwithdata.com.`

30. Kunin, Daniel, Jingru Guo, Tyler Dae Delvin, and Daniel Xiang. "Seeing Theory." Brown University. 2022. `https://seeing-theory.brown.edu.`

31. Kirk, Andy. *Data Visualisation: A Handbook for Data Driven Design, 2nd Edition.* SAGE Publications Ltd. 2019. `www.visualisingdata.com/book.`

32. Healy, Kieran. *Data Visualization: A Practical Introduction.* Princeton University Press. 2018. `https://socviz.co.`

Governance

In This Part

By reaching Part III: Governance, it means you recognize the influence, power, presence, and role of data on our lives and in our digital systems. There's also an optimistic hopefulness that society can off-ramp its current trajectory of algorithmic-based harms and carve new paths of inclusivity in data and tech. With a transparency push (Chapters 1–4) and by setting accountability as a requirement (Chapters 5–8), what's left to address is our action steps. We need to lay out a plan of attack on how to guard and defend transparency and accountability approaches. The digital space intentionally inserts a wedge between individuals using tech tools. And if we're not careful, our humanity will get erased along with our dignity. Those of us who have rebelled against tech-solutionism have managed in silos pushing for change, set off alarm bells with investigative reports, and published "controversial" scholarly articles. It has been little pokes to a well-established, well-funded web of systems and policies. No more.

To help operationalize your rebel tech resolve, I've shared a definition of governance as perceived by the tech industry's behaviors as well as my own adaptation. Reflect on how bureaucracy works against the will of the people while imagining tech that's anchored in putting people first.

Governance (n): bureaucracy.

—**Karen Hao, in "Big Tech's Guide to Talking About AI Ethics,"**
www.technologyreview.com/2021/04/13/1022568/
big-tech-ai-ethics-guide[1]

Governance (n): The administration of equity and decency.

—**Revised definition by Brandeis Hill Marshall**

The red tape of governance as we are living it must pass away. Society, meaning all of us, have to stop giving it oxygen to blossom, replicate, and disseminate. Aligning our focus on equity and decency-building can break our bondage to the systems as is. The compounding influence of algorithmic-based harms can be combatted with a coordination of people, platform, and policy interventions. Chapters 9–11 discuss what has been done and what I envision can be accomplished with our collective, cooperative, and sustained engagement.

Note

1. Hao, Karen. "Big Tech's Guide to Talking About AI Ethics." MIT Technology Review, 2021. www.technologyreview.com/2021/04/13/1022568/big-tech-ai-ethics-guide.

By the Law

Dr. Brandeis Marshall
@csdoctorsister

We're operating under the "separate, but equal" doctrine in tech. And by "we", I don't mean me.

Source: https://twitter.com/csdoctorsister/status/1392178830861901826

Tech moves fast. The law moves slow. Coping with these two extremes causes a host of varying intensities of friction for people familiar with tech, for those attuned to the law, and for everyone else in between. The mashup between tech and law is an unlikely pairing. Frankly it's debatable if this experiment of regulating algorithms, processes, and systems is viable, but there are a lot of people from all industries and sectors who want to give it an earnest try. The ability for the law to be misused and misinterpreted comes full circle; what has been flimsily considered legal to our physical world isn't a guardrail in digital spaces.

In this chapter, the extent in which the law is a useful aid, or a persnickety hindrance, in regulating tech is described for the reader to make up their own mind. Combatting algorithmic-based harms using the law misses more than it hits in the past, but there's hope with the adoption of impact assessments. We'll give a slate of suggestions on how the legal system can be more forceful in constructing more effective penalizing tactics when breaches to people's data, digital rights, and dignity occur.

Federal and State Legislation

The plight for tech responsibility is at the very beginning stage. With the prevalence of cameras in mobile devices and social platforms serving as a gateway to disseminate inappropriate content immediately, the tech industry and trillion-dollar tech companies, in particular, has come under heavy scrutiny. While General Data Protection Regulation (GDPR) and the California Consumer Privacy Act (*CCPA*) 2.0 have started to address tech companies' behaviors in their data practices, the Algorithmic Accountability Act of 2019 (`www.congress.gov/bill/116th-congress/house-bill/2231/text`)[2] and the subsequent Algorithmic Accountability Act of 2022 (`www.congress.gov/bill/117th-congress/house-bill/6580/text`)[3] focus on making the tech production process more transparent in order to enforce accountability statues that mandate federal oversight. The Federal Trade Commission (FTC) is tapped to facilitate this oversight and is in the best position to supply enforcement measures.

The Algorithmic Accountability Act of 2019 struck the first blow, based partially on the work done at the AI Now Institute (`https://ainowinstitute.org/aiareport2018.pdf`),[4] at breaking tech's brick wall to regulation and compliance. Admittedly, the proposal was scant on details, introduced to the U.S. House of Representatives during a divisive Congress and created without much input from those in the tech and coding communities. As soon as it was introduced, criticism ran rampant in the mainstream media and within tech-focused venues. The ensuing dialogue concentrated on how the act failed to capture the nuanced understandings of algorithmic design and computational thinking. The language read as abstract, while those of us in tech need specifics. In short, it was heavy on the legalese and light on the tech. The act collected digital dust until 2022.

With a new U.S. government administration and entering year 3 of a global pandemic, the original bill proposers introduced the Algorithmic Accountability Act of 2022 with key terms, a plan of action for eligible companies, and guidance on the components of impact assessments expanded. It's clear that many different tech voices contributed to the discussion, and their recommendations were incorporated into the revised bill. The difference between these two proposals are stark (check out the 2019 version[5] and 2022 version[6] to see the nearly 300 lines added).

The Algorithmic Accountability Act of 2022 made two significant strides forward in regulating tech at the federal level. First, in Section 2(8), the term "critical decision" is explicitly defined and specific applications that affected a consumer's life are listed, from education to legal services. This specification cements how an eligible company needs to be intentionally conscious of the impact of their products and services on people throughout their life, not just on sensitive groups. An eligible company will have a more difficult time claiming that their products and services aren't part of a critical decision system and side-stepping their digital responsibilities to their consumers. Second, in Section 4(a), the bill lists the 12 categories required as part of an eligible company's annual impact assessment. The fingerprints of those in the harm-reducing portion of the tech community are clearly imprinted on this section. The full software development life cycle and key computational aspects of the data life cycle are covered in clear but not overly methodical detail. It's three to four steps ahead of Canada's Algorithmic Impact Assessment[7], which is closer to a checklist than a tech versioning control system. While the term "ethics" isn't mentioned once, the connotation reverberates throughout this section. And I think this is for the best as opponents of the bill will want to quibble over "what is tech/ AI/data ethics?" in an attempt to redirect the discourse and defer doing the impact assessment work.

A glaring concern comes in Section 4(8) with the establishment of the Bureau of Technology. Attracting and retaining quality people from different ethnicities, gender identities, and so forth with the skillset outlined are big lifts. These people will be highly sought after by academic institutions, private, civic, and other government agencies. And given the detail requested as part of the impact assessments, it's improbable that 75 personnel is insufficient. An increased size, scale, and budget commensurate to the Internal Revenue Service would be better aligned with the urgency this Bureau requires.

At the state level, tech policy legislations centers consumers with a heavy emphasis on data privacy. Figure 9.1 displays the June 2022 status of data privacy legislation in the United States.[8] This map shows a stark reality of how long the road is for consumer data privacy protection rights; only five states (California, Colorado, Connecticut, Virginia, and Utah) have a bill signed into law, 31 states have stalled data privacy legislation, and 17 states have no data privacy bills even introduced. Even with full implementation and momentum of the EU's GDPR, U.S. legislation regarding data privacy remains in its infancy. It's going to take two to three generations at this rate to have all 50 states with comprehensive data privacy laws.

Now, when I compare data privacy legislation progress in relation to the U.S. Black population, a disturbing but expected story emerges. Figure 9.2 shows the Black population distributions according to the 2020 U.S. Census.[9] Black populations are most heavily concentrated in the Southern states (>25%) and reside in significant percentages (10%–24.9%) across the Midwest and Mid-Atlantic states.

Figure 9.1: State data privacy legislation status (as of March 2022)

Source: Taylor Kay Lively 2022 / International Association of Privacy Professionals

The five states that have passed data privacy laws disproportionally protect white communities. Protecting and defending Black, and I'd argue the tech health and safety of all minoritized communities, with respect to data privacy isn't a high priority at the state level. The people more likely negatively impacted by a lack of data privacy legislation are the same communities that are fending for themselves. With each of these bills, legislative procedures, and laws, I'm always left asking the same questions since protecting white communities always comes first even though white never appears in the text:

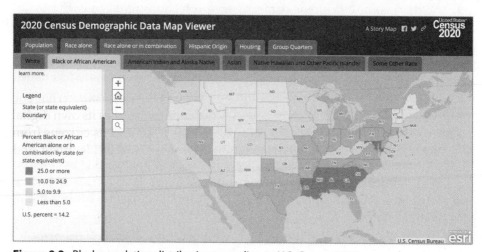

Figure 9.2: Black population distribution according to U.S. Census 2020

- How are Black people protected from further discrimination by automation? When will they be protected fully by the laws?

- How are Latinx people protected from further discrimination by automation? When will they be protected fully by the laws?

- How are Indigenous people protected from further discrimination by automation? When will they be protected fully by the laws?

- How are disabled people protected from further discrimination by automation? When will they be protected fully by the laws?

- How are LGBTQIA+ people protected from further discrimination by automation? When will they be protected fully by the laws?

- How are Asian people protected from further discrimination by automation? When will they be protected fully by the laws?

- How are Pacific Islander people protected from further discrimination by automation? When will they be protected fully by the laws?

- How are women, particularly non-white women, protected from further discrimination by automation? When will they be protected fully by the laws?

International and Transatlantic Legislation

Undoubtedly, there's an appetite to expand the regulation conversation beyond the U.S. centering of AI and data operations. The United States, in my opinion, has enough unfinished business concerning making data, AI, and tech regulation laws. My concern is that U.S. lawmakers will pour their time and energy into international and transatlantic legislation rather than preserving the digital civil rights of U.S. citizens. I don't want the U.S. to distract itself by playing world leader in foreign countries while simultaneously not leading domestically. So I'm including this short, and by no means exhaustive, section since for many, understanding the transatlantic perspective with respect to AI and data ethics is perceived as participating in global digital citizenship. What one country does informs and impacts how another country handles its own digital infrastructure as well as how each country decides to protect its citizens from algorithmic-based harms. Agreements among countries must be identified, and plans covering a multitude of scenarios must be settled so as not to introduce needless international conflict.

Let's start with providing a brief international landscape of AI. The recent AI Index report[10] found private investment in AI nearly *doubled* to $93.5 billion, with a B, in 2021 from 2020. The hunger and thirst for AI regulation skyrocketed from 2020 to 2021, with 71 percent more industry scholars publishing in data and AI ethics venues in addition to the plausibility of regulation of algorithms being more regularly discussed in mainstream media outlets.[11] You'd think the increase in private investment in AI would go toward regulation, compliance, and policies. No, a healthy portion went toward constructing more algorithms and boosting hardware systems in order to reduce the computational time of training AI models.

The concern for aligning data operations and AI algorithms, processes, and systems to an international code of ethics falls by the wayside; see, for example, the IEEE Code of Ethics and the ACM Code of Ethics[12–13]. The concern remains more country-first self-serving to U.S. interests than goodwill for participating in international digital citizenship. As of mid-2022, the White House's Fact Sheet on the transatlantic data privacy framework is just that—a framework.[14] It's like dog-earing a page in a book so that you'll remember where you should start reading when you pick up that book again. While the title says *data privacy framework*, the underlying concern for the United States is national security. The U.S. wants to ensure that data sharing among EU countries flows seamlessly, and in the event of a data-sharing disagreement, the U.S. will seek to resolve the dispute amicably. There's a focus on *what* the data privacy framework *would* do, not *how* or *when* it will get done.

The two disheartening revelations of the AI Index remain (1) the bizarre fixation on "improving" large language models when they are proven to be discriminatory, and (2) the lack of substantive representation of Latin, African and Pacific Islander countries. Upon first observation, large language models are for computational performance, optimization, and benchmarking junkies. They ignore the environmental impact of running many servers simultaneously on a singular electrical grid or the introduction of disparate impacts to different vulnerable communities. Upon second observation, it's as if there was a quota for the number of people from certain non-white countries who could participate on the AI Index committee, and countries below the equator line tended to have that invisible quota. Creating new approaches to addressing disparities and discriminations in data, AI and tech systems go to the bottom of the priority list. The meeting agenda always keeps equity for Latin, African, and Pacific Islander countries under "unfinished business."

The biggest proposed *and passed* international regulation in 2022 comes out of the European Union. The Digital Services Act (DSA) and the Digital Markets Act (DMA) extends the General Data Protection Regulation as a means of shaping universal online rules and guidelines to protect EU citizens, boost transparency and accountability protocols of data use, and curb illegal content (`https://digital-strategy.ec.europa.eu/en/policies/digital-services-act-package`).[15] Basically, they are attempting to carve out a safer online platform for EU citizens. Time will tell whether the DSA will provide useful, timely, and actionable transparency and public accountability measures to successfully challenge this safer EU online platform. And the DMA creates gatekeeper organizations on this platform to prevent monopolies and business bad actors. Since these gatekeepers need to be qualified, I see an introduction of another level to the online hierarchy, unstable and inconsistent self-regulation, siloing of activities by gatekeeper organizations, and smaller organizations still being excluded from participation. For more information on both these acts, refer to the press releases and supporting documentations (`https://ec.europa.eu/commission/presscorner/detail/en/ip_22_1978`[16] and `https://ec.europa.eu/commission/presscorner/detail/en/ip_22_2545`[17]).

Through all the regulation, both domestic and foreign, what has become apparent is how AI has been primed to absorb society's value systems and reflected it back to us. It can't fix a society that has been constructed with an exclusionary male-centric, white-centric, wealthy, able-bodied value structure. AI's increased acknowledgment of its source: data. Data is necessary for their algorithms, processes, and systems to function. Forming a comprehensive data strategy and plan is just as important as the algorithmic, analytics, and benchmarking work. There's an impending return to data stewardship (`https://yjernite.github.io/content/LangDataGov.pdf`).[18] The choices surrounding the data sources and their quality, selection of data tools, and enforcement of sound data integrity and data governance procedures are starting to take a more prominent role. The opportunity to deflate AI's influence from our society can happen to reconsider its use and craft meaningful legislation that will regulate that use, depending on the industry and sector.

Regulating the Tech Sector

The tech sector is actually a spectrum of industries, ranging from those who create tech products to those who use tech services in order to facilitate their own services. Also, the size of the companies within each industry varies, so the perceived and actual impact of client reach for startups, small businesses, medium-sized organizations, and Big Tech companies should be adjusted accordingly. In this book, I've concentrated the discussion of what constitutes the tech industry as Big Tech companies who are creating tech products. Both in the United States and internationally, the legal systems focus on devising proposed policies and regulations for these types of companies. With this framing in mind, the legal framework suggested here primarily considers the Big Tech–sized, tech-creating companies that are the focal points of existing regulation. Very big companies have very big regulatory issues that they themselves are unable to untangle, identify, and attempt to handle. For instance, Twitter was fined by the FTC for violating its own privacy rule—and ordered to pay a $150 million penalty.[19] Different variations of these issues crop up regardless of industry type.

Trust, fairer practices, and data privacy compliance represent the bulk of the legal framework disseminated thus far. This approach is limited in its ability to enforce, guard, and police ethics considerations because it's unable to cover the vast combinations of interdependent ethical tensions. For instance, in Figure 9.3, we've created a two-dimensional representation of how data, industries, and technology tools interact for a subset of industries. The large circular disk represents the data that's gathered, manipulated, and interpreted by each industry, such as the eight inner discs shown in the figure. Each industry (inner eight disks) processes data to inform industry-specific AI tools (outer eight disks). The data processing operates as follows: data is absorbed by a specific industry, to then be crafted for the specific industry's use and processing by customized AI tools. The bidirectional arrow denotes the information flow that needs to happen between the industry and its AI tools. The industries are relatively siloed as well as the AI tools that formed in response to the collected data. These AI tools straddle the larger data disc and the white background since they must take into consideration non-data factors like compliance and regulation issues and human factors. A more comprehensive legal framework for tech regulation has to apply pressure on more than the data and AI tools.

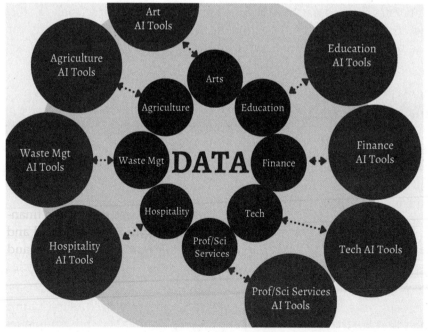

Figure 9.3: Data, some of the industries it affects, and the AI-based tools that are used

This figure has a lot happening, admittedly. First, it's important to emphasize that data use and AI tools have infiltrated every industry. Second, all of our concerns shouldn't be isolated to data use and AI tools—we need to respond to circumstances beyond the data. Third, industries are siloed, indicating that cross-industry knowledge sharing isn't a viable quick-fix option. And fourth, a broad stroke regulation that will cover all industries and sectors won't work. The regulations, penalties, and compliance protocols needed for the hospitality industry won't be the same as for the finance industry. And this is the expectation we, as the public, should insist the legal system to recenter as their core premise.

The legal field needs to demonstrate to tech that the tech industry is in their vise grip. Right now, Big Tech–sized, tech-creating companies don't care that they are for the most part being bad actors, and every digital citizen knows their playbook. The tech industry relies on the premise that the legal field won't be able to create legislation fast enough in order to stop them from (1) creating new technology, (2) technology being adopted by the public, and (3) the public being dependent on that technology so that any subsequent legislative attempts are deemed adversarial.

So, for instance, let's take mobile phones. The mobile phone was a convenience at first, for the wealthy. Now the world has recognized the mental health ramifications and bouts of addiction it can exploit. The remedies include but are not limited to: screen time usage apps, screen time break apps in order to tell you when to step away from your digital devices, and calm-inducing/sound apps that are designed in order to help you reduce anxiety. There are apps designed for you to continually engage with content like social platforms and the Internet. The world has devolved to a situation where tech has created a problem and continues to amplify that problem while providing possible mitigating interventions to that problem.

A similar situation is happening when it comes to algorithms, processes, and systems in the digital space. Our digital society has data that is being collected by people and that data is being massaged within the digital sphere unregulated. This type of conduct has been normalized to the extent that we are developing applications in order to decide which data is important to massage and which data isn't important to manipulate. In recent years, the mounds of data gathered has caused a digital storage issue, with environmental and financial cost impacts. Companies are realizing that a bunch of data collected and stored is useless and no longer want to fill up their filesystems, datacenters, and cloud services with junk data. But a company's data and data privacy policies created as a demonstration of being a responsible corporate citizen has caught them in a difficult situation. They can't abandon their company policies, nor can they avoid devising ways to track the provenance of all of this data through impact assessments.[20–21]

Given the rate of technological change, I recommend creating a new data equity-focused agency, that would be mirrored after the Centers for Disease Control and Prevention. This agency, I'll call the Center for Technological Civility (CTC), would be the national technological safety institute of the United States to help provide the needed guidelines and recommendations to the American public. CTC's main goal is to "protect the public health and safety through control and prevention" from technological harm in the United States and internationally. The CTC would challenge the digital circulation of misinformation and disinformation campaigns while overseeing the impact and ramifications of deepfakes, hate speech discourses, and other tech incivility efforts. It would better align the essence and intent of protecting all people from malicious tech design, implementation, and deployment than what's offered by the existing Federal Trade Commission, which focuses on the adverse legal impact to consumers due to business practices.

We need to cut tech off at the knees by banning certain types of algorithms, processes, and systems. The approach of designing technology to monitor existing technology is problematic. Validation of tech correctness for any algorithm, process, model, and/or system designed, implemented, and/or deployed requires human approval. Verification of results or outcomes produced from any algorithm, process, model, and/or system requires human approval. Simply stated, machines cannot monitor other machines. Human oversight at the tech stage is integral. Marginalized communities remain unengaged at the decision level regarding tech. Technologies must be designed, implemented, tested, and deployed by communities who are impacted by them.

Let me give an example of this: any software that is trying to suss out a person's emotions using their facial expressions. This type of research has been happening for generations. It has not been proven to be accurate or ethical or moral, yet this idea keeps appearing in the literature. Scholars from one generation to the next are reviewing these race science/eugenics-related papers. They should be shut down rather than entertained. And when these "tech innovations" appear in government and corporate sectors, they should be shut down and banned there too.

Any company designing or leveraging an algorithm, process, or system that does this type of work needs to be dealt with as a human criminal. Companies can no longer be permitted to use person/entity status during tax season but circumvent punishment when malfeasance has been done. Since the law doesn't start directly guarding against the exploitation and expansion into the digital air, we're seeing digital personal data privacy and digital civil rights violations that replicate the disparities as instituted by the Black codes, Jim Crow laws, and Civil Rights Act in recent U.S. history. I have several recommendations to thwart tech's dominance:

Prosecute for malcoding.   *Malcoding* is using algorithmic design and computational thinking to create code that digitizes harm-inducing ideas and outcomes, labeled as tech innovations, but has been proven to be a bad idea in prior literature. Malcoding instances include software libraries, methods, processes, and systems. The ability to turn off certain code that would be deemed malcode is possible. Computer programmers have used a familiar update routine to prevent it from executing. It's called deprecation. Let's reconfigure the codebase so that certain code elements are not allowed and prosecute people and companies who don't discontinue malcode use.

Prosecute data brokers.   Trolls and bots thrive on access to people's data. Regulate data brokers who compromise people and their sensitive data.

In recent years, prosecution for bad data dealings has become a reality using a framework called *algorithmic destruction*.[22] And the FTC has implemented it:

The Federal Trade Commission has struggled over the years to find ways to combat deceptive digital data practices using its limited set of enforcement options. Now, it's landed on one that could have a big impact on tech companies: algorithmic destruction. The premise is simple: when companies collect data illegally, they should not be able to profit from either the data or any algorithm developed using it. That is both the data (collected illegally) and the algorithm developed from it should be destroyed. The FTC has penalized companies like Cambridge Analytica, Everalbum, and WW International (formerly known as Weight Watchers) for this.[23]

Frankly, the term *algorithmic destruction* sounds great. Its punchy wordplay comes with an overtone of seriousness in addressing algorithmic-based data privacy breaches. Those in the legal profession have completed the three-piece puzzle to form the triangle: (1) data fuels algorithms, (2) algorithms fuel company profits, and (3) penalize companies by taking their profits, destroying their algorithms, *and* forcing them to delete the ill-collected data. It feels like for many years, many of us in data and tech communities have been telling those not in data and tech spaces that forcing companies to pay fines isn't enough. The algorithms, and especially the data outputs, are the real money-generating sources. We're dealing with the effects of algorithms created 15, 20, 30 years ago. Algorithms last for generations and so do the data outcomes. We all need to recognize that data has a shelf life and respond accordingly.

It's encouraging to realize that the term "algorithm" is no longer a scary only-tech-people-can-understand word. Thanks to many data, AI, and tech people participating in congressional hearings, testimonies, and panels for explaining algorithms and their impact on people and society. The countless examples of algorithms being misused and harming the average hardworking Jamar and Jennifer, not just the average Joe, has resonated. Taking a company's money doesn't change its behaviors. Destroying their sources of said money can be an integral tool to alter companies' choices, maybe. Good job. FTC, but . . .

This is only a first step. There are many algorithms that need destroying. Applying this approach one case at a time isn't fast enough given how quickly algorithms are integrated into digital systems. Let's go several steps further to build an algorithmic destruction infrastructure to provide remedies and resolutions to these and other questions: How do you assess whether the algorithm(s) as well as all the ill-collected data are destroyed? Will destroyed algorithms be cataloged somewhere, publicly, so that companies can destroy their own known bad algorithms? What happens if a company uses a known destroyed algorithm? And what's being done to prevent work-around algorithms that mimic the impact of those destroyed algorithms?

And last question while we're on this topic: when will Algorithm Destroyer positions open up in public, private, and civic sectors?

Yes, I'm encouraged and full of questions because seeing this approach applied frequently is in our digital society's best interest. I'd say we're in algorithmic destruction infancy or exploration phase. We need to reach a full-blown algorithm destruction era. We've burnt 0s and 1s, people, by using this approach three times in three years. Time is of the essence before tech figures out sidestepping maneuvers.

Create a legal framework for tech probationary jail, short-term banning, and long-term tech incarceration for algorithms, processes, systems, and tools.   Certain technologies need to be sidelined until their impact on society and its people can be determined. Place certain algorithms, processes, and tools in a virtual timeout where their functionalities are disabled and inoperable. This conduct is applied on social platforms when accounts/profiles are marked as incendiary. The same rules need to apply to tech products.

Create a legal framework for a company to experience probationary jail, short-term banning, and/or long-term incarceration   As with technologies, certain eligible companies need to be sidelined until their impact on society and its people can be determined. I suggest suspending their products and services for different intervals of time based on the degree of grievance. This conduct is already applied on social platforms when accounts/profiles are marked as incendiary. The same rules need to apply to eligible companies.

For the legal field, slow and steady is the norm. Making small steps toward the final goal is also a favorite go-to method of the U.S. legal system. Both approaches benefit tech's plan of domination. People can't exercise their free will of using an algorithmic-based approach or not if they've never been afforded the opportunity to use their agency and see the outcomes. By boasting about cases won, charges with convictions, money provided in settlements, and company revenue lost, the legal field can cripple bad actors in tech and make the statements loud and proud.

Three areas of vulnerability remain open that the law can attack: tech production processes, tech's applications, and tech's impacts. There's an opportunity to go a step further than deploying the algorithmic destruction approach being performed at the federal level. Companies, that are subjects of a legal investigation, charged or convicted, are typically permitted to continue providing their products and services without disruption to their consumers. This mode of operation allows companies to make money while still inflicting algorithmic-based harms. Instituting ways to disrupt their business operations while they are under litigation would at least stifle their ability to generate revenue and help to mitigate some of tech's harms.

I recommend that these companies be required to suspend their products and services that would fall under one of three degrees of disruption: probationary jail, short-term banning, or long-term incarceration. In probationary jail, a company's digital infrastructure would stay mostly intact. They would maintain access to the tech tools and platforms so that the company's employees, contractors, and vendors can still perform their duties. However, the strength and stability of the company's computing networks would be slowed down so there would be a delay of receiving and sending emails, for instance. Short-term banning would include the inconveniences of probationary jail in addition to pre-determined, yet limited high-traffic business hours experiencing restricted access to the company's digital infrastructure. For example, all the company's response times to operations would be delayed, and during 2 peak business hours, two to three times a week for eight weeks, the company would experience a halt in delivering their products and services to their customers. Lastly, for long-term incarceration, the company's digital presence would be suspended in hours to days segments over the course of weeks to months. Their whole digital infrastructure, including their website, company files, and email system, would be inaccessible to everyone during these blackout periods.

With each severity of disruption, the company's employees, contractors, vendors and customers would be impacted based on the egregiousness of the open litigation. It would also impact the solvency of the company. This would help incentivize companies to mitigate algorithmic-based harms so that they could retain their reputation with their customers as well as their workers.

Whether these suggestions are adopted or others are deemed more effective, it's crucial that the next steps be expeditious, steady, coordinated, and relentless. In the law. In the data and software development rooms. And in your everyday digital life.

Summary

Tech's growth rate far outpaces the law. The regulatory and compliance aspects of the law fail to keep up with tech. The law shouldn't. Tech is made up of data, algorithms, processes, and systems that shape what constitutes online platforms and digital spaces. The law should focus on these fundamentals of tech and stop being distracted by the application of technologies. Make data, algorithms, processes, and systems the focus of the legislation at the national and state levels, simultaneously. Transparency, accountability, and governance needs to impact the full supply chain of those who make the algorithmic decisions—from the coders to the CEO, not just the company's regulation and compliance officers. Bad actors and bad faith conspirators can't stay invisible, be unscathed, and coexist peacefully with the collective alignment to equity in data operations, algorithms, processes, and systems.

Notes

1. Hao, Karen. "Big Tech's guide to talking about AI ethics." MIT Technology Review. 2021.

2. Algorithmic Accountability Act of 2019. `Congress.gov`. 2022.

3. Algorithmic Accountability Act of 2022. `Congress.gov`. 2022.

4. Reisman, Dillon, Jason Schultz, Kate Crawford, & Meredith Whittaker. Algorithmic Impact Assessments: A Practical Framework for Public Agency Accountability. AI Now Institute. 2018. `https://ainowinstitute.org/aiareport2018.pdf`.

5. AlgoAcctAcct. DiffChecker. 2022.

6. Text Compare Online – Compare Text and Files Online. 2022.

7. Secretariat, Treasury Board of Canada. 2021. Algorithmic Impact Assessment Tool. 2021.

8. Lively, Taylor Kay. US State Privacy Legislation Tracker. `Iapp.org`. 2022.

9. United States Bureau of the Census. 2020 Census Demographic Data Map Viewer. 2022.

10. Measuring trends in artificial intelligence. Stanford University. 2022.

11. Wiggers, Kyle. Stanford report shows that ethics challenges continue to dog AI field as funding climbs. VentureBeat. 2022.

12. Code of Ethics. IEEE Computer Society. 2022.

13. Association for Computing Machinery. ACM Code of Ethics and Professional Conduct. `Acm.org`. 2018.

14. Fact Sheet: United States and European Commission Announce Trans-Atlantic Data Privacy Framework. White House. 2022. `www.whitehouse .gov/briefing-room/statements-releases/2022/03/25/fact-sheet-united-states-and-european-commission-announce-trans-atlantic-data-privacy-framework/#:~:text=The%20United%20States%20 and%20the,decision%20underlying%20the%20EU%2DU.S.`

15. The Digital Services Act Package: Shaping Europe's Digital Future. European Commission. 2022. `https://digital-strategy.ec.europa .eu/en/policies/digital-services-act-package`.

16. Digital Markets Act: Commission welcomes political agreement on rules to ensure fair and open digital markets. European Commission. 2022. `https://ec.europa.eu/commission/presscorner/detail/en/IP_22_1978`.

17. Digital Services Act: Commission welcomes political agreement on rules ensuring a safe and accountable online environment. European Commission. 2022. `https://ec.europa.eu/commission/presscorner/detail/en/ ip_22_2545`.

18. Data governance in the age of large-scale data-driven language technology. BigScience Research Workshop at FAccT. 2022. `https://yjernite .github.io/content/LangDataGov.pdf`.

19. Fair, Lesley. Twitter to pay $150 million penalty for allegedly breaking its privacy promises—again. Federal Trade Commission. 2022.

20. Allen, Anita L. Dismantling the "Black Opticon: Privacy, race, equity, and online data-protection reform." `yalelawjournal.org`. 2022.

21. Office of Oversight and Investigations Majority Staff: A review of the data broker industry: Collection, use, and sale of consumer data for marketing purposes. Committee on Commerce, Science, and Transportation. 2013.

22. Li, Tiffany. Algorithmic Destruction. SMU Law Review. 2022. `https:// ssrn.com/abstract=4066845`.

23. Kaye, Kate. The FTC's new enforcement weapon spells death for algorithms. Protocol. 2022.

By Algorithmic Influencers

Dr. Brandeis Marshall
@csdoctorsister

In tech, y'all are forever trying to do all
the things at scale instead of quality.

Source: Twitter, Inc.

Our society, globally, is enamored with artificial intelligence (AI). AI tools are donned the one-stop efficiency-making vaccine solution. No matter what is causing your organization to lose revenue, clients, and/or employees, there's an AI tool for that! The tech industry—specifically algorithmic influencers—touts these approaches as measurable ways to save the organization money in the long run while being able to quickly handle the volume of data coming into the organization. AI tool providers give "data-driven" evidence that their approach works. And AI tool customers are forced to hand over their data to make the AI tool possible. AI tools that eat data often hit bumps because they fail to take people into account.

In this chapter, we discuss tech's dominance in our society and, in particular, as a culture that excludes other solution options. The frequent narrative of being efficient in tech blinds us to harms constantly absorbed by minoritized communities. Governing the bureaucracy that lies within the tech community receives serious criticism. We, as global citizens, have this pesky habit of centering tech as a means to "fix" or "correct" problems. We do it with discrimination in data via algorithmic fairness models. We do it with online discrimination on platforms via content moderation. We slow down and take inventory of how we engage tech. We leave it to you to come up with answers. Because that's what's needed—you without tech.

Group (Re)Think

Algorithmic influencers, a play on the ever-popular phrase *artificial intelligence* (AI), is a concept that I've created to encapsulate the collection of people within an organization who peddle AI as *the* solution to economic, social, and political issues. The responsibility of specifying how AI is perceived and used in our society rests on everyone who is on the decision-making chain: software development teams, data teams, business operations, and organizational leadership. Leadership decides the organization's priorities and goals for their tech-based products and services based on budget constraints. Business operations from sales to public relations itemize how to measure and meet key performance indicators dictated by the leadership. Data and software development teams create the digital infrastructure to design and implement algorithms to satisfy the requests from the leadership team and business operations. Each member of this decision-making chain shapes how the others in the chain behave. They are all algorithmic influencers.

The power that makes algorithmic influencers so effective lies in the focus on a *use case* of the tech-based AI-assisted product or service to better people's everyday lives while stipulating that the use case extrapolates to be *useful* in many other cases. This one-to-many conditioning has made our society reliant on finding a tech-based solution. Let's review how the iPhone was presented to the world: "What's great about the iPhone is that if you want to check snow conditions on the mountain, there's an app for that. If you want to check how many calories are in your lunch, there's an app for that. And if you want to check where exactly you park the car, there's even an app for that. Yep there's an app for just about anything. Only on the iPhone." These are the words that accompanied the then-new iPhone 3G commercial (`https://youtube.com/watch?v=Tqw9biUyVc4`), back in early 2009.

We've been indoctrinated into a belief system that tech can do it all and solve all our problems. It took five years before this belief system had a name—and explanation.

Evgeny Morozov coined the term *technological solutionism* to describe this core belief system in his book *To Save Everything, Click Here*. Morozov "critiques what he calls 'solutionism'—the idea that given the right code, algorithms and robots, technology can solve all of mankind's problems, effectively making life 'frictionless' and trouble-free" (The Guardian Interview, March 2013).[1] A key concern repeatedly made by Morozov is the seemingly intentional unknown costs of these tech solutions in terms of the increasing power they command over our lives and the potential dampening of our critical thinking skills and social skills.

While the iPhone and app technologies definitely altered the way we engage with tech, algorithmic influencing happens at much smaller scales and in circumstances that aren't classically considered issues that a tech-based AI-assisted product would or could solve. For example, Moodbeam, a wristband that tells your boss if you are unhappy, helps managers check in on their work-from-home (WFH) team members.[2] The team member must agree to wear the wristband, press the orange or blue button depending on their mood, and download and configure the app that records the team member's response. If the WFH team member is unhappy, the manager can initiate a conversation. Now this tech is attempting to address the lack of in-person interaction and body language cues by introducing—really interjecting—a physical device that requires both the team member and the manager to engage with it in real time.

There are several assumptions made by these tech creators that presuppose emotions and social context can be patterned by algorithms. And it raises red flags: (1) the mood self-reporting of the team member is truthful, (2) the only mood options are either happy/okay or unhappy/not okay, (3) the collected mood data of each team member will only be used as a well-being gauge and not repurposed for another use like being weaponized against an employee on an annual evaluation, (4) the manager has the sufficient report, expertise, and workplace context to engage an employee who is unhappy, and (5) a team member's mood isn't time-sensitive. A team member could be unhappy in the morning and happy by the afternoon. Or vice versa. Or the mood could have nothing to do with the workplace. These assumptions often persist whether you have WFH or in-person employees as we reconstruct the workplace environment post-pandemic (McKinsey & Co. report, June 2020).[3]

As a data geek, we've got a few big problems with any tech that claims to algorithmically decipher social or emotional cues:

- A lack of clear procedures for keeping any sensitive data HIPPA-compliant (And if it's not considered sensitive data, what are the organization's protocols in making the data anonymized?)

- Unknown reliability and accuracy of the content recorded by the tech, such as unknown data quality

- Unknown usefulness of the collected mood data, such as uncertainty about data integrity

- Possible infringement of digital civil rights to uniquely identify a person or potentially be a basis of discrimination, such as data privacy

- A lack of clear procedures for how long or how many mood recordings we should store or archive per employee (Archiving data over time isn't cheap—cloud services are prime cyber real estate.)

The value-add of this data remains suspicious. Mood tracking isn't a new phenomenon, but the use of apps isn't all favorable. According to a 2018 National Institutes of Health (NIH) article,[4] "mood tracking apps offer many features for the collection and reflection stages, but lack adequate support for the preparation and action stages."

And then there's the obvious question: why can't the manager check in on team members without a mood tracking tech app? This is an excellent candidate for tech-not-needed.

The mental and emotional health aspect raises the complication level in tech circles. The perceived problem becomes difficult to solve because of what computational problem solvers like to do: break up the problem into smaller manageable parts. The codependent interplay between people and the app isn't amenable to making clear, isolated puzzle pieces that can be neatly reconstructed on computational demand. Let's consider another situation that's for the more analytically minded. AI scholars globally featured in the well-known *Wired*[5] to the lesser-known *Good News Network*[6] publications stipulate that AI can be unbiased or debiased as if discrimination can be taken out mostly or entirely by algorithmic means. The path to algorithms making more ethical decisions includes a set of familiar elements—you've guessed it: a mathematical formula that requires more "bias" and "unbiased" data examples! See Chapter 3, "Bias," for a deep dive on the effects of bias in physical and digital spaces.

Mathematical formulation of fixing social, economic, or political constructs falls into a pattern of attempting to separate the "good" from the "bad" based on preexisting assumptions. The "good" here refers to the influence, power, access, and opportunity to build wealth, provide benefits to humankind, or move toward a more democratic republic. The "bad" here refers to the systemic inequities that prevent the "good" from happening for all people in society. And lastly, there are certain assumptions all of us bring to our formulations of the world because we each come with a unique perspective. These three parts are evaluated to output a solution, or "the fix." So when analytically minded people observe social, economic, and political imbalance, it maps for them (or us) to an existing mathematical equation that can be solved.

Given my computer science background and scholarship in information retrieval, the goal of accentuating the "good," minimizing the "bad," and conceptualizing both in terms of assumptions is quite familiar. In fact, it's called the Rocchio algorithm,[7-8] created in 1971, that was designed for filtering, assessing, and retrieving documents related to a word or phrase. Briefly, Rocchio's algorithm is an iterative process used in refining the selection of perceived useful documents in a filesystem. It (re-)labels certain items relevant and other items not-so-relevant based on proximity to user-defined criteria. Rocchio's algorithm has three parts that's a weighted linear equation as described well in Chapter 9 of *Introduction to Information Retrieval*.[7] The application of Rocchio's algorithm is fundamental to web searching, but there are stark parallels on how we in data and tech approach fixing social, economic, and political constructs. Table 10.1 dissects Rocchio's algorithm into its main components: the equation's output ("the fix"), the user's original search request (the preexisting assumptions), the relevant documents (the "good"), and the nonrelevant documents (the "bad").

Table 10.1: Rocchio's algorithm explained (simply?)

MATHEMATICAL FORMULA ELEMENT	EXPLANATION
$\vec{q}_m$	The system's answer (usually a list of documents or websites that the system says matches a user's request for data/information); namely "the fix."
$\alpha\vec{q}_0$	The original user request (usually a list of words) that's valued at a weight, called α, that's > 0 but < 1; namely "the preexisting assumptions."
$\beta\dfrac{1}{|D_r|}\sum_{d_j \in D_r}\vec{d}_j$	The set of documents containing words similar to or exactly matching the words identified by the user's request. The words are highly frequent, valued at a weight, called β, that's > 0 but < 1; namely the "good."
$\gamma\dfrac{1}{|D_{nr}|}\sum_{d_j \in D_{nr}}\vec{d}_j$	The set of documents containing words similar to or exactly matching the words identified by the user's request. The words are highly frequent, valued at a weight, called γ, that's > 0 but < 1; namely the "bad."
$\alpha + \beta - \gamma = 1$	α (alpha), β (beta), and γ (gamma) are levers used to increase or decrease the value assigned to each part of the algorithm.

In short, the outcome we get is based on where we start and what we perceive as relevant minus what we perceive as not relevant. And we manipulate the outcome by changing how much value we place on where we start, what we perceive as relevant, or what we perceive as not relevant. Also, we manipulate the outcome by changing what we perceive as relevant or what we perceive as not relevant. And that's Rocchio's algorithm.

This key concept from 1971 keeps popping up in the research literature as if it's new. Nearly 50 years later, for example, the article "An Unethical Optimization Principle"[9] proposed an unethical optimization principle. The authors' "new" mathematical formula was presented as a way to prevent AI from making unethical decisions. But their formula $T(s) = A(s) - C(s) + Q(s)$ is reminiscent of Rocchio's algorithm wrapped in a private sector three-piece suit. $T(s) = A(s) - C(s) + Q(s)$ refers to a company's true risk-adjusted return as the risk-adjusted return minus the risk-adjusted costs plus any errors between returns. The definition of risk varies by company but centers on economic penalty as perceived by the company's shareholders. Economic penalty is only one form of risk to consider because public reputation of the company, for instance, can be at risk if unethical decisions are executed. How a company defines what it determines to be risky shapes how the company engages with constructing its products and services, interacts with its personnel, supports its customers, and sees its contribution or hindrance to improving humanity. Regardless, the $T(s)$ formula is assuming that returns, costs, and errors are monoliths. They are not.

$$\vec{q}_m = \alpha \vec{q}_0 + \beta \frac{1}{|D_r|} \sum_{\vec{d}_j \in D_r} \vec{d}_j - \gamma \frac{1}{|D_{nr}|} \sum_{\vec{d}_j \in D_{nr}} \vec{d}_j$$

Many of the approaches to humanize algorithmic work try to recapture our humanity by wanting to amplify what we perceive as relevant or good—that's adding optimal data and datasets with a perfection we haven't seen. On the other hand, we want to remove the undesired or bad elements we observe in the perceived not-relevant items. The rub is that while perceived relevant items have commonalities that overlap quite nicely, the same doesn't apply to items that aren't perceived as relevant. The ability to identify, isolate, and remove nonrelevant or bad items becomes even more challenging because there's an absence of a consistent pattern that defines its irrelevancy.

So what do we do now that we know these things? (1) Tell others, (2) check your tech solutionism at the door (refer to the questions posed throughout Part II, "Accountability," to get started), and (3) include others outside of tech to identify paths forward. Tech can help *and* hurt the situation. It's critical that we evaluate both sides before implementing tech approaches. We can reduce the harms to minoritized communities. The path forward is wayward, meandering and not conveniently standardizable. Minimizing harmful snafus and faux pas prioritizes human dignity. It arguably is a better business decision by increasing customer loyalty, employee retention, and potentially shifting/reducing human resources and public relations budgets.

The companies creating and releasing tech to the public know the harms that will be inflicted and calculate (predict) the amount and duration of backlash they'll receive from the public. Yet they deploy anyway. They have calculated that it will blow over. Time will defuse any anger. The negative press, costs, and other potential consequences can be absorbed by the company. Tech's playbook counterbalances any negative press with positive press that obfuscates their accountability and centers the oppressed as problem solvers. The go-to play is pushing a false narrative that the tech workforce hasn't reached demographic parity for Black people because there isn't "enough good Black talent—we can't find them." April Christina Curley,[10] former Historically Black College and Universities (HBCU) diversity specialist at Google, famously laid out on Twitter (December 21, 2020) the internal company messaging she experienced that entrenched discrimination of HBCU intern and employee candidates. Subsequent reporting revealed organizational and cultural issues with their Google Tech Exchange program.[11] A 60-minute meeting with a few Google leadership and several HBCU presidents,[12] intended to discuss Google company culture toward HBCUs and their students, resulted in a nothing-burger of a joint statement sent to CNN on January 31, 2021: "We are all encouraged about the future partnership. . . . The meeting paved the way for a more substantive partnership in a number of areas, from increased hiring to capacity building efforts that will increase the pipeline of tech talent from HBCUs."

By February 15, 2021, Google announced an initiative to teach 100,000 Black women digital skills[13]—using only Google products of course, as shown in Figure 10.1. A partnership with Black Greek sororities cemented their pipeline access to Black women for the training, interview preparation, mentoring, and networking plans. On June 18, 2021, the announcement "Apple and Google Award more than $50 Million to HBCUs"[14] hit the newsreels—one day prior to the inaugural federal observance for Juneteenth, when enslaved Black Texans were informed of their freedom on June 19, 1865, nearly 2.5 years after the Emancipation Proclamation was issued. This initiative aims to "build equity for HBCU computing education, help job seekers find tech roles, and provide opportunities to accelerate their careers." There's no mentioning of changes to Google's recruiting, hiring, or retention practices. There's no mention of changes to how their tech is designed with inclusion in mind. There's no mention of increasing the percentage of Black tech workers in managerial or C-suite positions by any date. The algorithmic influencers at these organizations, who are overwhelmingly not Black or women, keep doing what they have been doing. They will ultimately decide which algorithms get created, implemented, and executed, at scale.

The modus operandi is clear: our algorithms got us into this algorithmic siege on our humanity, and our algorithms will get us out. There's no standard practice of finding harms that exist or manifest in data. And the harms are considered blunt objects—affecting different communities and people the same, but that's far from the truth. Monolithic tech innovation breeds an octopus of mistreatment, misuse, and mistrust. Regaining that trust isn't the focus of many in tech or the structural sieges they concoct. It would be a happy or fortunate byproduct, though. The goal is to persuade us to take another chance, to try playing algorithmic roulette again. But everyone (in tech) knows, the House *always* wins.

Figure 10.1: False narration of the Black tech pipeline problem

Source: Twitter, Inc.

The call is to each of us, as algorithmic influencers, to go beyond the use case and seek out the usefulness of the tech-based AI-assisted product or services. Groupthink wants us to go along and *not* ask probative questions. Group re(think) allows us to reimagine *if* we'd recommend a tech-based AI-assisted product or service. Group re(think) has us consider whether tech solutionism is driving the project steps and phases, rather than the issue in need of a remedy. Group re(think) permits us to envision the tech house not winning so that the algorithmic mistreatment, misuse, and mistrust aren't scaled digitally. The preexisting assumptions, the "good" and the "bad" of mathematical formulation of fixing social, economic, and political ills are no longer siloed for easier computation. As algorithmic influencers, we consider the continuum of contextualizing the role tech *may* play in improving people's lives.

Flyaway Fairness

The reckoning of those affected by algorithmic impacts jumped into the national and international spotlight by the mid-2010s because the cases of harm—legal, moral, social, economic, or political—became too many for the tech community to make excuses for. In 2015, numerous news sources[15] reported on a disturbing phenomenon of gorillas displaying as part of photo search results when the keyword search included Black people on Google. This algorithmic harm reactivated recent history of when Black people were displayed like zoo animals, like the Belgium's Human Zoos of the Congolese people in 1958,[16] or when the COMPAS recidivism algorithm[17] was exposed in 2016, as we've already discussed in Chapter 1, "Oppression by. . ."

And in early 2018, at the then brand-new conference called Fairness, Accountability, and Transparency, Joy Buolamwini and Timnit Gebru presented their research on racial and gender biases aspects of commercial AI and facial analysis tools from Amazon, IBM, and Microsoft. "Gender Shades: Intersectional Accuracy Disparities in Commercial Gender Classification"[18] added a heavy dose of fuel to the algorithmic discrimination discourse from people in the tech, public, private, and civic sectors. This groundbreaking work *quantitively* demonstrated inequities, at scale, by automated decision systems used by government and nongovernment organizations. The backlash was severe and included online harassers, with trolls cyberbullying and discrediting the research once *The New York Times*[19] published an article about it in January 2019. Amazon issued a litany of criticisms—publicly, even after Buolamwini requested that they give them a preview of the research before its publication. Buolamwini responded with a detailed accounting days later, published on Medium.[20] The quantitative evidence is particularly threatening to the tech industry. It became rooted in a currency that tech understands: data (which they interpret as facts), performance metrics, and benchmarking (comparing outcomes from several algorithms). The misclassification of Black people as gorillas in 2015[15] and the imbalanced automated recidivism scoring system in 2016 were cast as rare instances of unintentional tech harms. It checked the first two tech currency buckets—data and performance metrics. But Gender Shades checked all three, with the research led by a person holding multiple minoritized identities, and directly adversely affected by the tech. Gender Shades as research and the treatment of its scholars couldn't be swept under the rug. It was a tipping ripple that turned into a wave referendum on who is building these automated systems and how our humanity is being compromised one algorithm at a time.

Algorithmic Fairness

The social justice and tech worlds collide. Much of the national and international attention still focuses on how white privilege harms non-white people, while ignoring how white privilege uplifts white people. We need deeper understandings and redress of how white privilege uplifts white people. But like we'd said before: tech as an industry stays singular in its pursuit to persuade us to take another chance on playing algorithmic roulette. They hope the outcome will be different. Everyone (in tech) knows, though, that the House *always* wins. They turn the negative into a positive—fiscally supporting the dominant male culture and white supremacy while avoiding addressing the bulk of the concerns/harms exacerbated through tech solutionism.

The narrative and discussions surrounding fairness in algorithms are troublesome. Avoiding bias as well as fairness in and of technology are misnomers. Bias exists in unquantifiable and varying degrees. We, at least in the computer science continuum of data science, are attempting to create fairness and bias computationally aware metrics. But in what situation has everyone agreed that they were treated fairly? "Life isn't fair" is a common colloquialism.

Since we, as a human race, have yet to experience fairness in the physical world, then there is no model to represent it in the digital world. The tech industry has reduced the discrimination in automated decision systems and data/algorithms more broadly to accurately portray what scholars want to do—which is to computationally minimize discrimination. What does this really mean? Discrimination, injustice, "bias," and its synonyms become a mathematical problem where they search for a mathematical solution. And they've coined it "algorithmic fairness."

Algorithmic fairness has been defined by many scholars like Cathy O'Neil in her book *Weapons of Math Destruction*[21] and Virginia Eubanks in her book *Automating Inequality*.[22] (Seriously, add both to the book club and widen your eyes to the spectrum of systemic inequities, if you haven't read them.) Cynthia Dwork, in her 2018 talk at Microsoft Research (www.youtube.com/watch?v=g-z84_nRQhw), said that "we don't have a straight mathematical answer for where we're going to get the metric." Fairness, algorithmically, tends to be broken down into three general definition characteristics[23] for computer scientists:

- **Treating similar individuals similarly:** If two people are deemed similar across their attributes by way of a similarity distance measure (like Euclidean distance), then both people should receive comparable outcomes. On its face, this is unachievable. Two people can be similar to each other and have very different outcomes. And similarity is another situational and contextual notion. For example, two Black women with PhDs walk into their consulting agency; are they similar? If this sounds bonkers and dehumanizing, it is.

- **Never favor a worse individual over a better one:** In the case of ordering people based on some arbitrary criteria, the "worse" person can't have a higher ranking than the "better" person. If your mind immediately goes to a meritocracy framing, then you understand this. And you know that meritocracy as our society operationalized it is another relabeling of white supremacist thought. You have to do it the white way for it to be considered worthy of merit.

- **Calibrated fairness:** Fairness is a distribution based on merit. Well, who decides merit? And how is this fair? For example, with 100 applicants for a job, 80 are white and 20 are Black. To calibrate you decide you'll interview the top 10 percent from each racial group. So you interview 8 white people and 2 Black people. You've just calibrated an 80 percent chance of hiring a white person. And yes, this example should remind you of W.E.B. DuBois's book *The Talented Tenth*—which stipulated a ceiling on what Black progression can be and internalizes white supremacist thought (`http://moses.law.umn.edu/darrow/documents/Talented_Tenth.pdf`).

All the definitions, whether they are based on statistics, computing, or some other field, funnel to the same conclusion. Fairness is in search of making equality, not equity. But things are equal due to differences in political, social, economic, and computational contexts. Mitchell et al.[24] said it best: "While mathematical definitions in the algorithmic fairness literature discussed . . . may be able to certify the fair allocation of decisions across a population, they have nothing to say about whether any of the available actions are acceptable in the first place." And let us not forget the compounding nature and effects of these actions and decisions.

A real limiting condition is the binary yes-or-no framing of high-profile algorithmic fairness approaches. There's no room for examination or investigation of the disparate impacts of a person or situation having satisfied multiple criteria simultaneously. As a Black woman, Kimberlé Crenshaw coined and developed intersectionality in 1988.[25] It serves as a means to describe the interdependence of race, class, gender, and other individual characteristics and how different forms of discrimination and privilege manifest. In a situation, scholars force choices with cascading effects that aren't accounted for downstream of the algorithmic process like assessing individual fairness versus group fairness or addressing inequities in the dataset versus classification algorithm. Pairwise evaluation in computing sits at the core of these approaches. The pattern is "If it's not A, then it's B." Our society doesn't work like that. In real life, "If it's not A, then it could be any combination of B, C, D, . . ."

Broadening Fairness

Fairness is contextual. "Model Cards for Model Reporting,"[26] published by Google Ethical AI researchers in 2018, gives us a framework to document this context. The goal and process is straightforward for those in tech: perform a preprocessing step to an automated/AI model to reveal the capabilities and, more importantly, the limitations of that model so that the limitations may be addressed by the developers before moving forward in the software development life cycle. Face and object detection model cards (`https://modelcards.withgoogle.com/model-reports`) are shared as demonstrations of how to record the model's input and output, model architecture, performance evaluation, trade-offs, and limitations. It provides a workspace, or in the pre-Internet days a scratchpad, to capture potential impacts and harms of the model. It's like an executive summary for automated models that includes code, visualizations, and narrative.

The Model Card Toolkit (`https://github.com/tensorflow/model-card-toolkit`) was born and exists as an open source JSON schema (available in GitHub) to make adoption easier for developers. Other companies mimicked this framework soon thereafter: the Google-Microsoft-IBM joint venture called Responsible AI Licenses (RAIL; `www.licenses.ai`), the multi-institution-born SECure framework (`https://montrealethics.ai/secure-a-social-and-environmental-certificate-for-ai-systems-2`), and PriceWaterhouseCoopers' Responsible AI Toolkit (`www.pwc.com/gx/en/issues/data-and-analytics/artificial-intelligence/what-is-responsible-ai.html`), just to name a few.

Frameworks and toolkits are only as good as how they are integrated into business operations. The transparency sought in designing these frameworks clarifies the gaps innate to quantitative. Transparency notions fall off a cliff when honing in on how the developers decided which model's input and output, model architecture, or performance evaluation process to follow. That's the secret sauce—that's what developers need to better understand. So let's back up and be more rigorous in our qualitative assessment in this fairness estimation processing:

- Which fairness definition are we operating under? Refer to the three descriptions provided in the previous section: (1) Treating similar individuals similarly, (2) Never favor a worse individual over a better one, and (3) Calibrated fairness. And we'll be crossing our fingers that the dev team reaches a consensus on the definition choice.

- What are our fairness expectations? How do we know if we've reached our fairness goals? Noting an "improvement" in the absence of ground truth has empty worth, especially to minoritized communities.

- How do we assess the disparate impact of our fairness goals? Demonstrating an approach as perceivably fair can shift or direct privilege or harm to another group. Unearthing hidden fairness issues is like finding and correcting one computer bug just to have hundreds more reveal themselves. Realizing the limits of fairness helps us to see it as an option rather than the solution.

It's encouraging that existing automated models and algorithms are getting a second glance by software developers. The premise of this second glance, however, remains tech-skewed. A tech solution will be chosen so the underlying intent is still trying to justify the final automated model selection using quantitative calculations. And there's a large void in where these frameworks are applied in practice and to what degree they help achieve fairness goals.

The discourse around fairness became complicated very quickly in the tech arena. So the tech industry does what it always does—shift to a more suitable (e.g., tech manageable) problem. Enter Explainable AI, a $3.5 billion industry as of 2020. Explainable AI is intended to translate what a machine is doing so that people can understand it. It's a play on transparency with a hint of fairness:

if you can explain what the computers are doing, then people won't perceive that the computers are being unfair. SHapley Additive exPlanations (SHAP)[27] hit NeurIPS (Conference and Workshop on Neural Information Processing Systems) 2017 like a ton of bricks as an exemplar case of Explainable AI. Lungberg and Lee's scholarly work[28] provided an explanation model for machine learning predictions. Using game theory as a backdrop, SHAP calculates and explains the contribution of each feature to a prediction. It's a method to reverse-engineer calibrated fairness. SHAP values are complicated to compute (in fact, NP hard), but essentially they numerically define how far away a feature's actual value is from that feature's predicted value. Imagine an (x, y) plot with a bunch of points scattered (these represent the actual values). Now imagine drawing a straight diagonal line that cuts across these points as evenly as possible, meaning we have an equal number of points on the left side and the right side of that line. This line represents the predicted values. If the actual point is to the left of the line for a certain x-coordinate, then we calculate a negative SHAP value. Otherwise we calculate a positive SHAP value. SHAP, at its core, imposes a fairness allocation equation by way of that straight linear line identifying predicted values. And Explainable AI didn't squelch more transparency and better fairness calls from within and outside the tech community.

IBM's AI Fairness 360 (`https://aif360.mybluemix.net`), released in late 2018, provides a more comprehensive full-stack fairness model that intends to mitigate bias (not discrimination) in datasets and classifiers. The combination of demos, tutorials, videos, APIs, resource libraries, and GitHub software repositories lays out a path to adopt the tech. Because it's open source, there's lots of encouragement to add to GitHub. As a software developer, you can get your name associated with contributing to the algorithmic fairness materials. The perception is that you're doing tech for good, but the rationale for doing this work isn't always pure. And the jury is still out whether algorithmic fairness systems are good for tech or whether they further bury and codify inequities. These software developers are operating as algorithmic influencers—just like what we've seen when it comes to social media influencers. Social media influencers have a large and broad audience; their reach is gigantic, so what they share with their followers cascades deeply and quickly. The knife cuts both ways, though. A correct or harmful message gains traction for them. Promoting the correct message is the desired outcome, but when the statements misrepresent the truth it's impossible to retract. (Remember how Black women scholars were erased from the *60 Minutes* episode about facial recognition in 2021? If not, check out the racial and gender discrimination in facial analysis snippet (`https://twitter.com/csdoctorsister/status/1394136497805275136`).

Software developers are tech rock stars with a lot of sway on which open source GitHub repositories are adopted and adapted by fellow developers. And people who develop software packages that others find valuable gain a certain tech capital that's stronger, more covert, and lasts longer than social capital on a platform. As long as algorithmic fairness garners developer-beneficial tech capital, algorithmic influencers will create, amplify, adopt, and adapt algorithmic fairness approaches. This is a cynical point-of-view and leans into the white tech-bro bravado, hard. Give examples to the contrary.

Practically, algorithmic fairness scholars and practitioners would be seeking ways to evaluate how their approaches impact people. That's a sociological effort. Or how their approaches impact business. That's an economic and political effort. They instead examine how their approaches impact tech, which can't mathematically equation fairness. It doesn't make sense. Compounding this nonsense with the dearth of racial/ethnic and gender representation on data teams and lack of people-driven checks and balances automated decision system regulation/screenings, it's no mystery why algorithmic fairness as a movement shifts to a trend. We've reached an evolution stage that calls on companies to use these algorithmic fairness frameworks, toolkits, and systems with such regularity that their use is adopted and documented for third parties, such as the public, to scrutinize. Minimizing what they call bias as a proxy for discrimination and inequities needs clear messaging—how much time is saved by deploying these algorithmic fairness approaches or how much HR and/or PR monies is saved by choosing one of these algorithmic fairness approaches. We can't escape our capitalistic society, right now, so it'll be easier to make the business case to answer the holy grail question of why we should add algorithmic fairness checks to their tech building machine. We're currently battling the inefficiency response—it costs time, company money, and employee talent resources to bother integrating fairness. And the public doesn't understand (or care to understand) the impact of unjust scaled tech solutions.

As tech culture races to "move fast and break things," let's shift the goalposts to "move intentionally and make tech fairer for vulnerable communities." It's an unpopular and hard sell, for sure. Recall that you are an algorithmic influencer with the power to ask pointed questions about how fairness is evaluated and assessed within your team and organization. Reinforcing the information-gathering process of the algorithmic implementations purporting fairness around the most vulnerable communities reverberates to all those in the decision-making chain. A fairness development life cycle that's in alignment with the software development life cycle can bring clarity to where social, economic, political, and technical strategies are valuable. This "something-is-better-than-nothing" framing for algorithmic fairness breeds chaos and could be introducing harms outside the scope of existing mitigation approaches. We're experiencing the collective backlash of interdisciplinary inaction with regard to fairness every time we log on to a platform.

Moderation Modes

Content moderation, according to Grimmelmann,[29] consists of the "governance mechanisms that structure participation in a community to facilitate cooperation and prevent abuse." Figure 10.2 presents the backbone of content moderation approaches. User-generated content enters the platform or another digital system where a series of machine learning algorithms are executed to automatically screen and vet the appropriateness of the content. If the content doesn't raise any platform governance issues, the content is posted. If the content violates the platform's governance guidelines, the content is labeled as sensitive content, not posted, or removed depending on the perceived severity of the media. Otherwise the content is considered potentially problematic, then it's forwarded to human content moderators to review manually and decide on whether the content can be posted. The pain point for handling content moderation on platforms is how to deal with the fast influx of user-generated content.

We're in a vicious cycle of more data begets more data. Controlling data/content has become a top priority for platforms, which use a combination of human content moderators and automated content moderation practices, as detailed in Gillespie's *Custodians of the Internet*.[30] Human content moderators were deemed sufficient given the manageable content generation rate of the early Internet. However, manual content screening soon couldn't keep up with the rate of user-generated content. Automated content moderation strategies were built to help handle the additional workload and, in theory, conduct the moderation more efficiently. Some particularly offensive content, like child pornography, takes a severe psychological toll on human content moderators, and automated content moderation algorithms can protect people from manually screening that content.

> **NOTE** Facebook and Twitter have received frequent attention related to labor issues regarding their content moderation practices. Facebook's content moderators have spoken out about the lack of mental health support[31] and overall unconducive work experience (`https://twitter.com/RMac18/status/1382366931307565057?s=20`). Paul M. Barrett's 2020 report on content moderation and consequences[32] calls for Facebook to make content moderators in-house employees, rather than third-party contract workers, and to triple this workforce, among other recommendations.

Still, content moderation remains difficult. Content exists that algorithms can't discern because the nuances of our culture aren't as predictable as once believed. Social, economic, political, technical/algorithmic, gender, and racial factors all impact Black women. Society's approach is to silo these factors and address them one at a time with the mindset that solving the individual factors will help solve all the issues.

Most approaches seek to standardize the pain points, meaning that the newly enacted solutions are supposed to affect all the communities in the same way. Standardizing the identification and handling of perceived and actual problematic content thrives on establishing a sameness criterion, demonstrating consistent patterns of inappropriate content and a universal effective routine for solving the problems—which doesn't work in our global society, where we're much more multicultural in our demographic composition.

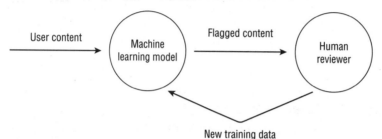

Figure 10.2: How content moderation works

Source: Devin Soni 2019 / Towards Data Science

This isn't an addition problem of disparate impacts. It's more like a multiplication problem of disparate impacts. The end result of the simplistic approach is inconsistent moderation practices that silence Black women.

Double Standards

Content moderation operates simultaneously in two directions: (1) ways in which a user interacts with the platform, and (2) ways in which the platform interacts with the user. For instance, blocking a user is an exemplar of content moderation practice that allows a user to directly control their interactions with the platform. Both Twitter and Facebook implemented this control similarly. For Twitter's blocking rules,[33] "[b]locking only works if the account you've blocked is logged in on Twitter. For example, if the account you've blocked isn't logged in or is accessing Twitter content via a third party, they may be able to see your public Tweets." Facebook limits interactions through blocking protocols[34] so the blocked account won't be able to see anything the other account posts on its timeline, tag you, send an invite, try to friend, or start a conversation. Mutual followers/friends provide an avenue for the blocked accounts to see each other's content, yet doesn't infringe on those mutual connections' digital rights from posting content.

On the contrary, when the platform is in the driver's seat, content moderation practices lean on more heavily automated decision systems and protocols. The balance between social structures and technical processes collide. Reply tweets, by their opaque design and implementation, are candidates for online harassment violations. On Twitter's Offensive Content page,[35] it states that "[p]eople are allowed to post content, including potentially inflammatory content, as long as they're not violating the Twitter Rules".[36] It's important to know that Twitter does not screen content or remove potentially offensive content. But then further down the web page, it states that "[i]f your Tweet reply is identified as using potentially harmful or offensive language, we may ask you, via a prompt, if you want to review it before sending." The tweet originator is part of an implicit protected class over the tweet commenter. The tweet commenter is notified that their content has been reviewed and potentially deemed violating the platform's rules. The tweet originator doesn't receive the same treatment. In essence, one can interpret that uncomfortable conversations are discouraged by the platform. One way to circumvent Twitter Rules and uneven content moderation practices is to use the quote tweet feature.

Nominally, content moderation is subject to platform standards and guidelines, such as Facebook's Community Standards.[37] At Facebook, 23 different categories make up their content moderation guidelines, covering violence and criminal behavior, safety, objectionable content, integrity and authenticity, intellectual property, and content-related requests and decisions. Facebook broadly details what content is deemed inappropriate, yet refrains from sharing how their standards are enacted.

For example, Carolyn Wysinger, a high school teacher in Richmond, California, had her Facebook comment deleted within 15 minutes for hate speech even though she was responding to Liam Neeson's anti-Black remarks (www.usatoday.com/ story/news/2019/04/24/facebook-while-black-zucked-users-say-they-get- blocked-racism-discussion/2859593002).[38] While promoting a revenge movie, the Hollywood actor confessed that decades earlier, after a female friend told him she'd been raped by a Black man she could not identify, he'd "roamed the streets hunting for Black men to harm" (www.usatoday.com/story/life/people/2019/02/04/ liam-neeson-reveals-shocking-racially-charged-past/2766111002).[39]

The actor's remarks were not removed. Violence against Black men, for being Black, isn't content designated to be removed from the platform, but calling white men fragile is considered hate speech? According to Facebook's 23 categories, it seems that Liam Neeson's content breached both their Violence and Incitement and Hate Speech policies. It's unclear which community standard policy Wysinger's post violated.

Women are called fragile, weak, and sensitive regularly, yet that speech isn't marked as hate speech. Or, was it the word "fragile" in conjunction with "white men" that triggered the automated content moderation algorithms? We don't know, because transparent contention moderation algorithms, processes, and practices elude us. We do have access to Facebook's Community Standards Enforcement Report[40], which is heavily sanitized, presenting aggregated and summarized data.

At Twitter, 15 rule categories[36] are covered under the content moderation umbrella. These are divided into four groups: safety, privacy, authenticity and enforcement, and appeals. The content moderation decisions are swift and harsh for Black women.

Consider the case of Shana V. White, currently the Senior Associate, CS Equity and Justice Initiatives at the Kapor Center. As a computer science educator with 16 years of experience, she engages her over 25,000 Twitter followers as a vital advocate for teachers and marginalized communities. It started when Jason S. Campbell, a supporter of Rick Santorum, posted a video clip of Rick Santorum's speech on Twitter stating his belief that Native American culture isn't in American culture (https://twitter.com/JasonSCampbell/status/1386685340522536961?s=20), as shown in Figure 10.3.

Figure 10.3: Original tweet post by CNN's Rick Santorum saying that "We birthed a nation from nothing. I mean, there was nothing here. I mean, yes we have Native Americans but candidly there isn't much Native American culture in American culture."
Source: Twitter, Inc.

White was permanently banned from the platform on April 26, 2021, for her comments as screen captured by another Twitter user, Shea Wesley Martin, displayed in Figure 10.4. White had responded to Campbell, who supported former Senator Rick Santorum's disinformation narrative about Native Americans. She appealed and her account was restored that evening. Days later, on May 4, 2021,

White once again issued a comment in defense of a marginalized community and was permanently banned again. After three appeal attempts and a Black woman advocating for White's Twitter account restatement, she announced her return to Twitter on May 27, 2021 (`https://twitter.com/ShanaVWhite/status/1397873437197078530?s=20`).

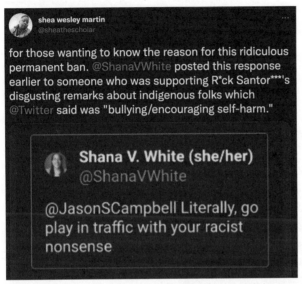

Figure 10.4: Twitter response to alleged community code violation: "For those wanting to know the reason for this ridiculous permanent ban. @ShanaVWhite posted this response earlier to someone who was supporting R*ck Santor***'s disgusting remarks about indigenous folks which @Twitter said was 'bullying/encouraging self-harm.'"

Source: Twitter, Inc.

So a post sharing disinformation about the United States's history remains viewable to the public (~9.8M views), but a snarky and sarcastic comment results in the profile's permanent ban? The initial post seems to violate the Platform Manipulation and Spam policy. Like Facebook, Twitter's Transparency Report[41] is also heavily sanitized, presenting aggregated and summarized data. It's untraceable on why the original post by Campbell didn't violate misinformation or disinformation campaigning rules.

White's response seems to have violated Twitter's Suicide/Self-Harm policy. However, again, we don't know what triggered this violation because transparent contention moderation algorithms, processes, and practices elude us. From April 26, 2021 to May 20, 2021, White received three notification emails from Twitter that listed which of their policies they believe she violated.

Notification #1

From: Twitter `<notify@twitter.com>`

Date: Mon, Apr 26, 2021 at 11:15 AM

Subject: Your Twitter account has been suspended

To: Shana V. White (she/her)

Hello Shana V. White (she/her),

Your account, ShanaVWhite has been suspended for violating the Twitter Rules.

Specifically, for:

Violating our rules against promoting or encouraging suicide or self-harm.

You may not promote or encourage suicide or self-harm. When we receive reports that a person is threatening suicide or self-harm, we may take a number of steps to assist them, such as reaching out to that person and providing resources such as contact information for our mental health partners.

If you are having thoughts of self-harm, suicide, or depression, we encourage you to please reach out to someone and request help. Our Safety Center has a list of resources you can consult for a variety of reasons, including depression, lone-liness, substance abuse, illness, relationship problems, and economic problems. You can find those resources here: `https://about.twitter.com/safety/ safety-partners.html#mental-health/us.`

Please know that there are people out there who care about you, and that you are not alone.

The tweet itself is referenced: Shana V. White (she/her) @ShanaVWhite @ JasonSCampbell Literally, go play in traffic with your racist nonsense.

Note that if you attempt to evade a permanent suspension by creating new accounts, we will suspend your new accounts. If you wish to appeal this suspension, please contact our support team.

Notification #2

From: Twitter `<notify@twitter.com>`

Date: Tue, May 4, 2021 at 6:53 PM

Subject: Your Twitter account has been suspended

To: Shana V. White (she/her)

Hello Shana V. White (she/her),

Your account, ShanaVWhite has been suspended for violating the Twitter Rules.

Specifically, for:

Violating our rules against promoting or encouraging suicide or self-harm.

You may not promote or encourage suicide or self-harm. When we receive reports that a person is threatening suicide or self-harm, we may take a number of steps to assist them, such as reaching out to that person and providing resources such as contact information for our mental health partners.

If you are having thoughts of self-harm, suicide, or depression, we encourage you to please reach out to someone and request help. Our Safety Center has a list of resources you can consult for a variety of reasons, including depression, loneliness, substance abuse, illness, relationship problems, and economic problems. You can find those resources here: `https://about.twitter.com/safety/` `safety-partners.html#mental-health/us.`

Please know that there are people out there who care about you, and that you are not alone.

The tweet itself is referenced: Shana V. White (she/her) @ShanaVWhite @ MattWalshBlog Please go jump into a lake of fire you racist.

Note that if you attempt to evade a permanent suspension by creating new accounts, we will suspend your new accounts. If you wish to appeal this suspension, please contact our support team.

Notification #3

From: Twitter Support `<support@twitter.com>`

Date: Thu, May 20, 2021 at 2:58 AM

Subject: Case# 0207320655: Appealing an account suspension - @ShanaVWhite [ref:_00DA0K0A8._5004w28zjd8:ref]

To: shana V. White (she/her)

Hello,

Your account has been suspended and will not be restored because it was found to be violating the Twitter Terms of Service, specifically the Twitter Rules against participating in targeted abuse.

In order to ensure that people feel safe expressing diverse opinions and beliefs on our platform, we do not tolerate abusive behavior. This includes inciting other people to engage in the targeted harassment of someone.

You can learn more about our rules against abusive behavior.

Thanks,

Twitter

In these content moderation snafus and the handful of others collected, it's the Black women who are responding to incendiary posts and then de-voiced as a consistent outcome. Black women who defend themselves or others are tagged as the agitators who need to be tone policed by white colonialists in powerful positions.

We don't know how much of this algorithmic misogynoir is ignited by content moderation algorithms or by fellow users' reporting their content. Still, the final decision of their content's appropriateness, regardless of the outcome, becomes part of the platform's online portfolio of their suspected and attributed violations (see Twitter's consequences section in their hateful conduct policy, as an example[42]). This is reminiscent of an online version of the U.S. criminal system, where once a person is tagged an agitator it is very difficult to reduce or remove that perception. Twitter lays out a ladder of content moderation enforcement options[43]—including tweet-level, direct message–level, and account-level, with permanent suspension being the most severe—but the escalation process for content moderation enforcement remains confusing.

Calling Out Algorithmic Misogynoir

While we are one human race, social, economic, and political constructs impose a hierarchy that centers white colonialist culture and white patriarchy through manipulation, coercion, or force. These social, economic, and political structures are not designed for equity. Rather, they're designed to de-value everything but white culture. As Gulati-Partee and Potapchuk discuss in their work on advancing racial equity, "[r]acial disparities are driven and maintained by public- and private-sector policies that not only disadvantage communities of color but also over-advantage whites."[44]

We exist in a global society that exudes anti-Blackness—and this is true for online spaces as well. The tech industry is monopolized by white men in ownership,[45] leadership,[46] and the workforce.[47] When building businesses, Black women are invested in at funding levels 20 times less than the median national funding level that includes all demographics of business owners. This demonstrates how much more difficult it is for Black women to raise the capital they need and stunts their revenue growth. Men account for 70 percent–80 percent of the tech leadership roles and workforce. This industry has built a well-documented culture of toxicity, where men hold all the cards and make all the rules and covert structural racism persists.[48-49] And this toxic tech culture perpetuates in the classroom with computer science education not very committed to changing its culture.[50] These circumstances make the pursuit of equitable practices tenuous at best.

Being a Black woman—offline and online—means existing on one of two extremes: (1) no one pays attention to what you say or how you say it, or (2) your words are fodder for scrutiny, surveillance, and judgment. Being simultaneously invisible and hypervisible is a consistent theme (as explored in Tressie McMillian Cottom's *Thick*[51]) and the result of part of what Moya Bailey calls misogynoir (Crunk Feminist Collective, March 2010[52]), the "anti-Black racist misogyny that Black women experience." The Abuse and Misogynoir Playbook[53] sheds light on a five-phase cycle of disbelieving, devaluing, and discrediting the contributions of Black women as the historical norm. Algorithmic misogynoir builds on Bailey's description to identify how these interactions play out online and in code for Black women.

In digital spaces, Black women's presence, experiences, and interactions include everything from communicating our accomplishments to sharing our trauma. But now, the interactions and responses come extremely quickly, from real, bot, and troll profiles from anywhere on the globe.

Black people and women are more likely to be the targets of online harassment than their white and male counterparts.[54] Black women have been criticized internationally for their scholarship, had platform posts removed for statements that aren't met with as much scrutiny as their white counterparts, and been suspended or banned from a platform for speaking out against any form of algorithmic discrimination.

Black women's distinct circumstances aren't recognized and centered. The 2018 Stop Online Violence Against Black Women report[55] showed how online campaigns using Facebook ads were created to disparage Black girls and women with sexualized memes, hashtags, and fake accounts to help spread disinformation ahead of and during the 2016 U.S. presidential election. And Charisse C. Levchek's *Microaggressions and Modern Racism* (https://link.springer.com/book/10.1007/978-3-319-70332-9) documents anti-Black racism at the micro and macro level, both via in-person and online interactions. Levchek points to racial slurs and other forms of hate speech done by micro-aggressors and macro-aggressors on the Internet. She specifically calls on organizations to enact policies and procedures to address instances of racism, penalize these micro/macro-aggressors, and support survivors of racism.

All this falls under what Ariadna Matamoros-Fernandez[56] calls "platformed racism," which is "a new form of racism derived from the culture of social media platforms—their design, technical affordances, business models and policies—and the specific cultures of use associated with them." Content moderation can work toward creating inclusive, welcoming spaces for Black women, but current practices embrace misogynoir and then deploy it algorithmically.

Here are a few more high-profile content moderation and online harassment instances.

- Dr. Safiya Noble's *Algorithms of Oppression: How Search Engines Reinforce Racism* was publicly criticized on Twitter[57] by a staff historian from the Institute of Electrical and Electronics Engineers (IEEE), an international professional society. The staff historian hadn't read the book prior to posting his commentary under the IEEE umbrella. The post was taken down only after public outrage.

- Joy Buolamwini, Timnit Gebru, Helen Raynham, and Deborah Raji's Gender Shades paper[18] on racial and gender discrimination in commercial facial recognition software drew sizable international critique from Amazon, which developed one of the technologies evaluated in the paper. Amazon went so far as to post their disagreement with the paper's findings on their blog.[58] Buolamwini responded using Medium articles like this to share their prior communications with each company about the racial and gender inequities in their facial analysis findings.

- Timit Gebru contended with online harassers[59] when discussing Duke University's PULSE AI tool,[60] a human face creation technology. Her pioneering work in algorithmic inequities in artificial intelligence were minimized, she was addressed as if she were too emotional or hysterical to be rational for the discourse, she endured mansplaining,[61] and experienced the earmarks of being treated unfairly like an angry Black woman.[62]

- Months later, Dr. Gebru advocated for more transparency about internal Google processes regarding research paper publication criteria. One of her papers, accepted for publication at a prominent international conference, was scrutinized by those inside of Google, but she did not receive clarification on the process or issues. She was abruptly terminated by the organization. As Dr. Gebru shared this experience in real time on Twitter, she was attacked again and again on Twitter after she was ousted by Google, yet her harassers retained their online profiles for months.

Data and Oversight

Current content moderation practices signal a trajectory that codifies algorithmic misogynoir. The existing public value failure (PVF) framework[63] articulates nine categories that delineate society's failure in providing a public value, such as rights, benefits, or privileges of citizens, by governments and policies.

The public values framework helps us tease out proposals that could make the internet safer for Black women. The framework tells us that an "equal playing field" is less desirable than collective actions and public policies addressing structural inequalities and historical differences in opportunity structures. It is thus important to regularly examine content moderation practices for Black women and other minorities.

It would be useful to disaggregate data by race/ethnicity and gender in content moderation guidelines, standards, practices, enforcement and legal requests. Sanitized and aggregated data hides the demographics of who flagged content, whose content was flagged, which guideline was breached by the content and how the automated content moderation algorithms decided on their outcomes. Much more work needs to be done to make transparent the automated content moderation tools, policies, and practices.

As platform engagements are an integral part of business and marketing activities, potential uneven content moderation enforcements can affect people's livelihood as well as damage their dignity and reputation online. It is also important to have independent oversight and public accountability reports and audits. This helps in establishing transparency as a central tenet of policy-making. Sharing and implementing consistent content moderation protocols are required for true transparency across sociopolitical systems. Accessible public discourse and responsive government actions can build trust with more effective communication streams. It may be helpful to have equal representation of Black women and other minorities in human content moderator teams. As public yet privately owned platforms, their users' ability to share content freely is seamless but determining the equitability of that distribution is questionable. The benefits of existing content moderation practices need to be documented, in which ways and to which communities. The ranking and prioritization protocols in content moderation benefit white communities more favorably than non-white communities. Black women, in contrast, experience punitive actions for vocalizing inequities on these same platforms.

These suggested best practices are directly contrary to what exists currently, the Global Internet Forum to Counter Terrorism (GIFCT),[64] a collaborative stating that they're "foster[ing] collaboration and information-sharing to counter terrorist and violent extremist activity online." The founding members are titans in the social media and internet community: YouTube (Google), Twitter, Facebook, and Microsoft. GIFCT's mission, vision and core values lack race, gender, class, and ableism considerations, therefore potentially infringing on progressive opportunities.

Gorwa et al.[65] eloquently describes how GIFCT's interlaced technical and political issues are grounded in opacity. We deduce that there are a series of matching and classification algorithms to handle perceived definitive (blocking, removal, etc.) and fuzzy (flagging, etc.) content moderation situations. What's missing in these approaches, however, is contextual understanding.

The specific engagements of the working groups, partnerships, and collaborations that are part of GIFCT aren't shared. Their transparency reports offer little detail on which algorithmic tools are being used in automated content moderation, or how individual users are the benefactors of this collective, resulting in the public value benefits to be unknown. Internal oversight has us on the never ending hamster wheel—ignoring, inflicting and enacting more harms than realized. It's time to add another structural support to governance: The People.

Summary

Tech's grasp on our society concerns most of us. The rockstar tech workers, or algorithmic influencers, guide every industry one software update, code version release or code library at a time. This digital power creates a tech capital that's more effective and impactful than social capital. Proper consistent checks and balances infrastructures elude us. Those of us "in" tech understand data and algorithms at a superficial level due to the pervasiveness of automated decision tasks. We can't trace all the possibilities of the decision tree. But we all "in" or "out" of tech want to desperately believe that tech can be a big part in saving us, at scale and quickly. Our humanity wants a dignified quick fix through algorithmic fairness, content moderation, and tech-regulated oversight. An elegant tech-driven suite of solutions we haven't algorithmically man-made. Algorithms aside we've hit a ceiling in what tech can and should do. The rest is up to us: to prioritize our dignity, for our humanity.

Notes

1. Tucker, Ian. "Evgeny Morozov: 'We are abandoning all the checks and balances." The Guardian. March 9, 2013. www.theguardian.com/technology/2013/mar/09/evgeny-morozov-technology-solutionism-interview.

2. Bearne, Suzanne. A wristband that tells your boss if you are unhappy. BBC News. 2021. www.bbc.com/news/business-55637328.

3. Boland, Brodie, Aaron De Smet, Rob Palter, & Aditya Sanghvi. "Reimagining the office and work-life after COVID-19." McKinsey & Company. 2020. www.mckinsey.com/business-functions/people-and-organizational-performance/our-insights/reimagining-the-office-and-work-life-after-covid-19.

4. Caldeira, Clara, Yu Chen, Lesley Chan, Vivian Pham, Yunan Chen, & Kai Zheng. "Mobile apps for mood tracking: an analysis of features and user reviews." National Center for Biotechnology Information. 2018. `www.ncbi.nlm.nih.gov/pmc/articles/PMC5977660`.

5. Knight, Will. "AI is Biased. Here's How Scientists Are Trying to Fix it." WIRED. December 19, 2019. `www.wired.com/story/ai-biased-how-scientists-trying-fix`.

6. Good News Network. "New Mathematical Formula Unveiled to Prevent AI From Making Unethical Decisions." Good News Network. July 5, 2020. `www.goodnewsnetwork.org/new-mathematical-formula-to-prevent-ai-from-making-unethical-decisions`.

7. Manning, Christopher D., Prabhakar Raghavan, & Hinrich Schütze. *Introduction to Information Retrieval*. Cambridge University Press. 2008. `https://nlp.stanford.edu/IR-book/information-retrieval-book.html`.

8. Wikipedia. "Rocchio Algorithm." Wikipedia. November 30, 2009. `https://en.wikipedia.org/wiki/Rocchio_algorithm`.

9. Beale, Nicholas, Heather Battey, Anthony C. Davison, & Robert S. MacKay. An unethical optimization principle. The Royal Society Publishing, 2020. `https://royalsocietypublishing.org/doi/10.1098/rsos.200462`.

10. Kirby, Donte. "April Christina Curley spoke out against racism at Google. Her story points to the struggles Black women face in tech." `Technical.ly`. January 22, 2021. `https://technical.ly/company-culture/april-christina-curley-google`.

11. Elias, Jennifer. "Google's program for Black college students suffered disorganization and culture clashes, former participants say." CNBC. February 21, 2021. `www.cnbc.com/2021/02/21/google-howard-west-program-faced-disorganization-culture-clashes.html`.

12. Alcorn, Chauncey. Google CEO and HBCU leaders discuss talent pipeline for Black tech workers. CNN Business. 2021. `www.cnn.com/2021/01/31/business/google-hbcus/index.html`.

13. Major, Derek. Google announces initiative to train 100,000 black women in digital skills by 2022. Black Enterprise. February 15, 2021. `www.blackenterprise.com/google-announces-initiative-to-train-100000-black-women-in-digital-skills-by-2022`.

14. Major, Derek. Apple and Google award more than $50 million to HBCUS. Black Enterprise. 2021. `www.blackenterprise.com/apple-and-google-award-more-than-50-million-to-hbcus`.

15. Pachal, Pete. "Google Photos identified two black people as 'gorillas'." Mashable. July 1, 2015. https://mashable.com/archive/google-photos-black-people-gorillas.

16. Boffey, Daniel. "Belgium comes to terms with 'human zoos' of its colonial past." The Guardian. 2018. www.theguardian.com/world/2018/apr/16/belgium-comes-to-terms-with-human-zoos-of-its-colonial-past.

17. Angwin, Julia, Jeff Larson, Surya Mattu, & Lauren Kirchner. Machine Bias. ProPublica. May 23, 2016. www.propublica.org/article/machine-bias-risk-assessments-in-criminal-sentencing.

18. Buolamwini, Joy, & Timnit Gebru. Gender Shades: Intersectional Accuracy Disparities in Commercial Gender Classification. Machine Learning Research. 2022. https://proceedings.mlr.press/v81/buolamwini18a/buolamwini18a.pdf.

19. Singer, Natasha. "Amazon Is Pushing Facial Technology That a Study Says Could Be Biased." The New York Times. January 24, 2019. www.nytimes.com/2019/01/24/technology/amazon-facial-technology-study.html.

20. Buolamwini, Joy. Response: Racial and Gender bias in Amazon Rekognition — Commercial AI System for Analyzing Faces. Medium. 2019. https://medium.com/@Joy.Buolamwini/response-racial-and-gender-bias-in-amazon-rekognition-commercial-ai-system-for-analyzing-faces-a289222eeced.

21. O'Neil, Cathy. Weapons of Math Destruction. Harlow, England: Penguin Books, 2017.

22. Eubanks, Virginia. "Automating Inequality: How High-tech Tools Profile, Police, and Punish the Poor". New York, NY: St. Martin's Press, 2018.

23. Ani Saxena, Nripsuta, Karen Huang, Evan DeFilippis, Yang Liu, David C. Parkes, & Goran Radanovic. How Do Fairness Definitions Fare? Examining Public Attitudes Towards Algorithmic Definitions of Fairness." Harvard University. 2022. https://econcs.seas.harvard.edu/files/econcs/files/saxena_ai19.pdf.

24. Mitchell, Shira, Eric Potash, Solon Barocas, Alexander D'Amour, & Kristian Lum. "Annual Review of Statistics and Its Application Algorithmic Fairness: Choices, Assumptions, and Definitions." Annual Reviews. November 9, 2020. www.annualreviews.org/doi/pdf/10.1146/annurev-statistics-042720-125902.

25. Crenshaw, Kimberlé W. "On Intersectionality: Essential Writings." Columbia Law School. March, 2017. https://scholarship.law.columbia.edu/books/255.

26. Mitchell, Margaret, Simone Wu, Andrew Zaldivar, Parker Barnes, Lucy Vasserman, Ben Hutchinson, Elena Spitzer, Inioluwa Deborah Raji, & Timnit Gebru. "Model Cards for Model Reporting." arxiv. January 2019. `https://arxiv.org/pdf/1810.03993.pdf`.

27. Lundburg, Scott. "Welcome to the SHAP documentation." SHAP. 2022. `https://shap.readthedocs.io/en/latest/index.html`.

28. Lundburg, Scott & Su-In Lee. "A Unified Approach to Interpreting Model Predictions." 31st Conference on Neural Information Processing Systems. 2022. `https://papers.nips.cc/paper/2017/file/8a20a8621978632d76c43dfd28b67767-Paper.pdf`.

29. Grimmelmann, James. "The Virtues of Moderation," 17 Yale Journal of Law & Technology, 42. 2015. `https://openyls.law.yale.edu/bitstream/handle/20.500.13051/7798/Grimmelmann_The_Virtues_of_Moderation.pdf?sequence=2&isAllowed=y`.

30. Gillespie, Tarleton. "Custodians of the Internet." Yale University Press. August 24, 2021. `https://yalebooks.yale.edu/book/9780300261431/custodians-internet`.

31. Messenger, Haley & Keir Simmons. "Facebook content moderators say they receive little support, despite company promises." NBC News. May 11, 2021. `www.nbcnews.com/business/business-news/facebook-content-moderators-say-they-receive-little-support-despite-company-n1266891`.

32. Barrett, Paul M. Who Moderates the Social Media Giants? A Call to End Outsourcing. NYU Center for Business and Human Rights. June, 2020. `https://bhr.stern.nyu.edu/tech-content-moderation-june-2020`.

33. How to block accounts on Twitter. Twitter Help Center. 2022. `https://help.twitter.com/en/using-twitter/blocking-and-unblocking-accounts`.

34. Unfriending or blocking someone" Facebook Help Center. 2022. `www.facebook.com/help/1000976436606344`.

35. Understanding how Twitter handles offensive or explicit Tweets. Twitter Help Center. 2022. `https://help.twitter.com/en/safety-and-security/offensive-tweets-and-content`.

36. The Twitter rules: safety, privacy, authenticity, and more. Twitter Help Center. 2022. `https://help.twitter.com/en/rules-and-policies/twitter-rules`.

37. Facebook community standards. Meta Transparency Center. 2022. `https://transparency.fb.com/policies/community-standards/?source=https%3A%2F%2Fwww.facebook.com%2Fcommunitystandards%2Fintroduction`.

38. Guynn, Jessica. "Facebook while black: Users call it getting 'Zucked,' say talking about racism is censored as hate speech." USA Today. April 24, 2019. www.usatoday.com/story/news/2019/04/24/facebook-while-black-zucked-users-say-they-get-blocked-racism-discussion/2859593002.

39. Deerwester, Jayme. "'Liam Neeson is canceled': Fans react to actor's story of urge for racist revenge." USA Today. February 4, 2019. www.usatoday.com/story/life/people/2019/02/04/liam-neeson-reveals-shocking-racially-charged-past/2766111002.

40. Community standards enforcement. Meta Transparency Center. 2022. https://transparency.fb.com/data/community-standards-enforcement/?source=https%3A%2F%2Ftransparency.facebook.com%2Fcommunity-standards-enforcement.

41. Rules enforcement. Twitter Transparency Center. 2022. https://transparency.twitter.com/en/reports/rules-enforcement.html#2020-jan-jun.

42. Twitter's policy on hateful conduct. Twitter Help Center. 2022. https://help.twitter.com/en/rules-and-policies/hateful-conduct-policy.

43. Our range of enforcement options for violations. Twitter Help Center. 2022. https://help.twitter.com/en/rules-and-policies/enforcement-options.

44. Gulati-Partee, Gita and Maggie Potapchuk. "Paying Attention to White Culture and Privilege: A Missing Link to Advancing Racial Equity." The Foundation Review. 2022. www.mpassociates.us/uploads/3/7/1/0/37103967/paying_attention_to_white_culture_and_privilege-_a_missi.pdf.

45. Project Diane 2021. Digital undivided. 2022. www.projectdiane.com.

46. Molia, Rani & Renee Lightner. "Diversity in Tech Companies." The Wall Street Journal. December 30, 2013. http://graphics.wsj.com/diversity-in-tech-companies.

47. Rooney, Kate & Yasmin Khorram. "Tech companies say they value diversity, but reports show little change in last six years." CNBC. June 12, 2020. www.cnbc.com/2020/06/12/six-years-into-diversity-reports-big-tech-has-made-little-progress.html.

48. Bell, Tiffany Ashley. "It's Time We Dealt With White Supremacy in Tech." Medium. 2020. https://marker.medium.com/its-time-we-dealt-with-white-supremacy-in-tech-8f7816fe809.

49. Chang, Emily. "Brotopia." Portfolio. 2019. www.penguinrandomhouse.com/books/547571/brotopia-by-emily-chang.

50. Nunez, Anne-Marie, Matthew J. Mayhew, Musbah Shaheen, & Laura S. Dahl. "Let's Teach Computer Science Majors to Be Good Citizens. The Whole World Depends on It." EdSurge. March 15, 2021. `www.edsurge.com/news/2021-03-15-let-s-teach-computer-science-majors-to-be-good-citizens-the-whole-world-depends-on-it`.

51. Cottom, Tressie McMillan. "Thick and Other Essays." The New Press. January 8, 2019. `https://thenewpress.com/books/thick`.

52. moyazb. "They aren't talking about me. . ." Crunk Feminist Collective. March 20, 2010. `www.crunkfeministcollective.com/2010/03/14/they-arent-talking-about-me`.

53. Turner, Katlyn, Danielle Wood, & Catherine D'Ignazio. "The Abuse and Misogynoir Playbook." Montreal AI Ethics Institute. January 27, 2021. `www.media.mit.edu/articles/danielle-wood-and-katlyn-turner-co-author-article-the-abuse-and-misogynoir-playbook-for`.

54. Vogels, Emily A. "The State of Online Harassment." Pew Research Center. January 13, 2021. `www.pewresearch.org/internet/2021/01/13/the-state-of-online-harassment`.

55. How the Facebook ads that targeted voters centered on Black American culture: Voter suppression was the end game. Stop Online Violence Against Women. 2022. `https://stoponlinevaw.com/wp-content/uploads/2018/10/Black-ID-Target-by-Russia-Report-SOVAW.pdf`.

56. Matamoros-Fernandez, Ariadna. "Platformed racism: the mediation and circulation of an Australian race-based controversy on Twitter, Facebook, and YouTube." Taylor & Francis Online. February 21, 2017. `www.tandfonline.com/doi/abs/10.1080/1369118X.2017.1293130?journalCode=rics20`.

57. Flaherty, Colleen. "Questioning 'Algorithms of Oppression'." Inside Higher Ed. February 6, 2018. `www.insidehighered.com/news/2018/02/06/scholar-sets-twitter-furor-critiquing-book-he-hasnt-read`.

58. Kleinman, Zoe. "Amazon: Facial recognition bias claims are 'misleading'." BBC News. February 4, 2019. `www.bbc.com/news/technology-47117299`.

59. Kurenkov, Andrey. "Lessons from the PULSE Model and Discussion." The Gradient. 2022. `https://thegradient.pub/pulse-lessons`.

60. Menon, Sachit, Alex Damian, McCourt Hu, Nikhil Ravi, & Cynthia Rudin. "PULSE: Self-Supervised Photo Upsampling via Latent Space Exploration of Generative Models." Proceedings of the IEEE Conference on Computer Vision and Pattern Recognition (CVPR). June, 2020. `http://pulse.cs.duke.edu`.

61. McClintock, Elizabeth A. "The Psychology of Mansplaining." Psychology Today. March 31, 2016. www.psychologytoday.com/us/blog/it-s-man-s-and-woman-s-world/201603/the-psychology-mansplaining.

62. Wikipedia. "Angry Black Woman." Wikipedia. November 26, 2014. https://en.wikipedia.org/wiki/Angry_black_woman.

63. Bozeman, Barry, & Japera Johnson. "The Political Economy of Public Values: A Case for the Public Sphere and Progressive Opportunity." *The American Review of Public Administration* 45, no. 1. 2015. https://doi.org/10.1177/0275074014532826.

64. Preventing terrorists and violent extremists from exploiting digital platforms. Global Internet Forum to Counter Terrorism. 2022. https://gifct.org.

65. Gorwa, Robert, Reuben Binns, & Christian Katzenbach. "Algorithmic Content Moderation: Technical and Political Challenges in the Automation of Platform Governance." Big Data & Society. January 2020. https://doi.org/10.1177/2053951719897945.

CHAPTER 11

By the Public

Dr. Brandeis Marshall
@csdoctorsister

Manufactured outcomes are a phenomenon in the data industry. The pressure to retrofit data supercedes established ethical compasses. This is why all of us need to insist upon a data conscience in dataops that'll anchor equity + not erode our empathy + decency. #DataEducation

Source: `https://twitter.com/csdoctorsister/status/` `1488507000648523776?s=20&t=3DvOzaZESjHeLrbXZhFJfQ`

Change is a choice. In 2000, a mustard seed percentage of the global population knew and understood what data and algorithms were. Now we have all sectors in every industry executing data-informed decision-making and distributing AI-inspired tools. All of this has been done within the span of one generation. But the "move fast and break things" mantra continues to damage people, so it's time to reframe tech's chant. Let us, as global citizens, move fast and break the algorithmic-based, damage-ridden processes, systems, and institutions. Let's build anew while tinkering and inventorying the gaps in existing structures. In this chapter, educating ourselves, our communities, and our society takes center stage. This repetitive loop begins with prioritizing the most vulnerable groups. We then move to (re-)mastering data civics. At all times, we must keep a firm finger on the pulse of our industry and focus on coordinating, collaborating, and cooperating with others who are part of the rebel tech collective.

Freeing the Underestimated

In Chapter 9 (By the Law) and Chapter 10 (By Algorithmic Influencers), we've seen the volume and veracity of contrived challenges to instituting change in our data and tech systems. On one hand, the law is designed to protect the white dominant culture's interest, in particular their physical identities. Perfecting this design has been alive since 1619 and continues to present day. The friction lies in when the non-white dominant cultures have interests that don't align with white culture, and non-white communities attempt to use the law to exact their agency. On the other hand, the law also is being used as a tool to enforce antidiscrimination in the digital space. Recent federal and state digital civil rights legislative proposals and bills are reminiscent of equal pay, anti-lynching, and other equity-seeking legislation campaigns. If history is our teacher, the lesson is that this fight for humanity and dignity in digital spaces using the tools of the law will take *over* 100 years. That's 99 years too long. While those who build tech and amplify its adoption, e.g., algorithmic influencers, try to confine any change of data and tech systems within the bounds of lines of code.

The minoritized, and implicitly labeled underestimated, members of our society—minoritized groups in particular—navigate the brunt of the white eurocentric culture's unwillingness to share in social, legal, political, and economic equity. The idea of non-white people taking any action to live as freely and unobstructed as white people do is met with staunch resistance. As a refresher, Jim Crow laws, referenced in Chapter 1, "Oppression By. . .," were a collection of statutes at the state and local levels that enforced racial segregation. They were justified by the separate but equal doctrine provided as part of the *Plessy v. Ferguson* (1892) U.S. Supreme Court decision. Jim Crow 2.0 refers to a modernization of Jim Crow laws for the digital space. Scholars like Ruha Benjamin, Simone Browne, Meredith Broussard, Jesse Daniels, Virginia Eubanks, and Safiya Noble describe not only the impacts of technology on minoritized groups but also the processing of racism, sexism, and otherism through algorithmic practices. Discrimination is a form of social control that has leaped quietly into data and tech systems and institutions. The full scale and prevalence of digitized discrimination isn't realized because it's such an insidious component of algorithms, processes, and systems.

The digital infrastructure provides a platform for the underestimated to shape a path to freedom and liberation while the scales of legal justice and algorithmic influencers slowly make progressive change. The underestimated are not waiting and making inroads leveraging the digital infrastructures that are trying to oppress them. The R&B group EnVogue sang it best in "Free Your Mind" (songwriters are Denzil Delano Foster, Gerald Edward Levert [rest in peace], and Thomas Craig McElroy):

Why, oh why must it be this way?

(Ohhh, ohhh, ohhh, ohhh)

Before you can read me

You got to learn how to see me!

I said...

Free your mind

And the rest will follow...

The song, specifically sharing Black women's lived experience, lays bare the frustration and irritation associated with being *othered*, treated as *less than* initially and called upon regularly to deliver the impossible. White colonized spaces smother every ethnicity, gender, social class, and disability status that doesn't support the white power, domination, and control point of view. U.S. systems and institutions target, and more aptly in the digital space criminalize, Blackness and Black people with such structural, consistent, and regular frequency. So as I focused on Black people's objectification in Chapter 1, I am centering Black people again. Black people are in the first wave to call out inequities, to be pushed aside when funds are distributed, and last to reap the equity they fought for with their unpaid long-term labor. (To avoid blowback for focusing on Black people and not including other communities, let me say that Black people aren't the only group facing, coping, and fighting discrimination. As a Black woman, I only feel comfortable discussing the Black experience.)

Wrapped around Black people, like a straitjacket, is this inferiority characterization in all areas of society: education, healthcare, housing, criminal system, and so on[1-2]. By global societal design and continued execution, Black people are draped in and carry the weight of being the generationally poor class and positioned as the "go-to gleeful and grateful workforce for the (white) affluent." So each generation teaches the next generation the call signs, actions taken, and lessons learned in coping with bigotry thrown in their faces. Through segregated municipalities, called Freedmen's towns in the United States, or a cluster of Black neighborhoods (`https://hbtsa.org`), Black people over the generations form close-knit local communities in attempts to keep prejudice at bay—or at least insulate themselves from the majority of its blowback.

But in the digital space, unaddressed prejudices in these structures are coded and then cemented into the digital infrastructure. This squarely puts Black people in harm's way. People are being reduced to data units—column and row entries in databases. These data are fueling algorithms, which become automated decision systems and tech-scaled discrimination. Black people wind up fighting invisible combatants that are digitally made and exponentially driven to coordinate with each other.

As I introduce in my essay published in *The Black Agenda* (https://us.macmillan.com/books/9781250276872/theblackagenda),[3] we all need to call these harms by a name *commensurate* with the impact: algorithmic assault. Let's name, describe, place, date, and timestamp them for every infraction, such as what has been discussed via COMPAS in Chapter 1 or facial recognition analysis in Chapter 7, "Circus of Misguided Analysis." Black people are attuned to the harmful impacts of these invisible digital combatants. Living with these algorithmic-based harms hurt us in unimaginable ways because of the compounding impact I described in Chapter 3, "Bias." The valiant and persistent fights are against the harms we can't see. Trusting data and algorithms and the systems that operationalize them isn't a productive path. Defending Black lives, amplifying Black voices, and demanding equity in digitalized forms of bigotry helps keep our humanity and dignity intact.

Chronicling algorithmic assaults require that Black people and all minoritized groups understand how these algorithms and systems operate. These structures weren't designed with you and me in mind. Minoritized groups see and experience gaps in tech. To learn them is to know them. To know them is to know how to combat the bad influences as a collective and better the lives of minoritized groups.

Digital infrastructures, with all of its disparities, are revolution platforms that are in the hands of the public. The public needs avenues that will activate their data understanding so that they can protect themselves, their families, and ultimately humanity. Becoming more comfortable with data and assessing which data/tech systems are causing harms requires an actionable framework of liberatory tactics and approaches. This will free the underestimated and, as a consequence, unshackle us all from white supremacy conditionings.

As a digital society, we have the data tools at our fingertips. We need the language and messaging to make data concepts more relatable. And that's what we're going to discuss next. Some may assign "public data literacy" or "public interest data literacy" to this notion as a way to connect it to public interest technology. But what I'm talking about isn't framed with an academic-minded underpinning. It's data literacy for the public with an intentional focus on data impact issues and causes that are important to the voting populace. I call it *data civics*.

Learning Data Civics

Data industry isn't going anywhere. The U.S. Bureau of Labor Statistics highlighted "Data scientists and mathematical science occupations, all other" as one of the top-10 fastest-growing occupations from 2020 to 2030.[4] By 2039, some 19,800 new positions in data science industries are anticipated, marking a 31.4 percent increase in employment opportunities. Data science industries, as categorized by the U.S. government, include computer systems design and related services, management of companies and enterprises, management, scientific and technical consulting services, scientific research and development services, and insurance carriers.[5] All are flourishing industries accounting for close to 60,000 jobs. Data science professionals in the industry regularly give insight to the field's evolution and expansion by sharing their tech stack (a collection of their often-used software libraries, tech tools, and tech services for their jobs), their employment status, years of experience, salaries, and such.[6–7]

But as I've emphasized time and again throughout this book, science covers a fraction of full realities of data management. Other fields like ethics, sociology, psychology, Asian studies, Black studies, Latin/Chicano studies, Indigenous peoples studies, political science, law, and anthropology need space and breadth to be embedding how we all manage data throughout the digital infrastructure. Dropping "science" from data science unshackles us from relegating data as a numbers-only construct and make it primarily a value equivalent to digital assets for algorithms, tools, and platforms leveraging computing principles.

Becoming a more conscious data citizen won't simply be a bonus or perk to your life, if you have time. It will be a requirement and essential to navigating everyday life. In fact, McKinsey & Company's study on the future of work skills[8] highlighted 56 skills they deem foundational and then categorized them into 13 skills groups. Three skills groups, housing 11 skills, fall under their Digital label: digital fluency and citizenship, software use and development, and understanding digital systems. Data literacy, alongside computational and algorithmic thinking, digital ethics, and data analysis, and statistics, are specifically named. Those of us in the data and tech industries are well aware of tech's power, presence, longevity, and the influence it has on our society for generations to come. The general public isn't cognizant of its importance and how to become responsive to tech's fast evolutions.

The road to public accountability is laid by shaping what I'm calling *data civics*. Data civics, in short, is public-facing data activities and operations, which amounts to a practice of managing and disseminating data understandings from an individual or an organization to the public in order to inform and enrich their lives. Table 11.1 outlines data civics' stages.

Table 11.1: Data civics stages

	SHORT DESCRIPTION	COMPONENTS
Stage 1	People's relationship to data	▪ You and data ▪ Data at home ▪ Data in the workplace ▪ Data in the Community ▪ Data Impacts on Society
Stage 2	Data's relationship with equity	▪ Equity-driven data collection (Chapter 5, "Messy Gathering Grove") ▪ Equity-driven data storage (Chapter 6, "Inconsistent Storage Sanctuary") ▪ Equity-driven data analysis (Chapter 7, "Circus of Misguided Analysis") ▪ Equity-driven data visualization (Chapter 8, "Double-Edged Visualization Sword") ▪ Equity-driven data storytelling (Chapter 4, "Computational Thinking in Practice")
Stage 3	Data's relationship to machines	▪ Social constructs ▪ Software ▪ Systems

Data civics disrupts and rattles the existing approaches to working with and managing data in the industry. Typically, the order of operation is reversed to build a scalable and generalizable system that can be applicable for a broad population. Those of us in data and tech have seen that this approach doesn't work. The results consistently show more than antidotal instances of algorithmic-based harms. And the public doesn't care about the broader population but how data directly affects their lives.

In Stage 1, people come first. Consider each component as a layer of an onion, starting from the inside and finishing with the outer layer, as shown in Figure 11.1. Each of our connectivity to data changes depending on the circumstance. "You and Data" focuses on your personal interactions with our digital devices, applications, and online presence on platforms, such as social media accounts, Internet search history, personal email, calendar, and cloud storage. Next, "Data at Home" extends our connection to data to our immediate and extended family, relatives and friends, including family calendar management, household bank accounts, healthcare, and financial management.

Then, "Data in the Workplace" encompasses how your job responsibilities and duties dovetail with data operations, policies, and practices. Most industries are doubling down on making AI and data a central factor in their business operations. As employees, contract workers, or business owners, we all must be continuing our education in how to work with data given our expertise. The continuing education can come through our respective professional societies, on-the-job experiences, professional development skills workshops, certification attainment, or degree attainment. But the onus is on you to upskill regularly.

Figure 11.1: Data civics Stage 1: people's relationship to data

Next, "Data in the Community" aims to connect data localized to neighborhoods, regions, and states. Social enterprises and organizations know and have gained the trust of community members and leaders to gather and synthesize data outcomes with the community in mind, such as the New Georgia Project.[9] Lastly, "Data Impacts on Society" concentrates on the national, international, and transatlantic reach of data's influences on technological changes and global societal implications, for example, the World Economic Forum.[10]

Each layer of this onion doesn't have to be handled by every person. Nevertheless, each of us should know that these layers exist. And frankly, the vast majority of people will engage in the last two layers sparingly, like during U.S. election cycles and when there's an infringement on their civil rights. By learning about data through Stage 1's lens, any digital citizen can be equipped with the ability to better evaluate content from various digital sources. Having an anchored handle on how data operates for themselves, their loved ones, and careers changes a person's perspective. There's a personal investment and subsequent engagement that grows over time.

Stage 2 pushes to effect change in the data industry. Those people are being continually informed in tandem and looking to grow their data muscles. Their goal is to assess the trustworthiness of data *before* it's cast as information, knowledge, wisdom, insights, or impact (refer to Chapter 8, "Double-Edged Visualization Sword," for an in-depth discussion). And in my humble opinion, Stage 2 is this book, especially Chapters 4–8. Every situation where there is room for interpretation, there is room for inequity to duplicate and scale. With due diligence at all levels of an organization, minimizing digital discrimination, oppression, and suppression can happen, be sustained, and not negatively impact business costs.

Lastly, Stage 3 has a tight hold on all sectors and industries across the globe, particularly in software and systems. The learning paths diverge as people niche down to one of the three subareas: social constructs, software, and systems. The National Science Foundation developed a clear representation for the software and systems portions, as shown in Figure 11.2.[11] As a taskforce made up of computer scientists, it's no surprise that the mechanics of working with data took priority. The social constructs surrounding data appeared at the top of their figure as "[ethics, policy, regulatory, stewardship, platform, domain] environment." Some of the disparate impacts of each of these environments are covered by books, notes, and articles, which appear as part of New York University's Center for Critical Race and Digital Studies (`https://critical-racedigitalstudies.com/publications`)[12] and the Social Science Research Council's Just Tech initiative (`https://just-tech.ssrc.org`).[13] Examining the social impacts and reverberating interconnected outcomes of managing data requires just as much attention as to the mechanics.

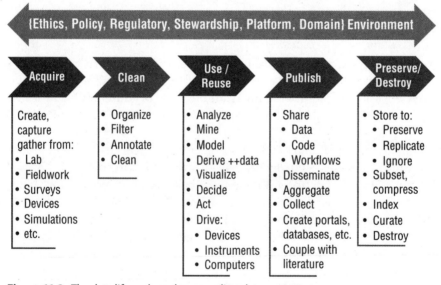

Figure 11.2: The data life cycle and surrounding data ecosystem

Source: Berman et al. 2016 / National Science Foundation / Public Domain

Those people who count themselves part of Stage 3 are *supposed* to be creating, executing, and maintaining vetted and trusted digital processes, systems, and structures from data. Instead, what has been dubbed and implemented as "data science" amounts to a reaction of companies collecting mounds of data from its customers and for its products and services without any way to extract meaningful insights. The existing work in computer science, statistics, and mathematics became the foundation for resolving the overwhelming data problem while perpetuating that the up-front expenses in building tech tools one time would be worthwhile in the long run. More often than not, the value proposition underperformed in practice.

Private, public, and governmental sectors couldn't duct-tape together computer science and statistics fundamentals to manage existing and new data needs by the early 2000s. Data programs emerged at higher education institutions and other educational organizations to train people in this new field[14], where 600+ programs exist as of February 2022. Adopting the current infrastructure of computing and statistics meant the dominant voices, approaches, and instruction in these spaces became the blueprint for data science: white/Asian, male, analytical-minded, and rooted in STEM. All of us are therefore seeing the manifestation of these choices.

The State of the Data Industry

As expected, the data industry is woefully overrepresented for some groups, marginalized for many groups and uncounted for other groups. In the Harnham Data and Analytics Diversity Report [15], the ethnic composition of data professionals remains rather homogeneous, with Asian respondents comprising 30 percent, Hispanic/Latin respondents accounting for 6 percent, Black/African American respondents constituting 3 percent, while white respondents make up 49 percent. The imbalance between the U.S. demographic representation in the data industry in Table 11.2 versus the U.S. population from the U.S. Census is stark, as displayed in Table 11.3. Since the Harnham report does not disaggregate their observations by ethnicity and gender, I begrudgingly imputed the female and male percentages using their observation that 27 percent of data and analytics professionals identify as women (see Table 11.2). And the Harnham report doesn't collect data identifying LGBTQ+ and other nongender conforming persons so there's a lack of accurate accounting according to gender identities. (From my research, there's a severe lack of recognition of non-male/non-female gender identities, with a number of acts and bills stalled that will support requiring their inclusion in surveys. There's so much work left to do.)

Table 11.2: Actual data industry representation by ethnicity/gender demographic (~2021)

	ASIAN	BLACK/ AFRICAN AMERICAN	HISPANIC/ LATIN	WHITE
Female	8.1%	0.81%	1.6%	13.2%
Male	21.9%	2.1%	4.3%	32.3%

Table 11.3: U.S. population representation by ethnicity/gender demographic

	ASIAN	BLACK/ AFRICAN AMERICAN	HISPANIC/ LATIN	WHITE
Female	5%	12.9%	18%	60%
Male	5.9%	13.4%	18.5%	61%

When demographic composition percentages in a particular industry are shared, the focus of so many within and outside that industry compare one ethnic group to another. That's the wrong focus. Frankly, it's narrow-mindedly divisive. The framing of the terms "underrepresented" and "underrepresented minorities" further codifies society's racial constructs. The dialogue needs to be anchored in seeing discrimination more fully—the racism, sexism, and all the other -isms happening in that industry. First, women and men are evenly distributed in the data industry, but they are the U.S. population. Second, the ethnicity backgrounds aren't evenly distributed in the data industry. If those of Asian descent can account for 6 percent of the U.S. population and 30 percent of the data workers, it's possible for Black and Latin people to make up a much larger percentage of data workers also. So in my ideal world if there were only two genders and four ethnicities, then each ethnicity and gender combination would be 12.5 percent. Because my goal is *equity*.

The notion of equity is a controversial one in many tech circles as the equity is a synonym for affirmative action or forced equality. The subsequent conversation veers toward more white-space comfortable terms like diversity, inclusion, and equality. *Diversity* asks who's in the room? *Inclusion* asks who's talking and speaking up in that room? *Equality* asks each person in that room to share their opinion about what's being discussed, and everyone speaks at the same time. *Equity* asks who's listened to in that room? I want a data industry where I would be just as likely to see another Black woman as I am to see an Asian woman. And I want each of our voices to be listened to at the same urgency and tenor of a white/Asian man in today's data industry (`https://twitter .com/csdoctorsister/status/1531628409016795138`).

There's bound to be discussion from people who raise their Confederate flag due to the percentages of white people in the data industry. They believe and amplify a fake narrative that white people account for 49 percent of the industry as compared to the 60 percent of the U.S. population as evidence of reverse racism. There is no reverse racism because according to the Harnham report, 65 percent–75 percent of leadership roles are held by men and 70 percent of head/VP roles are held by white people. White people still hold positions of authority, power, and influence.

Tech's toxicity, exclusionary practices for anyone not a white/Asian male and abysmal participation and representation percentages among Black people and other minoritized communities have bled over into the data industry. And hence the algorithms, processes, systems, and institutions within the data industry are a carbon copy of the tech community, including new and deeper harms than currently understood. Since many in the data community have leap-frogged over Stages 1 and 2, they realize that the nature of their work isn't vetted or trusted by the public. Jumping into Stage 3 reveals the depth of crisis response when they find out the ramifications of their work: lines of code, SQL scripts, and dashboards. And many people are choosing to dive into these data programs without calibrating their moral compass in alignment with Stages 1 and 2. Running to craft remedies and interventions are the first response because it's minimally invasive to their original work and serves to bandage symptoms of algorithmic-based harms.

It's time to swerve and veer in a different direction. Chapter 10, "By Algorithmic Influencers," pulls into focus the frictions and tensions that exist within the data and tech communities. But whether you are in Stage 1, 2, or 3, being critical of data uses and applications in technologies makes you at best an informed digital citizen and at worst a tech whistleblower. Either way, you'll need to know what this newfound impact awareness brings with it.

Living in the 21st Century

To live in the 21st century, you are managing your physical identities in the real world *and* the distinct, yet related, online identities that the U.S. laws aren't equipped to understand or guard us against tech approaches that do harm to certain groups. All of us have a digital footprint—either you engage directly through online services like banking, e-commerce, or medical records, or it's done for you via overt surveillance in public spaces.

While you can't dictate how the digitized pieces of your presence is processed by an algorithm, system, or organization, you can make it harder for your characteristics and behaviors to be tracked.

An attack on your online presence can go undetected for long stretches or never be known. An online attack of your finances, character, or other sensitive aspects can manifest as mental anguish. This attack can also turn up as denial of services. The law relies on a time-sensitive cause-and-effect sequence. Tech's effects on people vary across time intervals and move nonsequentially so that the trail leading back to tech can be lost or simply forgotten. This is what makes Jim Crow 2.0 difficult to capture and articulate in terms of the law.

I suggest that you can be safer in digital spaces and manage your online identities better. While it will be best if laws did the heavy lifting, this isn't the case now or in the near future. For those of you who post, reply, and share content via social media platforms, it's walking a fine line between sharing your unfiltered truths and being your authentic self, especially when you make it regularly known that you don't align with white supremacy. The sweet spot is to be present and consistent but not "famous." You want to be the B rather than the A student on social platforms. Your message gets shared and heard for traction but you're minimally harassed.

The inadequacies of law allow all of us—with targeted guidance—to exploit the vulnerabilities of algorithms, processes, and systems. And as global digital citizens we should and must take advantage of those vulnerabilities. We can severely cripple and suffocate the effectiveness of algorithms, processes, and systems with our actions by following these guidelines:

1. **Understand your limited choices.**   Because of legislation like the EU's *General Data Protection Regulation* and California Consumer Privacy Act (CCPA), users have more agency in how much of their personal data, e.g., Internet activities, is being tracked by a company's website. These Internet tracking tactics automatically store information about you, your location, and your preferences for the company's website you visited. Subsequent ads on your Internet browser, email marketing, and so on customize and target you based on this information. Companies can buy and sell this information without your consent. The four main types of Internet cookies are strictly necessary, preferences, statistics, and marketing. You can disable preferences, statistics, and marketing cookies if the website allows. It takes 10 seconds and helps limit the spread of your information within the digital landscape. It's well worth the time trade-off. You can't disable the necessary cookies, nor is there a comprehensive explanation of what quantifies cookies as "necessary," but hopefully with more public pressure, additional legislation would help clarify what constitutes necessary in terms of Internet cookies.[16]

2. **Be preemptive.**   When possible, your safety can be better controlled when you're on the offense rather than the defense. Every situation and its possible outcomes are predictable. But clearly sharing your actions and updates can help deter aggressive behavior by others. In pre-Internet times, we'd travel in groups. We're modernizing this concept for the digital space by selectively sharing location updates in real time. For instance, the 2020 U.S. presidential election season was contentious, particularly in certain states. For concerns over voter suppression and physical altercation at the voting booth, I publicly shared my voting experience (`https://twitter.com/csdoctorsister/status/1315614726538383360`).

   It can be overwhelming to figure out which posts are true or which are fake, as well as which accounts you're engaging with are actual people who are acting like jerks (trolls), and which are machines programmed to be jerks (bots). Bots are automated POS (pieces of software) whereas trolls engage in everything from cyberstalking to doxxing people as forms of intimidation.

NOTE Doxing devices from the term "dropping documents." It's a form of online harassment where a person finds and then publishes sensitive information about another person or people. The sensitive information includes government-issued identification, residential address, financial statements, and other forms of exploitation that result in malicious harms.

The key to protecting yourself is to hone your digital radar to detect what's likely a bot or a troll. Both digital nuisances on social platforms operate in very similar ways. They aren't followers to your social platform account, yet they attach quickly and fiercely to your post(s).

Bots are easier to identify since they are elementary algorithms intended for a singular purpose such as retweeting any post containing a particular hashtag.[17] Characteristics of bots accounts include:

- Computer-generated usernames
- Default profile banner images
- Abstract profile pictures such as an animal, plant, or artwork
- Little to no information in the profile description
- A timeline feed filled with shared posts and rarely an original post

These accounts tend to have many more accounts they are following than are following them. Of those who follow them, many are also bot accounts.

Trolls, on the other hand, require the public to understand their modes of operations and ways to avoid being lured into their traps. The frequency of Internet users witnessing trolling behavior on an everyday basis is a palpable 38 percent.[18] Table 11.4 contains actionable suggestions provided by five social platforms on subverting online trolls. Social platforms are paying more attention to helping their users in managing trolling behavior, but unfortunately trolls are getting craftier with every new feature offered by these social platforms.

Table 11.4: Troll subversion recommendations by social platforms

SOCIAL PLATFORM	RECOMMENDATION
Twitter (73 million U.S. users)	You can choose *who* can reply to your posts. Consider selecting one of the available options.
TikTok (80 million U.S. users)	Two features exist (as of 2022): (1) You can enable filters to review all comments before they post, and (2) you can rely on the platform's spam and offensive comments filter.

Continues

Table 11.4 (*continued*)

SOCIAL PLATFORM	RECOMMENDATION
Instagram (170 million U.S. users)	The guardrails aren't as robust. Be cautious of *who* you respond to via DMs and replies on your posts.
LinkedIn (180 million U.S. users)	Beware of the replies to your posts that are incoherent as well as accounts that part of your 3+ network.
Facebook (330 million U.S. users)	Keep your audience set to Friends and log out after each use. Bots and trolls like to attack when your account is inactive.

3. **Proactively avoid direct communication.**   Engaging in dialogue with faceless profiles with low numbers of followers isn't the best use of your time and energies. First tip: ignoring their replies, no matter how egregious, saves you from undue frustration and stops them from exploiting your platform to share their views. Second tip: when you can't muster the emotional strength to stay silent, screen-capture their response in your response. Following this tip significantly lessens the strength of their message because you've created a new instance that the algorithm can't trace back to them. Last, but certainly not least, your followers and supporters will sometimes take the lead in shutting down improper or inappropriate language targeting you.

4. **Use alternative language and spellings.**   Algorithms thrive on the reoccurrence of the same or similar words. It's therefore easy for you to confuse algorithms by using secular jargon, urban slang, and, for Black people, African-American Vernacular English (AAVE). Algorithms need terms to be frequently used in a short time frame in order to determine a recognizable pattern. And by the time the pattern is realized by algorithms, the jargon has shifted. Another popular strategy is to deflect from the original message with alternative positive messages like *Black brilliance, Black joy,* and *Rest is resilience.* Algorithms are susceptible to topic drift. When there is critical communication mass of one topic over another, the algorithm will direct its efforts in understanding the patterns of the popular topic, even when it's not the initial topic shared by the original poster.

5. **Stop engaging with rude profiles and organizations,**   If the online engagement becomes toxic or egregious, you have three strategies to distance yourself from the harm-inducing profile: mute the conversation or user, block the user, or report the post or user to the social platform. These strategies won't necessarily remove the profile from the social platform, but they significantly reduce the likelihood of you seeing their posts—about you or anyone else.

In each of these suggestions, the root of my recommendation is to give hate zero oxygen to propagate in digital systems and social platforms. It takes restraint, for sure. I don't trust these systems, not designed with me in mind, to protect me from harassers, so I devised my own plan of online survival. I chose to disrupt enough to be noticed but not to be permanently banned. It's my choice until the algorithms, processes, and systems can be dismantled and built from scratch. It's my choice in hopes that others will lead a similar path in their field, in their business, or at their workplace.

This choice of mine is reinforced by how the United States has handled the overgrown discriminatory activities where personhood status of non-white people (people like me) doesn't have their full digital civil rights within the digital landscape. It's as if each non-white person has an invisible asterisk beside their digital representation. Let me refer to this as a 1* person. Meanwhile a white person retains their digital civil rights and their digital representation has no asterisk, I refer to this as 1 person. You therefore are either counted as a 1* or a 1 person in this society — in both physical and digital spaces. This baked-in hierarchy structure efforts to combat discrimination are met with limited effectiveness. As an implicitly labeled 1* person, I therefore don't expect any *one* effort, activity or cause to reverse the impact of this baked-in hierarchy that mirrors what has been established in our physical world.

What's being eluded to here and in earlier chapters is that the original stain of the United States, the trafficking and enslavement of Africans from 1619 to 1863, and then the present everyday oppression of their descendants, Black Americans, provides the quintessential blueprint for deliberately overlooking discrimination. So I'm shepherding us through this original stain in the next section as a historical, social, legal, economic, and civic reminder of which power infrastructures still exist that enable the criminalizing of Black Americans. It's important to note, as you're reading, when and how these power structures were used as weapons against Black Americans. These are similar tactics being used against humanity within the digital space. You'll read the 1* and 1 personhood description again to emphasize how for some groups, personhood status remains conditional throughout our society.

Condemning the Original Stain

The law has failed minoritized communities in so many ways for so long. From the first invasion of the Americas and early iterations of the U.S. Constitution, enslaved African people were non-persons. Enslaved African people were considered only property—either an asset or a liability—of the dominant privileged class forming a new country to replace the existing Indigenous ones. By 1787, Black people were placed at the crux of the economic and political power infrastructure for the white-powered United States by baking into the Constitution Black people's personhood with the three-fifths compromise (Article I, Section 2, Clause 3,[19]). This compromise was repealed in 1868 (14th Amendment. Section 2,[20]) after the Emancipation Proclamation and Civil War that judged the morality of enslavement.

Black people's full humanity and liberation didn't come with the 14th Amendment. The mistreatment and conditionality of my ancestors' personhood and my own, through the law and societal interactions, can't undo the original stain of our constitutionalized oppression in 1776, 1787, 1863, and 1868. Black people's economic and political agency were denied explicitly in the late 1700s and implicitly with performative platitudes in the late 1800s. There hasn't been any consistency in extending and enforcing equity to Black people. The enslaved Africans of the 1600s through the 1800s, their Black ancestors of the 1900s and the Black people living in the 2000s are continually in pursuit of economic and political equity in the United States.

I believe that the tethering together of Black people as an unpaid forced workforce and economic asset available for bartering renders a Black person's personhood as a 1* count to the law[21]. I think of 1* as a representation of not being fully free, not fully seen as equal, and not treated with the same grace as our white counterparts. It's the discrimination in all systems and institutions. And Black people have been stuck at 1* status since 1863. Examples of 1* status appear in everyday life, across sectors and industries: mortgage lending,[22] tax system,[23] criminal justice system (https://naacp.org/resources/criminal-justice-fact-sheet),[24] tech,[25] and higher education,[26] just to name a few.

And then there's the antidotal situations that infuriate me like that of Joseph Thompson, who in the 1950s was operating MIT's Whirlwind computer as a high school graduate (https://news.mit.edu/2021/scene-at-mit-computing-pioneer-joe-thompson-technology-history-0203).[27] As the article states, Thompson was part of "an MIT push to meet the demands for skilled staff by recruiting from local high schools those students who were academically and socially exceptional, but for whom, for whatever reasons, college was inaccessible." College was accessible. It wasn't a priority. Colleges like Oberlin started accepting Black students in 1833 as well as Historically Black Colleges and Universities (HBCUs) accepting Black students starting in 1837, with many HBCUs opening after the Civil War. Yet, Joseph Thompson wasn't supported to attend college in Massachusetts or elsewhere, in order to work for MIT.

Laws dictated that Black people have to be paid if employed post–Emancipation Proclamation, but the pay did not have to be equal to that of whites. The Fair Labor Standards Act of 1938 required a minimum wage and "time-and-a-half" for working over the 40-hour workweek. The Paycheck Fairness Act of 2021 calls for equal pay victims of discrimination in the payment of wages on the basis of sex, and for other purposes and has yet to become law.[28]

If Black people aren't engaging in unpaid labor for white spaces, Black people are underpaid labor for white spaces.

Equal pay legislation isn't the only slow roll to equity. Lynching of Black people occurred before the Civil War and has continued to present day. Ida B. Wells-Barnett's *Red Record*[29] became the most well-known document accounting of lynching of Black people in the United States in 1895. The National Association for the Advancement of Colored People (NAACP) used her data journalistic work as the foundation for their campaign to make lynching a crime at the local, state, and federal levels. The Dyer Anti-lynching Bill was introduced in 1918, in response to the St. Louis Race Massacre the prior year by a member of the U.S. House of Representatives, Leonidas C. Dyer. While the bill passed the U.S. House in 1922, it was blocked by the U.S. Senate. After 100 years and 200 anti-lynching bill attempts later, the Emmett Till Antilynching Bill was approved by the U.S. Senate on March 7, 2022 and signed into law soon thereafter. The physical murder and public display of Black death took generations to provide a semblance of justice under the law. The digitized misrepresentation of Black people and our criminalization remains on full display online. The existing law and legal strategies, so far, supply no refuge.

Condemning the power structures enacted by history, social constructs, the law, economics, and civic engagement is the burden of all of us, not just Black people navigating the original stain of enslavement in the United States. The public needs and has the fortitude to exert intense unrelenting pressure on both those in the government as policymakers and those in the tech industry as algorithmic influencers for actionable, permanent digital safeguards. As we're mastering data civics and condemning discriminatory power structures, we all need guiding principles to operationalize our tech safety.

Tech Safety in Numbers

We the public, meaning all of us, are steering the tech ship toward the physical and digital society we want. You've chosen one of the options: (1) progressive change for equity, (2) maintaining the status quo, or (3) longing for the days of centuries ago. Because you're in this chapter, I'm assuming you're part of the first group, my group. The blueprint for our group hasn't been written and none of us knows where we'll end up. The journey, however, requires "stick-toitiveness," resilience, loud voices, deep (wealthy) pockets, role models, peer groups, and a larger community. What's for certain is that you and I are on the defensive line, preserving humanity and dignity as we fight to institutionalize equity and decency in our structures, systems, and institutions.

To increase the likelihood of us making progressive change for equity, we need clear goalposts. Kim Crayton (https://twitter.com/KimCrayton1) developed guiding principles[30] through her strategic business consulting work and her #causeascene podcast,[31] as shown in Figure 11.3.

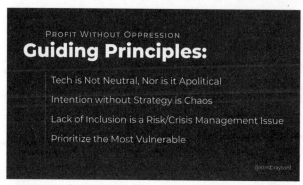

Figure 11.3: Profit Without Oppression's Guiding Principles, by Kim Crayton

1. **Tech is not neutral, nor is it apolitical.** While some in data and tech will argue this point, it is true. Making tech requires devising algorithms that manipulate data. Data that's digitized is a snapshot of what the data collector perceived as important, valuable, and worthwhile to share. Tech is subjective.

2. **Intention without strategy is chaos.** Throughout these chapters, antidotal examples, op-ed articles, and scholarly publications demonstrate the human toll of knee-jerk tech solutionism. People are harmed and lives are irrevocably damaged.

3. **Lack of inclusion is a risk/crisis management issue.** As we all learn, live, and experience the data industry, the consistent outcome of exclusionary practices leads to individuals and organizations trying to manage the damage. And in many cases, the offending party's choice is to wait for public outrage to diminish by staying silent or conduct internal investigations to appease the public. Regardless, it's money poorly spent because they could have chosen the equitable path and avoided a majority of the damage they inflicted.

4. **Prioritize the most vulnerable.** Vulnerable populations and groups aren't weak as the opposition implies. Vulnerable communities are impacted first, hardest, and longest by algorithmic-based harms. By prioritizing them, we make them our barometer in grounding our humanity and plight for equity. If the remedy, intervention, or reform doesn't benefit the vulnerable, then it's not worthy of doing.

While each of these principles are intended for tech but apply to all processes, systems, and institutions, they are critical foundations for those of us rebelling against the tech and data industry status quo. Also, the line between tech and data is so thin because they are interconnected as data serves as inputs and tech turns out to be our final output. Bonding over our collective data critical and skeptical lens grows after each new algorithmic-based harm reaches national or international prominence.

Finding rebel tech communities, in-person and/or online, isn't as hard in the 2020s as it was in the 2000s. Many communities (a list is available at www.datacareerpaths.com/resources,[32] including Black in AI, Queer in AI, Black Data Processing Associates) have organized as a means to provide psychologically safe spaces. Common themes focus on improving data and tech practices, resisting the excuses used to uphold the status quo, and finding alternative paths when tensions rise. The main benefit is knowing you aren't alone in pushing for equity in data operations, implementations, and practices.

Undoubtedly, retaliation will come. That's why you need a rebel tech community *inside* and *outside* of your current organization. Your experience will mimic the ones experienced by many Black women in the workplace. You may not be conditioned for these degrees and frequencies of aggressions, but in time and through your own experiences, you'll adapt. But don't cop out, get frustrated, and decide to "take a break." Black women can't take a break from being a Black woman, so you can't take a break from critiquing data practices and tech products regardless of your data civics mastery. If retaliation tactics are successful, then they will lead to a lack of inclusion, which will result in risk and crisis management issues. And risk and crisis management issues are costly in terms of time, resources, and personnel while also causing irreparable damage to any company's reputation.

For those who haven't had traumatic workplace experiences, Figure 11.4 showcases a familiar sequence of events.[33] At first, you'll be seen as advocate, change agent, and thought leader. Then, you'll be called a disruptor as you push for transparency, accountability, and equity-driven governance. The leap to the obstructionist and troublemaker label comes swift and sticks to you quickly. The retaliation tactics can overwhelm to the point of exiting the organization, in order to do it all over again in a new organization. In data and tech industries, however, there are resources like The Tech Worker Handbook (https://techworkerhandbook.org)[34] and tech unions like Alphabet Workers Union[35] to craft common messaging and build safety in numbers.

My cause is data education for the public, for those in data operations and software development, and for those shaping policies. Emily Hadley shared a slew of great resources back in 2020 on steps to being antiracist in the data industry (https://medium.com/towards-data-science/5-steps-to-take-as-an-antiracist-data-scientist-89712877c214).[36] Funnily enough, step 1 is educating yourself about being antiracist. As my parents always told me, "Education can never be taken away from you." Educating yourself on the areas you don't know is the key to success. It can be in the classroom, on the job, or through lived experiences. But education is the path out of neutrality.

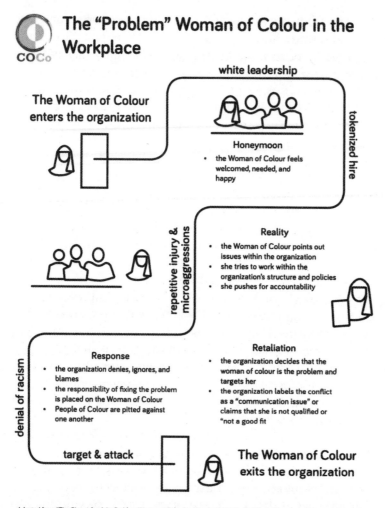

The "Problem" Woman of Colour in the Workplace

COCo

white leadership

The Woman of Colour enters the organization

tokenized hire

Honeymoon
- the Woman of Colour feels welcomed, needed, and happy

Reality
- the Woman of Colour points out issues within the organization
- she tries to work within the organization's structure and policies
- she pushes for accountability

repetitive injury & microaggressions

Response
- the organization denies, ignores, and blames
- the responsibility of fixing the problem is placed on the Woman of Colour
- People of Colour are pitted against one another

denial of racism

Retaliation
- the organization decides that the woman of colour is the problem and targets her
- the organization labels the conflict as a "communication issue" or claims that she is not qualified or "not a good fit

target & attack

The Woman of Colour exits the organization

Adapted from "The Chronicle of the Problem Woman of Color in a Non-Profit" by the Safehouse Progressive Alliance for Nonviolence
www.coco-net.org

Figure 11.4: Adapted from "The Chronicle of the Problem Woman of Colour in a Non-profit" by the Safehouse Progressive Alliance for Nonviolence

Hadley's steps 2 and 3 provide reading lists and direct calls-to-action to making a choice to do better right now in data operations. The act of continuing to learn how data and algorithms scale discrimination isn't a solo endeavor. We, as human beings, don't see when we've excluded someone else unless we're intentional and strategic in our interactions. Hadley's step 3 is a call to eliminate discriminatory algorithms. I argue that the industry can't eliminate these algorithms under the current systems and institutions. The best outcome is to minimize the use of discriminatory algorithms and systems because the current and long-standing design is to discriminate, oppress, and suppress people not in positions of power and influence. To eliminate discriminatory algorithms, we'll need to build from scratch.

Hadley's last two steps advocate for increasing diversity in the data industry and financially supporting Black-led organizations. Frankly, you should already be doing both of those advocacy actions. I implore you to raise the stakes by increasing diversity in the C-suite and leadership of data and tech companies and financially support Black-owned and Black-led nonprofit and for-profit organizations. All minoritized organizations and companies need the infusion of cash, subscribers, and customers.

Go beyond the bare minimum from now on. Make data a liberating force, not a gatekeeping one. Follow Profit Without Oppression's guiding principles. Become a better you to be better to other people.

Summary

Data won't stop being created, digitized, manipulated, and interpreted. All of us can't acquiesce to existing processes, systems, and institutions designed to further marginalize minoritized groups. We're battling for our dignity in digital spaces with the same indignant veracity as we do in physical spaces. Remember, change is a choice. Change also comes in different sizes. Choosing one ring on the humanity sphere, in data civics' Stage 1, causes ripples to the others. Choosing one algorithmic-based harm to combat impacts how others are recognized and addressed by the data/tech industry. Choosing to join forces with just one other person cements a rebel tech collaboration. Changes may come slow or they may come fast, using this grassroots approach. But what's certain is that change will come. The future will be under the domination of a few people with elaborate and intrusive algorithms. Or the future will be a multiracial, multigender, and multiclass cooperative society where its people participate and influence its direction.

Notes

1. Hannah-Jones, Nikole. The 1619 project: An origin story. One World Publishing. 2021. https://1619books.com.

2. Zinn Education Project. Rethinking schools and teaching for change. 2022.

3. Opoku-Agyeman, & Anna Gifty. *The Black agenda: Bold solutions for a broken system.* St. Martin's Press. 2022. https://us.macmillan.com/books/9781250276872/theblackagenda.

4. Dubina, Kevin S., Lindsey Ice, Janie-Lynn Kim, & Michael J. Rieley. Projections overview and highlights, 2020–30, Monthly Labor Review. U.S. Bureau of Labor Statistics. October 2021. `www.bls.gov/opub/mlr/2021/article/pdf/projections-overview-and-highlights-2020-30.pdf`.

5 Occupational Employment and Wage Statistics. U.S. Bureau of Labor Statistics. June 2, 2022. `www.bls.gov/oes/current/oes152098.html`.

6. State of Data Science 2021. Anaconda, June 2, 2022. `www.anaconda.com/state-of-data-science-2021`.

7. State of data science and machine learning 2021. Kaggle. October 14, 2021. `www.kaggle.com/kaggle-survey-2021`.

8. Dondi, Marco, Julia Klier, Frédéric Panier, & Jörg Schubert. Defining the skills citizens will need in the future world of work. McKinsey & Company. June 25, 2021. `www.mckinsey.com/industries/public-and-social-sector/our-insights/defining-the-skills-citizens-will-need-in-the-future-world-of-work`.

9. New Georgia Project. June 2, 2022. `https://newgeorgiaproject.org`.

10. Artificial intelligence for humanity. World Economic Forum. June 2, 2022. `www.weforum.org/communities/gfc-on-artificial-intelligence-for-humanity`.

11. National Science Foundation Computer and Information Science and Engineering Advisory Committee Data Science Working Group. Realizing the potential of data science. National Science Foundation. December 2016. `www.nsf.gov/cise/ac-data-science-report/CISEACDataScienceReport1.19.17.pdf`.

12. Publications & Public Works. Center for Critical Race and Digital Studies. June 2, 2022.

13. Just tech. Social Science Research Council. June 2, 2022.

14. Ryan Swanstrom. Data science colleges and universities. June 2, 2022.

15. Harnham Data and Analytics Diversity Report. Harnham Search and Selection Ltd. June 2, 2022.

16. Koch, Richie. Cookies, the GDPR, and the ePrivacy Directive. June 2, 2022.

17. Wojcik, Stefan, Solomon Messing, Aaron Smith, Lee Rainie, & Paul Hitlin. Bots in the Twittersphere. Pew Research Center. April 9, 2018.

18. Kunst, Alexander. Witnessing Internet trolling on selected media in the U.S. 2017. Statista. September 3, 2019.

19. Constitution of the United States: A transcription. National Archives. October 7, 2021. `www.archives.gov/founding-docs/constitution-transcript`.

20. The Editors of Encyclopedia Britannica. Fourteenth Amendment. Britannica. April 14, 2009. www.britannica.com/topic/Fourteenth-Amendment.

21. Martin, Bonnie. Slavery's invisible engine: Mortgaging human property. *Journal of Southern History* 76, no. 4 (2010): 817–866. www.jstor.org/stable/27919281.

22. Broady, Kristen, Mac McComas, & Amine Quazad. An analysis of financial institutions in Black-majority communities: Black borrowers and depositors face considerable challenges in accessing banking services. Brookings Institution. November 2, 2021.

23. Brown, Dorothy A. *The whiteness of wealth: How the tax system impoverishes Black Americans—and how we can fix it*. Crown Publishing. 2021.

24. Criminal Justice Fact Sheet. NAACP. June 2, 2022. https://naacp.org/resources/criminal-justice-fact-sheet.

25. Palladino, Valentina. Reverend Jesse Jackson calls out Silicon Valley for lack of racial and gender diversity. The Verge. March 19, 2014. www.theverge.com/2014/3/19/5525696/reverend-jesse-jackson-calls-out-tech-companies-for-lack-of-diversity.

26. National Academies of Sciences, Engineering, and Medicine. *Promising practices for addressing the underrepresentation of women in science, engineering, and medicine: Opening doors*. National Academies Press. 2022. https://nap.nationalacademies.org/catalog/25585/promising-practices-for-addressing-the-underrepresentation-of-women-in-science-engineering-and-medicine.

27. Weinstock, Maia. Scene at MIT: A Black computing pioneer takes his place in technology history. MIT. February 3, 2021. https://news.mit.edu/2021/scene-at-mit-computing-pioneer-joe-thompson-technology-history-0203.

28. 117th Congress. H.R.7 – Paycheck Fairness Act. Congress.gov. June 2, 2022. www.congress.gov/bill/117th-congress/house-bill/7.

29. Wells-Barnett, Ida B. *The Red Record: Tabulated Statistics and Alleged Causes of Lynching in the United States*. Project Gutenberg. February 8, 2005. www.gutenberg.org/files/14977/14977-h/14977-h.htm.

30. Crayton, Kim. Profit without oppression: Guiding principles. 2022.

31. The strategic disruption of the status quo in technical organizations, communities, and events. #causeascene. Podcast, June 2, 2022.

32. Find your resources: Data career paths. June 2, 2022. www.datacareerpaths.com/resources.

33. Page, Kira. The "Problem" woman of colour in the workplace. Centre for Community Organizations. March 8, 2018.

34. Ozoma, Ifeoma. The Tech Worker Handbook. June 2, 2022. `https://techworkerhandbook.org`.

35. Alphabet Workers Union. AWU-CWA Local 1400. June 2, 2022. `https://alphabetworkersunion.org`.

36. Hadley, Emily. 5 Steps to Take as an Antiracist Data Scientist. Towards Data Science. June 8, 2020. `https://towardsdatascience.com/5-steps-to-take-as-an-antiracist-data-scientist-89712877c214`.

APPENDIX

A

Code for *app.py*

This appendix displays the code blocks as described and discussed in Chapter 4, "Computational Thinking in Practice." Each code block is labeled alphabetically for more convenient reference.

A

```
# app.py

import glob           # a Unix style pathname pattern expansion software library
import os             # misc operating system interfaces library, done at start
import warnings     # warning control library, enables warnings to be displayed
import requests      # HTTP library, make requests to webpages

# web microframework library
from flask import (Flask,session, g, json, Blueprint,flash, jsonify,
redirect, render_template, request, url_for, send_from_directory)
# Flask supporting library
from werkzeug import secure_filename
```

B

```
# app.py

import textract #text extraction library
#text summary library, returns most representative sentences using
TextRank algorithm
from gensim.summarization import summarize

# TF-IDF features creation library
from sklearn.feature_extraction.text import CountVectorizer,
TfidfVectorizer
# Unsupervised learner for implementing neighbor searches library
from sklearn.neighbors import NearestNeighbors

import pdf2txt as pdf #converts PDFs to text files library
import PyPDF2 #ingest PDF into Python library, separate images and
texts, etc.

import screen #allowing this app.py to see and use screen.py methods
import search #allowing this app.py to see and use search.py methods
import hashlib #secure hashes library
```

C

```
# app.py

# ignoring user warnings that may creep up for the gensim module
-- technical issue for windows
warnings.filterwarnings(action='ignore', category=UserWarning,
module='gensim')

# This is a flask application with name variable, meaning this python
flask instance.
app = Flask(__name__)

#https://flask.palletsprojects.com/en/1.1.x/config/
app.config.from_object(__name__) # load config from this file , flaskr.py

# Load default config and override config from an environment variable
app.config.update(dict(
    USERNAME='admin',
    PASSWORD='7b4d7a208a333b46acdc9da159e5be7a',
```

```python
        SECRET_KEY='development key'))

app.config['UPLOAD_FOLDER'] = 'Original_Resumes/'
app.config['ALLOWED_EXTENSIONS'] = set(['txt', 'pdf', 'png', 'jpg',
'jpeg', 'gif'])

class jd:
    def __init__(self, name):
        self.name = name

def getfilepath(loc):
    temp = str(loc).split('\\')
    return temp[-1]

# login method to receive and validate username and encrypted passwords
@app.route('/login', methods=['GET', 'POST'])
def login():
    error = None
    if request.method == 'POST':
        if request.form['username'] != app.config['USERNAME']:
            error = 'Invalid username'
        elif app.config['PASSWORD'] != hashlib.md5(request
.form['password'].encode('utf-8')).hexdigest():
            error = 'Invalid password'
        else:
            session['logged_in'] = True
            flash('You were logged in')
            return redirect(url_for('home'))
    return render_template('login.html', error=error)

# logout method to securely end the active session
@app.route('/logout')
def logout():
    session.pop('logged_in', None)
    flash('You were logged out')
    return redirect(url_for('home'))
```

D

```python
# app.py (cont'd)

@app.route('/')
def home():
    x = []
    for file in glob.glob("./Job_Description/*.txt"):
        res = jd(file)
        x.append(jd(getfilepath(file)))
    print(x)
```

```python
        return render_template('index.html', results = x)

@app.route('/results', methods=['GET', 'POST'])
def res():
    if request.method == 'POST':
        jobfile = request.form['des']
        print(jobfile)
        flask_return = screen.res(jobfile)

        print(flask_return)
        return render_template('result.html', results = flask_return)

@app.route('/resultscreen' ,  methods = ['POST', 'GET'])
def resultscreen():
    if request.method == 'POST':
        jobfile = request.form.get('Name')
        print(jobfile)
        flask_return = screen.res(jobfile)
        return render_template('result.html', results = flask_return)

@app.route('/resultsearch' ,methods = ['POST', 'GET'])
def resultsearch():
    if request.method == 'POST':
        search_st = request.form.get('Name')
        print(search_st)
    result = search.res(search_st)
    # return result
    return render_template('result.html', results = result)

@app.route('/Original_Resume/<path:filename>')
def custom_static(filename):
    return send_from_directory('./Original_Resumes', filename)

if __name__ == '__main__':
    # app.run(debug = True)
    # app.run('127.0.0.1' , 5000 , debug=True)
    app.run('0.0.0.0' , 5000 , debug=True , threaded=True)
```

Code for *screen.py*

This appendix displays the code blocks as described and discussed in Chapter 4, "Computational Thinking in Practice." Each code block is labeled alphabetically for more convenient reference.

A

```
# screen.py

# Like in the app.py code, software modules are loaded in to help set up the
# software environment.
# No need to duplicate the code here!

# creates the ResultElement object, containing rank value and filename
class ResultElement:
    def __init__(self, rank, filename):
        self.rank = rank
        self.filename = filename

# function: access and return the filepath reformatted using forward
slashes
```

```python
def getfilepath(loc):
    temp = str(loc)
    temp = temp.replace('\\', '/')
    return temp


# function: recursively retrieves resume documents that are formatted as
# pdf, doc and docx. Each page of resume is captured separately and text
# extracted using extractText() for pdfs or textract.process() for MS Word
def res(jobfile):
    # create empty vectors to store files of different formats, text
    # from resumes, etc
    Resume_Vector = []
    Ordered_list_Resume = []
    Ordered_list_Resume_Score = []
    LIST_OF_FILES = []
    LIST_OF_FILES_PDF = []
    LIST_OF_FILES_DOC = []
    LIST_OF_FILES_DOCX = []
    Resumes = []
    Temp_pdf = []

    # iterate through the resumes directory, separately listing them
    # into vectors
    os.chdir('./Original_Resumes')
    for file in glob.glob('**/*.pdf', recursive=True):
        LIST_OF_FILES_PDF.append(file)
    for file in glob.glob('**/*.doc', recursive=True):
        LIST_OF_FILES_DOC.append(file)
    for file in glob.glob('**/*.docx', recursive=True):
        LIST_OF_FILES_DOCX.append(file)

    # ordering files by format type gives the coder a systematic way to
    # process files. It's slightly more efficient to do so as the method
    # is loaded
    # into the computer's memory/cache.
    LIST_OF_FILES = LIST_OF_FILES_DOC + LIST_OF_FILES_DOCX + LIST_OF_
    # FILES_PDF

    print("This is LIST OF FILES")
    print(LIST_OF_FILES)

    # print("Total Files to Parse\t" , len(LIST_OF_PDF_FILES))
    # iterate through filenames and parse files, executing format-
    # specific methods
    print("####### PARSING ########")
    for nooo,i in enumerate(LIST_OF_FILES):
        Ordered_list_Resume.append(i)
        Temp = i.split(".")
        if Temp[1] == "pdf" or Temp[1] == "Pdf" or Temp[1] == "PDF":
            try:
```

```python
                    print("This is PDF" , nooo)
                    with open(i,'rb') as pdf_file:
                        read_pdf = PyPDF2.PdfFileReader(pdf_file)


                    number_of_pages = read_pdf.getNumPages()
                    for page_number in range(number_of_pages):
                        page = read_pdf.getPage(page_number)
                        # main external method, we'll look under the hood
                        # later
                        page_content = page.extractText()
                        page_content = page_content.replace('\n', ' ')
                        # page_content.replace("\r", "")
                        Temp_pdf = str(Temp_pdf) + str(page_content)
                        # Temp_pdf.append(page_content)
                        # print(Temp_pdf)
                    Resumes.extend([Temp_pdf])
                    Temp_pdf = '"
            except Exception as e: print(e)
    if Temp[1] == "doc" or Temp[1] == "Doc" or Temp[1] == "DOC":
        print("This is DOC" , i)

        try:
            # main external method, we'll look under the hood later
            a = textract.process(i)
            a = a.replace(b'\n',  b' ')
            a = a.replace(b'\r',  b' ')
            b = str(a)
            c = [b]
            Resumes.extend(c)
        except Exception as e: print(e)


    if Temp[1] == "docx" or Temp[1] == "Docx" or Temp[1] == "DOCX":
        print("This is DOCX" , i)
        try:
            # main external method, it's called a few lines earlier
            # in this code
            a = textract.process(i)
            a = a.replace(b'\n',  b' ')
            a = a.replace(b'\r',  b' ')
            b = str(a)
            c = [b]
            Resumes.extend(c)
        except Exception as e: print(e)



    if Temp[1] == "ex" or Temp[1] == "Exe" or Temp[1] == "EXE":
        print("This is EXE" , i)
        pass


print("Done Parsing.")
```

B

```
# screen.py

Job_Desc = 0
LIST_OF_TXT_FILES = []
os.chdir('../Job_Description')
f = open(jobfile , 'r')
text = f.read()

try:
    tttt = str(text)
    # automate a summary of the text tttt by selecting a few
    # sentences/phrases
    # to represent the entire text. In this case, the text is a job
    # description.
    tttt = summarize(tttt, word_count=100)
    text = [tttt]
except:
    text = 'None'

f.close()
# create a word storage container for all non-stop words
vectorizer = TfidfVectorizer(stop_words='english')

# sort words from 'text' into this vectorizer container and process
# idf values
vectorizer.fit(text)
# uses this vocabulary to construct tf-idf-weighted document-term
# matrix
# each word is valued by its frequency (tf) adjusted for relevance
# (idf) in docs
vector = vectorizer.transform(text)

Job_Desc = vector.toarray()
# print("\n\n")
# print("This is job desc : " , Job_Desc)

os.chdir('../')
for i in Resumes:
    text = i
    tttt = str(text)
    try:
        tttt = summarize(tttt, word_count=100)
        text = [tttt]
```

```python
        vector = vectorizer.transform(text)

        aaa = vector.toarray()
        Resume_Vector.append(vector.toarray())
    except:
        pass
# print(Resume_Vector)
```

C

```python
# screen.py
    for i in Resume_Vector:
            samples = i
            # create a container that'll record the closest resume to
            # another resume
        neigh = NearestNeighbors(n_neighbors=1)
        # group resumes based on a resume's frequent words
            neigh.fit(samples)
            NearestNeighbors(algorithm='auto', leaf_size=30)
Ordered_list_Resume_Score.extend(neigh.kneighbors(Job_Desc)[0][0].tolist())

    Z = [x for _,x in sorted(zip(Ordered_list_Resume_Score,Ordered_list_
    # Resume))]
    print(Ordered_list_Resume)
    print(Ordered_list_Resume_Score)
    flask_return = []
    # for n,i in enumerate(Z):
    #     print("Rankkkkk\t" , n+1, ":\t" , i)

    for n,i in enumerate(Z):
        # print("Rank\t" , n+1, ":\t" , i)
        # flask_return.append(str("Rank\t" , n+1, ":\t" , i))
        name = getfilepath(i)
        #name = name.split('.')[0]
        rank = n+1
        res = ResultElement(rank, name)
        flask_return.append(res)
        # res.printresult()
        print(f"Rank{res.rank+1} :\t {res.filename}")
    return flask_return

if __name__ == '__main__':
    inputStr = input("")
    sear(inputStr)
```

Code for *search.py*

This appendix displays the code blocks as described and discussed in Chapter 4, "Computational Thinking in Practice." Each code block is labeled alphabetically for more convenient reference.

A

```
# search.py

# Like in the app.py code, software modules are loaded in to help set up the
# software environment.
# No need to duplicate the code here!

# creates the ResultElement object, containing rank value and filename
app = Flask(__name__)

app.config['UPLOAD_FOLDER'] = 'Original_Resumes/'
app.config['ALLOWED_EXTENSIONS'] = set(['txt', 'pdf', 'png', 'jpg',
'jpeg', 'gif'])

class ResultElement:
    def __init__(self, rank, filename):
```

```python
        self.rank = rank
        self.filename = filename

def allowed_file(filename):
    return '.' in filename and \
            filename.rsplit('.', 1)[1] in app.config['ALLOWED_EXTENSIONS']

import re, string, unicodedata # software libraries for regular
expressions, strings.
import nltk # natural language toolkit software library
import contractions # software library to handle English's contraction
structure
import inflect
# software library for pulling data out of HTML and XML files
from bs4 import BeautifulSoup
# software library for identifying words (tokens) in a stream of text
from nltk import word_tokenize, sent_tokenize
# software library that lists stop words for each language
from nltk.corpus import stopwords
# software library for finding the root words/meanings of words
from nltk.stem import LancasterStemmer, WordNetLemmatizer

def remove_non_ascii(words):
    """Remove non-ASCII characters from list of tokenized words"""
    new_words = []
    for word in words:
        new_word = unicodedata.normalize('NFKD', word).encode('ascii',
'ignore').decode('utf-8', 'ignore')
        new_words.append(new_word)
    return new_words


def to_lowercase(words):
    """Convert all characters to lowercase from list of tokenized words"""
    new_words = []
    for word in words:
        new_word = word.lower()
        new_words.append(new_word)
    return new_words


def remove_punctuation(words):
    """Remove punctuation from list of tokenized words"""
    new_words = []
    for word in words:
        new_word = re.sub(r'[^\w\s]', '', word)
        if new_word != '':
            new_words.append(new_word)
    return new_words
```

```python
def replace_numbers(words):
    """Replace all interger occurrences in list of tokenized words with
    textual representation"""
    p = inflect.engine()
    new_words = []
    for word in words:
        if word.isdigit():
            new_word = p.number_to_words(word)
            new_words.append(new_word)
        else:
            new_words.append(word)
    return new_words

def remove_stopwords(words):
    """Remove stop words from list of tokenized words"""
    new_words = []
    for word in words:
        # print(word)
        if word not in stopwords.words('english'):
            new_words.append(word)
    return new_words

def stem_words(words):
    """Stem words in list of tokenized words"""
    stemmer = LancasterStemmer()
    stems = []
    for word in words:
        stem = stemmer.stem(word)
        stems.append(stem)
    return stems

def lemmatize_verbs(words):
    """Lemmatize verbs in list of tokenized words"""
    lemmatizer = WordNetLemmatizer()
    lemmas = []
    for word in words:
        lemma = lemmatizer.lemmatize(word, pos='v')
        lemmas.append(lemma)
    return lemmas
# text processing routine in order — get the most "valuable" words
def normalize(words):
    words = remove_non_ascii(words)
    words = to_lowercase(words)
    words = remove_punctuation(words)
    # words = replace_numbers(words)
    words = remove_stopwords(words)
    words = stem_words(words)
    words = lemmatize_verbs(words)
    return words
```

B

```
# search.py
def getfilepath(loc):
    temp = str(loc)
    temp = temp.replace('\\', '/')
    return temp

def res(jobfile):
    Final_Array = []

    # longest common sequence method
    def lcs(X, Y):
        try:
            mat = []
            for i in range(0,len(X)):
                row = []
                for j in range(0,len(Y)):
                    if X[i] == Y[j]:
                        if i == 0 or j == 0:
                            row.append(1)
                        else:
                            val = 1 + int( mat[i-1][j-1] )
                            row.append(val)
                    else:
                        row.append(0)
                mat.append(row)
            new_mat = []
            for r in  mat:
                r.sort()
                r.reverse()
                new_mat.append(r)
            lcs = 0
            for r in new_mat:
                if lcs < r[0]:
                    lcs = r[0]
            return lcs
        except:
            return -9999

    def spellCorrect(string):
        words = string.split(" ")
        correctWords = []
        for i in words:
            correctWords.append(spell(i))
        return " ".join(correctWords)
```

```python
# match strings (partial and whole) to sentences in resumes
def semanticSearch(searchString, searchSentencesList):
    result = None
    searchString = spellCorrect(searchString)
    bestScore = 0
    for i in searchSentencesList:
        score = lcs(searchString, i) # find if search string is in a
                                     # sentence
        print(score , i[0:100])
        print("")
        temp = [score]
        Final_Array.extend(temp)
        if score > bestScore:
            bestScore = score
            result = i
    return result
```

C

```python
# search.py

    app.config['UPLOAD_FOLDER'] = 'Original_Resumes/'
    app.config['ALLOWED_EXTENSIONS'] = set(['txt', 'pdf', 'png', 'jpg',
'jpeg', 'gif'])

    def allowed_file(filename):
        return '.' in filename and \
            filename.rsplit('.', 1)[1] in app.config['ALLOWED_EXTENSIONS']

    Resume_Vector = []
    Ordered_list_Resume = []
    Ordered_list_Resume_Score = []
    LIST_OF_FILES = []
    LIST_OF_FILES_PDF = []
    LIST_OF_FILES_DOC = []
    LIST_OF_FILES_DOCX = []
    Resumes_File_Names = []
    Resumes = []
    Temp_pdf = ''
    os.chdir('./Original_Resumes')
    for file in glob.glob('**/*.pdf', recursive=True):
        LIST_OF_FILES_PDF.append(file)
    for file in glob.glob('**/*.doc', recursive=True):
        LIST_OF_FILES_DOC.append(file)
    for file in glob.glob('**/*.docx', recursive=True):
        LIST_OF_FILES_DOCX.append(file)
```

```
    LIST_OF_FILES = LIST_OF_FILES_DOC + LIST_OF_FILES_DOCX + LIST_OF
_FILES_PDF
    # LIST_OF_FILES.remove("antiword.exe")
    print("This is LIST OF FILES")
    print(LIST_OF_FILES)

    # print("Total Files to Parse\t" , len(LIST_OF_PDF_FILES))
    print("####### PARSING ########")
    for nooo,i in enumerate(LIST_OF_FILES):
        Ordered_list_Resume.append(i)
        Temp = i.split(".")
        if Temp[1] == "pdf" or Temp[1] == "Pdf" or Temp[1] == "PDF":
            try:
                print("This is PDF" , nooo)
                with open(i,'rb') as pdf_file:
                    read_pdf = PyPDF2.PdfFileReader(pdf_file)
                    # page = read_pdf.getPage(0)
                    # page_content = page.extractText()
                    # Resumes.extend(Temp_pdf)

                    number_of_pages = read_pdf.getNumPages()
                    for page_number in range(number_of_pages):

                        page = read_pdf.getPage(page_number)
                        page_content = page.extractText()
                        page_content = page_content.replace('\n', ' ')
                        # page_content.replace("\r", "")
                        Temp_pdf = Temp_pdf + str(page_content)
                        # Temp_pdf.append(page_content)
                        # print(Temp_pdf)
                    Resumes.extend([Temp_pdf])
                    Temp_pdf = ''
                    Resumes_File_Names.append(i)
                    # f = open(str(i)+str("+") , 'w')
                    # f.write(page_content)
                    # f.close()
            except Exception as e: print(e)
        if Temp[1] == "doc" or Temp[1] == "Doc" or Temp[1] == "DOC":
            print("This is DOC" , i)

            try:
                a = textract.process(i)
                a = a.replace(b'\n',  b' ')
                a = a.replace(b'\r',  b' ')
                b = str(a)
                c = [b]
                Resumes.extend(c)
                Resumes_File_Names.append(i)
            except Exception as e: print(e)
```

```
            if Temp[1] == "docx" or Temp[1] == "Docx" or Temp[1] == "DOCX":
                print("This is DOCX" , i)
                try:
                    a = textract.process(i)
                    a = a.replace(b'\n',  b' ')
                    a = a.replace(b'\r',  b' ')
                    b = str(a)
                    c = [b]
                    Resumes.extend(c)
                    Resumes_File_Names.append(i)
                except Exception as e: print(e)
            # Resumes.extend(textract.process(i))
            if Temp[1] == "ex" or Temp[1] == "Exe" or Temp[1] == "EXE":
                # print("This is EXE" , i)
                pass
```

D

```
# search.py

    # print("This is length of Resume Vector : " , len(Resumes))
    # # # print(Resumes[1][0:10])
    # for m , i in enumerate(Resumes):
    #     print("This is m : " , m , i[0][0:100])
    #     print("############################################################
###############")

    for m,i in enumerate(Resumes):
        Resumes[m] = nltk.word_tokenize(Resumes[m])
        Resumes[m] = normalize(Resumes[m])
        Resumes[m] = ' '.join(map(str, Resumes[m]))

    # identify the most valuable words within the job description
    jobfile = nltk.word_tokenize(jobfile)
    jobfile = normalize(jobfile)
    jobfile = ' '.join(map(str, jobfile))
    # Resumes2 = np.array(Resumes)

    # Resumes2 = Resumes2.ravel()

    # print(len(Resumes))

    # Resumes = ['microsoft is dumb' , 'google is awesome' , 'facebook
is cheater']
```

```python
        print("This is len Resumes : " , len(Resumes))
        os.chdir('../')

print("################################################################")
        # a = input("Enter String to Search : ")
        print("\n\n")
        print("Printing Scores of all Resumes...")
        print("\n")
        # find resumes that map to the job description (but do we find good
matches)
        result = semanticSearch(jobfile, Resumes)
        print("\n")
        print("Printing 1 Best Result.....")
        print("\n")
        print (result)
        print("\n\n")
        print("###############################################")
        print("\n\n")
        print(Final_Array)
        print("This is len Final_Array : " , len(Final_Array))
        print(Resumes_File_Names)
        print("This is len Ordered_list_Resume : " , len(Resumes_File_Names))
        Ordered_list_Resume = Ordered_list_Resume[1:]
        # print(Ordered_list_Resume)

        Z = [x for _,x in sorted(zip(Final_Array,Resumes_File_Names) ,
reverse=True)]
        flask_return = []
        # for n,i in enumerate(Z):
        #     print("Rankkkkk\t" , n+1, ":\t" , i)

        for n,i in enumerate(Z):
            # print("Rank\t" , n+1, ":\t" , i)
            # flask_return.append(str("Rank\t" , n+1, ":\t" , i))
            name = getfilepath(i)
            #name = name.split('.')[0]
            rank = n
            res = ResultElement(rank, name)
            flask_return.append(res)
            # res.printresult()
            # print(f"Rank{res.rank+1} :\t {res.filename}")
        return flask_return
```

Pseudocode for *faceit.py*

This appendix displays the pseudocode of Gaurav Oberoi's FaceIt software as described in Chapter 7, "Circus of Misguided Analysis." If you want to know how to swap one person's face with another, here are the general steps to accomplish that objective.

FaceIt: main computer program

(1) Import necessary ML/AI algorithm libraries into the computer program, e.g., `faceit.py`.

(2) Identify file paths for program's input and output data.

(3) Instantiate program's input and output data elements.

(4) Create methods to identify media (video and photo) segments.

(4.1) Methods to retrieve the video.

(4.2) Methods to extract frames from the videos.

(4.3) Methods to return all faces of the people's faces, both original and target for every media type to identify a person who may be located in that media.

(4.4) Store the output in pre-defined local file directories.

(4.5) Method to download an original/actual video from YouTube.

(4.6) Method to create video clips from extracted frames; to be performed in batches.

(4.7) Method to extract the facial characteristics from videos stored in your local directory.

(5) Provide method calls to support handling of program input and output.

(5.1) Preprocessing method calls to fetch, extract frames, and then extract faces.

(5.2) Create a directory containing faces of Person A and a directory containing faces of Person B on your local machine.

(5.3) Conversion step: The inputs are video files and faces of Person A and Person B.

(5.3.1) Using a robust open source machine learning model platform, such as TensorFlow (www.tensorflow.org) the preprocessed video files and video clips of the faces of Person A and Person B are supplied as the input layer into a deep learning algorithm, such as Generative Adversarial Networks (GANs).

(5.3.2) This algorithm then constructs a new set of video files that minimizes the features of the original face (Person A) while introducing and promoting the features of Person B's face.

(5.3.3) For each frame of the video files and each iteration of the algorithm with features associated with Person A's face that are being replaced by a feature associated with Person B's face.

(5.3.3.1) GANs perform these manipulations using a two-part iterative training process, which consists of a generator and a discriminator. The generator "learns" to create visual representations that look real, whereas the discriminator "learns" to tell real visual representations apart from fakes. Examples of this two-part training process exists in our physical environment: an art forger and an art critic or a criminal and a law enforcement professional, where the art forger and criminal are the generators, whereas the art critic and law enforcement professional are the discriminators.

(5.3.4) The algorithm executing the GAN concludes when a predetermined condition has been met which is ideally when the discriminator cannot identify any fake elements from the generator's visual representation.

(5.3.5) The algorithm's output is a set of doctored video files with Person B's facial features.

(6) Conduct formatting operations on pre-processed video, e.g., duration and size uniformity, as desired.

(7) Make a final video with side-by-side images of original and swapped frames.

(8) Write final video to a designated output directory and complete post-processing tasks.

(9) Execute the main program:

    (9.1) Perform preprocessing of videos and identify Person A and Person B.

    (9.2) Train the selected data learning model.

    (9.3) Perform the face swaps for each video frame.

    (9.4) Create a final video of showcasing the original and swapped video content.

(10) End of Program.

The Data Visualisation Catalogue's Visualization Types

This appendix contains the visualization types and picture representation as it appears on `https://datavizcatalogue.com`.

The appendix allows the seeing-reader to reference the different visualization types while reading the Chapter 8, "Double-Edged Visualization Sword" rather than having to access the website on a separate device. The captions indicate the frequently used visualization types seen in mainstream media and scholarly articles.

Figure E.1: The following data visualizations are displayed: error bars, flow chart, flow map, Gantt chart, heat map, histogram, illustration diagram, Kagi chart, line graph, Marimekko chart, multiset bar chart, network diagram, nightingale rose chart, non-ribbon chord diagram, open-high-low-close chart, parallel coordinates plot, parallel sets, pictogram chart.

Figure E.2: The following data visualizations are displayed: pie chart, point and figure chart, population pyramid, proportional area chart, radar chart, radial bar chart, radial column chart, Sankey diagram, scatterplot, span chart, spiral plot, stacked area graph, stacked bar graph, stem and leaf plot, steam graph, sunburst diagram, tally chart, timeline.

Arc Diagram   Area Graph   Bar Chart   Box & Whisker Plot   Brainstorm   Bubble Chart

Bubble Map   Bullet Graph   Calendar   Candlestick Chart   Chord Diagram   Choropleth Map

Circle Packing   Connection Map   Density Plot   Donut Chart   Dot Map   Dot Matrix Chart

Figure E.3: The following data visualizations are displayed: arc diagram, area graph, bar chart, box and whisker plot, brainstorm, bubble chart, bubble map, bullet graph, calendar, candlestick chart, chord diagram, choropleth map, circle packing, connection map, density plot, donut chart, dot map, dot matrix chart.

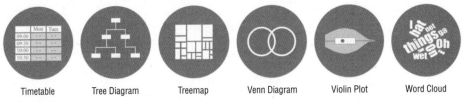

Timetable   Tree Diagram   Treemap   Venn Diagram   Violin Plot   Word Cloud

Figure E.4: The following data visualizations are displayed: timetable, tree diagram, treemap, Venn diagram, violin plot, word cloud.

APPENDIX

F

Glossary

This glossary is a list of six popular V's of Big Data terms that may be unfamiliar to the reader.

Value — The evaluation of the usefulness of gathered data for business. Data in its raw form isn't useful unless knowledge and insights can be harnessed for productive application.

Variety — The handling of structured, semi-structured, and unstructured forms of data for effective storage and analyses. Inconsistent data formats and data structures cause data and software development teams to find insufficient work-arounds to manage data translations.

Velocity — The increasing rate in which data is created, stored, processed, analyzed, and visualized. In one Internet minute, Google conducts 5.7 million searches. The speed of data is lightning fast.

Veracity — The assessing of data's quality and making informed judgments distinguishing between noisy data, erroneous data, degree of uncertainty, misinformation, and disinformation. Data with high variety, velocity, and volume will not be 100 percent accurate, so all of us need to account for imperfection.

Volume — The enormous quantity of data entering digital systems. Managing the scale of data requires different approaches, processes, and systems.

Variability — The degree of change in outcomes when the same data is applied to the same circumstances repeatedly. Ideally, data workers want the algorithmic-based outcomes to be consistent, especially when performing experiments. It provides evidence that generalizable observations can be stated with confidence and sets a precedent for making predictions. In practice, however, data is much more heterogeneous than the data industry would like to admit.

Index

LCS (longest common
   subsequence), 113
Rocchio, 234–236
shampoo algorithm, 89–91
topic drift, 276
well ordered collection, 88
alternative language/spelling, 276
Amazon AI hiring tool, 65–70
anthropometry, 18–19
   eugenics and, 20–21
   Tuskegee Institute and, 21
anti-Blackness, 4–5
antivaccine claims on Facebook, 30
apoliticalness in data, 49–50
app.py file, 101–103
   code blocks, 287–290
AUC (area under the curve), 107
authorship, data collection and, 126
Automated Résumé Screening
   System, 98–99
AWS (Amazon Web Services), 93

B
BeautifulSoup, 151
beliefs, opinions and, 30
Bertillon, Alphonse, 18–19, 20
Bertillon card system, criminal justice
   system, 19
bias, 61
   algorithmic practices, 65, 68
   Black people in keyword searches, 62
   business and, 65
   confirmation bias, 96
   data and, 65
   data-related roles, 64
   defining, 63–65
   example, 65–70
   flagging, 97
   implicit/explicit bias, 96
   information bias, 96
   people and, 65
   sampling bias, 96
   selection bias, 96
bias wheel, 70–73

Big Data, 150
   people plus algorithms, 169
   value, 313
   variability, 314
   variety, 313
   velocity, 313
   veracity, 313
   volume, 313
binary numeral systems, 17–18
bipartisanship in data, 49–50
Black codes, 5–7
   Black women's work life, 9–11
   Civil Rights of Freedmen in
      Mississippi, 6–7
Black population, 217–218
   U.S. Census 2020, 218
Black Twitter Project, 150
   Blacktags, 151
   handle removal, 152
   Hashtags, 151
   keywords, 151
   webscraping, 151
BlackTwitter, 32
   data reformat, 136–137
Brown, Henry Billings, 8
*Brown v. Board of Education of
   Topeka*, 11–12
Buolamwini, Joy, 254
Bureau of Technology, 217

C
CCPA (California Consumer Privacy
   Act), 216
   cookies, 120
cease and desist calls, 186
Center for Minorities and people with
   Disabilities in IT, 125
CIA (confidentiality, integrity,
   availability), 75
Civil Rights Act of 1964, 12
Civil Rights of Freedman in
   Mississippi, 6–7
cleaned datasets, evaluating, 169–177
cloropeth visualization, 205–206